Medieval Marriage

LITERARY APPROACHES, 1100–1300

Medieval Marriage

LITERARY APPROACHES, 1100–1300

Neil Cartlidge

D. S. BREWER

First published 1997
D. S. Brewer, Cambridge

ISBN 0 85991 512 3

D. S. Brewer is an imprint of Boydell & Brewer Ltd
PO Box 9, Woodbridge, Suffolk IP12 3DF, UK
and of Boydell & Brewer Inc.
PO Box 41026, Rochester, NY 14604–4126, USA

A catalogue record for this book is available
from the British Library

Library of Congress Cataloging-in-Publication Data
Cartlidge, Neil, 1967–
    Medieval marriage : literary approaches, 1100–1300 / Neil
Cartlidge.
        p.   cm.
    Includes bibliographical references and index.
    ISBN 0-85991-512-3 (hard cover : alk. paper)
    1. Literature, Medieval – History and criticism.
2. Marriage in literature.   I. Title.
PN682.M37C37   1997
809′.02–dc21   96–44585

This publication is printed on acid-free paper

Printed in Great Britain by
St Edmundsbury Press Ltd, Bury St Edmunds, Suffolk

Contents

Acknowledgements

Peter Dronke supervised my doctoral work in Cambridge. He has overseen the planning of this project and has given my work minute consideration for over five years. My debt to him is enormous. Jill Mann and Richard Axton offered me valuable advice just when I needed it – as did the examiners of my Ph.D. dissertation, Douglas Gray and James Simpson. Eric Stanley and Richard Beadle have also been very generous with their time; while Margaret Laing and Angus McIntosh taught me an immense amount in the few weeks I had with them in Edinburgh. I am very grateful to Morgan Dickson for reading some of my drafts so carefully; and to Kate Thomas for all her help and encouragement over the last couple of years.

I also owe thanks to the Jebb Fund and the Neil Ker Memorial Fund for financial assistance during the academic year 1994–5; to Wolfson College for bringing me to Oxford; and to the British Academy for the post-doctoral Research Fellowship which I currently hold.

A Note about Quotations

Some quotations have been silently repunctuated. In Middle English texts, the obsolete letters *yogh* and *thorn* have been regularized to ''y'', ''gh'' ''h'' or ''th'', as appropriate. All translations are my own.

Abbreviations

Adv. Jov.	Adversus Jovinianum
Archives	*Archives d'Histoire Doctrinale et Littéraire du Moyen Age*
ALMA	*Arthurian Literature in the Middle Ages: A Collaborative History*, ed. Roger Sherman Loomis (Oxford, 1959)
AN	Anglo-Norman
ANL	M. Dominica Legge, *Anglo-Norman Literature and its Background* (Oxford, 1963)
ANTS	Anglo-Norman Text Society
ASNS	*Archiv für das Studium der neueren Sprachen*
ASS	*Acta Sanctorum . . .*, ed. J. Bolandus et al., 62 vols, (Paris, [1863]–75)
Auch	The version of the Middle English *Guy of Warwick* contained in the Auchinleck MS (Advocates' Library, Edinburgh, MS 19.2.1., ff. 108r–175v), ed. J. Zupitza
AW	*Ancrene Wisse*
BHL	*Bibliotheca hagiographica latina antiquae et mediae aetatis: novum supplementum*, ed. Henri Fros, Subsidia hagiographica 70 (Brussels, 1986)
BL	British Library
BN	Bibliothèque Nationale
Caius	The version of the Middle English *Guy of Warwick* contained in Gonville and Caius College, Cambridge (MS Cl.A.8.107, ff. 1–271), ed. J. Zupitza
CB	*Carmina Burana*
CCCM	Corpus Christianorum, Continuatio Medievalis
CCM	*Cahiers du Civilisation Médiévale Xe–XIIe siècles*
CFMA	Classiques français du moyen âge
Cluny Studies	*Pierre Abélard; Pierre le Vénérable: Les courants philosophiques, littéraires et artistiques en occident au milieu du XIIe siècle: Abbaye de Cluny, 2 au 9 juillet, 1972*, Colloques internationaux du C.R.N.S. (Paris, 1975)
Court and Poet	*Court and Poet: Selected Proceedings of the Third Congress of the International Courtly Literature Society*, ed. Glyn S. Burgess, ARCA, Classical and Medieval Texts, Papers and Monographs 5 (Liverpool, 1981)
CSA	*Chanson de Saint Alexis*
DTC	*Dictionnaire de théologie catholique*, ed. A. Vacent, E. Mangenot, and E. Amann, 15 vols (Paris, 1903–50)
E&S	*Essays and Studies by Members of the English Association*
EETS	Early English Text Society

EHR	*English Historical Review*
EMEL	R.M. Wilson, *Early Middle English Literature* (3rd. edn, London, 1968)
ES	Extra Series
Fälschungen	*Fälschungen im Mittelalter: Internationaler Kongress der Monumenta Germaniae Historica: Munich, 1986*, vol. 5: *Fingierte Briefe, Frömmigkeit und Fälschung, Realienfälschungen*, MGH Schriften 33 (Hanover, 1988)
Fr. trans.	Modern French translation
FS Pierre Bec	*Mélange de langue et littérature occitanes en hommage à Pierre Bec . . .* (Poitiers, 1991)
FS Erich Köhler	*Mittelalterstudien: Erich Köhler zum Gedenken*, ed. H. Krauss and D. Rieger (Heidelberg, 1984)
IMEV	*The Index of Middle English Verse*, ed. Carleton Brown and Rossell Hope Robbins, (New York, 1943)
IPME	Peter Dronke, *Intellectuals and Poets in Medieval Europe* (Rome, 1992)
JEGP	*Journal of English and Germanic Philology*
JFH	*Journal of Family History*
JMH	*Journal of Medieval History*
JRMS	*Journal of Medieval and Renaissance Studies*
JWCI	*Journal of the Warburg and Courtauld Institutes*
LCL	Loeb Classical Library
LCM	*The Life of St Christina of Markyate: A Twelfth-Century Recluse*, ed. C.H. Talbot, Oxford Medieval Texts (Oxford, 1959, rpt. 1987)
Leuven Studies	*Peter Abelard: Proceedings of the International Conference. (Louvain, May 10–12, 1971)*, ed. E.M. Buytaert (Leuven and The Hague, 1974)
Linker	Robert White Linker, *A Bibliography of Old French Lyrics*, Romance Monographs 31 (University of Mississippi, 1979)
LLa	'On lofsong of ure lefdi'
LLo	'On lofsong of ure louerde'
LMAC	Henry Ansgar Kelly, *Love and Marriage in the Age of Chaucer* (Ithaca and London, 1975)
LPMap	*The Latin Poems commonly attributed to Walter Mapes*, ed. Thomas Wright (London, 1841)
LVMA	Peter Dronke, *Latin and Vernacular Poets of the Middle Ages* (London, 1991)
MÆ	*Medium Ævum*
Manual	*A Manual of the Writings in Middle English 1050–1400*, ed. J. Burke Severs and Albert E. Hartung, 9 vols (New Haven, 1967–)
MCL	*The Meaning of Courtly Love*, ed. F.X. Newman (Albany NY, 1968)
ME	Middle English
MeH	*Medievalia et humanistica*
MGH	Monumenta Germaniae Historica

Mittelalterbilder	*Mittelalterbilder aus neuer Perspektive: Diskussionsanstöße zu amour courtois, Subjectivität in der Dichtung und Strategien des Erzählens: Kolloquium Würzburg 1984*, ed. Ernstpeter Ruhe and Rudolf Behrens (Munich, 1985)
MlJh	*Mittellateinisches Jahrbuch*
MLN	*Modern Language Notes*
MLR	*Modern Language Review*
MMA	'Marriage in the Middle Ages', ed. John Leyerle, *Viator* 4 (1973) 413–501
MP	*Modern Philology*
MPHW	Peter Dronke, *The Medieval Poet and his World* (Rome, 1984)
MRS	*Medieval and Renaissance Studies*
MS	*Mediæval Studies*
MWB	Bella Millett and Jocelyn Wogan-Browne, ed. and trans., *Medieval English Prose for Women* (Oxford, 1990)
NGDMM	*New Grove Dictionary of Music and Musicians*, ed. Stanley Sadie, 6th edn, 20 vols (London, 1980)
NHC	*Northern Homily Cycle*: ed. C. Hörstmann, *Altenglische Legenden* (Heilbronn, 1881)
N&Q	*Notes and Queries*
NS	New Series
O&N	*The Owl and the Nightingale*
OE	Old English
OEMEP	Derek Pearsall, *Old English and Middle English Poetry* (London, 1977)
OS	Original Series
OSM	'Oreisun of seinte Marie'
PBA	*Proceedings of the British Academy*
PC	*Bibliographie der Troubadours*, ed. A. Pillet and H. Carstens (Halle, 1933)
PL	*Patrologiae cursus completus*, ed. J.P. Migne, 221 vols (Paris, 1844–64)
PP	*Le Petit Plet*
PQ	*Philological Quarterly*
Raynaud	*G. Raynauds Bibliographie des altfranzösischen Liedes*, ed. Hans Spanke (Leiden, 1980)
RES	*Review of English Studies*
RF	*Romanische Forschungen*
RMAL	*Revue du Moyen Age Latin*
RP	*Romance Philology*
RR	*Romanic Review*
RRTC	*Renaissance and Renewal in the Twelfth Century* [proceedings of a conference at Harvard, 26–9/11/77], ed. Robert L. Benson and Giles Constable (Oxford, 1982)
SATF	Société des Anciens Textes Français
SG	*Studia Gratiana*
SJ	*Seinte Iuliene: The Liflade ant te Passiun of Seinte Iuliene*, ed. S.R.T.O. d'Ardenne, EETS OS 248 (Oxford, 1961)

SK	*Seinte Katerine*, ed. S.R.T.O. d'Ardenne and E.J. Dobson, EETS SS 7 (Oxford, 1981)
SLC	*Scottish Legendary Collection*: ed. W. Metcalfe as *Legends of the Saints*, Scottish Text Society, 3 vols (Edinburgh, 1896)
SM	*Seinte Margarete*, ed. Millet and Wogan-Browne, pp. 44–84
Sm	*Studi medievali*
SMRH	*Studies in Medieval and Renaissance History*
SP	*Studies in Philology*
Spoleto Studies	*Il matrimonio nella società altomedievale: 22–28 aprile 1976*, Settimane di studio del centro italiano di studi sull' alto medioevo 24, 2 vols (Spoleto, 1979)
SS	Supplementary Series
TLF	Textes littéraires français
Trier Studies	*Petrus Abaelardus: Person, Werk, und Wirkung*, ed. Rudolf Thomas et al., Trierer Theologischen Studien 38 (Trier, 1980)
UGA	'On wel swuthe god ureisun of God almihti'
UL	'On ureisun of ure louerde'
ULC	University Library, Cambridge
UNCS	University of North Carolina Studies in the Romance Languages and Literatures
VCH	*Victoria County History*
VF	*Vox Feminae: studies in medieval woman's song*, ed. John F. Plummer, Studies in Medieval Culture 15 (Kalamazoo, Michigan, 1981)
WL	'Wohunge of ure lauerd'
ZFRP	*Zeitschrift für romanische Philologie*
ZFSL	*Zeitschrift für französische Sprache und Literatur*

Introduction

In this book, I shall argue that the representation of marriage in the literature of early medieval England can be characterized by a sophisticated interest in the affective nature of the conjugal bond. It was once commonly thought that in the Middle Ages, "the *mariage de convenance* was the normal arrangement in every class, from the noble to the peasant"; and even that medieval literature was never seriously concerned with marriage as a vehicle of the affections, only with adultery.[1] By contrast, I shall argue that, far from confirming anything cynical or casual in medieval attitudes towards marriage, the literature of the twelfth and thirteenth centuries reflects the idealism and psychological subtlety with which western society gradually defined a coherent, optimistic and abiding ideology of marriage in this period.[2] That is not to say that medieval writers could not also be uncompromisingly critical of marriage as an experience and as an institution: but they criticized it precisely because they felt that the relationship between marriage and the married could be a dramatic, exciting and even tragic one, and because its realities often clashed with their ideals. Virginia Woolf once described marriage as "the union of hearts and foundation of homes".[3] The cultural record does not support the notion that medieval society ever characteristically separated these two aspects in its ideology of marriage. Indeed, although the invention of the affective model of marriage has been claimed for many periods in history, I doubt that any culture can truly neglect the role of the "heart" in the formalization of sexual relationships.[4] I also hope to show how profoundly early medieval literature is animated by an awareness of the tensions between the social and emotional dimensions of marriage; and how seriously it examines marriage as a complex and important mechanism for expressing links between individuals.

It is particularly hard to study so fundamental a concept as marriage in a completely disinterested way. As Jack Goody has said, "none of us can entirely divest ourselves of our cultural clothing, nor is such nudity always

---

[1] Coulton, p. 630. For example, Moore, p. 436: "anyone stressing love as a free and spontaneous union between persons could not help but run into adultery in a society where love had virtually nothing to do with the union of persons in marriage". See also Wilcox, p. 324; Campbell, IV, 53.

[2] For the tenacity of medieval conceptions of marriage, see Brundage, *Law*, pp. 1–2, 579–94; Stone, pp. 15, 56.

[3] *Jacob's Room* in *Four Great Novels* (Oxford, 1994), p. 60.

[4] For example, Stone detects an affective watershed "in the middle and late eighteenth century" (pp. 259–60); and Foucault finds one in the Roman era (*Care*, pp. 77–80).

1

becoming. But one area where we need to exercise particular caution, indeed restraint, is in the study of the family itself, especially when examining the 'affective' aspects of the fundamental relations between its members, which we have all experienced from various angles".[5] The society with which I am familiar is one in which, relatively speaking, people marry late in life and with a small age-differential; and in which the economic and intellectual status of women is relatively high.[6] These are factors which make the relationship between married partners a complex one, and I am aware that, in stressing the affective importance of the conjugal bond to the medieval idea of marriage, I risk projecting this complexity back into the Middle Ages. Yet I am sure that the texts that I have chosen do demonstrate their own distinct sophistication in the face of the perennial human problem of defining and validating sexual relationships in terms of marriage.

My chosen approach by literary criticism is an especially hazardous one, for the study of literature as a witness to the sensibility of the past is, in Brooke's words, both a "fascinating" and a "treacherous field".[7] Literary sources demand a greater level of imaginative engagement than more purely factual ones, and their interpretation is thus more vulnerable to the modern reader's own prejudices and preoccupations. For the purposes of this book, I shall define literature simply by saying that literary texts tend to have a greater emotional and intellectual scope than historical records. I do not agree with John Baldwin's suggestion that while historians must concern themselves with "audience response and the relation of discourse to reality", literary critics need not.[8] All texts demand to be studied within their original context – so far as it can be determined. At the same time, it might be objected that a study of medieval literary texts based upon a specific social and legal structure such as marriage must necessarily result in too rigid a circumscription of their ideological and semiotic range. R. Howard Bloch, for example, has objected to the attempt to localize literature "within the context of an external historical referent" as an aspect of "philological enterprise" incapable of providing interpretations of the text "that would account for its specificity as literature".[9] However, in his own book on medieval misogyny, he insists that only "an analysis of the specific social, legal and economic determinants of [the twelfth century's] seemingly radical change in the politics of gender can account for the appearance of what since the late nineteenth century has been called 'courtliness' or 'courtly love' ".[10]

Marriage undoubedly was a live issue in this period, and I hope to show how this is reflected in medieval literature. Many texts place certain charges

---

[5] Goody, p. 2.
[6] Goody, pp. 8–9; Stone, pp. 415–16.
[7] Brooke, *Idea*, p. 22.
[8] Baldwin, *Language*, p. xxvii.
[9] Bloch, 'Medieval Text', p. 100.
[10] Bloch, *Medieval Misogyny*, p. 11.

upon particular ideas about marriage – often in ways which are strikingly discrepant with the nature of the discourses to which they ostensibly subscribe. Even in anti-matrimonial polemic, for example, a pristine ideal of marriage can be sustained in the suggestion that marriage on earth is the debasement of an essentially heavenly state. Far from diminishing the specificity of literary texts, I hope that my consideration of marriage will emphasize both the "discursive heterogeneity" of medieval attitudes towards sexual relationships, and the possibility of new perspectives upon texts so long analysed only in terms of love and, more recently, of gender.[11]

In using written records to approach so vast a field of ideology and practice as medieval marriage, it is always tempting to present too holistic a picture – to allow too little for the inflections of the author's time, locality, class, sources, genre, context and immediate purpose. In order to avoid this, I have limited the main body of this study to a number of texts belonging to three discrete English literary milieux of the twelfth and thirteenth centuries. One can be identified as early twelfth-century St Albans, while the other two belong to the next century and probably the West Midlands. The reception and circulation of these groups of texts was different in each case, but none of the definitive manuscripts are secular. Like most medieval books they are products of religious institutions, and as such, their composition is naturally biased towards material which either problematizes marriage or places a particular moral or ideological emphasis upon it. The paradox which has emerged most clearly in my reading of these texts is that even while several of these authors specifically subscribe to the established anti-matrimonial discourse inherited from patristic antiquity, their work nevertheless often betrays a sensitive and flexible approach to the intellectual value and emotional impact of marriage. Despite the predomination of texts designed in one way or another for religious use, the three groups do span a range of different types of discourse – hagiography and romance, devotional and didactic writing, lyric and debate. Given the nature of the evidence available, the works I have chosen to treat are perhaps as broadly representative of English literary culture in this period as is possible.

While recognizing the differing genres and environments in which each of these texts was composed or copied, I should like to stress, firstly, the richness and subtlety of all their treatments of marriage, and secondly, the underlying continuity of their thinking, both among themselves and within a larger western European context. With these purposes in mind, I should like to use the first chapter of this book to survey recent historical and literary critical approaches to medieval marriage, and to sketch briefly some of the developments in medieval thinking about marriage which lie outside the field of literature. The second chapter is intended to demonstrate the resonance of some of these new ideas about marriage in a few key, literary texts lying outside my chosen milieux.

[11] Baldwin, *Language*, p. ix.

CHAPTER ONE

Perspectives upon Medieval Marriage

1. Modern Theories of Medieval Marriage: The Two Models

The undue emphasis upon the utilitarianism of medieval marriage which has dominated historical accounts of sexual relationships in the Middle Ages originated as the by-product of a strand of scholarly romanticism. By minimizing marriage, the conceptual system of 'courtly love' made room for a fantasy of the hierophantic treatment of medieval women. Although the term "cortez'amor" occurs in a lyric by Peire d'Alvernhe, it was apparently first used in a specifically literary critical sense by Gaston Paris in 1883.[1] In Paris's work, as Bloch suggests, the theory of courtly love reflects his own homosocial and misogynistic tendencies.[2] Even so, the concept has had a long and complex history, as Roger Boase has clearly shown. He concludes his study by trying to syncretize all the different ways in which the idea of courtly love has been applied. Courtly love, he suggests, was "a comprehensive cultural phenomenon, a literary movement, an ideology, an ethical system, a style of life, and an expression of the play element in culture which arose in an aristocratic Christian environment exposed to Hispano-Arabic influences".[3] To treat the idea with such latitude is to weld together a number of aspects of medieval culture which I think are better kept distinct – such as the military ethos of "chivalry", the poetic ideal of "fin' amors", the customs of courtly "politesse" and the Ovidian tradition of love-casuistry. When the term 'courtly love' is indiscriminately applied to a range of medieval texts, it can only cause, as Dronke has said, "hopeless confusion".[4] Even though the concept now appears an artificial and inadequate guide to the relationship between literature and life in the Middle Ages, especially the early Middle Ages, it remains widely current, and still dominates 'layman's thinking' about the period.[5] However, what follows in this book is not

---

[1] Peire d'Alvernhe, 'Gent es, mentr'om n'a lezer . . .', ed. del Monte, pp. 99–104, line 58; Paris, 'Etudes'.

[2] Bloch, ' "Mieux" '.

[3] Boase, pp. 129–30.

[4] Dronke, rev. Buridant, p. 320; cf. Lazar and Lacy, pp. vii–ix; Robertson, *Preface*, p. 391.

[5] Donaldson rejects courtly love as a myth. Newman has pointed out (*MCL*, p. vii) that courtly love would have contradicted conventional medieval views on the psychology

another attempt to discredit the use of the term 'courtly love', but an attempt to put something in its place – to provide some ideas by which to structure readings of medieval texts in which marriage is thematically important.

The association of courtly love with a romantic marginalization of marriage was largely the achievement of C.S. Lewis, although as Henry Ansgar Kelly has said, "Lewis has been singled out for criticism not because courtly love was his invention – it was already a widespread delusion before his time – but because he wrote on it so well".[6] Lewis used the term to drive deep fissures between different classes of medieval society, between the sensibilities of the Middle Ages and of the ancient world, and between literature and actuality. Courtly love, he said, appeared "quite suddenly" in the lyrics of the troubadours.[7] He saw their erotic ethic as a conscious subversion of the prevailing ideological systems of the day – that is, the aristocratic and the ecclesiastical. Both these systems, he argued, valued marriage as a tool rather than as an ideal, and they "prevented the men of that age from connecting their ideal of romantic and passionate love with marriage".[8] In feudal society, "so far from being the natural channel for the new kind of love, marriage was

---

and theology of sexuality (for which see Bullough; Cadden). Benton has rightly stressed that in medieval law and custom adultery was regarded as a very grave offence (Benton, 'Clio', pp. 23–7; 'Court', pp. 587–8: cf. Brundage, *Law*, pp. 207–9, 247–8, 303–8). He also argued persuasively against the belief that the Court of Champagne provided a centre for the dissemination of ideas about courtly love ('Court'). Payen and Calin have suggested that the adulterousness of troubadour-lyric is purely notional: "le mariage rend la femme plus difficile d'accès et constitue un obstacle valorisant" (Payen, 'Mise', pp. 222–3; cf. Calin, p. 35). Robertson maintained that the notion arises from a misreading of texts which he believed to be wholly ironic and hostile to worldly love (e.g. *Preface*, e.g. pp. 30–31, 391–3, 446–8). Kelly has emphasized the preference for marriage in medieval romance (Kelly, *LMAC*, pp. 20–3; cf. Loomis, p. 189; Mathew, 'Marriage' pp. 132–5 and 'Ideals', p. 49). Dronke has argued that the love-experience expressed by the troubadours is a universal one (*MRELL*, e.g., pp. 39, 48, 180–1), concluding that "there is no evidence that [medieval] poets thought of love and marriage as incompatible' (rev. Schlösser, p. 58). Finally, Utley has devoted an article to the question 'Must We Abandon the Concept of Courtly Love?'. With regard to the term's continued use, Walsh has described it as a "ghostly presence" and a "bête noire" (*De amore*, p. 6). There are still books being written about courtly love. Jean Markale's *L'amour courtois: ou le couple infernal*, for example, was published as recently as 1987.

[6] Lewis, *Allegory*, pp. 1–43; Kelly, *LMAC*, p. 19; cf. Parmisano, p. 2: "after Lewis and largely because of him, few have ventured to deny that Church and poet, whether of 12th century France or 14th century England, were at odds over love".

[7] Lewis, p. 2; cf. de Rougemont, passim (e.g. p. 365); Campbell, IV, 62–3; Lefèvre, p. 92.

[8] Lewis, p. 13; cf. Lazar, p. 60: "pour les troubadours l'opposition entre fin' amors et amour conjugal est absolue et irréductible"; Lefèvre, p. 100: "l'amour courtois est par nature un amour adultère. Il ne saurait en être autrement. L'amour n'existe pas dans le mariage"; Wilcox, p. 324; Engels, p. 498; Schlauch, pp. 138–41; Loomis, p. 52.

rather the drab background against which that love stood out in all the contrast of its new tenderness and delicacy'';[9] while ''the general impression left on the medieval mind'' by the teaching of the Church ''was that all love – at least all such passionate and exalted devotion as a courtly poet thought worthy of the name – was more or less wicked''.[10] The troubadours, he argued, initiated a distinct and resilient ideal of romantic love in western society, an ideal defined by its absolute separation from the economic legitimacy of marriage.[11] By postulating a fundamental dislocation between the ideals expressed in literature and those actually governing medieval society, Lewis could portray the exaltation of love in medieval literature as a defiant counter-strain to the prevailing ideologies of the day. This aspect of Lewis's thinking could perhaps be seen as a development of Walter Pater's characterization of the twelfth century by ''its antinomianism, its spirit of rebellion and revolt against the moral and religious ideas of the time''. Pater goes on, ''in their search after the pleasures of the senses and the imagination, in their care for beauty, in their worship of the body, people were impelled beyond the bounds of the Christian ideal; and their love became sometimes a strange idolatry, a strange rival religion''.[12] Lewis was perhaps moved to endorse the earlier Oxford scholar's perception of the existence of a militant aestheticism in the Middle Ages by his own sense of scholarly beleaguerment in an apparently ever more philistine world.

A much more refined conception of medieval marriage in terms of these same two models – ecclesiastical and aristocratic – was offered by Georges Duby.[13] Duby suggested that the ethos of courtly love could be explained in terms of a policy evident among dynastic houses from the second half of the eleventh century onwards. In order to prevent the proliferation of heirs and the subsequent fragmentation of the patrimony, dynastic houses tended to allow only the eldest sons to marry.[14] Courtly love, he said, embodied the

---

[9] Lewis, p. 13. Cf. Engels, *Origins*, pp. 504–5: ''For the knight or baron, as for the prince of the land himself, marriage is a political act, an opportunity for the accession of power through new alliances; the interest of the House and not individual inclination [is] the decisive factor. How can love here hope to have the last word regarding marriage?''; Evans, p. 130: ''In a society practising dynastic marriage love was a disruptive force, antisocial and extramarital.''

[10] Lewis, p. 17. Cf. Campbell, IV, 43–53; Lazar, p. 13: ''Les préceptes de l'amour provençal, sa morale, son caractère adultère, sont absolument irréconciliables avec l'enseignement de l'Eglise''; Morris, *Discovery*, p. 108: ''the Church offered little to lovers, even to those with honourable intentions''. This notion has been challenged by Leclercq (*Monks*) and Parmisano.

[11] Lewis, pp. 3–4. Cf. Bezzola, p. 235; de Rougemont, pp. 33–5, 275; Campbell, IV, 54–5.

[12] Pater, p. 16.

[13] Duby, 'Mariage', pp. 20–6; *Medieval Marriage*, pp. 1–22.

[14] Duby, *Medieval Marriage*, pp. 9–12.

aspirations of the younger sons frustrated by this strategy.[15] Yet the ethics of youth clearly did not appeal only to the marginalized and landless. Powerful feudal *seniores* like Guilhem IX as well as petty lordlings like Bertran de Born used the conventions of literature to identify with the turbulent knightly 'companions' of their courts.[16] For example, in the *tenso*, 'Be me plairia . . .', Giraut de Bornelh suggests to Alfonso II, King of Aragon, that powerful men like him are too impatient and manipulative to be considered worthy lovers, while Alfonso defends himself by saying that he has only ever striven to win his lady's love in an honourable way. While it is possible that jealousy of the ''seigneurs'' intensified the glamour of martial and amorous enterprise, it seems to me that noblemen without extensive inheritances became literary paradigms most simply because they formed the lowest common denominator of heroic possibility. Their achievements were not hampered by their lack of rank, nor limited by the duties of wealth, kinship or government. They are ubiquitous in romance, not because they represent the dynamic outlook of a particular class, but because their potential as heroes is unobstructed by specific economic associations. Such figures were seen to be free to fight, to be holy or to love – in short, to express aspirations which were universal.

As to the Church, Duby recognized that theologians and canonists increasingly stressed the union of hearts in the marriage bond.[17] However, he insisted that this was only an accidental product of ''the Church's profound loathing for sex''.[18] In fact, the Church embraced a ''spectrum of opinion'', as James Brundage has put it, about the place of sex within marriage.[19] It was careful to distinguish moral rigorism from encratism, and vigorously campaigned against heretical movements which denied the dignity of marriage or the role of sex within it.[20] Duby also suggested that the Church only ''unintentionally tended to take a stand against the heads of households in matters of marriage, against the lay conception of misalliance, and, indeed, against male supremacy [in asserting] the equality of the sexes in concluding the marriage pact and in the accomplishment of the duties

---

[15] Duby, 'Dans la France'; *Medieval Marriage*, pp. 12–15, 105–9; *Knight*, p. 224; *History*, p. 76; 'Le mariage', pp. 36–7. Cf. Lazar, p. 14; Evans, p. 130; Payen, 'Mise', p. 225. This idea was suggested in the nineteenth century by Violet Paget: see Boase, pp. 24–5.

[16] Keen, p. 31.

[17] Brundage, *Law*, pp. 197–8, 234, 273–4; Goody, pp. 24, 48, 147–53.

[18] Duby, *Medieval Marriage*, p. 16; 'Mariage', pp. 25–6.

[19] Brundage, *Law*, p. 197; Baldwin, *Language*, p. 4.

[20] For example, Bernard of Clairvaux, *Sermones*, 65, 66. See Leclercq, *Monks*, pp. 6–9; Le Bras, *DTC*, cc. 2131–2, and 'Le mariage', p. 193; Glasser, pp. 19–20; Brundage, *Law*, p. 186. The Church was also reluctant to countenance the challenge to the sexual nature of marriage posed by the practice of *syneisaktism* – cohabitation without sexual contact (Elliott, *Spiritual Marriage*, pp. 32–6).

thereby implied''.[21] He saw no humanistic motives in the adoption of these positions. Indeed, he argued that the Church deliberately altered its definitions of marriage in order to disrupt the lay model of society.[22] For him, the history of medieval marriage is that of a struggle for power, of the conflict between what one might call the two utilitarianisms of marriage, ecclesiastical and dynastic. It was simply another aspect of ''the great political question of the age: the fierce struggle of the spiritual power to dominate the temporal''.[23] Yet, though marriage is indeed both an ideological and a political structure (a ''seminarium civitatis''), it is also a personal and emotional ideal (a ''seminarium caritatis'').[24] It represents a pattern of conduct by which individuals identify themselves and determine their duties in society – as was widely recognized within the medieval Church. Duby admits that his research was ''necessarily restricted to what was on the surface both of society and of institutions; to facts and events'', and pleads ignorance of ''the passions that moved body or spirit'';[25] but, in limiting his research to the evidence provided by those who possessed political power, he gives the impression that medieval marriage can only be understood in terms of political power.[26]

Similar polarities continue to dominate even recent critical thinking about the ''intellectual anthropology of marriage'' in the Middle Ages; only now they are assimilated to other oppositions – Latin/vernacular, clerical/demotic, literate/oral, law/liberty, and, above all, masculine/feminine. Stephen G. Nichols, for example, has equated the new millenium's increasing tendency to claim personal autonomy in marriage with an intellectual and philosophical rehabilitation of the feminine. He presents Marie de France, Constance of Le Ronceray and Heloise as champions of romantic love subversive as much in their gender as their ideology. He argues that these women used ''the resources of language, the marginal vernaculars like Breton and English, juxtaposed with the canonical (and legal) Latin, in a code-switching pattern intended to illustrate the possibility of integrating different attitudes towards love and marriage from those

---

[21] Duby, *Medieval Marriage*, p. 17. As Herlihy has pointed out (p. 86), the opposition between the two models of marriage cannot have been absolute: the Church's insistence on monogamy, for example, reinforced the dynastic emphasis upon the agnatic descent-line.

[22] Duby, *Medieval Marriage*, pp. 53–4; 'Mariage', p. 29: ''Pour juger. Donc pour régir.'' Brundage apparently endorses Duby's reasoning (*Law*, pp. 192–3), but later casts doubt upon the idea ''that the Church and its leaders were either cunning enough or farsighted enough to have implemented a long-range scheme to shape Christian marriage law so as to maximize the Church's material benefits'' (*Law*, pp. 586–7). Cf. Goody, pp. 42–7, 214–15.

[23] Duby, *Knight*, p. 12.

[24] For this antithesis, see Leclercq, *Monks*, pp. 20–1; Noonan, 'Power', p. 429.

[25] Duby, *Knight*, p. 8. A similar strategy is employed by Baldwin, *Language*, p. xvii.

[26] Duby has recently laid greater stress upon more purely ideological factors in the evolution of medieval marriage (*History*, p. 513).

officially sanctioned''.[27] Female speech was undoubtedly identified by medieval writers of both sexes with protest against the cruelties and inequities of medieval society. However, Nichols' rigid genderization of positions within the developing medieval dialectic of marriage not only places too much weight on too few voices, it also obscures the radically innovative processes at work within typically masculine discourses – legal, clerical and theological.

R. Howard Bloch's work, like Nichols's, is governed by a tendency towards binary structuralism in his views of language and society, often assimilated directly or metaphorically to polarizations of gender. Bloch also accepts Duby's predication of two dominantly opposed discourses of medieval marriage, the aristocratic and the clergiastic, represented for him by Guilhem IX d'Aquitaine and Robert d'Arbrissel respectively. However, he rejects the notion implied by Lewis that the courtly idealization of women was simply a "reactive ruse", as he calls it, designed to ennoble love and thus to "descandalize" it in the face of an increasingly strict Christian model of marriage.[28] Instead, he argues that "the conception of romantic love was not so much the product of ecclesiastic pressure upon a licentious aristocracy to respect the institution of marriage as it was a reaction on the part of a marriage-minded nobility against the increasing economic power of women".[29] He sees it, in other words, as a strategy designed to combat the new legal, political and proprietorial rights being attained by women in the eleventh century. By elevating women above the mundane, he argues, the romantic ethic sought to dissociate them from the exercise of power in the public sphere. "Although the discourse of courtliness, which places the woman on a pedestal and worships her as the controlling *domna*, seems to empower women along with an enabling femininity," Bloch argues, it should instead be seen as "yet another ruse of sexual usurpation thoroughly analogous to that developed in the early centuries of our era by the fathers of the early church. . . . Misogyny and courtly love are coconspiring abstractions of the feminine whose function was from the start, and continues to be, the diversion of women from history by the annihilation of the identity of individual women."[30] Bloch thus focuses on the establishment of 'courtliness' as a major cultural defeat for women, seeing in it the creation of an abiding model of gender-relations which effectively silenced feminine discourse. This account should be balanced by a recognition that the first three centuries of this millennium were also responsible for the elaboration of a sophisticated ideology of marriage as a framework for the relationship of two individuals, which in many ways contradicted the disenfranchisement of

[27] Nichols, 'Intellectual Anthropology', pp. 88–9.
[28] Bloch is also addressing the theories of Briffault (e.g. p. 96) and de Rougemont (e.g. p. 77).
[29] Bloch, *Medieval Misogyny*, pp. 195–6.
[30] Bloch, *Medieval Misogyny*, pp. 196–7.

women by the courtly ideal, and which has continued ever since to provide an authoritative site for criticism of it.

Lewis was content to assume too sharp a division between the sensibilities expressed in literature and those according to which medieval society was actually structured; Duby's pessimism about the viability of an archaeology of sentiment allowed him to identify the motivations of society too closely with its mechanisms; while Nichols and Bloch tend to subordinate medieval marriage to their own anatomizations of gender and the text. All these scholars have tended to define literary idealizations of human relationships during the Middle Ages only in terms of escapism, conflict, radical change and narrow oppositions between different classes, genders and institutions. In fact, attitudes towards marriage did not evolve solely within such prescribed ranges – neither solely in defiance of reality, in reaction to political exigency nor in deference to the medieval discourse of gender. They are also the expression of an organic intellectual development common to medieval society as a whole. As Christopher Brooke has argued, "what happened in the twelfth century . . . was a widening of the variety of sentiment, rather than the total *bouleversement* of human attitudes".[31] The ideology of marriage changed in this period not simply in response or reaction to political and religious pressures: it was enriched by a new attention to the nature of the relationships structuring society. The profound demographic, economic and political changes of the eleventh and twelfth centuries provided a stimulus for a re-evaluation of basic institutions, and, specifically, of the role of individuals within them.[32] Like Brooke's, then, my approach is designed to avoid too rigid a determination of "the medieval idea of marriage" by recognizing both the patchiness of medieval testimony and its challenging diversity.

As one of the ways in which people assess their allegiances to social ideals, literature was naturally an instrumental part of this process of re-evaluation.[33] It frequently sought to dramatize the question of how the bonds which necessarily link people together in any community can be validated emotionally and spiritually, by exploring the relationship between inward resolution and outward action. As Carolyn Walker Bynum has said, "inner with outer, motive with model, self with community, these aspects of the twelfth century go hand in hand . . . A new sense of self, of inner change and inner choice, is precipitated by the necessity to choose among roles, among

---

[31] Brooke, 'Marriage and Society', p. 19. Cf. Holmes, p. 648, and Dronke, *Poetic Individuality*, p. 23.

[32] I am thinking, for example, of the ties of monasticism and the religious life (Brooke, 'Marriage and Society', p. 27; Leclercq, *Love*; Bynum), of feudalism (Keen; Duby, *History*, pp. 3–31), of parenthood (Glasser, Fellows) and of friendship (Morris, *Discovery*, pp. 97–107; Mathew, 'Ideals'; Leclercq, 'L'amitié'). It was apparently only in the twelfth-century that medieval thinkers began to develop a comprehensive theory of the nature and value of a personal vow (Brundage, 'Votive Obligations', p. 78).

[33] Cf. Morris, *Discovery*, p. 45.

groups. A new sense of becoming part of a group by conforming one's behaviour to an external standard is necessitated by a new awareness of a choosing and interior self."[34]

2. Medieval Theories of Marriage: Canon Law and Theology

Although Bynum's formulation belongs to her analysis of the proliferation of new religious groups in this period, it is also a useful way of understanding the complex process which Duby labels a little too briefly as "the Christianization of marriage practices".[35] Indeed, one way of viewing this process is to see it as making marriage analogous to a religious calling. "What is the difference," asks a modern canonist, "between the intention required for ordination and the one required for marriage? Both sacraments . . . consecrate a person for a state of life and [each] brings with it heavy responsibilities."[36] Stanley Parmisano has argued that "in and through the Church's comparison of marriage to the extraordinary calling of virginity, marriage gradually assumed a dignity it had never known before . . . Now it was not simply compared to a religious order; it became an order in its own right, with surpassing, unborrowed dignity."[37] Goody has pointed out that the emphasis placed by the Church upon the importance of the affective engagement of the partners in the formation of the marital bond apparently contradicts its insistence upon the invalidity of divorce, no matter what the feelings of the partners.[38] This is less contradictory than it might seem, for in defining marriage as an absolute and lifelong commitment just like a religious vow, the Church made the participants' sense of inner consent seem particularly vital. At the same time, marriage itself served as a model for the definition of an individual's sense of a religious bond. As Leclercq has said, "it is because there can be no conjugal union without love that it became a metaphor of love for God".[39] Marital and religious commitments were mutually illuminated by their metaphorical interrelationship.[40] "Family

---

[34] Bynum, p. 107; cf. Waddell, 'Reform', p. 95.
[35] Duby, *Knight*, p. 48; 'Le mariage', p. 20.
[36] Örsy, p. 280.
[37] Parmisano, p. 76. Cf. Le Bras, 'Le mariage', p. 193.
[38] Goody, p. 25. He suggests (p. 188) that the Church's "view of marriage as an indissoluble tie . . . was intrinsic to its appropriation of marriage to the religious domain, to the domain of God". For the Church's policy on divorce, Brundage, *Law*, pp. 200–2.
[39] Leclercq, *Monks*, p. 3; cf. Herlihy, pp. 118–20.
[40] Bugge points out (p. 66) that "as early as the fourth century Ambrose reports that the rite for the consecration of virgins was similar to that used in the actual nuptial ceremony." Another facet of this process is Christianity's assimilation of kinship terms to spiritual ones: Goody, p. 194.

imagery, family models, in religious devotion and in daily experience: each echoed and reinforced the other.''[41]

Far from devaluing marriage or using it simply as a political tool, churchmen sought to construct for it a distinctive status, value and ceremonial, as for a religious order. This was the process by which, in Brooke's words, ''the celibate theologians of the eleventh and twelfth centuries . . . by some mysterious alchemy turned marriage into a sacrament''.[42] The presence of priests at marriage-celebrations evolved from a privilege, to a pre-requisite.[43] From late in the twelfth century it became customary in England and northern France for marriage to be performed at the doors of the church, generally as a preliminary to a mass celebrated inside.[44] From around 1100, a matrimonial liturgy began to evolve.[45] It became, in Parmisano's words, the point at which ''the Church's theology became itself a kind of poetry of love''.[46] All these developments formed part of an attempt to dignify marriage with a ritual apparatus of its own. This might be seen, in turn, as an attempt by the ecclesiastical authorities to win control over one of society's most fundamental institutions. The practice of using written records to assert the concrete existence of each marriage had yet to develop, and, in its absence, the more impressive the marital ceremony could be made to seem, then the greater the emphasis upon the finality of the union.[47] It was clearly in the Church's interest to support the stability of marriage in this way, if only as a way of establishing a standard of sexual

[41] Herlihy, p. 115.
[42] Brooke, 'Marriage and Society', p. 28: cf. Goody, p. 146; Brundage, *Law*, pp. 254, 431-2; Le Bras, 'Le mariage', pp. 193-4; Örsy, p. 29; Dominique Barthélemy in Duby, *History*, p. 128; Delhaye, 'Development', pp. 83-5. ''Sacrament is here used . . . in the sense in which scholastics were to define it between 1140 and 1150 – namely a rite which both symbolises and effects grace, of which they listed seven instances. The sacredness of Christian marriage was of course recognised from earliest times but no one dreamt of translating the *mysterion* referred to in the Epistle to the Ephesians (5: 32) by 'sacrament' in the scholastic and Tridentine sense'' (Delhaye, p. 85).
[43] Vogel, pp. 422, 426. Sheehan, 'Choice', pp. 26-8; Molin and Mutembe, pp. 28-9; Brundage, *Law*, pp. 190-91.
[44] Molin and Mutembe, pp. 36-7; Brooke, *Idea*, pp. 248-57; Lucas, p. 96. Brooke has suggested that ''the development of splendid church porches in the twelfth and thirteenth centuries owed something to new matrimonial fashions'' ('Marriage and Society', p. 29; 'Idea', pp. 253-6; cf. Le Bras, 'Mariage', p. 198). Similarly, Meyer (pp. 292-3) has suggested that the deep whetting-marks found in many German churches can be explained by ecclesiastical patronage of what had previously been a secular marriage-ceremony using a sword as a token of good faith: cf. *Ruodlieb*, XIV. 64.
[45] Barthélemy, in Duby, *History*, p. 124.
[46] Parmisano, p. 5. Cf. Kelly, *LMAC*, p. 293.
[47] It was only in the thirteenth century that marriage before a notary who made a formal written record was introduced in some Italian cities, and even then it seems to have been a custom only among the wealthy (Brundage, *Law*, p. 440, 502-3). For the development of literate culture generally, see Clanchy.

morality. Yet, at the same time, these developments in marriage-practice can also be seen, more importantly, as a reflection of the wider intellectual movement redefining marriage as a momentous act of consent. As Leclercq has remarked, "even the ritualization of marriage through external ceremonies and words helped to personalize and internalize conjugal union".[48]

It is striking that all these developments lie in the period directly following the Church's imposition of clerical celibacy.[49] It seems paradoxical that, just as theologians were establishing the Church's competence over marriage by sacramentalizing it, the same theologians were arguing that the clergy were better off without it.[50] It is possible that the noisy campaign against clerical marriage fostered a wave of antimatrimonial and antifeminist literature.[51] The establishment of clerical celibacy could at least partially explain the enormous popularity of Latin satires against women like Walter Map's *Epistola Valerii* and the anonymous *Dissuasio de non ducenda uxore*. Nevertheless, antifeminism is not a specifically medieval phenomenon, as Wulff points out, for the Middle Ages inherited the theme "whether to marry" ("ducendane uxor") from the traditional rhetorical exercises of antiquity.[52] Map's poem is an extravagant demonstration of virtuosity in this exercise, not a serious piece of propaganda. In this sense, it is, as Blangez says, a "hoax".[53] Similarly, Rigg points out that although the *Dissuasio* "seems to have enjoyed most popularity in university circles . . . it is concerned not with the obstacles that marriage places in the way of celibate sanctity or contemplative philosophy but simply with the inconveniences for the ordinary working man".[54] It makes no direct reference to the issues of Gregorian reform. By contrast, there are several works extant which vigorously express opposition to the principle of clerical celibacy.[55]

---

[48] Leclercq, *Monks*, p. 15.

[49] Gaudemet, 'Celibat', pp. 4–5; Brundage, *Law*, pp. 183–4. Clerical celibacy was already an issue at the Council of Nicaea (A.D. 325, Canon 33; Goody, p. 61; Perceval, pp. 51–2). In England, it was proclaimed at the Council of Westminster in 1102 (Canon 5; Goody, p. 134); and it became a widely-established principle "from the 1120s on" (Brooke, *Idea*, p. 68). Even so, clerical concubinage was still pervasive in practice even at the end of the twelfth century (Brundage, p. 404).

[50] Bynum, pp. 11–12; Brooke, *Idea*, pp. 63–4.

[51] Wulff, p. 35; Blamires, p. 4; McLaughlin, 'Peter Abelard', p. 311.

[52] Wulff, pp. 1, 15; Mann, *Geoffrey Chaucer*, pp. 50–1, quoting Quintilian, *Institutio Oratoria* II. 4. 25; Wiesen, pp. 113–15.

[53] Blangez, p. 393, "canular"; cf. Delhaye, pp. 79–82.

[54] Rigg, *Gawain*, p. 1; *History*, p. 236.

[55] For example, the Norman Anonymous, *De sancta uirginitate et de sacerdotum matrimonio*, pp. 204–9; the Latin poems, 'Consultatio sacerdotum', 'De concubinis sacerdotum' and 'De convocatione sacerdotum'; Adam de la Halle, *Jeu de la Feuillée*, 426–69; and *Renart le Contrefait*, 3193–6 (quoted, Flinn, p. 371). See also Gaudemet, 'Le celibat', pp. 13–17; Brundage, *Law*, p. 183.

The impulse for the reform-movement was not a sudden hostility towards marriage, but the growing conviction that the priest's vocation was different from that of the layman and that it should be seen to be different – that there should be "discretio ordinum".[56] As Honorius Augustodunensis put it, "the order of priests differs from that of laymen as much as light from darkness".[57] Fundamental to this conviction was the feeling that each order within society achieves its dignity only by being distinct from all the others. It was felt that priests were distracted from their essential functions by their concerns with property and family.[58] Clerical marriage was seen as a confusion of roles, and as a channel for abuses.[59] Pope Gregory VII, for example, declared that "the church cannot be freed from servitude to laymen, unless clerks can be freed from their wives".[60] The evolution of a pure ideal of marital union was perhaps only possible once it had been defined as a vocation exclusive of any other. The imposition of celibacy must have encouraged misogyny among the literate men of the Church, but, as Benton reminds us, "the preference for celibacy over marriage is so prominent in medieval religious writing that it is easy to overlook the underlying assumption that marriage was both normal and desirable for most people".[61] "The ideal of marriage", he adds, "if not always the reality, was that there should be love between the spouses". This was an idea which the Church's theologians actively encouraged.[62]

The Church's emphasis upon the feelings of the couple towards each other was not simply an attempt to diminish the importance of the sexual bond. It was an integral part of the re-evaluation of the individual's role within the institutions of society. One aspect of this development was the establishment of a legal tradition within the Church.[63] Law, like literature, can function "as ideological force and witness".[64] Codification requires definition, and the lawyers thus sought to pinpoint the essence of the marital contract, the effective moment in which a binding commitment was formed.[65] At the

---

[56] The phrase, and the argument, can be found in Gerald of Cambrai, *Acta Synodi Atrebatensis*, PL 142. 1299–1301 (written 1025); quoted, Duby, *Medieval Marriage*, pp. 18–19. Cf. Bynum, pp. 9–12; Goody, pp. 107, 133.

[57] "Quantum differt lux a tenebris, tantum differt ordo sacerdotum a laicis" (*De offendiculo*, 28; quoted, Waddell, 'Reform', p. 95).

[58] Cf. I Cor. 7: 32–5.

[59] Goody, pp. 81–2; Brundage, *Law*, pp. 214–15.

[60] "Non liberari potest ecclesia a servitudine laïcorum, nisi liberantur clerici ab uxoribus", quoted by Gaudemet, 'Célibat', p. 10.

[61] Benton, 'Clio', p. 21; cf. Leclercq, *Monks*, pp. 1–6. Cf. Gregory of Nyssa, *De virginitate*, 8 (quoted by Pagels, p. 84): "in saying this, let no one think we deprecate marriage . . . the common instincts of humanity plead sufficiently on its behalf".

[62] Cf. Parmisano, p. 5; Leclercq, *Monks*, pp. 58–9.

[63] Brundage, *Law*, pp. 177–80, 229–35, 256–60; Schnell, pp. 37–48; Moule, pp. vi–vii; Sheehan, 'Choice', p. 7.

[64] Dworkin, p. 11.

[65] Kelly contrasts the concern of legal writers about the sexual minutiae of relationships

beginning of this process stands Ivo, Bishop of Chartres (1091–1116). "Close study of Ivo's letters", says Carolyn Moule, "demonstrates that a single concept underlined all Ivo's understanding of the nature of marriage – that is *consensus*."[66] In his *Decretum*, Ivo quoted Pope Leo I's opinion that consent rather than consummation makes marriage, since even an unconsummated marriage fully symbolizes the relationship between Christ and the Church.[67] Moule argues that Ivo used the terms "consensus" and "sacramentum" almost interchangeably.[68] The implication of this association is that the sacramentality of marriage lies essentially in the consent of the individual. This is a radical interpretation in that it ignores the customary regard for parental approval, for the transfer of the dowry and for consummation. Ivo's insistence upon consent was perhaps not novel, for the principle that "consent rather than consummation makes marriage" ("nuptias non concubitus, sed consensus facit") had been articulated by the Roman jurist, Ulpian.[69] Yet, even if consent was the sole sufficient requirement for Roman marriage, "this should not be taken to mean", as Brundage reminds us, "that the other usual and customary elements of the marriage rites were irrelevent or immaterial. Betrothal, dowry agreement, the ceremonial procession of the bride and her attendants to the groom's house, the wedding feast, and other rituals constituted external manifestations of consent".[70] Moreover, the assumption in Roman law "that a girl was always in her father's gift," as Brooke points out, "made mock of this consent".[71] Ivo, by contrast, made *consensus* an inalienable principle, and thus located marriage firmly within the spiritual domain. He admitted, nevertheless, that physical union was at least a token for the creation of a union.[72]

A similar balance between the emphasis upon consent and the acknowledgement of consummation can be found in the *Decretum* of Gratian (fl. c. 1140). Noonan has stressed the personal against the social aspects of Gratian's conception of marriage, particularly his support for individual free

with the more "mystical code" expressed in other genres, particularly "writings on spirituality" (*LMAC*, p. 287). However, I think that even their sometimes inelegant analyses are rooted in an intellectual focus upon the *essence* of marriage, which is in its way highly susceptible to mysticism.

66 Moule, p. 3. Cf. Duby, *Medieval Marriage*, p. 43.

67 Ivo, *Decretum* 8. 74, 139 (PL 161. 599–600, 615); Leo, *Ep.* 167. 4 (PL 54. 1204–5): Brundage, *Law*, p. 188.

68 Moule, p, 8 ; Duby, *Medieval Marriage*, p. 42; Örsy, p. 280.

69 *Digest*, 50. 17. 30 (Krueger, p. 921); cf. 35. 1. 15 (p. 540); quoted by Brooke, *Idea*, p. 128. However, it has been suggested that such statements are Christian interpolations (see Clark, p. 30).

70 Brundage, *Law*, p. 34. On *consensus* generally in Roman and medieval law, see Gaudemet, 'Définition', p. 108; Le Bras, *DTC*, cc. 2134–7; Goody, pp. 86, 205–6; Herlihy, p. 8; Leclercq, *Monks*, pp. 1–2; Delhaye, 'Development', p. 86.

71 Brooke, *Idea*, p. 104; cf. Lucas, p. 66. Foucault resolves this contradiction diachronically (*Care*, pp. 72–80).

72 Moule, p. 22.

choice in opposition to family interests.[73] He shows how freely Gratian handled the authorities on this point, relying apparently more upon his own intuition than upon the legal tradition. For Gratian, the marital bond is essentially "an emotion-colored assent", and he designated it by a phrase from Roman Law – "affectio maritalis".[74] This phrase had formerly served only to distinguish marriage by its permanence and exclusivity from concubinage.[75] His employment of the term, by contrast, was "tinged with the sense of an emotional bond between the spouses, a mutual attachment and regard for the well-being and regard of one another".[76] Despite the "personalism" of his approach, Gratian argued that consummation did play an important part in marital union. In his theory of marriage, "consummation transformed the union into a 'sacrament' and hence made it indissoluble".[77] In this, Gratian was perhaps acknowledging the force of custom. Consummation was inevitably seen by many to be both the substantive expression of a couple's rights over one another and a guarantee of the possibility of procreation. In a similar way, the theologian, Hugh of St Victor (d. 1141), bound together marriage and "the office of marriage" (i.e. procreative sexuality) as a double sacrament: "Marital union lies in the bond of love. The office of marriage lies in the generation of children. Therefore conjugal love is a sacrament, and the sacrament among spouses is the commingling of the flesh."[78] In Hugh's eyes, the bond of love is sanctified by analogy with God's love for the soul: the sexual bond by analogy with Christ's love for the Church.[79] In a less abstract way, Hugh is also "personalistic", for he recognized the value of marriage in fulfilling the social and emotional needs of individuals.[80]

The "Parisian" theory of marriage championed and popularized by Peter Lombard (c. 1095–1160) completely subordinated sex to *consensus* in the formation of marriage: "The efficient cause of matrimony is consent", he declared.[81] Peter argued that betrothal differed from marriage not because it

---

[73] Noonan, 'Power'; 'Marital Affection', pp. 489–99; Sheehan, 'Choice', pp. 8–15; Kelly, *LMAC*, pp. 164–6.

[74] Noonan, 'Power', p. 425.

[75] Brundage, 'Concubinage', p. 2; Noonan, 'Marital Affection', p. 490.

[76] Brundage, *Law*, p. 239.

[77] Brundage, *Law*, p. 236. Cf. Le Bras, 'Le mariage', pp. 197–8; Helmholz, p. 26; Sheehan, 'Choice', p. 8.

[78] Hugh of St Victor, *De beatae Mariae virginitate*, PL 176. 874C: "Coniugium est in foedere dilectionis. Coniugis officium est in generatione prolis. Igitur amor conjugalis sacramentum est, et sacramentum in conjugibus est commixtio carnis." Cf. *De sacramentis*, II, 11, caps. 3, 7; Bugge, pp. 85–6.

[79] Hugh admitted, however, that sex was not essential to a true marriage (*De sacramentis*, II, 11, caps. 3–4).

[80] For example, *De beatae Mariae virginitate*, PL 176. 875A. Brundage, *Law*, pp. 197–8.

[81] Peter Lombard, *Sententiae*, IV, 27, PL 192. 910: "Efficiens . . . causa Matrimonii est consensus." This doctrine was theologically exigent, since the marriage of Mary and Joseph can only have been valid if consummation is not essential to marriage

was unconsummated but because it was a statement of future rather than present intention.[82] The consensual theory was repeatedly confirmed by Pope Alexander III, and became "the prevailing canonical doctrine throughout Europe".[83] It was made generally familiar by the matrimonial liturgy, and by its dissemination in handbooks of penance and confession.[84] By asserting that marriage was a wholly spiritual and emotional relationship rather than an economic or sexual one, the medieval Church not only gave itself greater licence to interfere in matrimonial matters, as Duby suggests: it also presented a model of society in which marriage was a more dignified and momentous event than it had been before. For example, preachers and hagiographers emphasized the potential of marriage as a channel for the moral improvement of its partners.[85] Penitential writers like Thomas of Chobham urged wives to be "their husbands' preachers" ("predicatrices virorum suorum"), for he thought that marital intimacy softened men's hearts better than clerical authority – "for no priest can so soften the heart of a man as can his wife".[86]

Yet the new definition of marriage had its side-effects. In recognizing unions formed either in breach of canon law or indeed entirely without any legal or ceremonial formalities, the Church created – or at least confirmed – a situation in which the validity of marriage now depended absolutely upon the nature of the thoughts and emotions of those concerned.[87] "Upon the assessment of those psychic factors depended the validity of their union, the legitimacy of their children, their own and their descendants' property rights, and the relationship of their families."[88] All of this was endangered by the possibility of 'contract' or 'clandestine' marriages, a phenomenon which was the inevitable result of "the simplicity of the Church in respect of consent".[89]

(*Sententiae*, 26, c. 910; cf. Hugh of St Victor, *De beatae Mariae virginitate*). The line of thought seems to originate with Augustine (Clark, p. 23). Cf. also Brundage, *Law*, pp. 264–5; Baldwin, *Language*, pp. 6–7; Sheehan, 'Choice', pp. 13–14; T.P. McLaughlin.

[82] *Sententiae*, 27, c. 912.

[83] Brundage, *Law*, p. 265, 268–70; Le Bras, *DTC*, cc. 2132–4; Herlihy, p. 81; Sheehan, 'Choice', pp. 14–15.

[84] Sheehan, 'Choice', pp. 19–33; Glasser, pp. 20–3. For example, Robert of Flamborough, II, iii, 55, p. 88.

[85] Farmer; Sheehan, 'Choice', pp. 24–5; Glasser, p. 27. Biblical precedents for the notion of marital improvement could be found in the Pauline deliberations on mixed marriages, I Cor. 7:14–6 and I Peter 3:1–7. For mixed marriages, see Brundage, pp. 195–6; they are prominent in Wolfram von Eschenbach's *Parzifal* and *Willehalm*.

[86] Thomas of Chobham, *Summa*, 7. 2. 15: "nullus enim sacerdos ita potest cor viri emollire sicut potest uxor". On Thomas himself, see Baldwin, *Language*, p. 2.

[87] For example, the *Magdalen College Pontifical* (Canterbury, 1150–1200): "Sufficit secundum leges solus eorum consensus; si solus in nuptiis forte defuerit, cetera omnia, etiam cum ipso coetu celebrata, frustrantur" (BN MS Lat. NA 306, f. 213v, quoted by Molin and Mutembe, p. 64, n. 3; Sheehan, 'Choice', pp. 28–9). See also Kelly, *LMAC*, pp. 163–8; Brundage, *Law*, pp. 239, 276–7.

[88] Brundage, *Law*, p. 414.

[89] Lucas, p. 94.

Uncertainty about whether or not a contract had been made frequently resulted in litigation, and continued to do so right into the early modern period.[90] Yet, so committed were Alexander and his successors to the principle of free consent in marriage, that they decreed marriages valid even at the expense of weakening their own control over them.

The policy of making consent the sole legal criterion for marriage was impracticable. Not only was it difficult to assess objectively, but it had to be related in practice to other factors, such as parental consent and economic circumstances. Moreover, it obstructed the Church's attempts to define marriage as a sacrament dignified by the presence of a priest and the performance of a ceremony.[91] The explanation seems to me to be that the sentimental prejudices of the Church's leaders outweighed political expediency. They only countenanced such practical contradictions in their marital policy because they were so convinced of the ideological consistency of what they taught, for they apparently felt that inward consent was so indispensable to the animation of outward ritual, that its absence rendered the visible formalities of marriage meaningless. For these reasons, they insisted upon consent as the primary factor in the creation of the conjugal bond, even though it was legally intangible. Measures were taken to discourage clandestine marriages, most notably at the Fourth Lateran Council of 1215; and they were frequently condemned in sermons.[92] However, it was not until the Council of Trent that such unions were pronounced absolutely invalid.[93] England did not subscribe to the Council of Trent, and thus retained much of the medieval canon law of marriage until

[90] Brooke, 'Marriage and Society', p. 26; Brundage, *Law*, pp. 335–7. The Church's recognition of clandestine marriages continued to provoke litigation even in the fourteenth century. Sheehan has shown, for example, that informal unions were at issue in 90% of the matrimonial cases brought before the consistory court of Ely between 1374 and 1382 (Sheehan, 'Formation'; cf. Helmholz, p. 5; Kelly, *LMAC*, pp. 169–72; Pedersen). As Stone has commented (p. 26), medieval churchmen could hardly have dreamed either of "the flood of litigation which [they] would unleash upon the church courts of Europe in the late Middle Ages, and later still in England" or "the perversion of [this] decree so as to facilitate male seduction of young unmarried girls". Jeremy Goldberg has recently doubted that "canon law was a 'seducer's charter' and that medieval marriage was inherently unstable" (p. 11). He argues that "by labelling any contract of marriage made other than in the approved manner at the church door as 'clandestine' the Church blurred the distinction that ordinary lay-folk may themselves have perceived between an informal 'engagement' and the binding contract of the 'handfast' or 'trothplight' " (p. 241). Yet what is so significant here is that despite the Church's gradual assumption of jurisdiction over marriage, it was still not prepared to legislate against such "informal engagements".

[91] Stone, p. 54.

[92] Brundage, *Law*, pp. 189–90. Banns became customary in England from the end of the twelfth century (Goody, p. 149; Sheehan, 'Choice', p. 15); and were formalized as a requirement by Fourth Lateran Council (1215; canon 51). For sermons, see d'Avray and Tausche, p. 81.

[93] Goody, p. 148; Vogel, p. 402.

the Marriage Act of 1753.[94] What is most striking about ecclesiastical teaching upon marriage during the twelfth and thirteenth centuries is therefore not its utilitarianism, but its impractical idealism, its often semi-mystical emphasis upon the essence of the bond, and its emphasis upon the emotional commitment of the marrying individual.

Brundage has raised the possibility that this was the Church's response to the dynamic literary idealism of the troubadours. However, as he says, "it is more likely that both the ethos of *fin' amors* and Alexander III's marriage decretals reflected a dawning consciousness of the importance of individual choice, coupled with a new awareness of marriage as a personal relationship".[95] In other words, the literary ethos of love distinctively expressed by the poets and romancers was parallel to the thinking of the canon lawyers and theologians, and neither opposing nor provoking it. The two 'systems' of thought share a similar consciousness and method of conception, rather than a direct relationship of cause and effect. The lyrics of the troubadours can thus be used to illustrate not a fundamental opposition between love and marriage in medieval society, but the coherence of literary analyses of love with legal and theological definitions of marriage. Moore has stressed the harmony between monastic, scholastic and 'courtly' definitions of the nature of love: "in the minds of most . . . love was the source of goodness, the effect of goodness, and goodness itself. It was a free act of the rational person – or rather of persons, for in its fullness, it was reciprocal, the mutual recognition of goodness and beauty. Its goal was the union of lovers, perhaps physical, but first of all the union of wills or hearts."[96] He explains what he sees as the failure of these three strands of thought to "synthesise" in terms of their solidification into narrow frames of reference.[97] Yet the differences in method and purpose of the three modes were profound, naturally preventing total coalescence, and they only make the coincidence of terms and ideas all the more striking.

One of the consequences of the canonical doctrine that marriages were formed solely by consent was the requirement which it placed upon the individual of the self-consciousness necessary to make an unambiguous personal commitment. By comparison, the most original aspect of troubadour-poetry in literary terms was neither its mysticism of love nor its emphasis upon unfulfilment, but its complex self-consciousness in the affirmation of an emotional bond. Like ecclesiastical thinkers, the troubadours were concerned with defining the essential moment in which such a bond was formed. We can perhaps see in the increasing sophistication of twelfth-century love-lyric and romance attempts to explore the subtle and complex process by which an individual recognizes in himself or herself the

---

[94] Stone, p. 15; Kelly, *LMAC*, p. 178.
[95] Brundage, *Law*, p. 333; also, pp. 239, 273–5.
[96] Moore, p. 434.
[97] Moore, pp. 442.

existence of a compelling link with another individual. It reflects a growing fascination with the psychological mechanisms which determine the relationships governing society.

3. Guilhem IX of Aquitaine: 'Champion of Adultery'?

The earliest identifiable troubadour, Guilhem IX, Duke of Aquitaine, is generally credited with the initial impulse for 'courtly love'; and his work is often the site for definitions of medieval attitudes towards sexual relationships.[98] The weakness of such approaches is not only that Guilhem can be seen as the representative of only a very limited group within medieval society, but also that what is most radically innovative about his work, as it seems to me, is not a consistent attempt to create any kind of counter-morality of love, but rather his application to love of ideas drawn from the currents of thought about law, relationships and the individual which were rapidly developing in the society of his time. For example, one of the most striking and fundamental aspects of his work is its exaltation of personal responsibility in the process of choice. He uses the metaphor of military allegiance to express a sense of the completeness of his engagement in love;[99] while at the same time he represents the difficulties of the service enjoined by the lady upon her lover as an equivalent to the emotional difficulty of reaching the point of resolution necessary for the formation of such a bond:

> Ma dona m'assaya e·m prueva,
> Quossi de qual guiza l'am,
> E ja per plag que m'en mueva
> No·m solvera[i] de son liam.[100]

When Guilhem says that his lady is testing him, he is referring to the trial of self-analysis, of which his song (as well as his resolution to love) is the product.[101] His declaration that he is his lady's liege-man has a triumphant air, because it represents the final achievement of emotional certainty. Guilhem's language is legal as well as feudal – "per plag que m'en mueva" (5), "en sa carta·m pot escriure" (8), "dels tortz q'ie·us clam" (30);[102] and

---

[98] Morris, *Discovery*, p. 109: e.g. Bezzola, pp. 152–7; Lefèvre, pp. 89–94.
[99] For example, 'Pos vezem . . .', 25–6: "Ja no cera nuils hom ben fis/ Contr' amor, si no l'es aclis . . .".
[100] 'Farai chansoneta . . .', 3–6; line 5, MS "solvera", em. Riquer, Bond: "My lady measures and tests me to find out in what way I love her, and never, whatever plea she moves against me, will I release myself from her bond." Doubts about this lyric's authenticity are discussed by Riquer, I, p. 124.
[101] Bossy argues that the twelfth century witnessed a vogue for "inner and confidential debate" (p. xix).
[102] Cf. Bond, p. 83.

it suggests that his conception of love, like the theologians' understanding of marriage, was modelled upon the legal concept of contract. He also imagines the experience of love in terms of a pattern of conduct, perhaps analogous to those patterns of conduct by which the new religious groups of the eleventh and twelfth centuries expressed their differing experiences of faith:

> Obedïensa deu portar
> A maintas gens qui vol amar;
> E cove li que sapchar far
> Faitz avinens,
> E que·s gart en cort de parlar
> Vilanamens.[103]

Even within the limitations of his profoundly egotistical poetry, Guilhem stresses the importance of reciprocality in the experience of love. He argues that only in the mutuality of consent can the finest joys of love be felt. "All the joy in the world is ours", he promises his lady, "if we love each other".[104] He is reminded by "the trembling hawthorn-branch" ("la branca de l'albespi . . . tremblan") of the morning when he and his lady crystallized their love:

> Enquer me membra d'un mati
> Que nos fezem de guera fi
> E que·m donet un don tan gran:
> Sa drudari' e son anel.[105]

The hawthorn-branch perhaps represents the emotional dialogue and uncertainty preliminary to the consummation of the bond in the Lady's gift of faith. With the phrase "drudari' e son anel" Guilhem identifies an inwardly founded disposition with an outward token, a identification implicit to the development of the marriage-ceremony. Like the canonists and theologians, however, Guilhem does not deny sex a place in the fulfilment of love, but it is only secondary to a moment of reciprocal consent in a higher, more mystical sphere. His declaration of desire has the air of an afterthought, a sidelong assurance that his love is healthily physical too:

> Enquer me lais Dieus viure tan
> C'aia mas mans soz so mantel.[106]

---

[103] 'Pos vezem . . .', 31–6: "Whoever wishes to be a lover must behave obediently to many people; and it is appropriate that he know how to do pleasing deeds, and avoid speaking in court like a churl."

[104] 'Farai chansoneta . . .', 33–4: "Totz lo joys del mon es nostre . . . s'amduy nos amam."

[105] 'Ab la dolchor . . .', 19–20: "Still it reminds me of a morning when we made an end to war, when she gave me a truly great gift, her intimacy and her ring."

[106] 'Ab la dolchor . . .', lines 23–4: "Still may God let me live long enough to get my hands under her mantle."

The conceptions which govern Guilhem's depiction of the experience of love – as a ritualized contract, as a pattern of conduct, and as a shared responsibility – are exactly those by which canonists and theologians sought to redefine the nature of marriage. His purposes were different, but it is not true, as Lazar thought, that his "conception de l'amour" was "nettement opposée à la morale chrétienne".[107] Yet the three songs from which I have been quoting depart somewhat from the tone characteristic of the rest of his corpus. Elsewhere he lays claim to a different persona: he is coarsely masculine, wittily boastful, cruelly satirical. He reinforces his claim to being a worldly and skilful manipulator of women – a "maistre certa" – by vaunting his conquests in relationships which are certainly not modelled upon marriage.[108] Thus, even if the ways in which he idealizes love parallel the ways in which the theologians idealized marriage, his attitude towards marriage as such is still, in Simon Gaunt's words, "exactly what one might expect from a man in his position. When they are not the subject of his bawdy jokes, he usually treats women as a form of currency in a masculine exchange, with little regard for the sanctity of marriage."[109] Yet Guilhem was no propagandist for adultery. His reference to the "leis de con" can hardly be seen as an attempt to glamorize illicit love. His attitude is salaciously unidealistic, and indeed, he balances his claims to a cynical prowess in sex by depicting female sexuality in terms of the misogynistic cliché of women's insatiability.[110] There is no systematic attempt in Guilhem's work to ascribe any sort of ethical value to love outside marriage. He draws attention to the illicitness of his amours only when his purpose is to deflate ironically, either himself or others, and never as an elemental part of his exaltation of the love-experience.

A strength of Guilhem's work is the dramatic way in which his two kinds of self-consciousness play against each other. The strutting, masculine arrogance by which he appeals to his male "companions" in his court might be seen as an attempt to play down the implications of apron-tied wimpishness and servility which might follow from his emphasis upon humility in love. In 'Farai chansoneta nueva . . .', Guilhem's declaration of allegiance in love is balanced by a roguish aside – "Don't think that I am drunk if I love my good lady."[111] By contrast, it is perhaps possible to see in 'Pos vezem de novel florir . . .' an attempt to distinguish cynical conquests in love unfavourably from the abstract and ideal relationships in which one finds true "joy":

[107] Lazar, p. 12.

[108] In 'Companho, farai un vers . . .', for example, he speaks of two of his vassals' wives as "mounts".

[109] Gaunt, p. 60. Cf. Lazar, 'Carmina', p. 252.

[110] In the Middle Ages, this idea was authorized by medical science: e.g. by Trotula in *De secretis mulierum*: see Bullough, pp. 495–6.

[111] 'Farai chansoneta . . .', 9–10: "E no m'en tenguatz per yure/ S' ieu ma bona dompna am . . .".

A totz jorns m'es pres enaisi
C'anc d'aquo c'amei non jauzi,
Ni o faray ni anc no fi.
C'az essïens
Fauc maintas res que·l cor me di:
"Tot es niens."[112]

In sum, the ideas which Guilhem expresses in his songs are fully consonant with the intellectual preoccupations and social concerns of his age. In the imaginative realms of love-poetry, the actual structures of society never seem very solid, and we should not take Guilhem's apparent lack of interest in them as an aspect of a literary or ideological programme. His work and that of his successors should not be seen as either the fountainhead or the spark for a new idealization of love to the absolute exclusion of marriage.[113] Although Guilhem's own matrimonial difficulties are well-known, there is no evidence that he was hostile to marriage as an institution, and no reason to think that his poetry systematically expresses any such hostility.[114] Far more significant is the way in which he presents what is perhaps a universal love-experience as a process of determining an emotional commitment and of expressing it in a ritualized moment of consent. His emphasis upon the inward determination of a social bond, both as a responsibility and as a privilege, is consonant with the treatment of marriage by many of the texts discussed in this book.

4. Andreas Capellanus: 'Adultery's Legislator'?

The *De amore* of Andreas Capellanus is often cited as a serious medieval commentary upon the nature and place of love in contemporary society. In particular, it has been treated as "the bible of Courtly love" and quarried for slogans which seem to support that concept.[115] To Douglas Kelly, for example, it "provides a norm with which to compare other works and to arrive at an understanding of how courtly love was conceived, at least as an

---

[112] 'Pos vezem . . .', 13–18: "Everyday this is the way it's been with me, that I've never delighted in anything I loved, and I never will, as I never did. Thus I consciously do many things, while my heart tells me: 'All [of it] is nothing'."

[113] Cf. Dronke, 'Guillaume IX', p. 247: "he is neither the founder nor even an exponent of *amour courtois*".

[114] Bond, pp. xxxi–xxxii; Duby, *Knight*, pp. 123, 158–9.

[115] Boase, p. 21; Moi, p. 11; Karnein, p. 324; Schnell, p. 12, n. 7. Walsh tentatively dates the work to "the middle 1180s" (p. 2). Karnein argues that it was only in the fourteenth and fifteenth centuries that it acquired its role as "quintessence de la conception courtoise de l'amour" ('Réception', p. 327; cf. Leclercq, *Women*, p. 147). The *De amore* was probably not known in England (Kelly, *LMAC*, p. 39). Dronke has recently argued that "Andreas the Chaplain" is a pseudonym borrowed from a now lost medieval romance, *Andreas of Paris*, and that the *De amore* was probably written in the 1230s ('Andreas Capellanus', pp. 53–6).

ideal, and what variations in interpretation and application are characteristic of it".[116] C.S. Lewis described it as a "methodical instruction in the art of love-making";[117] Lazar as a "codification de l'amour";[118] and W.T.H. Jackson as "a simple manual for those who wanted to love *honeste*, that is, like gentlemen."[119] Such descriptions credit the work with a unity and clarity of purpose it certainly does not deserve. Other critics have read it very differently. Bowden has drawn attention to its "obscene wordplay and harsh sexual fantasies".[120] Similarly, Coghill has detected an "unhealthy hatred of sexuality" at its core.[121] Donaldson interpreted it as a *jeu d'esprit*;[122] and Benton as "a work of the imagination" providing a framework for a set of "amusing fantasies";[123] while Robertson has argued that Andreas intended his work not as a guide to "idolatrous passion", but as an "ironic and humorous" critique.[124] Division of opinion about the *De amore*, as Schnell points out, tends to reflect divisions of opinion about the viability of courtly love itself.[125]

Andreas's attitude towards love and marriage is perhaps best characterized as a flippant cynicism, overlaid with mock-solemn didacticism. "Writing for a group of university-trained intellectuals," as Alfred Karnein puts it, "he applies the techniques of scholarly analysis to a literary topic, with the purpose, not of coming up with a serious codification, but rather of providing something in the nature of an amusing entertainment for those on his own intellectual level."[126] In other words, the *De amore* is a witty burlesque, depending for its humour on the discrepancy between its gravity of manner and its inconsequential matter. Andreas's elaborate and light-hearted mimicry was perhaps the natural response of an "amusing, vulgar, gossiping little *clerc*", as Dronke has aptly described him, to the sometimes pompous compendiousness of the scholastic method.[127] The *De amore* is primarily a commentary upon

---

[116] Kelly, p. 147.

[117] Lewis, *Allegory*, pp. 32–3.

[118] Lazar, p. 18; cf. pp. 268–78.

[119] Jackson, '*De Amore*', p. 244. See also Coppin, pp. 46–52; Schlauch, p. 141.

[120] Bowden, p. 81. See also Silvestre, 'Du Nouveau'; and Dronke, 'Andreas', p. 60.

[121] Coghill, p. 142.

[122] Donaldson, pp. 158–61.

[123] Benton, 'Collaborative Approaches', pp. 46–7; cf. 'Court', pp. 580–2.

[124] Robertson, 'Concept', p. 3; 'Subject', p. 161; *Preface*, pp. 393–448; 'Doctrine'; cf. Benton, 'Clio', p. 37.

[125] Schnell, p. 13.

[126] Karnein, 'Amor', p. 215. It is certainly unlikely that the *De amore* was addressed to "young men learning to become knights", as Duby suggests (*Knight*, p. 219). Baldwin argues that Andreas's audience was "equivocally located at the border of two worlds, clerical and lay" (*Language*, p. 20). Despite the prominence given to lay figures in the dialogues, I still find it unlikely that the *De amore* could have been appreciated by anybody without a rigorous training in Latin.

[127] Dronke, review of Schlösser, p. 60.

academic forms and literary themes: its analysis of love is a pretext rather than an issue. Andreas directly identifies amorous success with literary competence. As he put it, a suitor should desire to be able to "fulfil all the instructions of love with her [his beloved] – that is to say, those which can be found inserted in the treatises on love".[128] As Monson points out, "love for Andreas is not only an emotion or an activity . . . it is especially a discourse".[129]

In placing a premium upon rhetorical virtuosity rather than moral consistency, Andreas makes his own ethical position almost irrecoverable. Scholars who take him seriously often return repeatedly to the same loci, without recognizing contradictions elsewhere in the treatise, or that Andreas places a great deal of it in the mouths of personae.[130] None of these authoritatively reflect Andreas's own views: they are simply figures in a dialectical kaleidoscope giving temporary shape to certain ideas. Moreover, the authorities and traditions adapted by Andreas are so diverse that it is impossible to regard his work as the code or programme of any particular social or intellectual group.[131] Literary critics have enthusiastically recognized Andreas's debt to literary conventions. The treatise undoubtedly reflects some of the dynamics of love-poetry;[132] and it also contains pastiches of allegory and romance. These could well constitute a parodic commentary upon fashionable literary forms – in Karnein's words, "a hypertrophic exaggeration, and thus a critique of the conception of love prevailing in the vernacular literature cultivated in the princely courts".[133] Moreover, in method and humour, "the De amore takes its place in a tradition of love-casuistry which was already well established in both Latin and vernacular literature".[134] In particular, Andreas would have found a precedent for the flippant adoption of love as a subject for didactic form in a literary

---

[128] De amore, I. 2, 2, p. 34: "ut cum ea omnia compleat amoris mandata, id est ea quae in amoris tractatibus reperiuntur inserta."

[129] Monson, p. 78; cf. Moi, pp. 24–5.

[130] Schnell, pp. 13–14, 23; Robertson, Preface, p. 442; Cherchi, pp. 25–6. Lewis admits that Andreas speaks only through personae, but argues that the occurrence of any idea anywhere in the De amore is "tolerably good evidence that such an opinion was part of the body of floating ideas on the subject" (Allegory, p. 33). What is known about the historical Marie de Champagne, in particular, certainly does not accord with the notion that she openly advocated adultery (Benton, 'Court', pp. 587–9; Loomis, p. 51).

[131] Cf. Monson, p. 77.

[132] Cherchi, p. 25.

[133] Karnein, p. 326: "une amplification hypertrophiée et donc une critique de la conception de l'amour qui prévalait dans la littérature vernaculaire cultivée dans les cours princières". Cf. Monson, pp. 73–6.

[134] Dronke, review of Buridant, p. 319: cf., for the Latin tradition, Dronke, 'Pseudo-Ovid'; and for the vernacular, Jeanroy, Poésie lyrique, p. 259; Karnein, 'Réception'; Walsh, pp. 11–12, 23.

inheritance going back to the poet he describes as "wonder-making Ovid" ("mirificus Ovidius").[135]

What is less often recognized is that Andreas did not confine himself to strictly imaginative literature, but rather threw it into the melting-pot with forms and ideas plundered from the entire range of disciplines available to him. Law and theology are present in the *De amore* at least as tangibly as literature. They are in some ways even more susceptible to burlesque because, unlike imaginative literature even at its most earnest, they are not animated by any sense of play. In attempting to compile a definitive scholarly analysis of 'Love', it was inevitable that Andreas would find material most conveniently in treatises on what is at least a related issue – marriage. It is perhaps no coincidence that we find such a monumental and purportedly codificatory work on 'Love' only a few decades after Gratian, Hugh of St Victor and Peter Lombard, among others, had set a trend for the comprehensive concordance of opinions about marriage. The *De amore* certainly reflects the methods, jargon and generic conventions of contemporary scholastic treatments of marriage and sexuality.[136] The forms which Andreas exploited – analytical distinctions, letters on points of law (I. 6. 390– 4), decretal collections (II. 7), disputation (I. 6) and preceptive summaries like those of the penitentiaries (I. 6. 268–9; II. 8. 44–9) – were exactly those in which the Church's policy on marriage was developed and disseminated.[137]

Certain principles from the canon law of marriage recur in Andreas's codification of 'Love'. Like the canonists, he emphasized the importance of mutual consent: "for you should note that a lover does not relish anything from his beloved unless it comes from her voluntarily."[138] The word "relish" ("sapidum") is a reminder that the moral principle is here being adapted to an ethics of pleasure. Andreas made an exception to this rule only in the case of peasant women, permitting "at least a little force" ("modica saltem coactio") – a discrepancy which can be explained by the influence of the pastourelle.[139] Similarly, just as the canonists subordinated the principles of *consensus* and indissolubility to that of exogamy by making consanguinity adequate grounds for annulment (that is, a diriment impediment to marriage), so Andreas declares that consanguineous love-affairs cannot be countenanced under any circumstances by the rule of "amor".[140] In judging that a lady should not deny the love she has promised, he possibly reflects the

---

[135] *De amore*, p. 42, 8; cf. Robertson, *Preface*, p. 448; Carlson, p. 88.

[136] Schnell, pp. 86–126; Walsh, p. 22; Monson, pp. 69–73.

[137] Even Lewis admits (*Allegory*, p. 199) that, for Andreas, "the commandments of the god of Love for the most part were mere repetitions of the commandments of the Church".

[138] *De amore*, I. 2, 8, p. 36: "Nota etiam quod amans nihil sapidum ab amante consequitur nisi ex illius voluntate procedat."

[139] *De amore*, I. 11, 3, p. 222.

[140] *De amore*, II. 7, 18–9 (q. 7), p. 256. This observation is Lewis's (*Allegory*, p. 35).

emphasis upon betrothal in the canonical model of marriage: "And we firmly believe in the principle that if a woman bestows on a man the hope of her love or grants him other tokens of her love – he not being reputed unworthy of such love – the woman should be judged guilty of a serious offence if she then tries to deny him what he has long hoped for."[141] Andreas used such forms and ideas not in order to express an agenda of his own, but to construct a deliberately casuistical code from eclectic and disparate materials.

In Book II. cap. 7, he transforms the *De amore* into a "legal case-book".[142] The contrast between young and old discussed in the 20th *quaestio*, for example, is reminiscent of discussions about legal age-limits for marriage, and it is also a literary issue (for it animates a large number of jeux-partis, fabliaux and debates).[143] Yet Andreas (in the person of the Queen) does not resolve it in terms either of law nor literature, ceding competence instead to yet another discipline – medical science ("physicalis . . . inquisitio"). Similarly, while canonists and theologians often debated the problem broached in the 14th *quaestio*, of whether the wife of a husband long absent is unjustly deprived of her marital rights (especially with respect to the crusaders), the Countess's answer belongs to the realm of lyric and romance.[144] She judges that a lady should be pleased if her lord wins renown by his *prouesse*, as long as he does not risk the secrecy of their love by sending letters. In this way, Andreas blends 'literary' with 'non-literary' genres, freely crossing the boundaries between disciplines, and expressing in this way the infinite susceptibility of 'Love' to different intellectual methodologies.

It seems to me that the principle of the incompatibility of love and marriage, which is "authorized" within the *De amore* by Marie de Champagne and often quoted as a tenet of courtly love, also depends upon Andreas's confrontation of ideas from one discipline with those of another.[145] The male speaker in the seventh dialogue (the Higher Nobleman) suggests that it is impossible to confuse love with marital affection ("maritalis affectio") – a legal term familiar from Gratian.[146] Any marital couple ("quilibet coniugati"), he asserts, may feel affection for each another, but the deeper emotion of "love has no place between a husband and wife"

---

[141] *De amore*, II. 6, 34, p. 248: "Et firmiter credimus esse tenendum ut, si mulier alicui spem sui largiatur amoris vel alia sibi amoris primitiva concesserit, et ipse tali non reperiatur indignus amore, magna mulieris iudicatur offensa, si diu sperata denegare contendat."

[142] Benton, 'Court', p. 580; see also Schnell, pp. 49–80.

[143] *De amore*, II. 7, 47–8, p. 268; also, I. 445–57, pp. 172–4. Cf. Långfors, 20, 32, 33, 39, 42, 74, 97 and 131; Chaucer's *Merchant's Tale*.

[144] For example, Ivo of Chartres, *Ep*. 125, PL 162. 136–7; *Ep*. 245, PL 162. 251–3. The decretal 'Ex multa . . .' (Sept. 1201) abrogated the principle of marital debt by allowing a man to make a crusading vow without his wife's consent (Brundage, 'Crusader', p. 434; Rousseau, pp. 101–2).

[145] For example, Lewis, *Allegory*, pp. 35–6; and see Schnell, pp. 22–3.

[146] *De amore*, I. 6, 367–72, pp. 146–8.

("quum liquide constet inter virum et uxorem amorem sibi locum vindicare non posse"). The terms "marital affection" and "love" actually belong to different kinds of discourse – 'legal' on the one hand and 'literary' on the other. By contrast, the Higher Nobleman pretends that they denote two different kinds of relationship. He goes on to argue that, since partners in marriage achieve their desires without fear of opposition ("sine contradictionis timore"), their feelings lack the urgency of genuine love. This is a deployment of an Ovidian principle to which Andreas often resorts – "we always seek what is forbidden and desire what is denied".[147] The Nobleman develops it into a celebration of the challenge posed to love by adverse circumstances:

> Cunctis enim claret hominibus quod facilis rei optatae perceptio vilitatis parit originem, et contemptibile facit haberi quod totus prius mentis desiderabat affectus. Sed econtra, bonum quodcunque praestationis difficultate differtur, maiori quidem illud aviditate suscipimus et diligentiori studio reservamus. Rarus igitur atque difficilis amantis amplexus ferventiori cogit amantes mutuo amoris vinculo colligari, et eorum animos propensiori et adstrictiori affectione vinciri.[148]

Andreas suggests that marriage is cheapened by the rights of access which it confers – not because he really believed in the practical incompatibility of love and marriage, but because he felt that marriage is often too mundane a vehicle for the expression of the glamorous passion that stirs men to write. Like de Rougemont, Andreas is suggesting that within the realm of literature "happy love has no history . . . Romance feeds on obstacles, short excitations, and partings. Marriage on the contrary is made up of wont, daily propinquity, growing accustomed to one another."[149] As Archibald points

---

[147] *De amore*, I. 6, 7, p. 42: "Nitimur in vetitum cupimus semperque negatum." Cf. Ovid, *Amores*, III. 4, 17: "nitimur in uetitum semper cupimusque negata".

[148] *De amore*, I. 6, 361–2, p. 144: "It is clear to all men that easily achieving what one wishes makes it ignoble to undertake, and renders contemptible the possession of what was earlier the object of the whole mind's desire. By contrast, however, whatever goal is deferred by the difficulty of accomplishing it we pursue indeed with greater eagerness and preserve it with more diligent care. Thus when the lover's embrace is rare and difficult to earn, it causes the lovers to be bound by the mutual bond of love all the more fervently." Cf. II. 3 ("Qualiter amor minuatur"), 1, p. 230; Långfors, nos 22, 54, 67, 79, 106.

[149] de Rougemont, pp. 15, 292. However accurate as an assessment of the values of romance, de Rougemont's belief that romantic passion has been the touchstone of western society is plainly extreme. A more sober assessment of the endurance of the motif of marital renunciation in French literature is made by Tintignac. Medieval poets did themselves associate the satiation of desire with creative enervation: for example, Långfors, no. 86. Even so, there are exceptions: Wolfram von Eschenbach's lyric, 'Der helden minne . . .' is a celebration of waking with "ein offen süeze wirtes wîp" (line 19). However, I think it depends for its effect upon its subversion of the conventionally illicit love of the *alba*.

out "it is hard to go on telling stories about a knight once he is happily married, because the notion of impressing or winning his lady is no longer effective";[150] and in the same way, Calin has argued that the lyrical notion of *fin'amors* is essentially fed by "the notion of obstacle" and that marital and sexual circumstances are "accidental".[151] Yet even if the security of marriage is in this sense at odds with the demands of heroic trial and endeavour, early medieval literature in fact neither neglects the dramatic potential of this conflict nor ever seriously condemns marriage because of it.[152] The Nobleman's creation of a pseudo-canonical statement about the nature of marriage from what is more naturally an observation about the dynamics of literature is no more than a conceit.

The Lady argues more pragmatically that love is expressed best within a relationship which daily legitimizes it ("qui sine crimine quotidianis potest actibus exerceri") – that is, in marriage.[153] The Higher Nobleman replies by citing what he says is a dictum from "apostolic law", that a man who loves his own wife too vehemently should be regarded as an adulterer.[154] This saying is generally ascribed to the Neopythagorean philosopher, Sextus (or Xystus), but Christian authors such as Jerome, Gratian, Peter Lombard and Alan of Lille all quoted it with approval.[155] They used it, not to deny the dignity and legitimacy of marital love, but as a metaphor for the shamefulness of a husband's inability to show his wife sexual restraint. In canonical teaching, extra-marital sex is always wrong: but, within marriage, only excessively lustful behaviour was condemned.[156] The Nobleman, by contrast, uses the Sextan saying to justify his adulterous courtship. Andreas's argument is a patent manipulation, and it must have amused his original audiences. This aspect of Andreas's technique recalls Mann's characterization of Latin satirists like Walter of Châtillon or the Archpoet in terms of their relish for "the fluid use of rhetorical and intellectual argument, of language and of literary texts which seem to claim fixity".[157] Andreas's casuistry is as facetious as the Wife of Bath's – yet she has never been read as an authoritative commentator upon the sexual mores of her age.

---

[150] Archibald, p. 159. She quotes Malory's Lancelot (Vinaver, p. 161): "But for to be a weddyd man, I thynke hit nat, for than I must couche with hir and leve armys and turnamentis, batellys and adventures." Cf. Moore, p. 438; Dronke, 'Rise', p. 296.

[151] Calin, p. 35.

[152] See my discussion of *Erec et Enide* below.

[153] *De amore*, I. 6, 376, p. 148.

[154] *De amore*, I. 6, 383, p. 150: "vehemens amator, ut apostolica lege docetur, in propria uxore iudicatur adulter".

[155] Jerome, *On Galatians*, 5, PL 26. 443; *Adversus Jovinianum*, I. 49, PL 23. 281; Gratian, C. 32. q. 2. c. 2; Peter Lombard, *Sententiae*, IV, 31. 7, PL 192. 921; Alan of Lille, *Summa de arte praedicatoria*, 45, PL 210. 193; see Schnell, pp. 148–54; Walsh, p. 20; Boase, p. 59, n. 80; Delhaye, 'Dossier', pp. 70, 76–7; Morris, *Discovery*, p. 108.

[156] Schnell, p. 150.

[157] Mann, in Dronke and Mann, p. 180.

Though the *De amore* is largely the product of its author's fascination with style, method, and the manipulation of ideas, it also reflects some of the sensibility and ideology of serious discussions of marriage in law and theology. Coghill's allegation that "Andreas is incapable of conceiving of holiness of any kind" is a little unjust.[158] As Schnell has pointed out, Andreas speaks "of the union of lovers' hearts, just as do some contemporary moral theologians with respect to marriage".[159] For example:

> Amor enim duos quaerit fidei unitate coniunctos et voluntatum identitate concordes, alii autem quolibet amoris merito defraudantur et in amoris curia extranei reputantur.[160]

Such a formulation of love's purpose, with its accumulation of different terms signifying union, would have seemed no more alien to a Consistory Court of the real world than to the fictional 'Court of Love'. However, in this case Andreas immediately goes on to deny the affinity of this ideal with marriage:

> Sed et superveniens foederatio nuptiarum violenter fugat amorem, ut quorundam amatorum manifesta doctrina docetur.[161]

It seems to me that it was his very consciousness of the adaptability of his definition of 'Love' that led him to exclude marriage so specifically from his discussion. At this point, he is not really concerned with the distinction between marital and non-marital love, for he develops it no further. The connective "sed" marks a hasty parenthetical attempt to preempt any confusion between Andreas's amorous ideal and the theologians' marital one caused by their similarity of terms. He himself recognized the common ground of expression. In the 9th *quaestio*, he argued that it is difficult to distinguish marital and extra-marital love qualitatively because of the confusion caused by the common vocabulary in which they are discussed: "and therefore the equivocal vocabulary of this kind of discussion invalidates the process of comparison, associating [love and marriage] only by various superficial coincidences."[162] In other words, Andreas at least recognized that he shared many of the principles and sentiments which he expressed in terms of 'Love' with theologians and canonists writing about marriage.

---

[158] Coghill, p. 142.

[159] Schnell, p. 23: "von der Vereinigung der Herzen der Liebenden, wie es einige Moraltheologen seiner Zeit hinsichtlich der Ehe tun".

[160] *De amore*, II. 4, 4, p. 232: "For love aims at two persons bound together in the unity of faith and unanimous in the identity of their desires: the others are deprived of any virtue in love and are considered interlopers in love's court." Cf. I. 3, 2, p. 36.

[161] *De amore*, II. 4, 4, p. 232: "However, the development of marital union forcefully dispels love, as is clearly taught by certain lovers."

[162] *De amore*, II. 7, 21-2, p. 258: "Et ideo inventio ipsius sermonis aequivoca actus comparationis excludit et sub diversis ea facit speciebus adiungi."

Though the lyrics of Guilhem IX and the *De amore* have often been used to exemplify fundamental divisions in medieval sensibility, they better demonstrate the permeability of certain ways of thinking about marriage, not only between different literary genres, but also between different intellectual disciplines. Neither Guilhem nor Andreas were concerned with the ideologization of marriage, and the modern adoption of their works as paradigmatic medieval representations of sexual relationships has therefore only reflected their lack of interest in marriage. In place of their works I should now like to introduce in the next chapter four bodies of writings which seem to me to demonstrate less ambiguously some of the recurrent conceptions governing the treatment of marriage in early medieval literature. All four belong to the eleventh or twelfth centuries, and are drawn from France or Germany (and possibly in one case, from England). Each of these texts is profoundly engaged with the definition of marriage's function and value in society, and I hope that they will serve as illustrations of certain widespread conceptions in medieval literary approaches to marriage. In subsequent chapters I hope to show how many of the ideas which these four bodies of writing so dynamically express also inform my sample of texts from twelfth- and thirteenth-century England.

CHAPTER TWO

Literary Paradigms

1. *Ruodlieb*

C.S. Lewis's interpretation of the appearance of the first troubadours as a watershed of sensibility was perhaps natural because so little imaginative literature contemporary with them is now extant. A precious complement to our knowledge is the *Ruodlieb*, a romance which was written down in an idiosyncratic Latin during the second half of the eleventh century. Fragments of an autograph manuscript were discovered at the Bayerische Staatsbibliothek in 1803 in the book-bindings of various volumes from the monastic library at Tegernsee, which is perhaps where the work was written.[1] In 1830, a leaf from a fair copy probably written at the end of the eleventh century was found at the Austrian monastery of St Florian;[2] and further fragments from a Tegernsee volume were identified in 1981.[3] The extant text falls into 18 fairly substantial fragments, comprising nearly 2500 lines, of which many are defective, especially initially. Nevertheless, the *Ruodlieb* is a miraculous survival, and, in terms of marriage, an extremely illuminating one. Looking forward to the momentous ideological developments of the next century, it involves an ambitious attempt to capture a range of different attitudes towards love and marriage on a broad canvas. Even in its fragmentary state, it is clear that the work attempts to dramatize the whole course of a man's life on a grand scale.[4] It sets the quest for self-knowledge, not in a wilderness, like the romances of the later Middle Ages, but entirely within the structures of society. Crucial to it, for example, is the concept of the household, the *domus*.[5] Ruodlieb's life might be seen as a psychological journey illustrating a young man's passage from one household to another – from his parents' to his own. At the end of the romance in its extant form, his mother is still the lady ("domina") of his estate, but her frailty renders urgent his search for a woman to replace her in this role (XVI. 32). By

[1] Collected as clm 19486; Vollmann, pp. 23–42; Haug and Vollmann, pp. 1308–9.
[2] St Florian, Port. 22; Vollmann, pp. 43–4.
[3] Haug and Vollmann, p. 1309.
[4] Cf. Dronke, *Poetic Individuality*, p. 35.
[5] The concept is analysed by Foucault in the context of Greek society (where *oikos* equals *domus*): *Uses*, pp. 152–84. See also Duby, *Medieval Marriage*, pp. 3–4; *History*, pp. 35–155. It also emerges clearly from Ladurie's study of Montaillou.

postponing marriage, Ruodlieb is risking the failure of his line, the disintegration of his patrimony and the welfare of his dependants (XVI. 1-18) – whose interest in his marriage is sharply underlined by his decision to consult them in his choice of bride (XVI. 20-3).

From Ruodlieb's mother's premonitions of her own death and of his glorious marriage, we know that the hero will ultimately be fortunate in his choice (XVII. 89-118). His life is cast as a quest for the wisdom necessary to make this selection, and to fulfil honourably his duties as lord of his own *domus*. Having been exiled from his homeland, Ruodlieb receives his education in what might be seen as a model and macrocosm of the household, the court of the Great King ("Rex Maior"). He serves his adopted lord so well that he is rewarded, not only with gifts, but with wisdom – in the form of the Great King's gnomic and enigmatic proverbs. On his way home, Ruodlieb is further enlightened by two incidents exemplifying the relationship between a man's choice of marital partner and his duties to the *domus*; that is, the stories of the Young Husband and of the Old Husband.[6] In the first of these, the Young Husband is an exemplary figure: he wins his wife partly because he has served her previous husband so well. In the second, an Old Husband is cuckolded by his flighty young wife and then murdered by her and her lover. Throughout the romance, the noble household is presented, not only in feudal terms as a locus of political power, but also more profoundly as the source of health and harmony for everyone dependent upon it. This message is constantly underlined by the recurring image of the breaking of the bread, which graphically symbolizes the lord's control of the means of subsistence.[7]

In the story of the Young Husband, for example, it is by improving the quality of his predecessor's bread that the young man demonstrates his ability to govern a household:

> Puer inquit:
> "En, velut es, cunctis dives satis esse videris,
> Et tuus est panis solaminis omnis inanis,
> Furfuribus plenus, fuscus, lolio uel amarus.
> Si presentare mihi vis cuiusque farine
> Vel modium vel dimidium panes faciendum,
> Tot bene cribratos presentabo tibi panes
> Semine conditos apii vel sale respersos,
> Et preventuras aliquas lardo superunctas
> Atque coronellas compensabis uti menclas."[8]

---

[6] Respectively, VI. 25-116 and VII. 26 to VIII. 129. Dronke has emphasized the dramatic cohesion of these two tales (*Poetic Individuality*, pp. 48-9).

[7] Cf. Duby, *History*, pp. 14-16.

[8] *Ruodlieb*, VI. 77-86: "The young man said, 'Look at you, you seem rich enough to everyone, but your bread is absolutely tasteless. It's black with bran, and bitter with darnel. If you'll just give me a measure or a half-measure of any sort of flour to make

In making and breaking the bread, the young man improves the living-standards of every member of the household, and effectively usurps the old man's role as provider to his dependants – "he did this with such caution, and such care also, that neither the lord nor any of his dependants lacked anything".[9] The parsimony of the old man reflects not only his mean-spiritedness ("Rudis et inmitis, parcus, rarissime letus"), but also his incompetence, his slovenly mismanagement of resources.[10] He is too careless even to have his flour properly sifted. In marrying his widow, the young man formalizes the executive responsibilities for the household which he has already won by merit. At the beginning of Fragment VII, his hospitable breaking of the bread is portrayed as an almost sacerdotal gesture: .

> Panes ille secat et in illos distribuebat . . .
> Pro sacramentis pueros partitur in omnes . . .[11]

Indeed, Grocock believes that "what is described here is a ritual of lay communion deriving from pagan German roots as much as from the Christian eucharist".[12] Vollmann comments similarly that "in spite of its biblical and liturgical resonance, a comparison here between the bits of bread and the Christian sacrament of the Host is quite out of the question"; they are a token only of the deep friendship between the host and his guest.[13] Whether or not the poet was evoking any particular set of ceremonial customs, it seems to me that the significance of the incident is that the role of the *paterfamilias* is always and in essence a sacred one. The lord of the household quite literally gives his dependants their daily bread. It is a symbolism which Christianity adapted rather than invented in the Last Supper and in the Lord's Prayer.

Ruodlieb also uses the symbolism of the bread to demonstrate his respect for his mother:

> Non tamen in solio voluit residere supremo,
> Sed subiective matri dextrim, velut hospes,

some loaves, I'll present you with some, well-sifted, seasoned with parsley-seed and sprinkled with salt, and some *hors d'œuvre* smeared on top with lard, and you'll be able to place in your scales 'crownlets' as well as long, thin loaves.' " Note "preventurae" = '*hors d'œuvre*'; "menclae" = 'long, thin loaves'. In the medieval household, the blackest bread was eaten by the lowest in rank (Duby, *History*, p. 64).

9 *Ruodlieb*, VI. 97–8: "Tali cautela facit hoc tali quoque cura/ Ut domino nil deficeret nullive suorum". Cf. Joseph in the house of Potiphar (Gen. 39:6).

10 *Ruodlieb*, VI. 35: "coarse and harsh, miserly, and virtually never cheerful".

11 *Ruodlieb*, VII. 1, 10: "he cuts the bread and divided it among them . . . he shared it among all the servants, like the sacraments . . ."

12 Grocock, p. 217.

13 Haug and Vollmann, p. 1367: "trotz des biblisch-liturgischen Anklangs ist an eine Gleichsetzung der *offae* mit dem christlichen Sakrament des Herrenliebs nicht zu denken".

Atque libens totum sibi permisit dominatum;
Hec quod ei dederat, reverenter suscipiebat.
Incidens panem turbam partitur in omnem . . .[14]

Similarly, the Great King disguises his gifts to Ruodlieb as loaves of bread in a symbolic recognition of the young man's passage from honourable service to a sufficiency of his own. He tells the hero to break the golden bread with his mother, with his wife, and then with his friends. These instructions are never followed, but they are not a narrative loose end: rather, a clue to the significance of the Great King's gifts. By suggesting that Ruodlieb break the bread each time in a circle of duty and intimacy wider than the last, the King evokes the concentric structure of the household. As a token of the economic responsibilities of the landowner to his family and his dependants, bread serves as a reminder that Ruodlieb's inheritance is not only a privilege of nobility, but also a burden rigidly determining his duties. The story of the Old Husband who marries a young wife is an illustration of the consequences of allowing personal marital ambitions to outweigh the best interests of the house. In seducing the young wife, the redheaded man is only the agent of a calamity for which the Old Husband himself is more fully to blame. He is at fault in having selected as his partner a woman too foolish and shameless ("iuvenem stultam nimiumque procacem", VI. 121) to fulfil her responsibilities. On her account, the ruler of the household is reduced to a thief within it (VII. 120); his authority is destroyed; and – in an inversion of the Young Husband's ceremonious distribution of the bread – he proves himself unable to command even the service of the meal (VII. 122-6).[15]

The *Ruodlieb*-poet thus stresses the function of marriage as a guarantee of social, economic and dynastic cohesion, but he is also concerned to accommodate within this social vision a sense of marriage as the expression of a profound emotional bond between individuals. To this end, Fragments X to XIV are largely concerned with the marriage of Ruodlieb's comrade and kinsman to the "young mistress":[16]

Que dum procedit, ceu lucida luna reluxit.
Quam sollers esset, nemo discernere posset,
An volet, an naret, an se quocumque moveret . . .[17]

---

[14] *Ruodlieb*, XIII. 12-15: "However, he did not want to sit in the highest seat, but sat in a more humble position on his mother's right, just like a guest, and he freely allowed her to rule everything; and he received reverently what she gave him. Cutting up the bread, she divided it up among the whole company . . .".

[15] The *Ruodlieb* thus shares its hostility towards the jealous husband with romances like *Flamenca*, and *fabliaux* like the *Borgoise d'Orliens* or the *Castia Gilós*, without in any way endorsing the lovers' actions against him.

[16] Ruodlieb's comrade is described as his "contribulis", "consanguineus" and "nepos".

[17] *Ruodlieb*, X. 55-7: "who, when she went out, shone like the bright moon. She was so elegant that no one could tell whether she flew, or swam or moved herself at all."

These two lovers are admirable and exemplary figures, perhaps intended to prefigure in some ways Ruodlieb's own triumphant marriage. Their harmony of feeling is illustrated in the perfection of their dancing, in their evenness of play at dice and chess, in their reciprocal gifts of rings, and in their whimsical exchange of genders.[18] Meyer and Gellinek have seen their marriage as an example of "Friedelehe"[19] – that is, an informal union recognized in Germanic custom and distinguished from concubinage, but not involving the transfer of a dowry.[20] There is indeed no mention of a dowry, but, even so, the Kinsman's wedding is specifically approved by a substantial assembly of friends and relatives of both families, who take practical and economic factors carefully into account:

> Eius at ut matrem cernunt hec non renuentem
> Et genus amborum par posseque divitiarum
> Discutiunt caute, bene conveniant quod utrimque,
> Hanc desponsari sibi censent lege iugali.[21]

They are pleased that the young man is taking the opportunity offered by marriage to distance himself from a woman whom they describe as a filthy whore ("scortum turpe") – presumably a concubine.[22] Meyer also suggests that the dramatic way in which the bride states her rights as a partner in marriage is a response to the bridegroom's failure to respect her as his voluntary partner, his "Friedel".[23] When she is asked to draw the wedding-ring from the bridegroom's sword as a symbolic token of his right to kill her should she fail in her fidelity, she replies – "very shrewdly and aptly" according to the poet ("satis astute . . . et apte", XIV. 69) – that both partners should be equally bound. "Why should I keep better faith towards you than you towards me?" she demands.[24] There is no suggestion here that she is particularly heedful of marital equity on account of her rank or a specific set of social customs. Indeed, in referring to Adam and Eve, she makes it quite clear that reciprocal fidelity is a duty universal in marriage: "tell me", she demands, "where you read that Adam was allowed two Eves?"[25] The bridegroom recognizes the force of her argument, and they are

---

[18] Respectively, XI. 51-7; XI. 62-3 and XII. 22-6; XI. 63-72; XII. 27-8.
[19] Meyer, p. 280; Gellinek, p. 561-70.
[20] Herlihy, pp. 48-51.
[21] *Ruodlieb*, XIV. 60-3: "And when they saw that her mother approved, and that the families of the couple were well-matched in importance and wealth, they carefully investigated whether they would suit each other and decided that she should be betrothed to him according to the law of marriage."
[22] *Ruodlieb*, XIV. 26-35. For this practice, see Brundage, 'Concubinage'; *Law*, p. 297; Goody, pp. 75-81.
[23] Meyer, p. 287.
[24] *Ruodlieb*, XIV. 72-3: "Cur seruare fidem tibi debeo, dic, meliorem/ quam mihi tu debes?"
[25] *Ruodlieb*, XIV. 77: "Dic ubi concessas binas sibi Adam legeris Evas?"

duly married, to the joyous approval of the bystanders. This incident is not an illustration of a limited form of marriage in which the woman's status and mutual love were valued more greatly than was usual, but a model to Ruodlieb of the importance of reciprocal love, faith and dignity in any marriage. Though the kinsman's economic reponsibilities are not so grave as Ruodlieb's, his moral reponsibilities to his wife are no different. The romance thus carefully underlines the affectivity of the conjugal bond even within a carefully defined social and economic context.

2. *Le Mystère d'Adam*

The myth of mankind's departure from Eden has long provided an opportunity for expressing ideas about the nature of marriage.[26] Even Christ's teaching looks back to statements made in Genesis about the relationship between Adam and Eve. The expression which he uses of a married couple, "they are not two, but one flesh", surely alludes to Eve's creation from Adam's flesh.[27] Because "it is not good for a man to be alone", Eve is created for Adam as "a help-mate in his likeness".[28] However, after the Fall, she is stripped even of the dignity of being man's companion, and she is condemned to an earthly drudgery which is the token of her guilt. God tells her, "I shall multiply your hardships and your pregnancies: you will bring forth sons in sorrow, you will be in the power of your husband, and he will have lordship over you."[29] In this way, Genesis becomes the vehicle for contrasting images, not only of womanhood, but also of marriage. These ambivalences have resounded throughout Christian thinking about marriage.[30] Jesus himself taught that marriage is a divine institution – "what God has put together let no man put asunder".[31] Yet, to the disciples' question whether it might be better not to marry, he replied that, although not all can do without marriage, it is better to avoid it if possible – "those who are able to accept [celibacy], should do so".[32] He demanded from his followers the total rejection of worldly ties: "if anyone comes to me who does

---

[26] See Pagels; Bugge (esp. pp. 5–6); Bloch, *Medieval Misogyny*, pp. 22–9; Nichols, 'Intellectual Anthropology', pp. 71–83.

[27] Mt. 19:6: "non sunt duo sed una caro"; cf. Mark 10:8.

[28] Gen. 2:18: "non est bonum esse hominem solum: faciamus ei adiutorium similem sui".

[29] Gen. 3:16: "multiplicabo aerumnas tuas et conceptus tuos; in dolore paries filios et sub viri potestate eris et ipse dominabitur tui".

[30] Glasser, p. 3. Pagels speaks of "a durable double standard" (p. 28). Emblematic of this polarity is the contradiction between the Pauline and deutero-Pauline letters. The former are extremely disparaging about marriage, while the latter evaluate it much more generously (Pagels, pp. 16–18, 23–4).

[31] Mt. 19:6: "quod ergo Deus coniunxit homo non separet"; cf. Mark 10:9.

[32] Mt. 19:11–12: "qui potest capere capiat".

not hate his father, his mother, his wife, his sons, brothers and sisters – and even his own soul – he cannot be my disciple";[33] and he specifically excluded marriage from his image of heaven.[34]

As the arena of Christian discussion about marriage and sexuality, the myth of Adam and Eve facilitated the association of sexual relationships with sin.[35] In early Christianity, human sexuality was often interpreted as the literal embodiment of the first couple's disgrace. As Peter Brown puts it, "ascetic exegesis of the Fall of Adam and Eve tended to preserve, at the back of the minds of its exponents, a lingering doubt: society, marriage, and if not those, certainly sexual intercourse, were fundamentally alien to the original definition of humanity".[36] Marriage was regarded as a necessary bulwark for society against the corrosive influence of lust – "it is better to marry than burn", as Paul put it (I Cor. 7: 9) – and those who attempted to exclude it from the Christian commonwealth were pronounced heretical.[37] Even so, the Church's most influential figures were agreed that it was at least an inferior state, and their teaching on marriage is at best deeply apologetic. Ambrose, for example, described the marriage-bed as being overgrown with "the tangled brushwood of human frailty".[38] Jerome claimed: "I praise marriage, but only because it produces me virgins."[39] They did more than damn marriage with faint praise: they presented the emotional and physical ties of the family as challenges to the achievement of sanctity through virginity.[40] "If you conquer the household", declared Ambrose, "you conquer the world."[41] Jerome dramatically amplified Christ's call for independence from worldly ties into a memorably callous vignette:

> Licet parvulus ex collo pendeat nepos, licet sparso crine et scissis vestibus ubera, quibus nutrierat, mater ostendat, licet in limine pater

[33] Luke 14:26: "Si quis venit ad me et non odit patrem suum et matrem et uxorem et filios et fratres et sorores, adhuc autem et animam suam, non potest meus esse discipulus." Such statements were designed not so much as condemnations of family-feeling as dramatic ways of stressing the individual's duties as a a member of "the sectarian community" (Goody, pp. 87–90).

[34] Mt. 22:30; Mark 12:25; Luke 20:34–6.

[35] Bugge, pp. 14–15: "the force of the allegorical reading of Genesis was evidently sufficient to associate the spiritual fall of man with sexual intercourse itself".

[36] Brown, *Body*, pp. 399–400.

[37] See, for example, the so-called Twenty-First Canon of the Council of Gangra (c. 345, in Smith and Cheetham, 'Gangra'; Perceval, p. 101); also Hürsch, 'Alexiuslied'. As Elliott shows, the Church was also unwilling to allow its model of marriage to be desexualized by the ideal of a union without sexual contact (*Spiritual Marriage*, pp. 32–6).

[38] See Brown, *Body*, pp. 361–2.

[39] *Ep.* 22, 20, p. 94: "Laudo nuptias, laudo coniugium: sed quia mihi virgines generant."

[40] In this era, virginity was not seen as a distinctively female attribute (Bugge, p. 4).

[41] *De virginibus*, I. 12, PL 16. 206: "Si vincis domum, vincis saeculum"; Brown, *Body*, p. 342.

iaceat, per calcatum perge patrem, siccis oculis ad vexillum crucis vola!
Pietatis genus est in hac re esse crudelem.[42]

With Augustine came the idea that Man's postlapsarian and sexual nature
is the consequence of the loss of an original, psychological integrity. In John
Bugge's words again, "the emphasis upon a proud and *illicit* desire for
knowledge alone provides the Latin West with a sanitary alternative to the
motive of purely carnal lust. Theoretically, at least, the sin is purged of its
connotations of defilement; and the first effect of the sin, rather than the
ontological duality of two distinct sexes, becomes the loss of that primal
psychological integrity by which intercourse was possible without the
derangement and agitation of libidinous longing."[43] Elaine Pagels describes
Augustine's contribution as a "cataclysmic transformation" of the Christian
perspective.[44] He avoided the outright condemnation of human sexuality
only by discrediting human psychology. For Augustine, the myth of the
divine origin of mankind was an exemplum of the inadequacy, indiscipline
and inner division of the human mind.[45] If anything, he made marriage even
more marginal to the Christian world-view than it had been before. In *De
sancta virginitate* and *De bono conjugali*, he defined the utility of marriage in a
more positive way – "fides, proles, sacramentum" ("faith, children,
sacrament") – but his dark sense of humanity's constant and unconquerable
concupiscence ultimately denied even marriage the power to save it from the
corruption of the will.[46]

In the Middle Ages, marriage was re-formulated both as a public event
and as a sacrament. It was thereby restored to a central position in the model
of human experience. This heightened awareness of the role of marriage in
society stimulated a revised view of its role in the Fall. In the Anglo-Norman
Mystère d'Adam, for example, marriage is depicted neither as a reparation nor
as a defence, but as a mechanism fundamental to the universe as God
originally created it.[47] This twelfth-century play survives only in a single
manuscript, Bibliothèque municipale de Tours MS 927, a copy from which
the original ending is apparently lacking.[48] It begins with a dramatization of

---

[42] *Ep.* 14. 2, pp. 30–32: "Even if your little nephew clung to your neck, or your mother
with dishevelled hair and torn clothes showed you the breast at which you'd fed, or
your father lay across the threshold – go past him, trampling your father under your
heel, and without weeping fly to the standard of the Cross. In this case the way of piety
is to be cruel."

[43] Bugge, p. 27.

[44] Pagels, p. 97. Cf. Campbell, IV, 148–9.

[45] Brown, *Body*, pp. 396–427.

[46] Brown, *Body*, p. 426; Baldwin, *Language*, p. 4; Elliott, *Spiritual Marriage*, pp. 45–7.

[47] Cf. Duby, *Knight*, pp. 213–15.

[48] Legge dates it "c. 1140" and states that "it was almost certainly written in England"
(*ANL*, pp. 312, 321; cf. Bevington, p. 79). The manuscript probably belongs to the
thirteenth-century. Aebischer argues (pp. 21–5) that lines 945–1305 of the extant text
originally constituted a separate work (*Les Quinze signes du Jugement*). If so, then what

the story of Adam and Eve (lines 1–590). At the beginning of the play, they are introduced to each other by the divine "Figura" in such a way that a ceremony of marriage is clearly suggested.[49] The stage-directions require that they be stationed in ceremonial dress before a figure clothed as a priest (the "Figura").[50] His address to the new couple about the nature of their responsibilities to each other can easily be seen as a kind of marriage-sermon. According to Bevington, the actors would have been standing on the steps of the church during this scene; and this was the location increasingly chosen in the twelfth century for the performance of the matrimonial rite.[51]

The scene thus appears to be have been constructed with the wedding-ceremony and its significance specifically in mind. Yet the couple are placed not side-by-side before the priestly figure but with Adam a little in front. The dramatist stresses partnership and reciprocal love in his marital ideal, but he gives the husband sovereignty. Eve is told to accept his authority ("sa discipline", 36); and she accepts him both as her partner and as her superior in strength ("a paraille e a forzor", 44). God's command to Adam that he should rule her reasonably ("Tu la governe par raison", 21) is here more than an assertion of masculine rationality: it is a call for moderation in government. He must rule so well that "that between you there will be no dispute".[52] Indeed Adam's must be a reflection of God's own paternal authority. Although this dramatist is patronizing in that he does not permit Eve to share power in marriage, he does insist that she shares with Adam in its dignity:

> Ce est ta femme e tun pareil:
> Tu le devez estre ben fiël.
> Tu aime lui, e ele ame tei,
> Si serez ben ambedui de moi.[53]

Richard Axton has argued here that "the key words, 'aime' and 'ambe', repeated within a formal pattern, emphasize an ideal of mutual love".[54] Yet their reciprocal love for each another is subordinated to their joint love for God. The Figura's address is dominated by the concept of "conservage" (23)

---

survives of the original play concerns the Fall, the murder of Abel, and the succession of prophets, before breaking off in the middle of Nebuchadnezzar's account of the furnace.

[49] Axton, p. 120.

[50] Adam wears a scarlet tunic, while Eve is dressed in a white silken garment ("muliebri vestimento albo, peplo serico albo"). The priest wears a dalmatic, a deacon's outer robe (Axton, p. 117).

[51] Bevington, p. 79. Molin and Mutembe, pp. 36-7.

[52] *Mystère*, line 22: "N'ait entre vus ja tençon".

[53] *Mystère*, lines 11-14: "She is your wife and your partner: you should be faithful to her. You should love her and she you, and in this way you will both be mine."

[54] Axton, p. 120.

41

– that is, a joint service of the Creator.[55] In this sense, marriage is not made *by* God but *in* God. To marry is to participate in the continuum of his love. The Figura twice states that his precepts form the "law" of marriage: "Tel soit la loi de mariage" (24); "Car ço est droiz de mariage' (38). This is a remarkable assertion at a time when marriage-practices were still largely governed by custom rather than law. The process by which marriage came to be institutionalized in law was still in its infancy, Gratian's *Decretum* only being completed around this time.[56] It seems to me that this poet's presentation of this marital ideal as a legal blueprint testifies to the desire for order which must have lain at the heart of this dramatic expansion of the law. In this way, the poet makes marriage representative of his conception of a fundamental harmony in the whole of society.

Erich Auerbach has stressed the contemporary, even bourgeois, note in the *Mystère d'Adam*: "the ancient and sublime occurrence is to become immediate and present; it is to be a current event which could happen at any time, which every listener can imagine and is familiar with; it is to strike deep roots in the mind and emotions of any random French contemporary. Adam talks and acts in a manner any member of the audience is accustomed to from his own or his neighbour's house."[57] Not only does this endow the play with charm and intelligibility but it also makes the story of the Fall directly and immediately relevant to every individual in the audience. It becomes, in Axton's words, "a human tragedy with an intimate domestic meaning for a medieval lay audience".[58] Yet, as Auerbach has emphasized, the story of the Fall would simultaneously have had a profound eschatological significance to medieval Christians. It was the first stage in the cycle of Redemption – the "one great drama whose beginning is God's creation of the world, whose climax is Christ's Incarnation and Passion, and whose expected conclusion will be Christ's second coming and the Last Judgment".[59] This is exactly the significance of the *ordo prophetarum* which in the *Mystère* succeeds the stories of the Fall and Abel's murder. The prophets prepare the way for the Incarnation, the next great moment in the universal drama. Dominica Legge has suggested that in its original form the play would have ended with the Passion and Harrowing, but a more natural conclusion would be the Annunciation and Nativity.[60] The Incarnation would thus stand in a direct relationship of symmetry towards the Fall: a woman's flawlessness erases a woman's flaw; and the corrupted marriage of Adam and Eve is opposed by

---

[55] Cf. Godefroy, *conservage*: 'confraternité dans la servitude'.
[56] Early in the 1140s: Brundage, pp. 229–30.
[57] Auerbach, *Mimesis*, p. 151.
[58] Axton, p. 119.
[59] Auerbach, *Mimesis*, p. 158; cf. Duby, *Knight*, pp. 214–15.
[60] Legge, *ANL*, pp. 314–15: "In view of the interpolation of references to the redemption of Adam into several of the prophecies, it is tempting to see in it an Easter play, going down at least as far as the Harrowing of Hell." Cf. Aebischer, p. 23; and contra, Auerbach, p. 145.

the uncorrupted marriage of Joseph and Mary. Finishing in this way, the play would have completed the cycle of the creation, perversion and restoration of the marital ideal expressed in its opening scene.

The dramatist depicts Adam after the Fall as proudly and resentfully reproaching both his wife and the institution of marriage:

> Qui preirai jo ja qui m'aït,
> Quant ma femme m'a traït,
> Qui Deus me dona por pareil?
> Ele me dona mal conseil.[61]

The duty of counsel was indeed enjoined upon Eve as Adam's wife, but to his claim, "I have done wrong because of my wife", the Figura sharply rejoins, "You believed your wife more than me."[62] Adam erred in judgement. He confused the order of his duties of fidelity. In this, he transgressed the precepts outlined by the Figura at the beginning of the play just as surely as did Eve. Even if his sin was less direct, his responsibilities were the greater. Adam does not see this. He regards the sorrow imposed upon him as the punishment for his failure in governance as Eve's "dowry" ("duaire", 552). It is a sign of his unregeneracy that he is unable to recognize that evil came about not through God's conception of marriage or his creation of woman but through his own and his wife's inability to fulfil simultaneously their duties towards one another and towards God. Eve's attitude is quite different –

> Por quei ne fui al criator encline?
> Por quei ne tien jo, sire, ta discipline?
> Tu mesfesis, més jo sui la racine.
> De nostre mal long en est la mescine. . . .
> Mais neporquant en Deu est ma sperance.
> D'icest mesfait char tot iert acordance . . .[63]

It is fitting that the spring of contrition lies in Eve's heart rather than in Adam's. Her belated resignation to providence prefigures exactly this quality in the Virgin Mary – the agent of the future "acordance" of the Creator with mankind.

Thus, the *Mystère d'Adam* contrives to fuse Christian ambivalence towards marriage into a coherent and dynamic whole by focusing upon a single

---

[61] *Mystère*, lines 353–6: "And who will I ask to help me when my own wife has betrayed me – the woman God gave to me as a partner? She has advised me badly."

[62] *Mystère*, lines 422–3: "Jo ai mesfait par ma moiller. . . . Ta moiller creïstes plus que moi". According to St Bernard, Adam exacerbated his sins by reproaching Eve in this way: see Leclercq, *Women*, pp. 21–2, 27, citing *Sermones de diversis*, 102. 1.

[63] *Mystère*, lines 579–82, 587–8: "Why was I not obedient to my Creator? Why did I not, my lord, keep to your commands? You did wrong, but I was the root of it. The remedy for our wrong will be long in coming. . . . But nevertheless I place my hopes in God. The reconciliation after this wrongdoing will be truly sweet . . .".

paradox: although marriage is unquestionably good in its origins, it is nevertheless the channel by which evil comes to mankind. The dramatist depicts Satan as turning to the seduction of Eve only *after* he has failed in his temptation of Adam. This is a rare and distinctive motif.[64] It indicates that Satan turns to Eve only in order to attack Adam at his most vulnerable point – that is, in his relationship with his wife. When Adam accepts the apple from the hand of Eve it is with the words, ''I will trust you in this: you are my partner.''[65] In this way, the first two human beings are led to disobey God's word through their misunderstanding of the mutuality enjoined upon them. It could even be said that the dramatist's sense of humanity's distance from Eden is curiously uplifting because he recognizes that moral failure is the consequence, not simply of mankind's disposition to wickedness, but, more often, of its inability to resolve tensions between motivations which are good in themselves, but bad in the wrong order. In this version of the story, the first couple's exclusion from Paradise stands symbolically, not for mankind's exclusion from a state of sexual or epistemological innocence, but for its inability to live according to the pattern of perfection laid down at the beginning of time. In a sense, it is only because the law of marriage defined by God is such a high ideal, that the failure of human beings to live up to it is so inevitable and therefore so poignant. The dysfunction of the first marriage – the breaking of the first bond – symbolizes every dislocation of God's order caused since by the imperfection of mankind. The marriage of Adam and Eve becomes the vehicle for the assertion that life in this world is a tragic alienation from the ideal. Thus, what is ultimately most striking about this author's manipulation of the ancient myth is the intensity of his comprehension of a perfect and divinely-instituted order, of which marriage is certainly part.

3. *Erec et Enide*

Ever since Gaston Paris's seminal definition of ''amour courtois'' in an article on Chrétien de Troyes' *Lancelot*, Chrétien has frequently been invoked in discussions of medieval sexual relationships as a propagandist for courtly adultery – albeit a reluctant one.[66] Lewis, for example, argued that the *Lancelot* remained unfinished because of the author's distaste for the topic supposedly enjoined upon him by his patroness, Marie de Champagne – a ''genius bent to tasks unworthy of it by the whim of a fashionable woman'', as he put it.[67] However, the definition of Chrétien's ideological position in

---

[64] Woolf, 'Fall', p. 188.

[65] *Mystère*, line 313: ''Jo t'en crerra. Tu es ma per.''

[66] Paris, 'Etudes'.

[67] Lewis, p. 24; cf. more recently, Baldwin, who suggests that Chrétien had ''misgivings about the theme'' (*Language*, p. 32).

this work is made problematical not only by the incompleteness of the text, but also by the element of irony in his presentation of the hero. Despite Lancelot's military prowess, his love for Guinevere often reduces him to cutting an absurd figure – as when he is prepared to appear incompetent in the lists merely at his lady's pleasure (5654–708). Far from being an example to his class, Lancelot's behaviour is so much dictated by love that he is even willing to debase himself by riding in a cart like a criminal (320–77). These incidents demonstrate the depth of his devotion to his lady – and this is impressive in its way – yet Chrétien also uses them to show how Lancelot's feelings make him inconsistent, eccentric and unknightly. Love is shown to be capable of reducing even the mightiest of warriors to the most ignoble of deeds – "shame did not matter to him since Love commanded and desired it".[68] Lancelot is an illustration of the power of love: he is not a paragon of courtly behaviour.

Of Chrétien's other romances only *Cligés* celebrates an adulterous affair, but the author's purpose here is to demonstrate the inalienability both of a woman's love and of the sexual bond. Despite being married against her will and in love with Cligés, Fénice feels that it would be wrong to cuckold her husband once the marriage is consummated, however badly he might treat her:

> Qui a le cuer, cil a le cors,
> Toz les autres an met defors.
> Mes ce ne puis je pas savoir
> Comant puisse le cors avoir
> Cil a cui mes cuers s'abandone,
> Quant mes peres autrui me done,
> Ne je ne li os contredire.
> Et quant il est de mon cors sire,
> S'il an fet chose que ne vuelle,
> N'est pas droiz c'un autre i acuelle.[69]

Even though her marriage is clearly marked as an abrogation of her right to choose her own partner, she does not use this as a justification for sexual disloyalty. Indeed, she explicitly distances herself from what she regards as the dishonourable behaviour of Iseult, who gave her body to Tristan as well as to Mark.[70] The problem is solved by her nurse, who uses magical means to delude Fénice's husband into thinking that the marriage has been

---

[68] *Le Chevalier de la Charrette*, lines 376–7: "que de la honte ne li chaut/ puis qu'Amors le comande et vialt".

[69] *Cligés*, lines 3123–32: "Whoever has my heart will have my body – I don't want anybody else. But I've no idea how the one man to whom my heart is lost can have my body, since my father gives me to another, nor do I dare contradict him. And this other man is lord of my body, if he does anything with it that I don't want, it isn't right that I take anyone else."

[70] For example, *Cligés*, lines 3105–14; 5198–203; 5249–56.

consummated even though it has not. In this way, Fénice is ultimately able to sleep with Cligés without having to compromise herself, as she sees it, either by giving her body to a man who has not won her heart, or by sharing her body between two men. Even when she agrees to elope with Cligés she refuses to do so in a way that would bring public disgrace upon them. She escapes her husband only by shamming death – and not before she has endured the kinds of torments at the hands of the physicians more typical of the ordeals of virgin-martyrs:

> Quant des corroies l'ont batue,
> Tant que la char li ont ronpue
> Et li sans contreval li cort . . .
> Lors dïent que il lor estuet
> Feu et plonc querre, qu'il fondront,
> Qu'es paumes gitier li voldront,
> Einçois que parler ne la facent.
> . . . N'encor ne lor est pas assez
> De ce que li plons est passez
> Par mi les paumes d'outre en outre,
> Einz dïent li cuivert avoutre
> Que, s'ele ne parole tost,
> Or endroit la metront an rost,
> Tant que ele iert tote greslie.[71]

Her resistance to such pains underlines the purity of her motives. The romance ends happily with what Chrétien clearly sees as the fitting realization of the lovers' relationship in marriage:

> De s'amie a feite sa dame,
> Car il l'apele amie et dame,
> Et por ce ne pert ele mie
> Que il ne l'aint come s'amie,
> Et ele lui tot autresi
> Con l'en doit amer son ami.[72]

In *Erec et Enide*, Chrétien's purpose also involved a serious and coherent consideration of the boundaries of social and sexual obligation, and here he

---

[71] *Cligés*, lines 5905–15, 5923–9: "When they have beaten her with scourges so much that her flesh is torn and her blood pours down . . . They say that they have to ask for fire and lead, in order to melt the lead and pour it into the palms of her hands, before they can get her to talk. . . . And still it is not enough for them even when the lead has passed right through her palms, from one side to other, and the base knaves say that, if she doesn't talk soon, they'll stick her on a grill straight away, until she's completely roasted."

[72] *Cligés*, lines 6633–8: "He has made his lover into his wife, and so he calls her both lover and wife, so that she will never lose his love for her as his sweetheart, and in just the same way she loves him as if he were her lover."

chose to do so entirely within the framework of marriage.[73] Lewis argued that this was "almost certainly an early work" because in it "the later rules of love and courtesy are outraged at every turn". It shows no signs of being apprentice-work, however, and deserves full attention as the most subtle and complex of all Chrétien's treatments of marriage. Looking beyond what is perhaps the natural pattern of romance as a process of heroic trial ultimately rewarded by marriage, he dramatized in *Erec et Enide* the implicit contradiction between the ethics of individual endeavour and the social responsibilities of marriage.[74] The 'natural pattern' is completed in the first movement of the poem (27–2214), in which Chrétien describes how Erec's prowess and the beauty of the poor vavasour's daughter wins him a bride, and her the honours of the stag and the sparrowhawk. As Frappier remarks, "this prelude has the unity of a *lai* and is in itself a fair 'conjointure' ".[75] Indeed, Chrétien himself stresses the self-sufficiency of this preliminary section. At line 1796, he declares, "here is the end of the first part of the poem".[76] In continuing the action beyond the wedding, the story perhaps offered Chrétien a chance to examine the feelings of a man torn by the antagonistic demands of marriage and chivalry. Yet Chrétien adapted what he inherited. His claim that storytellers were fragmenting and corrupting the tale ("depecier et corronpre", 21) is an assertion not only of his own right to tell it, but also a revelation that he was altering its composition in order to place his own emphases upon it. Sparnaay conjectured that the next section of the story, the couple's quest, was a development of two originally discrete motifs: in one, the trials of adventure exonerate a wife suspected by her husband of infidelity, and, in the other, a knight demonstrates his prowess to a doubting lady.[77] The basic strength of the story undoubtedly lies in the way in which these parallel testing-processes conflict with and ultimately reinforce each other. The interest of Chrétien's version, however, lies not only in whether or not Erec and Enide can win back each other's confidence, but also in what way they need to redefine their relationship in order to do so. Enide's capacity for fidelity and Erec's ability to earn it are never properly in doubt, for Chrétien emphasizes their virtues from the very beginning of the

---

[73] Lewis, *Allegory*, p. 25.

[74] Moore cites Chrétien, oddly, in arguing that courtly writers "had nothing to say about the growth of love that should follow early infatuation. Chrétien could only say, in effect, that his lovers lived happily ever after" (p. 438). This could not be less true.

[75] Frappier, p. 165; Paris describes it similarly as "un petit roman fort agréable" (rev. Foerster, p. 158).

[76] *Erec et Enide*, line 1796: "ici fenist li premiers vers". See Roques, edn, p. ix, n. 1; Sparnaay, pp. 66–72.

[77] Sparnaay, pp. 101–4. He cites Orilus and Jeschûte in Wolfram von Eschenbach's *Parzifal* as a model for the first motif; and *Le Bel Inconnu* for the second (Malory's *Book of Gareth* (pp. 180–91) and his tale of *La Cote Male Tayle* (pp. 284–90) are further examples of the latter).

romance.[78] In this sense, neither character really needs to be tested or proved.[79] Instead, their estrangement becomes an opportunity for Chrétien to raise questions about the parameters of their relationship in love, marriage and *courtoisie*.

In the Welsh analogue, *Gereint Son of Erbin*, the hero is motivated to vanquish the uncourtly knight Edern by the recollection of the way in which he was insulted by him.[80] By contrast, Erec's victory over the corresponding figure, Yder, is attributed to the inspiration given him by Enide:

> Erec regarde vers s'amie,
> qui molt dolcemant por lui prie:
> tot maintenant qu'il l'ot veüe,
> se li est sa force creüe . . .[81]

At this stage, Chrétien emphasizes that Erec's feelings for Enide intensify his martial prowess: they are entirely compatible with his heroic exploits. Once won, however, Enide becomes the innocent occasion of his apostasy from chivalry. The contrast is heightened in order to illustrate the paradox that in literature marriage generally marks the *end* of individual endeavour in both senses of the word: it represents both the prize and the conclusion of the hero's career.

The difficulty of reconciling marriage with individual endeavour is translated by Chrétien into a psychological state: the moral problem is expressed as a kind of illness. Married life saps Erec's commitment to chivalry and makes him indolent and unmanly: "He no longer cared for the tournament, only for dallying with his wife" (2433–4).[82] Indeed, he becomes so feckless that he is content to stay in bed for most of the day (2442–3). The implication is that Erec is emasculated by marriage – undermined by it, not only in his heroic individuality, but also in his masculinity. In this he recalls the arguments of the hero of a ninth- or tenth-century Latin romance, *Waltharius*, who excuses himself from marriage on the grounds that his anxiety for his wife and children will make him less valorous:

> Namque voluptatem quisquis gustaverit, exin
> Intolerabilius consuevit ferre labores . . .[83]

The values celebrated in *Waltharius* are much more clearly those of a brotherhood of warriors, but even in *Erec et Enide*, we can sense the

---

[78] For example, 1484–6.

[79] See contra, Roques, p. xviii.

[80] For the relationship between the two romances, see Foster, p. 193; Goetinck, p. 13; Loomis, pp. 29, 55.

[81] *Erec et Enide*, lines 907–10: "Erec looks towards his beloved, as she softly prays for him: as soon as he sees her, his strength is increased".

[82] *Erec et Enide*, lines 2433–4: "N'avoit mes soing de tornoier:/ a sa fame volt dosnoier".

[83] *Waltharius*, lines 156–7: "For once a man has tasted pleasure, he will afterwards be accustomed to find labours unbearable."

continuing importance of this martial and masculine ethos in the emphasis placed upon the opinion of his peers:

> Ce disoit trestoz li barnages
> que granz diax ert et granz domages,
> quant armes porter ne voloit
> tex ber com il estre soloit.[84]

In this way, the conflict between marriage and individuality might also be seen as the expression of the tension between the ethos which feudal society inherited from its Germanic past and its more recent attempts to define roles for women.[85]

In Chrétien's *Yvain*, Gawain (Gauvain) urges the newly-married hero to remember their companionship and to avoid the trap of luxury:

> Comant! seroiz vos or de çax . . .
> qui por leur fames valent mains?
> Honiz soit de sainte Marie
> qui por anpirier se marie!
> Amander doit de bele dame,
> qui l'a a amie ou a fame,
> que n'est puis droiz que ele l'aint
> que ses los et ses pris remaint.
> Certes, ancor seroiz iriez
> de s'amor, se vos anpiriez;
> que fame a tost s'enor reprise,
> ne n'a pas tort, s'ele despise
> celui qui devient de li pire
> el rëaume dom il est sire.
> Or primes doit vostre pris croistre.
> Ronpez le frain et le chevoistre,
> s'irons tornoier moi et vos,
> que l'en ne vos apiaut jalos.[86]

---

[84] *Erec et Enide*, lines 2455–8: "All the nobles said that it was a great shame and pity that such a knight as he had been did not wish to bear arms."

[85] Cf. Paris, rev. Foerster, p. 165; Loomis, p. 190; Sparnaay, p. 78.

[86] *Yvain*, 2486, 2488–504: "What? Will you be one of those who devalue themselves because of their wives? By Saint Mary, shame upon him who marries only to degenerate! Anyone who has a lover or a wife, should be improved if she is a beautiful lady, because it's not right that she love him once his reputation and worth are exhausted. Certainly, you'll still grieve for her love, if you degenerate; since a woman soon withdraws her favour, and rightly so, if she comes to depise the man who is lord of her realm and grows worse because of her. Now your first duty is to increase your worth. Break the bridle and the halter, and then we go tourneying, you and I, so that no one can call you a jealous man." Cf. *Ywain and Gawain*, lines 1455–78. Noble describes this argument as "specious but plausible" (p. 53). It has to be more substantial than that, for it is the basis of the challenge to marriage in *Erec et Enide*.

MEDIEVAL MARRIAGE: LITERARY APPROACHES, 1100–1300

Erec illustrates Gawain's point, and the two romances clearly complement each other. Indeed, Loomis argues that the thematic coherence of *Erec et Enide* and *Yvain* is so pronounced that they must have been the products of "a single mind" even before Chrétien's redactions.[87] However, the conflict between marriage and personal endeavour was an anxiety characteristic of the age. Gawain's proverbial evocation of the charm of a pleasure deferred ("Joie d'amors qui vient a tart/ sanble la vert busche qui art") also recalls the arguments deployed by Andreas Capellanus, for example, in support of the notion that marriage belittles love by conferring facility of access.[88] Like Andreas, Chrétien deduced from the sentimental conventions of lyric and romance that there is nothing ennobling about love once it is readily satiable. In this sense, the appeal of the problem he chooses to dramatize depends on how far these literary conventions epitomize the common impulses of humanity.

Eventually, Enide comes to hear about Erec's fall into disrepute. She is especially grieved by them because she regards herself as its agent. In *Gereint*, Enide is accused by her father-in-law of instigating the hero's recreance: in the French romance, Enide accuses herself (p. 206). Indeed, the worth of Chrétien's heroine is demonstrated by her very sensitivity to criticism of her husband: it hurts her so deeply only because she identifies so completely with him. One morning, she inadvertently wakes him with her tears and self-reproaches – but, insists Chrétien, she intended no ill ("mes ele n'i pansoit nul mal", 2485). At first, she tries to hide the reason for her unhappiness. Her prevarication annoys Erec, and she reluctantly tells the truth. She tells him unreservedly about the damage to his reputation, and even suggests a course of action:

> Or vos an estuet consoil prandre –
> que vos puissiez ce blasme estaindre
> et vostre premier los ataindre –
> car trop vos ai oï blasmer.[89]

This awakens in Erec a grim resolve. "Lady," he declares, "you're right", and with that, he curtly orders their immediate departure from the court.[90] Thus Erec goes off, leading his wife with him, to suffer whatever adventures might befall:

[87] Loomis, p. 55. A clear argument for the existence of a lost corpus including stories like those of Erec and Yvain is that they are associated both in the *Mabinogion* and in the *Erec* of Hartmann von Aue, even though these works are apparently based on versions other than those by Chrétien.

[88] *Yvain*, lines 2521-2: "The joy of love which comes late is like a green log burning." Cf. *De amore*, I. 6, 361-2, p. 144.

[89] *Erec et Enide*, lines 2562-4: "Now you should accept some advice – that you try to erase this reproach and regain your former reputation, because I have heard you criticised too much."

[90] *Erec et Enide*, line 2572: "Dame . . . droit en eüstes."

Erec s'an va, sa femme an moinne
ne set ou, mes an avanture.[91]

Erec's motivation has puzzled many scholars.[92] In *Gereint*, the author directly states that the hero was motivated by his suspicion that "she was meditating love for another man in his stead".[93] Chrétien makes no such explicit statement about Erec's feelings. "Is it therefore to punish her that Erec conducts himself so harshly towards her?" asks Lazar, "But is she really to blame? Is not Erec solely to blame for the reproaches murmured by the other knights?"[94] "For the modern reader," agrees Noble, "it is hard to see where she has erred."[95] According to Zaddy, "the question is a thorny one, and remains unresolved, since Chrétien has neglected to tell us what motivates the departure of his hero".[96] Sheldon argues that "if Enide has been guilty of no fault which can excuse her husband's behavior, then Chrétien's account makes Erec guilty of a really unprovoked and unreasonably harsh, not to say cruel, treatment of Enide, and such cannot have been the poet's intention".[97] By contrast, some critics have been quite willing to justify her treatment. Paris accepted that she was responsible for her husband's recreance.[98] Küchler and Coghlan have endorsed her own belief that she had been proud (2600-6).[99] Woodbridge held that "Enide's *forfet* was in the distrust of her lord's prowess"; and Noble similarly that it "lies in doubting Erec";[100] while Brogyanyi suggested that Erec's "vengeance and anger" are justified by his "didactic" purpose.[101] Others have accepted that Erec's behaviour is indeed petulant. According to Lazar, "his violent reaction is that of an angry man, his masculine pride wounded".[102] Nitze regarded his gesture as an assertion of sovereignty.[103] For Zaddy, "self-regard, and its

---

[91] *Erec et Enide*, lines 2762-3: "Erec departs, taking his wife with him, he knows not where, but wherever chance may take him."

[92] See Ménage's summary of scholarship.

[93] *Mabinogion*, p. 207. Nitze thought this an *ex post facto* and conventionalized explanation of a complex motive (p. 473).

[94] Lazar, p. 201: "Est-ce donc pour la punir qu'Erec se conduit si durement à son égard? Mais est-elle vraiment coupable? Erec n'est-il pas le seul responsable des reproches que chuchotent les chevaliers?"

[95] Noble, p. 26.

[96] Zaddy, p. 179: "la question est épineuse et reste encore à résoudre, car Chrétien a négligé de nous dire ce qui motive le départ de son héros".

[97] Sheldon, p. 115.

[98] Paris, review of Foerster, pp. 162-3.

[99] Küchler, p. 87; Coghlan, pp. 28-9.

[100] Woodbridge, p. 440; Noble, p. 26; cf. Hoepffner, p. 445.

[101] Brogyanyi, pp. 417, 420-1.

[102] Lazar, p. 209: "sa réaction violente est celle d'un homme en colère, blessé dans son orgueil masculin".

[103] Nitze, p. 448.

demands, explain everything about Erec's conduct'';[104] while Frappier thought Erec "deeply wounded in his pride and knightly honour, all the more because he recognizes the truth of the criticism, and he avenges himself by adopting a course of cold, imperious, laconic severity".[105] For Bogdanow, "the crisis is best accounted for not in terms of psychology or morality, but rather in terms of his acting out sentiments attributed by troubadours to their cruel ladies".[106] Finally, Sheldon ingeniously suggested that, hearing only Enide's final words, "How unfortunate it was!" ("Con mar i fus", 2503), Erec misinterpreted them as an expression of discontent. He only provisionally accepts her explanation that her words expressed her concern for him, forcing their departure in order to test the truth of it.[107]

Yet, the issue is surely not so complex, for Erec's decision to depart is clearly motivated directly by Enide's suggestion that he should mend his reputation. It is not as a punishment that she is forced to accompany him. Erec can only demonstrate his prowess by finding room within their relationship to do so. For her husband to be rehabilitated as she wishes, it is necessary that she sacrifice the privileges of his infatuation, and share in some of his hardships. At the same time, it seems to me that Erec's resolution is also a selfish and impulsive gesture, as his surliness suggests. In fleeing to the magical wilderness of romance – conventionally the arena of solitary, masculine endeavour – Erec seeks to reaffirm himself as an individual and as a man. The gesture represents an individual's response to the difficulty of learning to accept the intimate criticisms inevitable in marriage. He is harsh with Enide because he identifies her with her beauty's power to seduce him from himself: he sets barriers between them as he steels himself against the effect she has upon him. In realistic terms, this is entirely unjust to Enide personally, but then, as Vinaver says, Chrétien's romances cannot be classified "as examples of psychological realism in the modern sense of the word. Chrétien lets the characters enact a line of argument that happens to interest him, no matter what kind of characterization, real or unreal, may emerge as a result."[108] He is not concerned with whether or not Erec acts with justice, and we are not meant to blame him for his insouciance: the initiation of the quest is simply a movement in the psychological drama of accepting marriage's claims upon the self.

Chrétien thus interprets the shared quest not simply as a test of his prowess and her fidelity, but as an image of the process of mutual accommodation in marriage. In order to do this, he emphasizes the continuing validity of their marital relationship, despite the disruption of their married life. This is why

---

[104] Zaddy, p. 184: "l'amour-propre, et ses exigences, explique tout dans la conduite d'Erec".
[105] Frappier, p. 170.
[106] Bogdanow, p. 81.
[107] Sheldon, pp. 119–20, 124.
[108] Vinaver, p. 30.

Erec troubles to commend Enide to his father's care in the event of his death (2721-7); and why he insists that she wear her best clothes (2576-8).[109] Chrétien identifies Enide's clothes all the more directly with her married status in that it is only at the point of becoming Erec's bride that she casts off her torn white shift and assumes the Queen's fine clothes.[110] By contrast, Geraint tells Enid to wear her worst in order to humiliate her: in his pride and jealousy, he no longer honours her as his wife (p. 207). In the adventures which follow, Enide amply proves her fidelity, and Erec his prowess. Yet, Chrétien has never allowed his audience to doubt that they can do so. What is perhaps more important is the sense of spiritual progress in Erec's and Enide's passage through trial, the feeling of reconciliation by shared experience. Auerbach suggested that the essential significance of the series of adventures typical of romance is as "a fated and graduated test of election, . . . the basis of a doctrine of personal perfection dictated by fate".[111] In this way, the adventures of Erec and Enide tend to an illumination of their relationship rather than to an alteration of its terms. Indeed, there seems to be nothing essentially different in the way they enjoy each other after their reconciliation:

> Ansamble jurent an un lit,
> et li uns l'autre acole et beise:
> riens nule n'est qui tant lor pleise.[112]

Their abandonment to love only seems more acceptable because they have endured hardship together as well:

> Tant ont eü mal et enui,
> il por li et ele por lui,
> c'or ont feite lor penitance.[113]

The incident which clinches their reconciliation is so structured as to allow Enide to demonstrate that her love for Erec is so exclusive that her loyalty extends even beyond his death. Weakened by his wounds, Erec has fallen unconscious as if he were dead ("con s'il fust morz", 4569). Enide is so grief-

---

[109] Cf. Kelly, p. 344; Sparnaay, p. 82. Noble, however, explains Enide's fine clothes as "tempting bait, likely to provoke the sort of incidents which will allow Erec to prove himself" (p. 19). The same incidents occur in *Geraint* even without such raiment, so this is clearly not a very compelling explanation. Noble also suggests that Enide is well-dressed as "a visible symbol of his status": Erec's status, it seems to me, is not at issue.

[110] Bender argues bizarrely that, in *Erec et Enide*, "Chrétien glorifie la compatibilité parfaite de la beauté et du mariage" (p. 35).

[111] Auerbach, p. 136.

[112] *Erec et Enide*, lines 5200-2: "They lie together in the same bed, and each embraces and kisses the other: there is nothing else which could delight them so much."

[113] *Erec et Enide*, lines 5203-5: "They have endured so much pain and trouble, he for her and her for him, that now they have done their penance."

stricken that she is on the point of suicide when the couple are discovered by the Count of Limors and his men. They assume that Erec is dead, as Enide does, and take him back to Limors, where they place him on a bier in the middle of the hall (4642–4708). The Count meanwhile tries to persuade Enide to marry him. Neither flattery nor threats avail him, and he eventually strikes her (4788). Erec revives in the commotion just as his wife is declaring her devotion to his memory in extravagant terms:

> "Ahi!" fet ele, "ne me chaut
> que tu me dïes ne ne faces.
> ne criem tes cos ne tes menaces.
> Asez me bat, asez me fier:
> ja tant ne te troverai fier
> que por toi face plus ne mains,
> se tu or androit a tes mains
> me devoies les ialz sachier
> ou tote vive detranchier."[114]

Chrétien turns what follows into a little comedy, with the people of Limors shouting "Run away! Run away! Look out for the dead man!" ("Fuiez! Fuiez! Veez le mort", 4840) and struggling to escape. Yet the incident also allows him to establish Enide as a model of conjugal devotion. Though she is motivated to suicide in part because she blames herself for her husband's death, her willingness to sacrifice herself so absolutely for her love is also the expression of a vocation just as profound as any saint's. It is possible that her imaginative references to torture (as well as Fénice's sufferings at the hands of the physicians) constitute a deliberate allusion to the traditional tortures of martyrdom. In this way Chrétien places the ideal of marital fidelity directly in competition with ethics of saintliness. Enide remains true to her husband, even when she thinks he is dead and has the option to remarry. Chrétien implicitly suggests that marital union is inviolable, even by death. However, in *Yvain* he does not condemn Laudine for marrying so rapidly after her husband's death – marrying her husband's slayer at that. His representation of Enide's total commitment to her husband is a consciously romantic ideal, rather than a blueprint for marriage in the real world. Whether or not Chrétien endorsed the principle of marital indissolubility, he at least recognized its sentimental appeal.

By contrast, Peter Noble asserts that "Chrétien is not just an apologist for marriage and love in marriage, [but] their advocate".[115] He

---

[114] *Erec et Enide*, lines 4806–14: " 'Ah!' she declares, 'I don't care what you do or say to me. I'm not afraid of your blows or your threats. You can beat or hit me as much as you like: I will never find you so cruel that I will ever do anything at all for you, even if right now with your own hands you should tear my eyes out or dismember me alive.' "

[115] Noble, p. 7.

thinks "Chrétien's argument is . . . that the love which Erec and Enide feel for each other is sufficient to withstand all their troubles, both external and between themselves. This love is the force which turns them from a selfish inward looking couple to a mature, responsible couple, who are admired by all."[116] Chrétien is hardly so didactic: the various impulses and aspirations of people in love and marriage provided him with the raw material of drama, but he felt himself under no obligation to resolve the tensions he outlined.[117] In any case, he probably inherited a plot in which these concerns were already implicit.[118] Even if the climax of Erec's and Enide's quest results in an affirmation of the importance of marital fidelity, the problem with which it begins – the difficulty of balancing commitment to marriage with endeavours in other spheres of life – remains a valid one.

It is to this issue that Chrétien returns in the bizarrely named episode with which the action of the romance effectively ends, the Joy of the Court ("Joie de la Cort"). The knight Mabonagrain is condemned by a vow to his lady to fight all comers in defence of their enchanted garden: Erec defeats him and sounds the horn which dispels the enchantment. Paris thought it "impossible to imagine anything more absurd, more incoherent, and at the same time less interesting than this story: moreover the poet prolongs it by adding a considerable number of useless details and tells it with a wearisome prolixity".[119] According to Murphy, "This dismissal has spurred subsequent critics to justify its inclusion, to interpret the episode as coherent in itself and necessarily linked to the rest of the romance."[120] Frappier, for example, thought that "the ideal marriage of Erec and Enide provides a contrast to the all-absorbing and anti-social relationship of Mabonagrain and his mistress, as well as to the fatal spell which binds Tristan to Iseut".[121] Scully suggested that Chrétien was "thinking of the the new convention of courtly love which insisted upon the initiation of the select few to certain rules of behavior and the acceptance of almost occult tenets about the effects of love. Into this closed mystical world Erec steps in the painful struggle to win *Joie*."[122] According to Roques, "the moral, if it is necessary to draw one, is that the profoundest and most joyous love is not the exclusive love which subordinates all life to it, but the love which

---

[116] Noble, p. 27.

[117] Cf. Küchler, p. 83; Morris, *Discovery*, p. 135.

[118] Loomis, p. 56.

[119] Paris, rev. Foerster, p. 154: "impossible d'imaginer quelque chose de plus absurde, de plus incohérent, et en même temps de moins intéressant que ce récit, allongé d'ailleurs par le poète à grand renfort de détails inutiles et raconté avec une fatigante prolixité."

[120] Murphy, p. 109.

[121] Frappier, p. 170. Compare, for example, Payen, 'Mise', p. 223; Noble, p. 26; Hoepffner, p. 448; Press, p. 534; Murphy, p. 117; Scully, pp. 87–8.

[122] Scully, p. 84.

takes life into account and is satisfied in having made every moment of it lovelier".[123]

Like the newly married Erec, Mabonagrain is imprisoned by his inordinate feelings for a woman. Murphy describes him as "the image of Erec's immoderate ardor in early wedlock".[124] Chrétien perhaps deliberately stressed this identification: in the Welsh analogue, the maiden of the "Joie" sits on a chair, while in Chrétien's version, she is lying on a bed, a symbol of luxury in love. As Nitze shows, the garden ("vergier") of the "Joie de la Cort" is a transformation of a Celtic prototype, often an enchanted island, where a "fairy-mistress" binds a hero to the pleasures of her bed.[125] It was thus implicitly an image of a man's enslavement to desire. Yet Mabonagrain is not precisely "a heightened replica" of the unregenerate Erec, for he gains his liberty only at the cost of defeat: Erec asserts his liberty only in order to recover his renown.[126] As Bogdanow points out, "Mabonagrain in contrast to Erec is never guilty of *recreantise*. In fact it was Mabonagrain's reputation that made Erec's victory in their battle such a signal triumph and enabled him to recover his *premier los* [his previous reputation]."[127] Indeed, Mabonagrain argues that recreance would have been a cowardly evasion (6048-51).

It seems to me that his state in the "vergier" corresponds not to Erec's brief period of uxoriousness, but to the earliest stage of Erec's courtship – the period in which Erec was still able to associate the deeds of arms with the expression of his love. In Mabonagrain's case, however, the trial of his prowess proves endless, and he becomes trapped in a cycle of blood-letting. In this way, Chrétien suggests that there is no return for Erec to the simple dynamic of romance that associates the inspiration of love with the demonstration of valour. This is a primitive stage of the nobleman's progress, valid in its time, but only stagnating once prolonged. The problem of reconciling individual values with the wider responsibilities here represented by marriage cannot be answered simply by the refusal to proceed to more complex states of life.

The *hortus conclusus* implicitly recalls the Earthly Paradise[128] – particularly in Chrétien's description of the enchanted fruit, for example (5698-704) – and Mabonagrain is indeed a pristine figure in that he represents the idealistic system with which the romance begins. Like the author of the *Mystère d'Adam*, Chrétien used the idea of a garden to establish a model. Mabonagrain's garden is not an inverse Eden. He and his beloved remain an

---

[123] Roques, p. 379: "la leçon, s'il faut en tirer une, c'est que l'amour le plus profond, le plus fécond en joie, n'est pas l'amour exclusif qui se subordonne toute la vie, mais celui qui tient compte de la vie et se tient satisfait d'en avoir embelli tous les instants".
[124] Murphy, p. 115.
[125] Nitze, pp. 461-70.
[126] Murphy, p. 117.
[127] Bogdanow, p. 89.
[128] Barron, p. 41; Murphy, pp. 113-15; Scully, p. 81.

ideal couple, depite Erec's intrusion: his valour, her beauty and their mutual devotion are beyond question. The limitation of what they represent is precisely the limitation of any ideal – its insulation from the real world. In releasing them from their enclosure, Erec perhaps enacts the way in which, as a storyteller, Chrétien himself released ideals into society. He emphasizes that in restoring Mabonagrain and his beloved to Evrain's court, Erec produces the "joie de la cort"; and indeed, this phrase is used in a contemporary text to denote the delight caused by entertainers at court.[129]

Chrétien thus offers no simple answers to the problems he poses: indeed, he uses Mabonagrain to turn his back on any brittle and simplistic idealism. He represents the *rapprochement* of Erec and Enide as an entirely individual process, not as an exemplary pattern. They are educated not by any method, but by chance – "aventure". If they are in any way exemplary it is in their willingness to face experiences together and to learn from them. While Erec and Enide at least develop, Mabonagrain and his beloved remain imprisoned in their enchanted garden. There is something rather immature, even infantile, about the relationship described by Mabonagrain's "amie":

> Ancor estoie anfes asez,
> et il ert biax et avenanz.
> La feïmes noz covenanz
> antre nos deux, tex con nos sist.
> Einz ne vos rien qu'il ne volsist,
> tant que amer me comança,
> si me plevi et fiança
> que toz jorz mes amis seroit
> et que il ça m'an amanroit . . .[130]

By contrast, Enide evokes a much more adult, responsible relationship.[131] While Mabonagrain's "amie" evokes his appearance and manner, Enide praises Erec's qualities as a knight and as a man:

> – Bele cosine, il m'espousa,
> si que mes peres bien le sot
> et ma mere qui joie en ot.
> Tuit le sorent et lié an furent
> nostre parant, si com il durent . . .

---

[129] *Eructavit*, 34.

[130] *Erec et Enide*, lines 6222–30: "I was still quite young, and he was beautiful and courteous; then we made the covenant between us, just as it suited us. At that time, I never wanted anything that he did not want, so that he began to love me, and thus pledged and promised me that he would always be my lover, and that he would bring me away here."

[131] Murphy suggests (p. 117) that the affinity between Enide and the maiden signifies their moral correspondence.

> car il est chevaliers si buens
> qu'an ne porroit meillor trover . . .[132]

In this way, perhaps, Chrétien takes us from the romantic microcosm in which he has expressed some ideals and raised some problems about love and marriage, to the brink of reality.

4. The Letters of Abelard and Heloise

Abelard and Heloise are often cast as the heralds of a new age, the age of humanism and individualism, tragically oppressed by the mechanistic ideology of the Gothic world. Pater, for example, argued that "the opposition into which Abelard is thrown, which gives its colour to his career, which breaks his soul to pieces, is a no less subtle opposition than that between the merely professional, official, hireling ministers of that system, with their ignorant worship of the system for its own sake, and the true child of light, the humanist, with reason and heart and senses quick".[133] Campbell saw in them a premonition of "the great theme that was in time to become the characteristic signal of our culture: the courage, namely, to affirm against tradition whatever knowledge stands confirmed in one's own controlled experience"; they affirmed "the majesty of love against the supernatural utilitarianism of the sacramental system of the Church".[134] Even Gilson saw them as great souls, trapped in the clash between passion and conscience: "it is absolutely certain that it is their innermost selves about which Abélard and Héloïse instruct us; and if they sometimes lie to themselves, they never lie to us".[135]

Yet the "greatness" of Abelard and Heloise is better sought in the substance and consistency of their ideas than in the tragic splendour of their circumstances.[136] By praising them too enthusiastically for their detachment from the standards of their age, for their emotional defiance and intellectual precocity, these scholars perhaps only stimulated some to doubt the authenticity of their correspondence.[137] Reluctance to accept the ascriptions

---

[132] *Erec et Enide*, lines 6242–6, 6248–9: "Fair cousin, he married me with my father's full knowledge and to my mother's joy. Our relatives knew all about it and were happy about it, as they should have been . . . For he is so worthy a knight, that no one could find a better."

[133] Pater, p. 5.

[134] Campbell, IV, 53–63, at pp. 54–5.

[135] Gilson, p. 117.

[136] Cf. Georgianna, 'Any Corner', p. 248.

[137] Gilson was able to dismiss the doubts of an earlier generation of scholars (pp. 145–66). More recently, Muckle doubted the authenticity of Heloise's first two letters (*MS* 15, p. 67) and her arguments against marriage reported in the *Historia* (*MS* 12, pp. 173–4). Robertson accepted "no reason whatsoever for thinking that the letters attributed to Heloise in this collection were actually composed as genuine letters by her" (*Abelard*,

"may be motivated, even if largely unconsciously, by the doubters' disquiet at certain 'profane' passages encountered there", as Dronke suggests.[138] What Robertson, for example, found so incredible was exactly Gilson's notion of the letters' candid sentimentality. Identifying emotional engagement with an anachronistically modern self-indulgence, he argued that there is "no justification whatsoever for regarding the history either as a record of romantic passion or as a revelation of Abelard's 'psychological development' ".[139] In fact, these documents constitute a very serious attempt to address issues of universal as well as personal significance, but it is an attempt necessarily grounded in the feelings of the authors. Heloise's insistence on the permanence and strength of her love for Abelard, for example, is not simply a "sentimental" declaration, nor even primarily a "triumphant affirmation", but a means to an end, an important part of her rhetorical strategy to persuade Abelard of the need to define the parameters of their relationship.[140]

For them, the value and nature of marriage were burning issues, not only before they entered it, but also afterwards when Abelard's castration and their withdrawal into separate cloisters made the definition of their relationship particularly problematic. In their correspondence, they tried to establish mutually acceptable definitions, firstly, of the relationship between love, marriage and the aspirations of the individual, and, secondly, of the point at which intellectual communion is no longer an obligation of the conjugal bond. In other words, they discuss the nature of marriage in a way typical of their age. It is certainly true that there is nothing so anachronistic or anomalous about their treatment of marriage as to support the belief either that the correspondence was a later forgery, or that Heloise was only fictionally a participant in it. Their letters give dramatic substance, for example, to Egbert of Schönau's defence of marriage against the Cathars:

> Virum et mulierem conjunxit Deus, qui secundum institutiones divinarum legum coram Ecclesia ineunt foedus conjugale, et tales per hominem separandi non sunt. Fit quidem nonnumquam ut tales migrent pariter ad monasticam vitam, et separatas abinvincem mansiones eligant, quatenus Deo liberius servire possint; sed talem separationem Deus operatur, non homo, et quidem tales non omnino

p. 121). Other doubters are Benton ('Fraud'), Silvestre ('Liebesgeschichte') and Fraioli. The authenticity of the letters has been defended by Dronke (*Women Writers*, pp. 108–9; 'Heloise, Abelard', pp. 323–32) and Newman (pp. 135–44). Newman goes so far as to accuse the doubters of "*a priori* notions", "outright misogyny" and even "gratuitous sexual fantasy" (pp. 121, 128).

[138] Dronke, 'Abelard', p. 249; *Women Writers*, p. 108; 'Abelard and Heloise', pp. 249–50.
[139] Robertson, *Abelard*, p. 121. Dronke has described Heloise's 2nd Letter as a "lacerating self-portrayal" ('Heloise's *Problemata*', p. 308). It seems to me that this "self-portrayal" is justified by her need to settle these issues in terms of her own experiences.
[140] Dronke, *Women Writers*, p. 117.

abinvicem discedunt, neque rumpitur inter eos vinculum conjugale, quia indivisa in eis manet unitas mentium. Nam quanto liberius divinae dilectioni vacant tanto purius atque firmius se invicem diligere possunt.[141]

It is the clarity of their thinking as well as its intensity that should strike the reader. Abelard's *Historia Calamitatum* and the letters are private documents, shaped by personal experiences.[142] However, they are also public ones, stamped both by a consciousness of the world's attention;[143] and by exacting standards of literary expression.[144] Indeed, what is most impressive about this correspondence is the intellectual consistency with which it distils general principles from individual circumstances.[145] In attempting to resolve the difficulties of their own situation, Abelard and Heloise lucidly and memorably contrast their different ideas about the nature of marriage. Their discussion is clearly structured by verbal and thematic parallels; by

[141] Egbert of Schönau, *Sermones contra Catharos*, 5, PL 195. 27: "God joined a man and a woman together, who enter a conjugal contract before the Church according to the decrees of the divine laws, and no man can separate them. Indeed it often happens that such a couple both progress to the monastic life, and choose dwelling-places apart from each other so that they can serve God more freely; but such separations are made by God, not man, and in fact a couple like this do not entirely leave each other, nor is the conjugal bond between them broken, since they remain undivided in their unity of minds. For the more freely they occupy themselves with divine love, the more purely and firmly they can love each other." It is a haunting coincidence that Egbert here uses one of Heloise's characteristic idioms, "quanto liberius . . . tanto purius atque firmius".

[142] Cf. Dronke, 'Heloise's *Problemata*', p. 308. According to Verbeke, Abelard "represents an important stage in the progressive disclosure of human subjectivity" (pp. 1–2). Letters became increasingly candid as the Middle Ages progressed: Leclercq, 'L'amitié', p. 409; Morris, *Discovery*, p. 79; McLaughlin, 'Abelard as Autobiographer', p. 487. Even so, medieval letters in general remained "self-conscious, quasi-public literary documents, often written with an eye to future collection and publication" (Constable, p. 11). This is still true of the *Epistolae duorum amantium*, which Könsgen argued were a genuine record of a historical relationship (pp. 80–5) – a relationship which Dronke tentatively accepted might be "not unlike Abelard and Heloise as they must have been before the tragedy" ('Abelard and Heloise', p. 272). This is a purely literary collection, its impression of temporal development being simply the impression given by patterns in the sequence – just as in Elizabethan sonnet-sequences.

[143] Heloise frequently heightens her appeals to Abelard by calling God and the world to witness: "ut omnibus patet" (70/29), "noverunt omnes" (70/30), "Deus scit" (70/43), "Deum testem invoco" (71/10): see Dronke, *Women Writers*, p. 116. Even so, it seems that the letters did not begin to circulate widely until the mid-thirteenth century. Newman explains (p. 134) that Heloise might have been reluctant to allow extensive publication during her own lifetime, if only for the sake of the reputation of the Paraclete and its priories.

[144] Dronke, *Women Writers*, pp. 107–8.

[145] Cf. McLaughlin, 'Abelard as Autobiographer', pp. 480–1. This is as true of the 'religious' letters as of the 'personal' letters: see Georgianna, 'Any Corner'.

symmetries of structure, style, mood and method; and even by a series of literary allusions to the same text, Lucan's *Pharsalia*.[146] Though they held different opinions about the compatibility of marital affection with religious devotion, they both accepted the absolute indissolubility of their bond. This idealistic, yet abstract, conception of marriage is entirely consistent with the nature of the public debate about marriage in this period.[147]

The simplest argument for the authenticity of the letters is that they are linked stylistically and thematically to other works which no critic has attempted to detach from the Abelardian canon (including, for example, Heloise's *Problemata*).[148] In the *Historia Calamitatum* (an autobiographical account of Abelard's misfortunes purportedly designed to console an unnamed and possibly fictive friend[149]), Abelard recounts how Heloise opposed his project of marriage. Her reasons were, firstly, that it would not secure him his immediate end, the placation of her guardian, and, secondly, that it ran counter to an ideal of intellectual and philosophical detachment which he had already expressed in his *Theologia Christiana*.[150] This is how Abelard reports Heloise's opposition to their marriage in the *Historia*:

> Ut autem hoc philosophici studii nunc omittam impedimentum, ipsum consule honestae conversationis statum. Quae enim conventio scholarium ad pedissequas, scriptoriorum ad cunabula, librorum sive tabularum ad colos, stilorum sive calamorum ad fusos? Quis denique sacris vel philosophicis meditationibus intentus pueriles vagitus, nutricum quae hos mitigant nenias, tumultuosam familiae tam in viris quam in feminis turbam sustinere poterit? Quae etiam inhonestas illas parvulorum sordes assiduas tolerare valebit? Id, inquies, divites possunt quorum palatia vel domus amplae deversoria habent, quorum opulentia non sentit expensas nec quotidianis sollicitudinibus cruciatur. Sed non est, inquam, haec condicio philosophorum quae divitum, nec qui opibus student vel saecularibus implicantur curis divinis seu philosophicis vacabunt officiis.

---

[146] *Historia*, 191/3–7, (*Pharsalia*, VIII. 94–8); *2 Ad Abaelardum*, 78/28–9 (*Pharsalia*, II. 14–5); *2 Ad Heloisam*, 92/32–3 (*Pharsalia*, VIII. 84–5). Von Moos, 'Cornelia'.

[147] I am thinking, for example, of the dependency of papal marriage policy upon the almost unverifiable factor of *consensus*.

[148] Luscombe, 'From Paris', p. 280; Dronke, *Women Writers*, p. 108, 'Heloise's *Problemata*', p. 295, and *Abelard*, pp. 247–60. Luscombe has concluded: "There seems to be no reason to believe that any of the pieces that are included in the collection were touched up or rewritten, lengthened or shortened, altered or forged, by a third party. The problem we are left with, and may never dispel, is that of knowing whether the letters were at first written for dispatch, separately and successively, with each provoking a reply and further correspondence until Abelard met Heloise's requests in full; or whether the collection arose from a compact between Heloise and Abelard jointly to share, compose and exchange their thoughts, experiences and principles in fictive correspondence" ('From Paris', p. 278).

[149] Brooke, p. 110; Morris, *Discovery*, pp. 97–8.

[150] Luscombe, *School*, p. 18.

> Unde et insignes olim philosophi mundum maxime contemnentes, nec tam relinquentes saeculum quam fugientes, omnes sibi voluptates interdixerunt ut in unius philosophiae requiescerent amplexibus.[151]

Heloise quotes St Paul's recommendation of celibacy in I Cor. 7:27-34 as a precedent for this contrast between an ideal of thoughtful serenity and the "troubles" of married life. Paul's phrase "tribulation of the flesh" implicitly recalls God's curse upon Eve for her part in the Fall of Man – "I will increase your hardships" ("multiplicabo aerumnas tuas", Gen. 3: 16). Since the troubles of marriage could so readily be interpreted as the universal inheritance of women for their kinship with Eve, they naturally became a commonplace of patristic and medieval teaching on female virginity.[152] Yet Heloise is thinking chiefly not of her own potential for trial and indignity in marriage, but Abelard's. Her real inspiration is classical and literary, rather than Christian and theological. In elaborating the theme of "tribulationes carnis", as Bella Millett says, "patristic writers show an obvious debt to classical literary tradition. The idea had been touched on more than once in Greek tragedy; the view that a wise man should not marry was common to many of the philosophical schools of antiquity, including the Epicureans, Stoics and Cynics; and from at least the fifth century B.C. the disadvantages of marriage had been a standard rhetorical topic".[153] The assumption lying behind both the pagan and Christian traditions of matrimonial criticism is that it is an individual's prerogative to safeguard his spiritual integrity by avoidance of mundane troubles and emotional distractions.[154] However, this

---

[151] *Historia*, 186/30-187/8: "However, even without mentioning the hindrance to philosophical study, consider the very conditions for a virtuous way of life. For what harmony can there be between students and serving-women, between desks and cradles, between books or tablets and distaffs, or between pens and spindles? For who could finally remain intent upon sacred or philosophic meditations and endure the wailing of infants, the lullabies of the nurses soothing them, and the noisy crowd of servants, both male and female? For who would be able to tolerate the constant unseemly filth of little children? You will say that the rich can do so, whose palaces and large houses contain refuges: being wealthy they are not troubled by expenses or tortured by daily cares. But I would say that the philosopher's circumstances are not those of a rich man: those who concentrate on money and involve themselves in worldly concerns will not be free for divine or philosophical offices. Therefore the famous philosophers of the past greatly despised the world, and, not so much relinquishing the world as fleeing it, banned all pleasures for themselves, and found peace in the embrace of philosophy alone."

[152] Hansen; Millett, *HM*, p. xxxiv.

[153] Millett, *HM*, pp. xxxiv-v; cf. Hansen, pp. 218-19; Brundage, p. 65; Delhaye, 'Dossier', p. 68; Wiesen, pp. 113-16; Blamires, pp. 3-4; Foucault, *Care*, p. 154. Cf. Map, *Epistola Valerii* ("Amicum habui, uirum uite philosophice"); Andreas, *De amore*. III, pp. 296/34-299/37, 304/62-306/64; Hugh de Folieto, *De nuptiis*. In the Middle Ages, wisdom was often equated directly with monasticism: Leclercq, *Women*, pp. 139-50; Blamires, pp. 3-4.

[154] Foucault, *Care*, pp. 39-68, 157-8. Cf. Gregory of Nyssa (*De virginitate*, 3: quoted by

"philosophical" ideal of the pagan world was predominantly masculine in character. This bias was inherited by the Christian era. Medieval polemics against marriage (*dissuasiones de non ducenda uxore*) are often cast as admonitions by devoted male friends, and often became vehicles for misogyny.[155]

The immediate occasion for Abelard's presentation of the same ideas in the *Theologia Christiana* was his attempt to syncretize pagan and Christian philosophy in support of his arguments about the nature of the Trinity.[156] To justify this, he drew heavily upon St Jerome's antimatrimonial treatise, *Adversus Jovinianum*. Jerome had recommended celibacy by appealing not only to biblical precedents, but also to the literary and philosophical authorities of the pagan world. As Delhaye points out, "only Abelard's direct use of the *Adversus Jovinianum* can explain the inclusion of the appeal to Holy Scripture in the *Theologia christiana*, since it sits uneasily with a line of argument intended to exalt the chastity of pagans".[157] Abelard was one of the first medieval writers to make extensive use of the *Adversus Jovinianum*.[158] Like Jerome, Abelard appeals to the examples of David, Samson and Solomon, and to the sapiential books of the Old Testament.[159] He then states:

> Hiis et consimilibus rationibus incitati, philosophi continentiae sibi proposuerunt uitam, tum ut philosophiae penitus uacare possent, tum plurimum ne eorum fortitudo muliebrium illecebrarum mollitiis ener-uata succumberet, uel filiorum affectu ad illicita uel turpia quaedam cogerentur, uel labem aliquam infamiae quam ex propria non haberent uitam, uitiis uxorum contraherent.[160]

Pagels, p. 83): "he whose life is contained in himself either escapes [sufferings] altogether, or can bear them easily, having a collected mind which is not distracted from itself; while whoever shares himself with wife and child often has not a moment to give even to regretting his own condition, because anxiety for those he loves fills his heart".

[155] For example, Map, *Epistola Valerii*; Peter of Blois, *Ep.* 79; Hugh de Fouilloy, *De Nuptiis*. Book III of Andreas's *De amore* is addressed to one Walter, and as a dissuasion from love in general, it covers similar ground. Analogues in later medieval literature are the dissuasion of Justinus (*The Merchant's Tale*, IV. 1521–65); and Rabelais, pp. 310–12. See Mann, *Geoffrey Chaucer*, pp. 51–2. The *locus classicus* is Juvenal, *Sat.* VI. Friendship seems to have been particularly in vogue among the professionally celibate – the monks: Leclercq, 'L'amitié'; *Love*, pp. 180–1; Morris, *Discovery*, pp. 97–107.

[156] Verbeke, pp. 6–7; Luscombe, *Peter Abelard*, p. 19.

[157] Delhaye, 'Dossier', p. 72: "seule la présence sous les yeux d'Abélard de l'*Adversus Jovinianum* peut expliquer dans la *Theologia christiana* la mention de l'argument d'Escriture Sainte car il ne se raccroche que malaisément à une argumentation dont le but est d'exalter la chasteté des païens".

[158] Schmitt, p. 262; Delhaye, 'Dossier', p. 71.

[159] Abelard, *Theologia*, II. 89–91, pp. 171–2.

[160] Abelard, *Theologia*, II. 95: "Urged on by these and similar reasons, the philosophers proposed a life of continence for themselves, firstly so that they could be completely free for philosophy, and then, more importantly, lest their strength of mind should fail and be weakened by the sweetness of female snares; or lest they be driven by fatherly

Still following Jerome, he goes on to cite the "philosophers", Cicero, Socrates, Herodotus, Epicurus and Sextus (or Xystus), and, finally, Theophrastus (II. 97–100). In quoting the Theophrastan passage as a moral admonition to Christians and to philosophers alike, both Jerome and Abelard seem remarkably insensitive to the selfishness and bigotry of this misogynistic tirade against women's conduct in marriage. According to Theophrastus, wives are avaricious, covetous, narcissistic, adulterous, domineering and quarrelsome; they deprive a man of his time, his money, his friends, and his authority; and a servant gives better service. It is paradoxical that, in advocating the purest of Christian and scholarly ideals, Jerome and Abelard unleashed upon the middle ages a text which was to exert "a quasi-hypnotic influence on medieval antifeminism".[161]

Jerome, Abelard and Heloise all refer to the same constellation of authorities,[162] and all three deliberately blur the distinction between the serenity of the celibate Christian and the *otium philosophicum* of the unmarried scholar. However, as Delhaye points out, "for the two lovers it is not a matter of reference to a Christian ideal or to the canon laws enjoining continence upon them. What is at issue is how to escape the obligations of a social condition. The Christian authors as well as the pagan ones allied with them here agreed in arguing against marriage, but the spirit in which they gave their advice was totally different. St Paul advocated virginity and Theophrastus unregulated love."[163] Heloise is not arguing for continence, but for a relationship based absolutely on the continued expression of mutual free will. It was an ideal perhaps based on the Ciceronian ideal of pure disinterest in friendship.[164] Abelard reports her as arguing "that it would seem more precious to her and more honourable to me to be called a lover rather than a wife, so that only love would keep me with her, rather than the constrictive force of any

affection to do base or illegal things, or lest they suffer any stain of disgrace because of their wife's vices, which they would not have suffered on account of their own way of life."

[161] Mann, *Geoffrey Chaucer*, p. 49; cf. Blamires, p. 11.

[162] Common to all three are the references to St Paul, Cicero, Theophrastus, Seneca and Socrates. Delhaye has "vraiment trop l'impression que les paroles rapportées ici ne sont pas d'Héloïse mais de l'auteur de la *Theologia christiana*" (pp. 73–4). It seems perfectly credible to me that the concordance between the passages reflects an attempt by Heloise to reinforce her arguments by an appeal to the teachings of the man she sought to persuade.

[163] Delhaye, 'Le Dossier', p. 75: "il ne s'agit pas pour les deux amants de se référer à un idéal chrétien ou à des règles canoniques qui leur enjoignent la continence. Il n'est question que d'échapper aux obligations d'un état social. Les auteurs chrétiens comme les païens allégués ici seront d'accord pour déconseiller le mariage mais l'esprit dans lequel ils donnent ce conseil est totalement différent. Saint Paul préconise la virginité et Théophraste l'amour libre."

[164] Cf. Gilson, p. 57; Newman, p. 150; Dronke, *Women Writers*, p. 117. See Mathew, 'Ideals'.

marital bond''.[165] Like Chrétien de Troyes and Andreas Capellanus, Heloise makes a distinction between the states of wife and lover. Like them, she did so because she was anxious to define the relationship between the institution and the feelings of the individuals it binds. She believed that marriage was only morally valid as long as it is an expression of the emotional commitment of the partners to each other. Unless she was ''amica'' and ''amie'', she saw no value in being ''uxor'' and ''fame''.

Luscombe has suggested that in Heloise's day, concubinage was a practicable possibility: ''at a time when concubinage was not socially disreputable but when the prohibitions of clerical marriage and other laws of marriage were still being sharpened, [it] is not so daringly original nor so old-fashioned as to be implausible''.[166] Brooke has suggested that Heloise's preference for concubinage ''echo[es] a world in which there was a real choice between being a wife and being a concubine''.[167] He argues that concubinage remained a social norm in chapters of secular canons for much of the twelfth century, despite the reform movement. Heloise ''was brought up in a cathedral close, where relationships of love were known and accepted, where marriage in the strict sense was alien and forbidden; and marriage was something of the outside world, a contract of convenience among worldly, landed folk, to sustain and enhance the fortunes of their families''.[168] Yet even if cathedral closes had been ''strangely little touched by the immensely powerful propaganda of the age for clerical celibacy'', Heloise herself could hardly have been unaware of the tide against clerical sexuality in the Church as a whole.[169] Canons were still acting illegally in keeping concubines and Abelard's career beyond the cathedral close would inevitably have been harmed. Moreover, there seem to be two kinds of ''concubinage'' at issue here – the respectable ''chapter-concubinage'' involving a household, children and a certain permanence – and what Roman law would have seen as concubinage – a temporary relationship in which the concubine's rights were virtually none. As far as Heloise is concerned, the former differs very little from marriage: she objects to the indignity of household cares and the burden of reciprocal duties, all of which would have been as much part of this formal concubinatory relationship as of marriage itself. The other kind of relationship, characterized by impermanence and the woman's lack of rights is what Heloise invokes. Such unions would not have been thought morally acceptable, even in cathedral chapters. She may have felt that

---

[165] *Historia*, 189/11–13: ''quam sibi carius existeret mihique honestius amicam dici quam uxorem ut me ei sola gratia conservaret, non vis aliqua vinculi nuptialis constringeret''.
[166] Luscombe, 'From Paris', pp. 252–3.
[167] Brooke, *Idea*, p. 91.
[168] Brooke, *Idea*, p. 261.
[169] Brooke, *Idea*, p. 113.

Abelard would be able to save his career if he could renounce her whenever necessary. It is unlikely, however, that concubinage would left Abelard in any better position than marriage. The Church was becoming increasingly hostile to all forms of clerical sexuality. For example, the First and Second Lateran Councils of 1123 and 1139 specifically proscribed clerical concubinage as well as clerical marriage.

The clue to Heloise's attitude lies in Abelard's description of his attempt at reconciliation with her guardian.[170] He refers to her in this passage as a commodity, offered in satisfaction for something Abelard speaks of as a crime ("dolus", "proditio", "me . . . accusans"). She is at once the woman corrupted ("eam . . . quam corruperam"), and the woman corrupting, the agent of Abelard's downfall. She is presented not as an individual, but approximated to the demonic ideal of medieval misogyny, the eternal Eve. Attempting to establish a sympathy with her guardian, Abelard reminds him "how catastrophically women have degraded even the most eminent of men from the very beginnings of the human race".[171] What Heloise feared above all else was exactly this dehumanization of their love. She saw the voluntarism of an unformalized relationship as a buttress against it. She played ideals of aloof and dignified scholarship against the riot and indignity of a household because she feared the deindividualization of a woman in marriage. As she saw it, a wife can only be a sexual distraction, a mother and a domestic worker, and never a lover, a friend or a fellow-scholar.[172]

Heloise thus consistently shows herself willing to sacrifice her own interests in order to safeguard Abelard's respect for her individuality. To Robertson, this seemed incredible – a masculine fantasy of having one's cake and eating it – but it is entirely logical.[173] What Heloise really wants from Abelard, as becomes entirely clear from her letters, is an intellectual and emotional communion – "unitas mentium", to use Egbert's phrase. Such relationships are not founded upon obligation, and she is prepared to waive her rights over Abelard's means and his household in order to ensure that their relationship remains pre-eminently a disinterested one. In parallel with the popes, theologians and lawyers who taught that marriage was essentially and sacramentally a consensual matter even at the expense of destabilizing it in practice, Heloise insisted that only the purity of her motives could justify her relationship with Abelard, even if that obliged her to sacrifice her own security within it. She declares herself willing to precede Abelard even into Hell ("ad Vulcania loca").[174] This is neither an idle profanity nor a mystical

---

[170] *Historia*, 185/8-16.
[171] *Historia*, 185/12-13: "quanta ruina summos quoque viros ab ipso statim humani generis exordio mulieres deiecerint".
[172] Jean de Meun suggests that Heloise rejected marriage so that she as well as Abelard would be free to study (8783-4).
[173] Robertson, *Abelard*, p. 90.
[174] 1 *Ad Abaelardum*, 72/41-2.

gesture of abnegation, but, as Dronke has pointed out, an allusion to Alcestis as a model of conjugal devotion.[175]

It seems ironic that Heloise should argue against marriage by turning to a body of ideas so unflattering to herself as the material from the *Adversus Jovinianum*, and that she should be so willing to commit herself to Abelard with no guarantee as to her own future welfare. As Mann says, "the more passionately Heloise argues against her own interests, the more apparent is the contrast betweeen the picture of woman painted by Jerome and Theophrastus on which she founds her case, and the self-sacrificing loyalty that drives her to argue it".[176] Heloise uses the image of Charybdis to suggest that by marrying she will shamelessly and irrevocably submerge Abelard in obscenity ("obscoenitatibus istis . . . impudenter atque irrevocabiliter").[177] This is profoundly disturbing. It suggests that she really saw herself in terms of antifeminist stereotypes as Abelard's Eve, bound ineluctably by her feminine nature to demean the man she loved. Heloise's perception of herself as both harmful and innocent ("plurimum nocens . . . plurimum innocens", 72/4–5) recalls Walter Map's accusations against women in the *Epistola Valerii*: "a woman is cunning when she wants to do harm, which is always; and often when she is ready to help, she hinders, whence it happens that she does harm even when she doesn't want to".[178] It is also hard not to think of the refrain from Abelard's emotive interpretation of Dinah's tragic fate: "Woe is me, I have betrayed myself!" she sings.[179] Heloise was perhaps too ready to blame herself for her husband's recreance, like Chrétien's Enide. However, in presenting the *Historia Calamitatum* as a parable of pride and its fall, Abelard certainly invites this interpretation of her role. Even at the beginning of their affair, he depicts himself as a scholarly *chevalier récreant* drawn from his studies by "the mental distraction, or indeed, disturbance" caused by his obsession with Heloise.[180]

In her second letter to Abelard, Heloise raises some of these concerns. She still feels responsible for the tragedy which led to their separation. "O how wretched I am to have been born the cause of so terrible a crime!" she exclaims, "It is the supreme characteristic of women to be harmful to the

---

[175] Dronke, *Women Writers*, p. 120. Newman, by contrast, thinks there is "a kind of mystical surrender, an ecstasy of abnegation about this sacrifice" (p. 152).
[176] Mann, *Geoffrey Chaucer*, p. 52. By contrast, Jean de Meun argues that she understood "les meurs feminins . . . Car tous essaiés les avoit" (8776–7).
[177] *Historia*, 188/9. Charybdis is a common allusion in medieval misogyny: e.g. Marbod of Rennes, *Liber Decem Capitulorum*, III. 58–9; Map, *Epistola Valerii*, p. 290; Hugh de Fouilloy, *De nuptiis*, c. 1202.
[178] *Epistola Valerii*, p. 304: "femina . . . artificiosa nocere cum uult, quod semper est; et frequenter cum iuuare parat obest, unde fit ut noceat et nolens".
[179] Lines 7–10: "Ve mihi misere per memet prodite!" See Dronke, *Poetic Individuality*, pp. 117–18.
[180] Gilson, p. 7. *Historia*, 184/13–14: "animi mei occupatio, immo perturbatio".

supremest of men!''[181] She explicitly compares herself with Eve and Delilah. The Devil, she says, used marriage to make her the means to Abelard's destruction:

> Et calidissimus tentator hoc optime noverat, quod saepius expertus fuerat, virorum videlicet ruinam in uxoribus esse facillimam. Qui denique etiam usque ad nos consuetam extendens malitiam, quem de fornicatione sternere non potuit, de coniugio tentavit; et bono male est usus, qui malo male uti non est permissus.[182]

Abelard disagrees: she was the agent, not of his destruction, but of his conversion to a truly religious life. In turn, their marital bond assured her own salvation. Marriage, he insisted, is benign: unbelieving husbands are turned to Christianity by the counsel and example of their wives;[183] and the prayers of women for their husbands are privileged with a special grace.[184] In these arguments, he reveals what is a characteristic aspect of his consideration of the nature of their marriage – his tendency to assert its validity only within the context of the afterlife. He does not deny the force of his debt to Heloise. Indeed, he admits that it extends beyond death, for he makes its honouring a matter only to be resolved when they are reunited before God.[185] He tries to stifle her rebellion against their separation in orders by insisting that she can only be his by sharing a heavenly companionship won by piety, humility and resignation to God's will. The climax of this strategy of deferment is his reminder to Heloise that she is now no longer solely his bride, but Christ's as well. Implicitly recalling the cynicism in which he initiated their relationship, Abelard suggests that his love never rivalled Christ's in unselfishness.[186] To some, his responses have seemed cold.[187] Yet I

---

[181] 2 *Ad Abaelardum*, 79/29–30: "O me miseram in tanti sceleris causa progenitam! O summam in viros summos et consuetam feminarum perniciem!" Cf. in the *Historia* (191/3–7) Heloise's allusion to Lucan's description of the fall of Pompey (*Pharsalia*, VIII. 94–8).

[182] 2 *Ad Abaelardum*, 80/3–8: "The most crafty of tempters knew very well from frequent experience that it is through their wives that men are most easily ruined. Eventually he extended his accustomed malice towards us: unable to overthrow you by fornication he attacked you through marriage. Thus he wrought evil through a good thing, when he was prevented from doing evil through an evil thing."

[183] In particular, the example of Clovis: 1 *Ad Heloisam*, 76/5–9. Cf. I Cor. 7:14; I Peter 3:1–7; Farmer, 'Persuasive Voices'.

[184] 1 *Ad Heloissam*, 75/39–41; he specifically compares himself to Nabal (74/1–2; 1 Sam. 25).

[185] Father Muckle (p. 58) regards Abelard's refusal to be "drawn into her spiritual affairs" as "the proper thing". Abelard, he thinks, would have left that to her director.

[186] 2 *Ad Heloissam*, 83/22–4.

[187] Most famously, by Mark Twain, who said that she wrote "in the unweighed language of unwavering affection, he in the chilly phraseology of the polished rhetorician" (*Innocents Abroad* (1869); quoted, Robertson, *Abelard*, p. 217). Cf. Brooke, pp. 113–15,

think that they are an honest and consistent attempt to address Heloise's anxieties and reconcile her to the intensity of his religious faith. He attempts to answer her idolatry with self-effacement, and her uncertainty about the nature of their relationship with an ideal of immaculate spiritual union.

By contrast, Heloise felt that Abelard was bound by their marriage to allay her distress in their present life. Having shown herself determined to guarantee their community of mind even by taking the veil, she felt that it was wrong for the veil itself to be used as a reason for their failure to communicate.[188] In adopting the religious life, Heloise confirmed the end of their marriage as an economic, social and sexual relationship. Yet, since she had always regarded their bond as an intellectual and emotional one, she could see no reason why her love for him should not remain the governing principle of her life.[189] Her letters express her desire for a mutual agreement about the continuing nature of their affective bond. Even in the superscription to her first letter to Abelard, she indicates her uncertainty about the roles they should play towards each other by addressing him with a series of paradoxes:

> Domino suo immo patri, coniugi suo immo fratri, ancilla sua immo filia, ipsius uxor immo soror, Abaelardo Heloisa.[190]

Dronke defines Heloise's purpose in this equivocal salutation as an "attempt to convey the gamut of relationships that she and Abelard have experienced".[191] Her evocation of the variety of their roles is not only a static observation made for expressive effect: it captures what is the essence of her concerns, her uncertainty about her status.[192] In her valediction, she shows how her feelings transcend such problems of definition, for she addresses him simply as "unice" – her only one. Abelard rises to this challenge. He

---

who describes Abelard's 1st Letter as "a feeble thing"; similarly, according to Radice, Abelard "does not allow himself to enter imaginatively into Heloise's plight" (p. 27).

[188] Although Heloise could have consented to Abelard's withdrawal into a monastery without entering a convent herself, it was perhaps seen as more proper that she should share his resolution. Compare, for example, the opinion of Gregory the Great (*Ep.* VI. 48) quoted by Roscelin of Compiègne (p. 67): "Nam cum unum utriusque corpus conjugii copulatione sit factum, indecens est partem converti et partem inde in saeculo remanere." ["For when one body is made two by the carnal bond, it is improper for one part of it to remain within the world and the other to forswear it."]

[189] Cf. Brooke, p. 101; Moule, pp. 118–19.

[190] 1 *Ad Abaelardum*, 68/1–2: "To her lord, or rather her father, to her husband or rather her brother, from his slavegirl or rather his daughter, his wife or rather his sister – to Abelard from Heloise."

[191] Dronke, *Women Writers*, p. 112.

[192] In his scurrilous letter against Abelard, Roscelin uses the ambiguity of Abelard's clerical and sexual status to suggest that he is a "homo imperfectus" (p. 80). He insinuates that a man who cannot say what he is, is nothing.

designates her as his "sister once dear in the world, now supremely dear in Christ",[193] and thus balances her sense of a relationship disintegrated into a parcel of contradictory roles with an emphasis upon its progression – "cara . . . carissima".

Heloise invokes Abelard's duties to her in a number of different ways. Although he designed the *Historia* to console a friend, she says, he has done nothing to console his dearest friends ("amicissimae"), his wife and her community.[194] She insists that as the sole founder ("solus fundator") of the convent, he alone can be their spiritual guide.[195] The exaggerated description of the wilderness which Abelard's settlement supplanted here stands as an index to the community's dependence upon him.[196] Moreover, she suggests that his spiritual obligation to the community may be discharged most effectively in his special relationship with her:

> Atque ut ceteras omittam, quanto erga me te obligaveris debito pensa ut quod devotis communiter debes feminis unicae tuae devotius solvas.[197]

Heloise suggests that the philosophical ideal of an intellectual companionship ("amicitia"), which they shared at their marriage, might be revalidated in Christian terms by Abelard's adoption of the role of moral guardian to her community. The Church Fathers were prepared to write works of encouragement and consolation for holy women, so why, she asks, is Abelard too heedless of God, of their love and the Fathers' example, to do the same for her?[198] It is clear from the *Historia Calamitatum*, that Abelard was attracted by the prospect of being Heloise's "provost", to use Mary McLaughlin's term – "the faithful servant, guide and collaborator of the 'deaconess' ".[199] His caution is perhaps explained by the taint of scandal ("detrimentum

---

[193] 1 *Ad Heloissam*, 73/39–40: "soror in saeculo quondam cara, nunc in Christo carissima".

[194] 1 *Ad Abaelardum*, 69/11–19.

[195] 1 *Ad Abaelardum*, 70/22. Cf. *Problemata*, cc. 677D–678D.

[196] 1 *Ad Abaelardum*, 70/24–8. Heloise's description may deliberately evoke Lucan's description of the ancient, pagan grove (*Pharsalia*, III, 399–425).

[197] 1 *Ad Abaelardum*, 70/17–19: "And even passing over the rest, consider the nature of the tie, by which you have bound yourself to me, so that what you owe to all these dedicated women you can repay the more dedicatedly to the one who is yours alone."

[198] 1 *Ad Abaelardum*, 70/20–2, 70/24–5: "Quot autem et quantos tractatus in doctrina vel exhortatione seu etiam consolatione sanctarum feminarum sancti patres consummaverint . . . nec reverentia Dei nec amore nostri nec sanctorum patrum exemplis admonitus, fluctuantem me . . . consolari tentaveris."

[199] McLaughlin, 'Peter Abelard', p. 325. Abelard was probably influenced by the examples of Jerome and Origen. Brooke suggests that the Abbesses of the Paraclete remained fully autonomous, despite Abelard's hostility to the authority of women, because Heloise felt Abelard to be irreplaceable: "she might well have thought it intolerable to be under the direction of another man" (p. 98). We may also guess that Heloise's own unique standing endowed her office with a prestige which sanctified the independence of her successors.

famae'') caused by his continued association with the Paraclete – in particular, the allegation that he was still improperly besotted with his former lover.[200] The *Regula* for the Paraclete which he eventually addressed to her is the evidence that he eventually recognized the force of this claim upon his powers.

The climax of Heloise's petition is the identification of his obligations with the indissolubility of their conjugal bond:

> Cui quidem tanto te maiore debito noveris obligatum, quanto te amplius nuptialis foedere sacramenti constat esse astrictum et eo te magis mihi obnoxium, quo te semper ut omnibus patet immoderato amore complexa sum.[201]

Heloise's use of the word sacrament here is highly significant, for even a decade later, as Brundage says, "theologians contemporary with Gratian were not agreed on the question of whether it was a sacrament at all and, if it was, what implications that might have for marital indissolubility".[202] Not only is Heloise sure that it is a sacrament, but also that it is indissoluble, even in circumstances which made sexual union impossible.[203] She completely denies sex any place in the constitution of marriage. Indeed, she specifically distinguishes "concupiscentia" and "libido" from "amicitia" and "amor".[204] Nevertheless, as Dronke says, Heloise's use of the notion of debt undoubtedly involves an allusion to the traditional interpretation of I Cor. 7:3 ("uxori vir debitum reddat/ similiter autem est uxor viro") as a statement of the obligations of each partner to fulfil the sexual needs of the other.[205] At a basic level, it is perhaps this loss of these conjugal rights to which Heloise refers by such phrases as "rem perdidi" (68/6) and "quanta in te amiserim" (70/30). Her intention in describing her amorous dreams about Abelard was not to cater for the salaciousness or romanticism of posterity, but to emphasize the exacerbation of her distress by her deprivation of a sexual outlet. Heloise's dilemma parallels a situation which was often

[200] *Historia*, 206/6–12.
[201] 1 *Ad Abaelardum*, 70/26: "Indeed you must recognise that you are bound to me by a debt all the greater in that you are also constrained by the sacramental bond of marriage: you are the more liable to me because, as is clear to everybody, I have always been tied to you by a limitless love." Significantly, Jean de Meun translates the phrase "nuptialis foedus sacramenti" as "la beauté du sacrement du mariage" (35).
[202] Brundage, p. 254.
[203] At this time, the canon law of this issue was in flux, and there were regional variations (Schnell, pp. 96–7). Ivo of Chartres and Burchard of Worms would apparently have allowed separation on the grounds of impotence (Brundage, *Law*, p. 202). Gratian, however, would not (Makowski, pp. 107–8).
[204] 1 *Ad Abaelardum*, 72/22–3.
[205] Dronke, *Women Writers*, p. 116. Cf. *Problemata*, cc. 727D–728A, quoting Augustine, *De bono conjugali*, PL 40. 377. Roscelin also discusses the matter in his letter to Abelard (p. 67). See Brundage, *Law*, p.198.

discussed by canon lawyers, as well as dramatized in lyric – that is, the case of the woman unfairly deprived of her marital rights by her husband's departure on crusade.[206] This issue is also discussed by Andreas Capellanus, though much more playfully.[207] He and the lawyers all conclude that in this case a woman is not justified in deserting her husband. In doing so, they subordinate the principle of mutual sexual obligation to a sense of the spiritual indissolubility of the marital tie.

In describing how much she has lost in Abelard, Heloise constructs a demanding ideal of conjugal devotion. The man she loved is so absolutely central to her experience that she was prepared to obey him in everything, to waive her right as his partner to economic support – "in you, I sought only you, coveting only yourself and nothing of yours. I was not expecting either the bonds of marriage, nor any kind of dowry".[208] She was ready to subordinate all her own pleasures and wishes in life to his. Indeed, she was ready to forgo for him even the greatest honours imaginable in the world:

> Deum testem invoco, si me Augustus universo praesidens mundo matrimoni honore dignaretur totumque mihi orbem confirmaret in perpetuo possidendum, carius mihi et dignius videretur tua dici meretrix quam illius imperatrix.[209]

She goes on to argue that a woman who marries for material reasons is prostituting herself:[210] only an unassailable conviction of the absolute worth of one's partner can validate the marital bond. She describes this ideal of conjugal respect as a "a holy error and a blessed delusion", for inevitably very few fully justify it. However, in her own case she believes that her admiration of the man she loves is entirely commensurate with his qualities. Perhaps in this, she illustrates in herself the fanaticism she recommends. She

---

[206] Monfrin compares Heloise's letters with the *chansons du croisade* ('Problème', pp. 421–3).

[207] *De amore*, II. 7, q. 14.

[208] 1 *Ad Abaelardum*, 70/43–71/1: "in te nisi te requisivi, te pure non tua concupiscens. Non matrimonii foedera, non dotes aliquas expectavi." Cf. *Speculum Virginum* VII. 554–6 (p. 209): "Martia Catonis filia cum quereretur ab ea, cur post amissum maritum denuo, non nuberet, respondit non se inuenire uirum, qui se magis uellet quam sua." [When Martia, daughter of Cato, was asked why she had not remarried after the recent death of her husband, she replied that she had not found a man who wanted her more than what was hers.]

[209] 1 *Ad Abaelardum*, 71/10–14: "I call God to witness that even if Augustus, the ruler of the whole world, deigned to honour me with marriage, and confirmed me in perpetual possession of all the earth, it would still seem sweeter and more honourable to me to be called your whore than his empress." There are many analogies to this hyperbole. Significant perhaps are Jerome's *Ep*. 22, in which he recommends "superbia sancta" in these terms: "si ad imperatoris uxorem concurrit ambitio salutantium, cur tu facias iniuriam viro tuo?" (p. 84); and Lucan's *Pharsalia* V, 727–31. Cf. also Könsgen, 46/82.

[210] 1 *Ad Abaelardum*, 71/14–18.

locates the essential force of the marital bond so completely in the affective and intellectual realm as to suggest that for most people marriage can only be validated by a leap of faith.

Although both Abelard and Heloise use the trials of marriage to contrast with an ideal of philosophical tranquillity, they also conceived the conjugal bond in curiously metaphysical terms. After their marriage and separation, Heloise attempted to assimilate their marital union to their original ideal of philosophical communion. She argued that the only dimension in which marriage could ever be valid was an intellectual one, and therefore, that as long as Abelard recognized the sacramental truth of their marriage, he was bound to accept her conviction of the continuing validity of their shared intellectual life. His understanding of their marital tie was more literally metaphysical. He felt that their life in this world was entirely provisional, and he was only prepared to define their intimacy in terms of the next.[211] He also felt that, as a nun, Heloise should subordinate her earthly bond with him to her heavenly marriage with Christ. In the correspondence, Abelard and Heloise thus attempt to address the difficulties raised by their circumstances by contrasting not only their intellectual and religious aspirations but also their differing models of the conjugal bond.

5. Summary of Issues

What emerges from these texts is the importance of marriage, not only as an economic and social convention, but also as a field of emotive ideals. The *Ruodlieb*-poet carefully balances his sense of marriage as the foundation of the household with an emphasis upon the affective harmony of the partners. He specifically rejects a double standard of fidelity. In his model of marriage, husband and wife are equal in duty and honour. Similarly, the dramatist of the *Mystère d'Adam* presents marriage as a relationship of mutual faith towards each other and towards God, which he describes as "conservage". Though emphasizing Eve's subordination to Adam, he does not diminish her active responsibility or individual dignity: indeed, he portrays her as recognizing better than Adam the nature and consequences of the Fall. In the *Mystère d'Adam*, marriage is presented as a divine institution, a perfect ideal which mankind is tragically unable to realize. For the Anglo-Norman dramatist, as for Abelard and Heloise, marriage is so absolute a bond between individuals that it conducts both good and evil without resistance. Abelard and Heloise agree that marriage is essentially neither an economic nor a sexual relationship. Heloise insists that it is a disinterested intellectual and emotional bond, while Abelard sees it as an instrument of the divine will – the

---

[211] For example, he frightened Heloise by making preparations for his death: 1 *Ad Heloissam*, Muckle, 76/40–77/1.

expression of God's touch upon their lives. He renounces marriage on earth only by expressing an imaginative ideal of its reflection in heaven. Though disagreeing about the continuing nature of their marital tie on earth, Abelard and Heloise were both certain of its absolute indissolubility.

As an ideal, marriage competes with other models of status and conduct as a claim upon the aspirations of the individual. Early medieval literature often dramatizes such confrontations between marriage and other models such as those of faith, wisdom and military prowess. An outstanding example is the *Erec et Enide* of Chrétien de Troyes; other texts which seem to me to be inspired by essentially the same impulses and concerns are discussed in the next chapter. This dramatic tension in literary depictions of marriage perhaps reflects a general sense of the importance of personal choice – the possibility of defining marriage as a vocation. This was expressed as an interest, not only in the formation of the marital bond, but also in the conservation of its dignity. As the social institution which fundamentally defined the status and experience of most people, the creation and evaluation of marriage, both as a fact and as an ideal, was an urgent prerogative for every individual. Though criticism of marriage readily associated itself with satire and misogyny, its popularity as a theme in the early Middle Ages might still be seen as the expression also of a sense of conflict between individual achievement and the inevitable ties of duty and loyalty. Similarly, Guilhem IX's dramatic emphasis upon love as an emotive personal commitment might be seen as an attempt to express a sense of it as a commitment in competition with others. These confrontations in literature between the principles of individuality and marital or affective cohesion only underline the depth of medieval anxiety about the nature of the conjugal bond.

It is perhaps inevitable that marriage almost only ever becomes a literary theme when it is problematized in some way, either itself as an ideal, or as a reality in conflict with other ideals. Such an observation possibly motivated Andreas Capellanus's exclusion of marriage from the sphere of love. He suggests that, in regularizing love, marriage empties it of its appeal as something "rarus" et "difficilis".[212] Indeed, "the attitude that insensibly arises out of legal obligation", as Thomas Hardy put it, is perhaps "destructive to a passion whose essence is its gratuitousness".[213] Heloise felt this: for she expressed her determination to be bound to Abelard only by love, and not by the hollow bond of matrimony alone. None of the texts which I shall discuss in the rest of this book are straightforward descriptions of married life. They express a new sense of the dignity and importance of marriage only in terms either of a vocation in conflict with other vocations or as a sublime ideal often poignantly contrasted with reality. It might seem strange that in attempting to demonstrate in early medieval literature a

---

[212] *De amore*, I. 6, 362, p. 144.
[213] *Jude the Obscure* (1895, rpt., London, 1985), p. 256.

fascination with certain concepts of marriage, I discuss texts which generally tend to exploit it as a foil for other ideals, as a symbol, or as the subject for criticism. Indeed several of the texts I treat are avowedly anti-matrimonial. Yet it is in answer to these dynamic challenges to its identity that marriage emerges so clearly as an issue deeply concerning medieval writers.

CHAPTER THREE

The St Albans Psalter

1. Introduction

The *St Albans Psalter* conserved at the St Godehardskirche in Hildesheim is one of the earliest surviving examples of what Bischoff describes as "a new genre of religious illuminated manuscripts", a psalter "introduced by full-page pictures from the life of Christ". As he says, "precious books of this kind, which served the purpose of prayer and contemplation, were painted principally for princely and higher noblewomen until the advent of the books of hours".[1] However, this codex is exceptional in that it was associated, not with a wealthy *domina*, but with Christina, the daughter of an Anglo-Saxon burgher, who became an anchoress, and eventually the foundress of a priory at Markyate, near St Albans.[2] It appears to have been designed (or at least adapted) either for her use or in her honour.[3] Talbot suggests that it "was altered perhaps and completed during the course of its preparation to conform to her interests".[4] Nearly all the obits in the calendar refer to members of Christina's family, friends and associates; and the addition of seven entries for female saints may indicate that the owner felt a particular spiritual affinity with them.[5] As Pächt points out, Juliana, Amalberga and Fritheswitha were all "involved in situations with their husbands or importunate suitors which have a remarkable likeness to those found in the life of Christina of Markyate".[6]

---

[1] Bischoff, p. 223; cf. Pächt, *Rise*, p. 21; Bullington, pp. 47–8; Salter, p. 11; Clanchy, pp. 191–6. Bischoff dates the manuscript "c. 1115"; Pächt et al. suggest 1119–23 (p. 5); and Holdsworth 1140–6 (p. 190); while Talbot suggests that at least parts were written "some time after 1155" (p. 26).

[2] Her biographer describes her as a "virgo . . . orta nobiliter in civitate huntendonie"; this is probably no precise indication of rank. Her father, Autti, seems to have been wealthy and influential, but only within a municipal and mercantile sphere (Talbot, pp. 10–13). Moule describes Christina's parents as "substantial burgesses of Huntingdon" (p. 51).

[3] Millett has recently suggested that "the manuscript is a compilation which seems to have been designed for more than a single user". Its range of languages and use of pictures "implies a hierarchy of literacy" ('Women', p. 92).

[4] Talbot, p. 26.

[5] Talbot, p. 24; Pächt et al., pp. 27–8; Holdsworth, p. 185. Christina's own obit is also present in the manuscript.

[6] Pächt et al., p. 26. Cf. Talbot, p. 24. Talbot also sees references to Christina's interests in two of the drawings (pp. 25–6).

Christina's life-story was recorded in a text written at the Abbey of St Albans before or shortly after her death.[7] This is now only incompletely preserved in Cotton Tiberius E. 1, a manuscript damaged in the Ashburnham fire of 1731, but apparently lacking a substantial part of Christina's Life even before then.[8] What makes this text so exceptional is that it is a biographical rather than a hagiographical portrait.[9] As Talbot says, "the usual desire to edify, to speak only of the supernatural qualities of the Saint, to borrow from or draw parallels with the lives of other saintly persons is conspicuous by its absence. There is in the narrative a frankness, a vigour of expression, and an economy of words that must reflect a direct contact with Christina herself."[10] It recounts Christina's resolution to celibacy; how she resisted the advances of Ralph Flambard, Bishop of Durham; and how, to avenge his frustration, he instigated a young nobleman called Burthred to press for her hand in marriage. Betrothed against her will, Christina was determined not to allow their union to be consummated. Her parents tried to change her mind, "sometimes by flattery, sometimes by scolding, with gifts or with grand promises, and even with threats and intimidation".[11] The Bishop of Lincoln initially upheld Christina's vow of celibacy, but was subverted by her father's bribery. Eventually she fled, seeking refuge firstly with an anchoress, and then with the hermit, Roger. After some years, Burthred released her from the betrothal; Roger died; and Christina sought protection with an unnamed clerk, an associate of the Archbishop of York. Christina and this man were strongly attracted to each other, and she was barely able to resist either his advances or her own desires. As Dronke points out, it is especially striking in the context of Christina's dramatic struggle to live in celibacy that she should be willing to admit the force of her own sexuality.[12] Nevertheless, she surmounted this challenge, and with the death of her enemy, the Bishop of Lincoln, found herself free to do as she wished. She eventually made her profession at the Abbey of St Albans, where she enjoyed an intimate relationship with the Abbot, Geoffrey – a relationship expressed intellectually and spiritually, but apparently deeply founded upon mutual physical attraction.

In terms of literary history, the *St Albans Psalter* stands at a crossroads, for as well as being associated with Christina of Markyate, it also contains one of the four extant copies of the Old French *Chanson de Saint Alexis*. It thus marks the intersection between two distinct literary traditions, in both of which

---

[7] Christina was still alive in 1155–6: Talbot, pp. 6, 10. Talbot suggests that the *LCM* was composed during the abbacy of Robert Gorham (1151–66).

[8] Talbot, p. 3.

[9] Moule, p. 48, n. 3.

[10] Talbot, p. 6. Cf. Dronke, 'Heloise's *Problemata*', p. 312.

[11] § 8, p. 46: "modo blandiciis, modo obiurgacionibus, interdum muneribus amplisque promissis, necnon minis atque terroribus".

[12] Dronke, 'Heloise's *Problemata*', p. 312.

marriage is a primary concern. On the one hand, Christina is one of the pioneers of female mysticism in England; and on the other, the *Chanson de St Alexis* is the best-known and probably the finest moment in the long tradition of stories about this saint. In this chapter, I shall be concerned not so much with the *Psalter* itself, as with the combination of literary traditions represented by it. As Talbot says, the French poem seems to be "an incongruous intruder on the Latin psalms", for the inclusion of a vernacular saint's life within a Latin psalter is strikingly unusual.[13] However, it was probably a bold and deliberate choice. As Bullington has emphasised, the *Psalter* seems to have been entirely composed according to a conscious scheme.[14] Talbot suggests that the presence of the *Chanson* may be explained by the way in which it "mirrors exactly the experiences of Christina". Indeed, he sees its presence as conclusive proof of her association with the *Psalter*, and he describes the poem as "a kind of *pièce justificative* of her action in leaving her husband and retiring to the hermitage".[15] Otto Pächt describes it similarly as a "symbolic memento of the owner's personal story". As he says, one has either to assume "that in Christina's case reality was moulded strictly according to a literary pattern, so to speak as an 'Imitatio Alexii,' or else to infer that the story of Alexis was introduced 'after the event' as a meaningful allusion and suitable parallel to Christina's own experiences".[16] At the very least, in associating Alexis with Christina, the *St Albans Psalter* testifies to the resonance of his legend as a model of religious sensibility in the twelfth century.

The story of Alexis was very widespread: there are versions in several ancient languages and in nearly all the medieval vernaculars of western Europe.[17] Indeed, Alexis might be described as a paradigm of the many saints who dramatically exemplify the confrontation between the affective ties of the family and the individual's compulsion to sanctity.[18] In the analysis which

[13] Talbot, p. 26.

[14] Bullington, pp. 51–6, 224–6. She suggests that the "editor" of the *St Albans Psalter* might well have been Geoffrey of Le Mans. Moreover, she argues that the relationship of the *CSA* to the Psalter suggests that the French poem was intended to play some part in a para-liturgical performance (pp. 2, 105–27, 205–15). As she points out, it was Geoffrey's enthusiasm for drama which led to his profession at St Albans (Talbot, p. 28). Hemming has recently argued that the Ashburnham MS of the *CSA* is also likely to have been associated in some way with the Abbey of St Albans (p. viii).

[15] Talbot, p. 26. Cf. Legge, *ANL*, p. 243; Schmolke-Hasselmann, p. 19; Wogan-Browne, 'Clerc', pp. 70–1; Gnädinger, p. 48. Bullington notes (pp. 1–2, 222–3) that the Prologue to the *CSA* and its accompanying miniature place more emphasis upon the drama of Alexis's marriage than upon his ascetic ideal.

[16] Pächt et al., pp. 136–7.

[17] According to Odenkirchen (p. 11), there are versions of his Life in "Greek, Syrian, Arabic, Armenian, Ethiopian and Latin" as well as in "Provençal, Catalan, Spanish, Portuguese, Italian, English, German, Russian, Norwegian, etc.". For the Latin lives, *BHL* 286–301a, pp. 37–40.

[18] Flight from marriage, either before or after the wedding-feast, occurs in the legends of

follows, I have tried to avoid too exaggerated an assessment of the distinctiveness of the *Chanson* by recognizing that many of its characteristics were traditional. What makes it so exceptional is the sensitivity and lyrical energy with which it balances the different sentimental impulses held in tension by these long-exploited narrative resources. Indeed, in the permutations of this single narrative tradition, we can see new attitudes towards marriage and celibacy unfold. As Leclercq has remarked, hagiography "enables us to study the evolution of thought and practice by tracing down the constant emphasis laid by the collective memory on certain models".[19] In this chapter I shall also discuss St Alexis's analogue in romance, *Guy of Warwick*. Although Guy lies outside the *St Albans Psalter*, his legend is an intrinsic part of the Alexis-tradition, for it represents its ultimate translation into the field of secular literature.

2. The Development of the Legend of St Alexis

Gaston Paris placed the *Chanson de Saint Alexis* at the fountainhead of French literature ("il ouvre dignement l'histoire de la poésie nationale"), assigning it on linguistic grounds to the middle of the eleventh century.[20] However, Pächt has persuasively argued that the poem actually belongs to the next century, and to England: "If . . . there are no objections from the linguistic side to dating the French original as late as 1120 – i.e. not much earlier than the date at which it was written down at St Albans – there would be a strong case for regarding St Albans, towards which we have a unique combination of circumstances converging at this time, as the location of the birth of the Alexis poem in Old French."[21] The St Albans redaction is generally thought to represent the earliest of all the vernacular versions of the legend, although T.D. Hemming has recently challenged this assumption in favour of the Ashburnham copy.[22]

The *Chanson de Saint Alexis* tells how the saint was born the only and long-desired son of a wealthy Roman count named Eufemian. Once educated, Alexis is placed in the Emperor's service. A noble and beautiful heiress is

many saints (for other examples, see de Gaiffier). The *Vie de Saint Euphrosine* in particular appears to be modelled quite closely upon the *CSA*, even to the point of verbal similarities, but the protagonist in this case is female. Mirroring Alexis's bride, her prospective spouse is a "distraught, humiliated, yet ever faithful fiancé" (McCulloch, p. 77; see also Storey, '*Vie de Saint Euphrosine*'). In the *Vita Sancti Licinii* of Marbod of Rennes, the saint escapes the marriage imposed upon him by his family, when his bride is struck with leprosy.

[19] Leclercq, *Monks*, pp. 39–40.
[20] Paris, edn, Intro. p. vi.
[21] Pächt et al., p. 143.
[22] Hemming's argument is that the Ashburnham copy is least affected by what he sees as the Church's attempt to appropriate and tame the legend (pp. xxv–xxvii).

chosen by his family to be his bride. On the very night of their wedding, however, Alexis flees Rome, stopping only briefly to explain his reasons to her, and to leave her his sword-knot and a ring. He takes a ship bound for Laodicea ("Lalice"). From there, Alexis goes to Edessa ("Alsis"), where he spends seventeen years in poverty, fasting and prayer. Although his father sends out many messengers in search of him, the two who come to Edessa do not recognize him on account of the changes wrought by his ascetic regime. By the agency of a miraculous speaking statue, his sanctity is revealed to the people of Edessa. Alexis, however, fears the corrupting influence of their adulation;[23] and flees once more, returning to Laodicea and taking a ship for Tarsus ("Tarson"). A miraculous storm blows up and the ship is driven back across the Mediterranean to Rome. There, meeting Eufemian, Alexis begs for charity in the name of his lost son. Not recognizing him, his father allows him to sleep under the stairs ("suz le degrét") of his house.[24] Alexis spends a further seventeen years in pious self-mortification. Sensing that his death is imminent, he calls for ink and parchment, and writes an account of his life. Another miraculous voice reveals the presence of the saint in the city. He is found, already dead, in Eufemian's house. When his identity is revealed, his wife and family lament. Finally, Alexis is interred in the church of St Boniface in Rome, where many miracles of healing occur at his shrine.

In its economy and sureness of expression, resonance of phrasing, and intense concentration on its essential themes, the *Chanson de Saint Alexis* is strikingly beautiful. At the same time, it is stark and remote. Its characters are simple and stereotypical, and its narrative is awkward and spare. "Yet, this does no discredit to the artistry of the Alexis-poet," comments E.R. Curtius, "for naturalistic, psychological characterisation was alien to the devotional art of the eleventh century."[25] Patrick Vincent would argue, by contrast, that the poem *does* have psychological depth. Alexis's wife and family are depicted, he says, "not as puppets in a sorrowful drama . . . but as real people".[26] Curtius is too sweeping in denying psychological sensitivity to the literature of this period, but the poem does not, as Vincent suggests, search out hearts.[27] The lamentations of Alexis's father, mother and bride upon his departure and rediscovery are profoundly moving, but not as a consequence of the poet's original sympathy. Indeed, he adds no new ideas to those by which the family express their grief in the Latin prose *Vita Sancti*

---

[23] *CSA*, 188: "D' icest' honur nem revoil ancumbrer".

[24] It seems to me likely that the poet imagined an external wooden staircase to the first storey entrance of a hall, like that described in *LCM*, § 25, p. 76. This arrangement was increasingly common in aristocratic houses of this period (Wood, pp. 328–35).

[25] Curtius, 'Interpretation', p. 119: "Das würde ja nun nichts gegen die Kunst des Alexiusdichters besagen, denn die hieratische Kunst des 11. Jahrhunderts kennt keine naturalistische, pyschologisierende Characteristik."

[26] Vincent, p. 531.

[27] Cf. Peter Dronke, *Poetic Individuality*, pp. 1–32.

Alexii.[28] The effectiveness of these speeches depends on the intensity of the poet's concentration on their essential, and yet conventional, themes – the disappointment of the father's dynastic ambitions, the possessive, obsessive affection of the mother for her child and the unnatural widowhood of the abandoned bride. To have complicated these themes would have been to have diluted them, for the poem is lyrical in its power and uncomplicated in its perspectives.

This singleness – indeed selfishness – of perspective has drawn some challenging criticism of the poem from Emil Winkler. He was inspired by its ostentatious austerity to compare it with "church-processions" and "glass-covered and incense-covered relics" – images which do justice to its cold and ceremonious beauty.[29] At the same time, he believed that it is "philosophically and morally impoverished". For him, "the piety of the *Chanson de Saint Alexis* is neither ardently mystical nor compelling" but, instead "superficial" ("aüßerlich").[30] The hero goes through his trials without inner conflict, without regret and without pity: "Dispassionately, Alexis watches his family's distress."[31] It is true that the poem lacks any real sense of moral conflict, but this is a consequence of the poet's emphasis on the marvellous indeflectibility of the saint's desire for God. The value of the family-relationships which he is prepared to sacrifice are the measure of his piety and resolution. He enacts the principle expressed by St Ambrose: "If you conquer your household, your conquer the world."[32] It is also true that Alexis seems to show no regret for the pain he causes his family. In disappointing his father, mother and bride by his departure, he demonstrates his independence of the ideals which they represent – worldly status, family affection and conjugal love.

It would be less easy to defend Alexis for his lack of respect for the sacraments of the Church. As Winkler puts it, "frivolously, half-heartedly, almost with inward reservation, he seals the bond which the Church held sacred".[33] In fact, as it is depicted in the *Chanson*, the saint's marriage is not

---

[28] *ASS*, July 17, pp. 251–3. It seems likely that this standard Latin version of the saint's life was prepared for the community of St Alessio founded at Rome in 977 by the Greek émigré, Sergius, Archbishop of Damascus (Hamilton, p. 269; Mölk, p. 162). For convenience I have used the edition by Odenkirchen, pp. 34–51. For detailed analysis of the *CSA*'s relationship to the various redactions of the Latin prose life, see Pächt, pp. 127–35.

[29] Winkler, pp. 588–9: "kirchliche Umzüge . . . glasbehütete und weihrauchumwogte Reliquien". Curtius uses the analogy of a painted diptych in discussing the poem's structure ('Interpretation', p.124).

[30] "'arm an philosophischen und sittlichen Werten . . . des Alexiusliedes Frömmigkeit ist nicht mystisch glühend noch hinreißend".

[31] "Teilnahmlos sieht Alexius den Schmerz der Angehörigen . . . .".

[32] *De virginitate*, I. 12, PL 16. 206: "Si vincis domum, vincis saeculum."

[33] "Leichtfertig, mit halbem Herzen, fast mit innerem Vorbehalt schließt er den Band, den die Kirche doch geheiligt hält."

formally sanctified by the Church. No mention is made of the participation of a priest or of the performance of a liturgy; and this is in contrast with the *Vita Sancti Alexii*, where we are told that the marriage was performed "by the most venerable of priests" ("per manus honoratissimorum sacerdotum").[34] The poet explicitly remarks upon the sanctity of baptism (29–30), but not of marriage. The reason for this is perhaps that the *Chanson* pre-dates the general inclusion of marriage in the list of the sacraments.[35] Early in the Middle Ages the Church's blessing upon marriage was a privilege, not a necessity.[36] Indeed, in his description of the marriage, the poet emphasizes that it is a business-arrangement – merely an elegant contract between two aristocratic families.[37] However, canonists and theologians did not allow one partner to enter a religious life unilaterally, as does Alexis. They insisted that the decision should be mutual and that both partners withdraw from the world together. Indeed, anyone making a unilateral withdrawal might well have been ordered to resume cohabitation with his or her spouse.[38] The simplest and most persuasive of Winkler's indictments is his suggestion that Alexis's manner is objectionably uncharitable: "Alexis scarcely takes enough time in the bridal chamber to give his bride any Christian instruction, and to share with her a small part of his enlightenment. What an egotistical asceticism!"[39]

Curtius suggested that Winkler treated the text "with the relish for impressionistic, empathic interpretations typical of our era",[40] and Hatzfeld amplified this criticism, arguing that "medieval theory and philosophy of life have always to be consulted in order to make modern interpreters sure of themselves. If there is disagreement between the medieval standards, so far as they are clearly recognisable, and the modern interpretation, then the modern interpretation is wrong."[41] I think it a rash assumption that the

---

[34] *Vita Sancti Alexii*, 2.7, Odenkirchen, p. 37.

[35] Brooke, *Idea*, pp. 273–80.

[36] Vogel, p. 422.

[37] Lines 41–58. The marriage is presented as a contract between the two fathers (41–7). It is made "gentement" and "belament" (47–8) – an indication that the marriage was splendid with wealth, not with sanctity. The immediate reference of the phrase used at line 58, "tut aveir terrestre", is the marriage just described.

[38] For example, Peter Lombard, *Sententiae*, IV, 27, PL 192. 912. Makowski, p. 101; Brundage, *Law*, pp. 202, 289; Schnell, p. 115; Leclercq, *Monks*, pp. 19–20.

[39] Winkler, p. 588: "Kaum daß Alexius im Brautgemach sich Zeit nimmt, die Braut christlich zu ermahnen und auch ihr ein wenig Teil zu geben an seiner Erleuchtung. Welch eine selbstsüchtige Askese!" Gnädinger remarks that the figure of Alexis scarcely ever lacks "ihre provokatorische Kraft und den Stachel der Anstößigkeit" ("its provocative power and the sting of offensiveness", p. 4). Winkler might have been even more offended by a metrical Latin life, 'Duxit Romanus vir . . .', (ed. Wagner), which tersely describes the parting "Illa flet, a flente se proripit ille repente" (line 104).

[40] Curtius, p. 135: "mit der impressionistischen Einfühlungsfreude unserer Zeit".

[41] Hatzfeld, p. 326.

literature of any given era will always live up to that era's theoretical and philosophical "standards". In any case, how are we to construct these "standards", if not by trusting and codifying our own responses to a range of texts? Hatzfeld's conception of the "interpretation" of a text is a simplistic one, for many literary texts are ambivalent, expressing and sometimes resolving their authors' ideological and emotional tensions. The *Chanson de Saint Alexis* expresses just such tensions, in this case with respect to marriage. The disturbing elements of the poem so provocatively identified by Winkler certainly exist within it. Not only do they contribute to its fascination, but they might also be said to have shaped the subsequent evolution of the legend in western Europe. This legend appealed to medieval authors because it offered them an opportunity to analyse their own ambivalence towards marriage. The egotism of the hero is a premise, not a flaw, for the impulse to sacrifice one's social obligations to a personal ideal is an intrinsically selfish one.

In his churlishness to his bride, Alexis is a cousin to Chrétien's Erec. Though the ideals which motivate the hero to overturn the normal pattern of married life are very different, the gesture in each case expresses a sense of friction between the realms of individual endeavour and social engagement. While *Erec et Enide* balances marriage against chivalry, the legend of St Alexis dramatizes a more ancient problem. It contains the germ of the contradiction between Christian asceticism and the Christian ethic of marriage which vexed the Church for so long. Every new redaction seems to attempt to resolve this tension in one way or another. The eleventh-century version is perhaps unique in its power because it balances rather than resolves different sentimental impulses.

In the context of Winkler's comments, Gerhard Eis has argued that "this kind of asceticism, as it is exhibited in Old French song of Alexis . . . did not correspond to the human and artistic characteristics of the medieval Christian".[42] In its coldness and cruelty, he suggests, the *Chanson* demonstrates its debt to a species of Christianity which was foreign to that of the Middle Ages. He points to the tale's Syrian origin, and suggests that the French poem merely inherited the Gnostic values of its sources.[43] He suggests that the aspects of the poem to which Winkler found himself unsympathetic would have seemed equally alien to the poem's medieval audience: "everything that seemed to Winkler's fine sensitivity an 'egotistical' and 'soullessly didactic' asceticism" he says, "actually also struck the people of the western Church as something foreign and cold".[44]

---

[42] Eis, p. 232: "diese Art Askese, wie sie in dem afrz. Alexiuslied vorliegt, . . . der menschlichen und künstlerischen Persönlichkeit des mittelalterlichen Christen nicht gemäß war."

[43] Bugge (p. 152) describes Syria as "the classic homeland of . . . encratism". The influence of Catharism is discussed as a possibility – and convincingly rejected – by Sckommodau (p. 179).

[44] Eis, p. 233: "Was Winkler mit feinem Gefühl als 'selbstsüchtige' und 'lehrhaft-

MEDIEVAL MARRIAGE: LITERARY APPROACHES, 1100-1300

Yet, the distinction between an ancient, encratistic Christianity of the Near East and the orthodox Christianity of the western Middle Ages is not so easy to make. Elaine Pagels speaks of the "deep ambivalence toward sexuality . . . that has resounded throughout Christianity for two millennia".[45] At the forefront of Gregorian reform, men like Guibert of Nogent (c. 1064–c. 1125) and Peter Damian (1007–72) did not hide their extreme abhorrence of sexuality.[46] The story of St Alexis was not at all alien to Peter Damian's sensibilities, for he made it the subject of one of his sermons.[47] Another medieval interpreter was the tenth-century Adalbert of Prague, who stressed in his *Homilia in Natale S. Alexii Confessoris* the glory of Alexis's ability to resist the impulse of natural emotions:

> O quanta constantia quantaque ejus fuit patientia! Quis enim narrare poterit quantas tentationes, quantosve fluctus in sui sacratissimi pectoris arcano pertulerit dum patrem pro se tanto moerore affici conspiceret, sciret etiam matrem nocte dieque in fletu et gemitu perdurare?[48]

Those who spurn marriage on earth, he concludes, will be united with God in Heaven and be numbered among the ranks of the Lamb. Early in the twelfth century, in a sermon on the text "Blessed are those who are called to the wedding-feast of the Lamb" (Apoc. 19:9: "Beati qui ad coenam nuptiarum Agni vocati sunt"), Honorius Augustodunensis similarly focused upon the saint's imperviousness to the grief of his loved ones:

> patris dolorem, matris moerorem, dulcis sponsae suspiria, lugentis familiae pro se lamenta flebiliter et pacienter sustinuit . . .[49]

Honorius speaks a little more regretfully than either Peter or Adalbert. Indeed, he describes the girl espoused to Alexis as his "noble bride worthy of much praise" ("nobilis sponsa multa laude digna"). Yet he is prepared to

seelenlose' Askese bezeichnet, . . . all das hauchte auch schon den Menschen der abendländischen Kirche fremd und kalt an." He is building upon Hürsch's argument that the spirit of the *CSA* contravenes the orthodox evaluation of asceticism made by the Fathers and upheld by ecclesiastical Councils. Clearly, however, the recurrence of such pronouncements is testimony to the endurance of the rigorist ascetic ideal and there is no evidence that these legislations succeeded in stifling it.

[45] Pagels, p. 29.

[46] Brooke, *Idea*, pp. 70–4; Brundage, *Law*, pp. 185–6.

[47] Peter Damian, *Sermo* 28, Lucchesi, p. 162; PL 144. 653.

[48] Adalbert of Prague, PL 73. 897; *ASS*, July 17, 257–8: "O what constancy and what patience he showed! For who could tell what temptations, what disturbances he endured within his most holy breast, while he looked upon his father so afflicted with grief for him, and while he knew that his mother lived night and day in tears and lamentation."

[49] Honorius Augustodunensis, *Dominica II. Post Pentecosten, Speculum Ecclesiae*, 1043–50, at 1046B: "He patiently and dolefully endured the sorrow of his father, the grief of his mother, the sighs of his sweet spouse, and the laments of his family mourning for him." For Honorius, see Flint, Garrigues.

84

quote Mark 9:43 ("if your hand offends you, cut it off") as a metaphor for the rejection of family-ties. Finally, Peter Lombard raised the case of Alexis in his *Sententiae*, using the saint as an example of how it was permitted to those who had made marital vows to "leave without the consent of the women to whom they are plighted, and instead, enjoy continence".[50] However, he made this dispensation conditional upon non-consummation.[51]

It might be objected that all these are exceptional cases. Adalbert was writing specifically for a monastic community dedicated to St Alexis. He made his profession in the Roman monastery of St Alexis soon after its foundation in 977 by the Greek émigré Sergius, Archbishop of Damascus.[52] Peter Damian's sympathy for Alexis is explained by his special agenda, for he believed that marriage was unworthy of the clergy; Honorius is writing an exhortation to virginity; and Peter Lombard is addressing the legal problems suggested by the saint's example. It might be argued that all four authors are representatives of a conservative spirituality to be distinguished from the mainstream of Christianity in the Middle Ages. To the laity, the spirit of St Alexis might have seemed just as alien as Eis suggests. It seems hard to believe, however, that the opinions of literate intellectuals like these were so insulated that they found no response in the beliefs of the population as a whole. As Brooke points out, the progress of Catharism in the twelfth century would hardly have been so rapid were it not closely related to a widespread popular impulse to asceticism.[53] The very existence of so many vernacular versions of the Life of Alexis implies that the distinction between conservative and popular spiritualities cannot be sharply drawn.

A more serious objection to the idea that what seems rebarbative in the *Chanson* does not belong to the Middle Ages at all, is that many of the features to which Winkler took objection are actually absent from the two pre-medieval versions of the story still extant. The earlier of the two Syriac versions translated by Amiaud and dated to the fifth or sixth centuries is extravagant in its asceticism, as one might expect.[54] It tendentiously reads malice into the motives of Alexis's parents and seems to take smug satisfaction in the confusion caused by the saint's behaviour. The Greek version published by Rösler is equally confirmed in its asceticism.[55] It is

---

[50] Peter Lombard, *Sententiae*, IV, 27, PL 192. 911: "li[nqu]ere . . . sine consensu suarum sponsarum, et e converso, continentiam profiteri".

[51] *Sententiae*, c. 912: "hoc autem conjugatis nullatenus licet."

[52] Hamilton, pp. 285–8.

[53] Brooke, *Idea*, p. 72.

[54] Although the Man of God in this legend is never named, Amiaud describes it (p. I) as "sans doute l'histoire véritable originale et par elle-même complète du saint auquel on a donné le nom d'Alexis".

[55] Rösler, 'Alexiusprobleme', pp. 508–11: "Obwohl die Hs., in der er erhalten ist, wahrscheinlich erst aus dem 12. Jh. stammt, halte ich es für sicher, daß das Original,

languidly world-weary, and reflects, as Odenkirchen suggests, "a civilisation ancient in its intellectual exhaustion".[56] Yet, in neither version does Alexis return to Rome, for both finish with the saint's death at Edessa. They lack everything contained in 186–625 of the eleventh-century *Chanson*. Alexis has no wedding-night confrontation with his bride. Instead, he flees before the wedding is solemnized. Thus, the bizarre and problematical features which truly distinguish the medieval legend of Alexis – his callous treatment of his bride and his voyeur-like contemplation of his family's grief – do not derive from early Christianity or from the Near East at all. Even if these elements of the story were introduced in order to reinforce an original spirit of encratism, they are nevertheless medieval features, and it is in terms of medieval sensibility that they must be understood.

The scribe of an eleventh-century copy of the later Syriac version of the Life of St Alexis appears to have been aware of the existence of both forms of the legend – the short form with the saint's death at Edessa, and the expanded form with his return and death at Rome.[57] He tries to reconcile them by suggesting that Alexis did indeed die and was buried at Edessa, but that, by divine and mysterious means, God took him from the tomb and brought him back to Rome, in fulfilment of the saint's wish and the prayers of his family that they should be re-united before his death. In effect, he suggests that the later form of the legend was evolved in order to take into account the continuing claims of affection upon Alexis by his wife and family. In making this suggestion, he betrays his own opinion that it was natural and necessary to do so. Clearly, there has been a shift of sensibility. In the earliest Lives, the saint's rejection of his wife and parents is absolute. It is not complicated by any sympathetic interest in their feelings about his departure. They stand as challenges to his resolution, which, once faced, trouble him no more. In the later form of the legend, his piety is glamorized by the poignancy of what they suffer as a result of his devotion to a higher ideal.

Several scholars have explained this expansion of the Life of St Alexis as an embellishment inspired by the Life of St John Calybite.[58] This saint fled his family for Jerusalem, and, having returned home to Rome, died in a hut near the family home. If St Alexis's Life had been closely modelled upon St John's, one would have expected the town of Edessa to have been supplanted in imitation by the much more famous and holy city of Jerusalem. There are

von dem sie eine späte Abschrift mit zahllosen orthographischen Schnitzern ist, die ursprüngliche Fassung der Legende war" (p. 508). The manuscript concerned is Venice, Marcianus, Cod. VII. 33.

[56] Odenkirchen, p. 30.

[57] Amiaud, p. 10.

[58] St John Calybite, *ASS*, January, I, 1029: Sckommodau. p. 174; Klausner, *Nature*, p. 27, n. 4.; Stebbins, 'Les grandes versions', p. 503; Amiaud, p. LXXI; Uitti, p. 277; Hemming, p. xii.

such variants, but they are exceptional.[59] Although there are clear correspondences between the two stories, we can hardly assume a relationship of direct influence wherever there is a coincidence of detail between two saints' Lives. The constantly recurring themes and motifs of hagiography more often demonstrate the consistent and universal appeal of certain ideas, than direct relationships between texts. The only relevance of the legend of St John Calybite to this study is that, like the new version of the legend of St Alexis, its shape depends upon the impulse to make the story as satisfying as possible, in literary as well as devotional terms.

Both stories exemplify the narrative structure which Charles Altmann has defined as characteristic of the *vita* of the confessor-saint. He argues that, while the *passio* of the martyr is "diametric" in structure, the *vita* is "gradational": "the saint begins as part of a group; as the text advances he progressively separates himself from that group until he is eventually proven to be utterly exceptional. At this point he returns to the group, but instead of becoming reintegrated into it, the original group now redefines itself around the saint."[60] The *passio* is imbued with the defiantly antagonistic spirit of the persecuted Church: by contrast, the emphasis of the *vita* upon the inner conflicts and outer loyalties of the individual saint reflects the tolerance of the post-Constantinian era.[61] The medieval version of Alexis's Life might be described as the result of an attempt to assimilate the original story of the Man of God to the gradational model. Yet the new legend subtly alters the message of the old. In the earliest versions of the story, the still nameless saint is exceptional only in seeking to efface – indeed to erase – his own individuality. In the later versions, the stark contrast between this world and the next is softened and obscured by the development of a social drama around it – "a widening of the paradigmatic context by means of intensive fictionalization", as Uitti has called it.[62]

The truth is that the old story of St Alexis was rather inert and undramatic. In order to heighten its appeal, its revisers adopted some of the methods and sensibility of romance. The relationship between Christian hagiography and the genre known as Greek romance has long been recognized. "In some of the earliest accounts of non-martyr saints," as Alison Goddard Elliott says, "the imprint of Greek romance is clearly discernible, since the authors appeared to have turned to such tales for structure and incident when they came to fabulate the lives of their Christian heroes."[63] For example, the

---

[59] Rösler, *Fassungen*, pp. 31–4. The French S-version includes a diversion to Jerusalem (197–220). In the Latin version printed by Maßmann as 𝔄, the saint travels via Pisa, Lucca and Jerusalem.

[60] Altmann, p. 6.

[61] Altmann, p. 3.

[62] Uitti, p. 277.

[63] Elliott, *Roads*, p. 46. Festugière has stressed the role of folklore in the development of hagiography. Romance also tends to be a literate development of folkloric motifs. The

brothel-scenes of the *Vita S. Mariae Meretricis* are analogous to those in the romance of *Apollonius, King of Tyre*. According to Elliott, "the motif of flight from an unwelcome marriage or suitor is present in most Greek romances", but Alexis was further romanticized by the adoption of a miraculous storm to blow him half-way across the Mediterranean. Such wonderful winds and storms are a blatant narrative device used in several Greek romances.[64] Although, in this case, the pious might have interpreted the storm as the miraculous expression of the divine will, many would have accepted it only as a mechanism – an infringement of probability justified by the desire to develop the story in a certain way.

The storm serves to bring the saint back to Rome – and specifically, back to his wife and family. In this sense, Rome could be described as the sentimental centre of the story. The invention of the saint's return there may be seen as an attempt to focus its emotional impact. It may also express a belief in the continuing validity of the sentimental relationship between Alexis and his wife and family, as the Syriac scribe suggests. Most simply, it is an assimilation of the legend to the fundamentally cyclical pattern of romance-narrative. Alexis's secret return naturally balances his secret flight. It allows a dramatic scene of recognition – *anagnorisis* – reminiscent of so many in Greek romance.[65] As readers, we are eager to witness the enlightenment of his wife and family. We feel the story gain in momentum as it approaches its resolution. Only when the saint has been identified does it feel properly complete. The loose ends of the narrative left by his departure are tied up by his return and recognition. Moreover, in devotional terms, only when Alexis is identified can he be honoured as patron and intercessor. The family's discovery of their lost loved one symbolizes the re-discovery by those who witness it – directly, like the people of Rome, or, indirectly, like those who read or hear of it – of the faith in God which his example inspires. Thus, the use of a familiar narrative pattern of immediate appeal made the legend both devotionally and aesthetically more satisfying. It intensified its appeal not only to the devout but also to the doubtful.

Barron has suggested that the "lasting appeal" of popular stories derives "from the universal nature of the emotions which the listener is invited to

coincidence of imaginative material indicates a shared public – as Legge argues of the relationship between medieval romance and hagiography ('Anglo-Norman'; cf. Pearsall, 'Capgrave', p. 121). The similarity of the methods by which this material is disposed indicates, more significantly, a parallelism of sensibility.

[64] Elliott, *Roads*, p. 86: e.g *Apollonius*, 12, 39; *Aithiopika*, I. 22; *Chaereas and Callirhöe*, III. 3. The addition of the storm might have been justified by the precedent of Jonah. However, if the debt had been direct, one would expect it to have been acknowledged. In fact, one Middle English version (Laud) does associate Alexis with Jonah, but this is probably an original attempt to dignify the story. Another narrative device perhaps inherited from Greek romance is the discovery of the saint's identity by means of a letter on his corpse: see *Aithiopika*, II. 6, 10.

[65] For *anagnorisis*, see Cave.

share by identifying with the hero (or, quite commonly, heroine) in the exploration of experience through feeling rather than conscious thought".[66] In this way, romance characteristically exploits the perennial fascination with strong and primal emotions. In many cases, its improbable convolutions of plot are introduced only in order to serve this fascination. For example, in the *Leucippe and Clitophon* of Achilles Statius, the apparent death of the heroine allows the hero to indulge in a grotesque excess of melodramatic grief. "Yet, now, since Fortune denies me the kisses of your lips, come then, let me kiss your butchered neck."[67] Leucippe is not dead, of course, for that would obviate a happy ending. By utilizing such ingenious intricacies of plot, the author allows his audience to contemplate a wide range of emotions as they respond to apparent events, yet with the assurance that all of them are inconsequential. Indeed, we are flattered in knowing better than Clitophon that his grief will prove chimerical in the inevitably agreeable resolution of the tale. "Secure in this belief," as Arthur Heiserman says, "we can take particular pleasure in the sufferings of people who are more beautiful, brave and magnificently unhappy than we are. At the same time, their superiority to us compels us to take their sufferings seriously. Perhaps these paradoxical mixtures of superiorities and inferiorities makes for that paradoxical mix of 'identification' and 'aesthetic distance' that helps us to enjoy the imitation of pain."[68]

In the accumulation of improbable events, we identify now with one character, now with another, sometimes sharing in a certain emotion and sometimes imagining ourselves as its object. This last kind of identification – the somewhat narcissistic fantasy of imagining how others might in certain circumstances love or grieve for ourselves – is what the legend of St Alexis offers us in the years he remains unidentified at home. Again, there is a possibility of reception on two levels. While, the devout might have seen the saint's voyeur-like detachment as a model of resistance to the degrading influence of earthly affections, many others would have identified with Alexis in the splendid heroism of being able to catalyse so magnificent a tragedy. Related to this is the choice of the moment of departure by the saint – his wedding. In the early versions of the story, his marriage simply represents the culmination of his earthly good-fortune. No more affronting moment could be chosen to stress his scorn for wealth and worldly happiness. Similarly, Elliott has suggested of the lives of the desert saints that the motif of "the flight from the wedding feast can be viewed as symbolic of the saint's entire rejection, summing up and encapsulating the full oppositional range between saint and society. The marriage festivity," she goes on, "contains in microcosm all that the saint is fleeing – not just sexuality, but civilisation."[69]

---

[66] Barron, p. 3.
[67] *Leucippe and Clitophon* (Reardon, pp. 170–284) V. 7, pp. 236–7.
[68] Heiserman, p. 82.
[69] Elliott, *Roads*, pp. 92–101.

When the story was recast as a hagiographic romance, the gesture of contempt also took on an air of heroism. Romance frequently exploits the momentousness of wedding-festivities in order to throw decisive events into heightened relief.[70] The rejection of marriage becomes a gesture of calculated flamboyance, demonstrating the protagonist's independence and strength of spirit. The legend of St Alexis was so successful in the Middle Ages because his distinctive gesture of renunciation came to be read, not only as an exemplification of contempt for the world, but also as a brave sacrifice to a grand ideal.

At the same time, its call to virginity was assimilated to what Foucault has described as the "new erotics" discernible in Greek romance – a system of values no longer derived from the ancient balance of the "political and virile domination of desires", but now organized "around the symmetrical and reciprocal relationship of a man and a woman, around the high value attributed to [pre-marital] virginity, and around the complete union in which it finds perfection".[71] Marriage in the earlier legend of St Alexis is no more than a token for the society which the saint rejects. In the medieval version, by contrast, we are intensely aware of its significance in its own right. This is because, when read as a romance, and not as an *exemplum*, the dramatic impact of the legend largely depends upon our sympathy with the feelings of the bride – and with her understanding of the nature of her marriage. The extent of the hero's glory is measured by the pain which we feel him to have caused in her by rejecting her earthly, yet legitimate, love. It is no wonder, then, that in the corpus of medieval versions of the legend, the bride plays an ever more important and complex role.[72]

In returning Alexis to Rome, the innovators of the medieval legend implicitly admit the validity of the affective claims upon him by his parents and his bride. They emphasized the holiness of his parents' marriage. Euphemian and his wife are depicted, on the one hand, as being rewarded for their faith by the birth of a son destined for saintliness, and, on the other, as being punished with grief for their inability to recognize the significance of his behaviour. Yet, this inconsistency does not mar the tale. It seems poignant that having achieved so much, Alexis's parents are unable to make the final leap of faith.

Even more complex are the reasons justifying the saint's return to his wife. She – unnamed in both the *Chanson de Saint Alexis* and the prose Latin *Vita Sancti Alexii* – chooses to remain in the home of her parents-in-law. She plainly does not feel that her entry into her new family has been invalidated by the bridegroom's sudden departure. Even so, it is hard not to see this as a

---

[70] For example, *Aithiopika* V. 19 (Reardon, p. 443); cf. Dronke and Alexiou.

[71] Foucault, *Care*, pp. 228–232, at p. 228 and p. 232.

[72] On the increased role of the bride in the "Alsis"-group, see Elliott, *Vie*, intro.; for the other French versions, see Stebbins, 'Grandes versions'; for the English ones, see Klausner, *Nature*, pp. 28–34.

slightly artificial way of ensuring the symmetry of the story. When her husband returns, she is still where he left her. The reunion was a deliberately created eventuality in the plot. It reflects the fascination of audience and redactors with the complex and problematical nature of the couple's feelings towards each other. No doubt interest in the *dénouement* of the story was intensified by the hope – or fear – that like any secular hero of romance, Alexis would declare, not only his own identity, but also his love for his lost bride, and thus bring the story to a comfortable conclusion. Heiserman defined as "a convention of romance . . . the extraordinary and admirable character whose dominant value, marital fidelity, is jeopardized by fate".[73] It was according to this model that the innovators of the legend developed the character of Alexis's bride.[74] That she loves and suffers is both (romantically) glamorous and (spiritually) glorious for her husband, but her own stature is increased by the medieval legend's emphasis upon her sacrifice. In ascetic terms she is scorned, while in romantic ones, she is exalted. The poet of the *Chanson de Saint Alexis* thus found an implicit dramatic tension in the contradiction between the legend's original asceticism and the romanticism of its development. The poet's sustainment of this tension is largely responsible for the impact and effectiveness of this version of the legend.

3. The *Chanson de St Alexis* and its Treatment of Marriage

I have discussed the evolution of the medieval legend of St Alexis in such detail not because I wish to suggest that the *Chanson de Saint Alexis* is merely the product of an organic tradition, but because it is only possible to assess its originality and coherence of vision by taking into account the materials with which the poet worked. He himself signals his awareness of the weight of time upon his pen. The poem begins (1–10) with an evocation of a lost and beautiful Golden Age:

> Bons fut li secles al tens ancïenur,
> Quer feit i ert e justise e amur . . .[75]

---

[73] Heiserman, p. 51.

[74] In one analogue of the story of St Alexis, that of St Anastasia, a husband and wife separate and dedicate themselves to religion due to the death of their children. While on pilgrimage twelve years later, they are brought together. She recognizes him and becomes his companion. Without admitting her identity, she remains with him for twelve years until her death. Anson has argued that this tale "represents the first stage in the gradual transformation of a religious legend exemplifying worldly renunciation for the love of God into a domestic fable of the devotion of chaste wives to their husbands" (p. 15). Perhaps a similar process was at work in the legend of St Alexis.

[75] *CSA*: lines 1–2: "The world was good in that ancient time, when there was faith and justice and love."

Now, it continues, things are different; the world is old and frail; and everything changes for the worse.[76] None of this, strictly speaking, is relevant to the poet's specific location of events in post-Constantinian Rome. The allusion to the passing of generations may be no more than a graceful embellishment, impressing us with a sense of the grandeur of time. A restive audience might have been settled by this reminder of its lowliness. Yet it seems to me that these ten lines establish the key to the whole poem. Its theme, succinctly, is Paradise.[77] The poet's notion of Paradise is not the remote and radically opposed world of early, ascetic Christianity, but an immanent and ideal world, underlying – in the same way as the Past underlies it – the world of our experience. This more humane comprehension of the two worlds is the basis of a more refined and emotional kind of asceticism than is to be found in the early Alexis-legends.[78] These could only be callous and destructive in their dogmatism. Paradise for them is the last resort from the unloveliness of human life. By contrast, Paradise in the *Chanson* is the embodiment of the ideals by which human life is sanctified.[79] The poet reassures us that there is another world, a better world, and that, although it is given to very few to practise consistently the ideals upon which it is constructed, ideals – moral and emotional – have real force before God.

Marriage is one of these ideals. In the ascetic perspective of the *Chanson de Saint Alexis*, it is not only the base alternative to a better life, but also a spiritual bond too fine to be adequately realized on earth. The poet states quite specifically that Alexis and his bride are joyfully re-united in Paradise:

[76] Lausberg has argued that all of this is a reformulation of biblical and patristic sources, especially I Tim. 6:11. Indeed, he speaks in terms of a "biblische Koordinierung" (p. 53). His case for specific sources is convincingly rejected by Sckommodau. Scheludko (p. 194) and Vine Durling (p. 464) have pointed out that the ages of Noah, Abraham and David were hardly golden. Scheludko suggests, however, that these men are imagined as "elders", illustrating the depth of time in their human antiquity.

[77] Indeed it finishes in the same key:

> En icest siecle nus acat pais e goie,
> Ed en cel altra la plus durable glorie! (*CSA*, 623–4)

[78] Note that in the *Chanson de Saint Alexis*, the saint abandons the world, not because he despises it, but for its fragility and imperfectibility:

> An ices[t] secle nen at parfit' amor:
> La vithe est fraisle, n'i ad durable honur;
> Cesta lethece revert a grant tristur'. (*CSA*, 68–70)

[79] It will be clear from this that I disagree with Auerbach's characterization of the poem (*Mimesis*, pp. 111–19). In the saint's fixity of purpose, he argues, "Everything else has vanished, the whole sweeping infinity of the outer and inner worlds, with its innumerable possibilities, configurations and strata." This seems to me much more applicable to the ancient versions of the legend, and, indeed, Auerbach does talk in terms of an intellectual rigidification *inherited* by the poem from antiquity. To my mind it is exactly a new sense of "possibilities, configurations and strata" which *distinguishes* the eleventh-century poem from earlier versions.

Sainz Alexis est el ciel senz dutance,
Ensembl'ot Deu e la cumpaignie as angeles,
Od la pulcela dunt se fist si estranges;
Or l'at od sei, ansemble sunt lur anames:
Ne vus sai dirre cum lur ledece est grande.[80]

None of this is to be found in the standard Latin version, the *Vita Sancti Alexii*, nor indeed in the Ashburnham copy of the *Chanson* (A).[81] It does recur in a Latin poem which is closely related to the Old French one and probably derived from it, 'Pater Deus ingenite . . .':[82]

Sic ambo coram domino
Conjunguntur perpetuo.

Donet nobis solatia
Horum beata copula!
Sponsus cum sponsa pariter
Custodiat nos firmiter![83]

In another Latin version, this time in prose and printed by Maßmann as 𝔄, the endurance of the relationship after death is heavy-handedly underlined by a gruesome transformation of an image from the Song of Songs. After the bride's death she is placed in a tomb with the saint, who "moved his arm across so that his beloved bride could, as it were, have his left arm under her head and his right arm embracing her"[84] Although the *Chanson* is much more subtle, it also seems to suggest that marriage cements a union of individuals even after death. As Dyan Elliott points out, virginal marriage could in this way provide "a dramatization of the consensual nature of the bond," so that "in the hands of Western hagiographers, virginal marriage became the vehicle of complex theological doctrine, while expressing a less orthodox, perhaps popular belief, which projected the marriage bond beyond the grave".[85] Petit de Julleville saw justification in the poem's suggestion of heavenly reconciliation for thinking that the poet imagined the saint to have

---

[80] *CSA*, lines 606-10: "St Alexis is certainly in heaven together with God and the hosts of angels, with the girl towards whom he was so aloof; now he has her with him, [and] their souls are together: I cannot say how great is their joy."

[81] In the Latin version, there is only the evocation of the bride's perpetual grief – "Amodo capiat dolor qui finem non habeat" (Odenkirchen, p. 49).

[82] The editor, Assman, suggested that the Latin poem was the source of the French poem. Rychner convincingly argued the reverse.

[83] Str. 5-7: "Thus the two are joined perpetually before God. May their holy bond give us solace, and both bride and groom constantly watch over us!"

[84] Maßmann, p. 163: "brachium . . . transposuit ut quasi dilecta sponsa leuam sub capite dextram se amplexantem haberet". Cf. Cant. 2:6; 8:3. This feature recurs in the German versions printed by Maßmann as A, F and H. The version itself is rarer and more ornate than the 'standard' version printed by the Bollandists: it is likely to be both later and more local.

[85] Dyan Elliott, pp. 67-73, at pp. 67 and 73.

loved his bride as she loved him: "he wants to win her in heaven by his vigour, and, by means of a double sacrifice, deserve both for himself and for her an eternal reunion"[86] The poem constantly invites this romantic reading. Alexis does say quite specifically that his flight is an attempt to secure his bride:

> cum fort pecét m'apresset!
> S'or ne m'en fui, mult criem que ne t'em perde.[87]

However, this can hardly be seen as a lover's self-sacrificing heroism. Rather it is a kind of spiritual possessiveness – a jealousy as to his wife's fate. Alexis behaves as he does because he desires heaven for himself. In his concentration on his own salvation, he is prepared to disregard the ties of loyalty and duty which human beings customarily hold dear. The tale challenges our normal conceptions of good behaviour in order to remind us that devotion to God outweighs all earthly responsibilities. This conflict of interests is inevitably disturbing. Torn by the difficulty of overcoming earthly affections and responsibilities, a believer might feel tragically alienated from God. The tranquillity of the saint in his resolution would appear to be a miracle of spiritual strength. Thus, as much as we are appalled by the saint's insensitivity to the feelings of those who hold him dear, we admire it, because it is a measure of his wonderful piety:

> Soventes feiz lur veit grant duel mener
> E de lur oilz mult tendrement plurer,
> E tut pur lui, unces nïent pur eil.
> Danz Alexis le met el consirrer;
> Ne l'en est rien, si'st a Deu aturnét.[88]

In short, even if the *Chanson de Saint Alexis* intensifies the saint's relationship with his wife, it remains a disturbing poem, just as Winkler argued, because, in his super-humanity ("ultra humanas vires"), Alexis is necessarily and essentially inhumane.[89]

The bride's reverence for her departed husband, like her beauty and birth, is an index to her desirability. The better the wife Alexis rejects, the greater his sacrifice. Her excellence is a terrible temptation, testing and demonstrating his outstanding holiness.[90] Baudouin de Gaiffier has read more into it

---

[86] Petit de Julleville, p. 13: "il veut la conquérir au ciel par violence et mériter pour elle et pour lui le réunion éternelle par la vertu d'un double sacrifice".

[87] *CSA*, lines 59–60: "How strongly sin oppresses me! If I do not flee from it now, I greatly fear that I will lose you because of it."

[88] *CSA*: lines 240–5: "Often he watched them showing great sorrow for him, weeping piteously: and all of this was for him, never for anything else. St Alexis considered all this: but it is nothing to him, for he is entirely turned to God."

[89] Peter Damian, *Sermo* 28, ed. Lucchesi, 130–1, p. 165.

[90] Cf. Sckommodau, p. 177: "Die Braut, die er dann vor sich sieht, ist für ihn – um es ohne Umschweife zu sagen – nicht mehr als ein Objekt der Verführung."

than this. He equates the bride's amenability with her approval of his departure. Answering one of the most awkward of Winkler's charges against the saint, de Gaiffier argues that, "given the bride's acquiescence, Alexis does not infringe the ecclesiastical measures condemning those who separated without the consent of their spouses".[91] Hagiographically parallel to the motif of flight, he suggests, is that of the chaste or "spiritual marriage".[92] In both cases, as he shows, the protagonists are typically wealthy, well-born and constrained to marry. When, before departing, Alexis persuades his bride to join with him in chastity, the two motifs are smoothly assimilated. The saint is thus able to reject married life without rejecting marriage.

Yet, though later redactions of the legend place more emphasis upon the stated feelings of the bride, in neither the *Chanson de Saint Alexis* or the *Vita Sancti Alexii* is her opinion made at all clear. Indeed, she does not reply to her husband's wedding-night homily – or her reply is not reported – and she continues to lament his departure as she could not were she in full accordance with his wishes. Even so, there is an element of truth in de Gaiffier's suggestion that at a spiritual level, Alexis's marriage remains valid despite his physical separation from his wife.[93] The significance of his gesture of renunciation is symbolic rather than exemplary. The legend does not suggest that the saint's unilateral rejection of marriage is a model of behaviour to the common man. Rather Alexis's flight is a dramatic externalization of a devout Christian's sense of a conflict between the longing for purity of mind and body, and the trials and indignities of life on earth. His marriage is never realized within the bounds of human society, but instead translated to heaven, where it represents a perfect state of tranquillity beyond and after the frailty and troubles of this world – as if in that "happy ever after" achieved by the heroic couples of romance. In its first lines, with its evocation of the Golden Age, the *Chanson de Saint Alexis* introduces both a sense of loss and the concept of a "far, far better place". In this atmosphere lives the "lost" marriage of Alexis and his bride – only ever to be recovered in the far-off after-life of individual longings. The poem perhaps offered a dream of perfect serenity in marriage – both to the monks and nuns in their cells meditating upon some spiritual union in the hereafter, and to lay-people hoping for an end to their trials in the here-and-now.

The saint's devout and single-minded impulse to flee carnal contact is thus balanced by the bride's characteristic and admirable fidelity. By reuniting

---

[91] de Gaiffier, p. 194: "vu l'acquiescement de la jeune mariée, Alexis ne tombe pas sous les censures ecclésiastiques condamnant ceux qui se séparent sans l'aveu du conjoint". Cf. Jodogne.

[92] Bugge, pp. 72–4; Brundage, *Law*, p. 75; and Dyan Elliott.

[93] Cf. Mölk, p. 168: "la texte ne permet pas de douter qu'Alexis et son épouse sont liés, l'un à l'autre, du lien d'un mariage légitime"; Gnädinger, p. 46. Indeed, Alexis's marriage was cited along with the Virgin Mary's to justify the idea that consummation is not essential to the validity of a marriage (Delhaye, 'Development', p. 86).

them only in heaven, the poet is able to depict both characters as having won their deserts. Through his piety, Alexis wins heaven: through her fidelity, the bride wins her husband. After his departure she compares herself, not only in the *Chanson de Saint Alexis* but also in the *Vita Sancti Alexii*, to the turtle-dove, which was supposed to remain faithful to its mate even after death.[94] The simile is attractive as a romantic protestation of love, but it has a further significance. In the *Chanson de Saint Alexis*, as we have seen, the validity of marriage extends beyond death. In the context of eternity, a second marriage is an impossibility, because it would confuse the relationship of souls in the after-life.[95] It is therefore not surprising to find the image of the turtle-dove also occurring in Alan of Lille's *ad status* address to widows in his *Summa de arte praedicatoria*.[96] The idea of marital reunion in heaven so beautifully expressed in the *Chanson de Saint Alexis* is an illustration of the belief that marriage is a unique and final commitment for each individual. Peter the Venerable perhaps sought to express a similar belief when he suggested to Heloise after her husband's death that God would preserve him for her; and a thirteenth-century chronicler suggested that Abelard, like the Alexis of Maßmann's 𝔄-version, reached out to embrace his bride when she was admitted to his tomb.[97] What is particularly striking about the marriage of Alexis and his bride is that it remains so eternally binding, even though they never consummate it or live formally together. The ceremony which unites them is the product of dynastic policy, not of their consent, and yet both Alexis and his bride are prepared to accept that it unites them forever.

These issues come to a head in the question of the significance of the tokens which Alexis gives to his bride as he leaves her on their wedding-night.[98] In the *Vita Sancti Alexii*, the saint hands over "his gold ring and his *renda* – that is, the end-part of the belt which he wore – wrapped in a veil and in a purple cloth".[99] In the *Chanson de Saint Alexis*, the tokens are his sword-knot and a ring – "les renges d'espethe" and "un anel" (72–3). All three items – the ring, some sort of belt-buckle or fastening for a sword, and the cloth or veil – can be associated with the wedding-ceremony;[100] and two of them, the sword and the ring, play symbolically active roles in the wedding-ceremony

---

[94] *Vita Sancti Alexii*, 4.25, Odenkirchen, p. 39; *CSA*, 148–9; cf. *Vie de sainte Euphrosine*, 765. See Gnädinger, pp. 74–82.

[95] Cf. the question put by the Sadducees in Luke 20: 27–40. Christ here confutes the Sadducees by stating that marriage has no force in heaven.

[96] PL 210. 109–98 at 194C.

[97] *Ep.* 115, ed. Constable, I. 307–8; Dronke, 'Abelard and Heloise', *IPME*, pp. 267, 285–6.

[98] For detailed discussion of these tokens, see Legge, 'Renges'; and Fotich. The tokens are clearly depicted on f. 29r of the *St Albans Psalter*.

[99] *Vita Sancti Alexii* 2.15, Odenkirchen, p. 37: "anulum suum aureum et rendam, id est caput baltei, quo cingebatur, involuta in prandeo et purpureo sudario".

[100] See Schmolke-Hasselmann. The ring played a formal part in Roman marriage-ceremonies: Herlihy, p. 7. For the use of the sword see Meyer; de Gaiffier, p. 193.

depicted in the *Ruodlieb*. It seems logical to assume that they represent a statement by the saint about the nature of his relationship with his bride in the future. Fotitch argues that the gift of the ring "very clearly" signifies "the breaking of the marriage-bond".[101] There is some support for her reading in the fact that the Ashburnham copy of the *Chanson* specifically describes the ring as the couple's wedding-ring ("cel anel dunt il l'ot espusee", line 73).[102] However, in the *St Albans Psalter*, there is reference only to a ring ("un anel"), and this suggests that it is a new gift, and therefore a new pact of faith. Alexis also commends his bride to God ("a Deu l'ad comandethe", line 73) – an ambiguous phrase in the circumstances, which could be interpreted either as an empty valediction, or as an assertion of the saint's continuing concern for the welfare of his wife. In contrast to Fotitch, de Gaiffier argues that the tokens are "signs of the inviolability of their union".[103] Both scholars agree that the ring should be understood as a symbol of perpetual fidelity, but they draw opposite conclusions about the significance of its use as a parting-gift in terms of the marriage of the saint and his bride. However, in addition to its association with the wedding-ceremony, rings had a broader significance as one of the commonest tokens of recognition among the conventions of romance;[104] and it seems to me that the poet of the St Albans *Chanson* is at pains to overlay the matrimonial significance of the ring with the romantic suggestion that their love endures despite their separation. In the later versions of the legend, the ring commonly becomes the only token exchanged and ever more explicitly a means to recognition in the romantic style.[105] In the French versions, S, M and Q, for example, the ring is halved, so as to become an infallible token of identification.[106] It would surely have indicated to most members of the audience – even the first audience of the eleventh-century *Vie* – that Alexis and his bride expect to meet again. The bride certainly interprets it in this way, for she tells us after his death that she has long expected his return:

> Sire Alexis, tant jurz t'ai desirrét,
> E tant lermes pur le tuen cors plurét,
> E tantes feiz pur tei an luinz guardét.

---

[101] Fotitch, p. 503. In Chaucer's *Clerk's Tale* (IV. 862–8), Griselda confirms the end of her marriage by returning her wedding-ring to her husband.

[102] Hemming, p. xxiv.

[103] de Gaiffier, pp. 189–90: "signes de leur union indéfectible." Cf. Gnädinger, p. 46; Tintignac, p. 22.

[104] Thompson, H. 94; Kelly, *LMAC*, p. 232.

[105] The NHC-version, for example, tells "how he gaue his golde ringe/ To his wife att[e] his partinge/ And saide it[e] suld be takeninge/ Between thaim att[e] thaire first[e] metinge" (401–4).

[106] Of Q, Elliott says (*Vie*, p. 19), "the poet seems obsessed with the division of the wedding ring, describing this incident in loving detail and returning to it later in his tale (it is the only possession Alexis retains in exile)".

> Si revenisses ta spuse conforter,
> Pur felunie nïent ne pur lastét.[107]

The twist is that her grief is premature, for the couple *are* ultimately re-united – not on earth, but in heaven. The gift of the ring thus comes to stand not only for the cessation of the couple's contact with each other on earth; not only as a gage of mutual fidelity: but also as a symbol of the eternal and metaphysical force of the marital bond.

Later versions of the legend of St Alexis, both in French and in English, freely accept the challenge to explain away the emotional and ideological tensions contained in the saint's relationship with his wife and family.[108] In the French R-version, for example, Alexis's bride replies to his exhortation to chastity with the words "Why then, sir? Is marriage then a sin?" The saint takes this opportunity to preach directly on the relative values of virginity and marriage: 'No, not at all,' he said, 'but it is a wise man who renounces this good for a greater one. Virginity is much better.'[109] The later versions attempt not only to justify the saint's behaviour but also to make him more sympathetic. Charles Stebbins has argued that the thirteenth-century author of the French O-version "reveals a more imaginative, artistic and humane sensitivity" than the St Albans poet, because "he has stressed the humanity of St Alexis as well as his sanctity, and this makes his character not only more sophisticated . . . but also much more vivid".[110] Character-development in the French S-version is also much fuller than in the *Chanson*. The saint is fully aware of the impact of his actions upon those around him. This Alexis, argues Alison Goddard Elliott, "has not wholly denied his humanity". His character is "softened by love – his love for the girl and hers for him".[111] Indeed, the poet tells us (1093–1100) that the bride's privilege of receiving the document ("cartre") from the hand of her dead husband is an illustration of

---

[107] *CSA*, lines 471–5: "My husband Alexis, I have desired you for so long, cried so many tears for you, and kept so long away from you. If you return to comfort your wife, that would be no crime or weakness." There has been considerable debate over the meaning of line 475. None of the manuscripts give a satisfactory reading. It seems likely – as Storey's reading suggests – that the bride is arguing that it would not have been to Alexis's discredit if he had returned to her. Perhaps by this she expresses her willingness to share with him a life of chastity. In this line, she confronts her statement earlier at line 108: "Pechét le m'at tolut." She accepts that his desire to be free of sin justified his flight, but she does not see that sin would have prevented him from returning.

[108] For bibiliographical details of these texts, see the Appendices.

[109] R, ed. Paris, lines 214–18: " 'Comment, sire? Es donkes peché mariage?' 'Nenil,' fet il, 'mès cil est sage Qui let cel bien por un graignor. Virginité est mout meillor' ".

[110] Stebbins, 'Etude comparative', p. 379: "témoigne d'une sensibilité plus imaginative, artistique et humaine . . . il a souligné l'humanité de saint Alexis aussi bien que sa sainteté, ce qui rend sa caractère non seulement plus développé . . . mais encore bien plus vivant".

[111] Elliott, *Vie*, pp. 22–48, at pp. 42, 36.

the "loyalty" which "every man owes his wife" (1094).[112] The legend has now been wholly emptied of its original force, for it now reinforces precisely the institution which the "original" Alexis so contemptuously rejected. Elliott concludes that "the version of the *Chanson de Saint Alexis* contained in S reflects the twelfth century's growing concern with love and women, with problems of conscience, and with the individual".[113]

The Middle English versions of the legend characteristically assert the validity of the saint's marriage.[114] In the Vernon redaction, the author insists that the couple were married "in godus lawe", a phrase which recurs in the Laud/Trinity and Titus versions.[115] "Atte here spousyng, I wott," adds the author of the Titus-text, "there stode Beshoppys felle and prestes goode";[116] and the Laud-version dignifies the wedding with an even greater ecclesiastical presence: "As custume was & shulde be, Thai maden gret solempnite, The Pope & his conseile."[117] In the *Scottish Legendary Collection*, the poet affirms the sanctity of marriage by emphasizing that God instituted it in Paradise.[118] These late medieval transformations of the Alexis-legend are primarily motivated by a fascination with the pathos of the protagonist's tragic peripeteia. That the saint be honourably married is important to them only because his glorious marriage contrasts with the pitiful state into which his piety drives him.[119] In contrast to the ancient versions of the legend, they are not even remotely encratistic. Although they recognize that Alexis's renunciation of marriage is the result of an admirable conscientiousness, their dramatic impact nevertheless depends upon the assumption that marriage is a normal and fortunate state. They did not expect their audiences to congratulate the saint for securing his integrity: but rather to commiserate with him for his alienation from the normal courses of life in human society.

4. St Alexis and Guy of Warwick

The Anglo-Norman romance, *Gui de Warewic*, is effectively a secularization of the Alexian motif of marital renunciation: it is the culmination of the process by which the legend had been adapted to the sentimental needs of a wider audience.[120] The hero's abandonment of his bride is the central dramatic

[112] Line 1094: "loiaute . . . tout home doivent a la moiller porter."
[113] Elliott, *Vie*, p. 43.
[114] The earliest of these is thirteenth-century; the latest, fifteenth. See Appendix A.
[115] Vernon, 55; Laud/Trinity, 105; Titus, 60.
[116] Titus, 61–2.
[117] Laud, 166–8.
[118] SLC, 10–18.
[119] For example, Vernon, 157–62; Laud, 241–4.
[120] Dated by Ewert (pp. iii–vii) 1232–42. He argues that *Gui de Warewic* was an original creation – "sans doute créé de toutes pièces par le poète anglo-normand". Conlon has suggested that this was only the "definitive version" of a traditional story "based on

moment of this lengthy and eclectic work, and it provides a distinctive structure for what is otherwise "a tissue of romance commonplaces".[121] Klausner has described Guy's story as "a secular pastiche of elements from the legend of St Alexis".[122] Indeed, *Gui* even opens with a verbal resonance of the *Chanson de Saint Alexis*. Its reference to the virtues of the past in terms of "verité, . . . fei e lealté" ("truth, faith and loyalty") evokes the triad found in the exordium to the *Chanson* – "feit . . . e justise e amur" ("faith, justice and love").[123] The first half of *Gui* is dominated by the hero's quest to accumulate a reputation glorious enough to win the hand of his lord's daughter, Félice: but, shortly after marrying her, Guy is struck by the ungodliness of his past life, and, like Alexis, he resolves to abandon his bride. The moment of his conversion comes as he stands on a tower and gazes at the firmament.[124] This setting beautifully illustrates the contrast between the transience of this world and the infinity of the next which lies at the heart of the *Chanson*.[125] Guy departs on a solitary pilgrimage to the Holy Land, only returning home to reveal his identity to his wife shortly before his death.

Just as in the legend of Alexis, a sword and a ring are the tokens exchanged at their separation (7711-26). The dying Guy uses the ring which Félice gives him as a token of his identity; and the sword which he gives her is destined for their young son, Reinbrun. Like Alexis, Guy passes directly from his confrontation with his bride to a journey by sea (7731-2); and afterwards, his

some legendary battle between the Saxons and the Danes" (p. 41; cf. Ward, p. 471). He points out (p. 47) that there was a Felicia in the family of the Earls of Warwick at the turn of the twelfth century, perhaps indicating that the legend was already established – at least in some form – even before 1232. Crane rejects (pp. 16-17) Ewert's notion that the poem was an ancestral romance (pp. iv-viii). For the manuscripts of *Guy*, see Ward, pp. 471-501.

[121] Barron, p. 75; Crane, pp. 92-117; Legge, p. 165. The poem is analogous at various points to a number of other legends and romances: see Ewert, p. viii, n. 1; Conlon, p. 14, n. 6.

[122] *Nature*, p. 17; 'Didacticism', p. 103.

[123] *Gui*, 1-12 (Caius 14); *CSA*, 2. Later French versions of the *CSA*, such as S and Mb retain this triad, and my impression is that these poems depend for their effect upon the familiarity of the older version to the ears of their audience. Only a wide oral currency can explain the complex textual affiliations of the four manuscripts of the *CSA*. S and Mb deploy the phrases of the *CSA* repetitively and in patterns, as if with the deliberate intention of creating a refrain-like effect. It is therefore possible that even the poet of *Gui* felt able to make quite subtle verbal allusions to his hagiographical model.

[124] *Gui*, 7563-94; Auch., 21/1-3; Caius, 7395-7. Caius does not mention a tower, although, just as in the other versions, Guy's view of the firmament succeeds a day's hunting.

[125] This is clearly expressed as a rhetorical contrast:

> La mortel vithe li prist mult a blasmer
> De la celeste li mostret veritet . . .
> La vithe est fraisle; n'i ad durable honor;
> Cesta lethece revert a grant tristur. (*CSA*, 63-4; 69-70)

father sends messengers to seek him (7815–6). Athelstan's dream in *Gui* recalls the vision of the custodian at Edessa; and Guy's meeting with the Emperor's entourage recalls the saint's encounter with Euphemian's.[126] Guy accepts charity from his wife and spends his last years living near his family-home.[127] After his death his corpse exudes an odour of sanctity and effects miraculous cures.[128] Finally, like the saint, the hero is reunited with his wife in heaven.[129]

Yet even if the creation of the romance was decisively structured by the precedent of St Alexis, it naturally also celebrates values which are quite alien to hagiography.[130] In the first half of the romance, Guy's wonderful heroism is the expression of his love for Félice. She initially rebuffs his suit because he is not a knight;[131] when he is made one, she rejects him because he has not yet won renown;[132] and when he does so, she still delays their union by suggesting that marriage will make him soft and uxorious:

> Si sur totes riens vus amasse,
> E l'amur de mei vus grantasse,
> Tant deviandriez amerus
> Que tut en serriez pereçus;
> Armes ne querriez mes porter,
> Ne vostre pris enhalcier;
> Jo mesferaie, ço m'est avis,
> Se par mei perdisez vostre pris.[133]

---

[126] *Gui*, 10925–55; 10945–66; Klausner, 'Didacticism', p. 106; *Nature*, p. 41.

[127] Guy's death in the hermitage recalls St John Calybite: but cf. Marie de France's 'Eliduc'.

[128] *Gui*, 11579–88 (Auch. 294/8–12, Caius 10960–3). The *odor sanctitatis* was a common motif, and not exclusively associated with saints (Klausner, p. 27, n. 1). However there are also verbal resonances:

> Nuls hom qui ait enfermeté,
> Qui de cel odur ne sait sané. (*Gui*, 11, 587–8)

> N'i vint anferm de nul' anfermetét,
> Quant il l'apelet, sempres n'en ait sanctét. (*CSA*, 556–7)

Cf. S 1273–4; Mb 1078–9. The Bollandist *Vita* has a similar phrase: "omnes infirmi quacumque infirmitate detenti tacto corpore sancto curabantur" (111–12).

[129] *Gui*, 11629–30 (Caius, 11060–1); cf. *CSA*, 606–8.

[130] Crane, p. 12.

[131] *Gui*, 617–28; Auch./Caius, 378–413.

[132] *Gui*, 685–98; Auch./Caius, 735–48.

[133] *Gui*, 1061–8: "if I loved you above everything else, and if I granted you my love, you would become obsessed with love and thus grow idle. You won't want to bear arms, nor enhance your honour. I would be doing wrong, I think, if because of me your reputation was harmed." Cf. Auch. 1140–2:

> Namore wostow of armes loue,
> No comen in turnament no fight.
> So amerous thou were anon right.

Félice's dissuasion recalls both Erec's period of recreance and Gawain's warning to Ywain.[134] It might also be seen as a transformation into knightly terms of the anxiety expressed by Heloise that a wife is an obstacle to her husband's endeavours. The repulses Guy receives from Félice prefigure his own rejection of married life, and thus the gesture of marital renunciation is validated in terms of romance well before Guy realizes it as an act of piety. Félice insists that he win her hand through outstanding martial prowess, but at the same time argues that marriage is an obstruction to its continued practice. By articulating ideals which are at odds with her role, she expresses the tension fundamental to the impact of the motif of marital renunciation – the tension between the two sides of marriage as both the aim and the enervation of an individual's participation in society.

Perhaps the most fundamental difference between the legend of the saint and that of the hero is that when Guy leaves his bride, she is already pregnant with their son, the inheritor of his lands and chivalrous prowess.[135] Nevertheless, Alexis and Guy had apparently become so blended in popular consciousness that one of the Middle English versions of the legend of St Alexis seems to make what Klausner calls the "monstrous mistake" of having the sàint consummate the match:[136]

> In to a chaumbur he com full ryght,
> And redy there he founde hys bryght;
> And toke here in his armys twoo,
> And downe they layde bothe twoo.
> "Dame," he sayde, "nou it ys soo
> Of fflessche ar wee all so,
> Noue may we be gladde of this lyffe,
> For thowe art bothe moder and wyffe . . ."[137]

Klausner's suggestion of "a backwards contamination from the *Guy* tale" is the only possible explanation for this anomaly. That such a confusion could occur demonstrates that the essential appeal of these stories lay not in the differing ideals of the two protagonists, but in what they shared, the melodramatic glamour of their departure.

As in the *Chanson de Saint Alexis*, the creator of *Gui* suggests that by accepting the hero's decision, the abandoned wife can participate in its fruits: "Of all the good works which I myself will do," promises Guy, "I will give you half the benefit."[138] His departure seems no less arbitrary for this, and

---

[134] Chrétien, *Erec et Enide*, 2492–502 (Barron, p. 77; Hopkins, p. 85) and *Yvain*, 2486–504.
[135] *Gui*, 7559–62 (Auch 19/7–9).
[136] Klausner, *Nature*, p. 49; 'Didacticism', p. 108.
[137] Titus, 87–94.
[138] *Gui*, 7633–4: "De tuz les bens que mes ferai/ La meité de tut vus granterai"; cf. Auch. 26/10–2, Caius, 7429–30.

indeed, the poet makes no attempt to soften the elements of "Selbstsüchtigkeit" (to use Winkler's word) implicit in the hero's unilateral decision to abandon his bride.[139] Her father Rohaud calmly suggests that she should regard his sudden departure as a test of her devotion – as if she should patiently accept the same role as Alexis's bride.[140] Guy himself claims that his motivation is contrition for the deaths he has caused in her honour. His sense that his life has been blighted by its bloodshed (7604–30) recalls the case of Mabonagrain, who was likewise compelled by his bond with his beloved to practise arms in an essentially destructive way. Guy even blames Félice for the deaths of his friends, Torold and Urry, in the course of his quest for the honour of her hand (1555–66). Despite this, he continues to maim and kill even in the second phase of his life.[141] The saint's journey into poverty seems to have been to assimilated to the martial ethic of the crusades.[142] Indeed, Guy directly contrasts the value of military activity dedicated to God with those deeds which were inspired by his profane love for a woman:

> Gui comence dunc a penser . . .
>   que tanz homes aveit oscis,
> Turs e citez par force pris,
> E cum aveit sun cors pené
> Loinz en estrange regné
> Pur une femme qu'il tant amat,
> Pur qui tant mals duré ad;
> Mais unc pur sun criatur,
> Qui fait li ad si grant honur,
> Ne s'entremist de lui servir . . .[143]

---

[139] Winkler, p. 588.

[140] *Gui*, 7787–8 (Auch. 37/1–6, Caius, 7504–9). Rohaud perhaps testifies to the author's consciousness of the Constance/Grizelda theme (see Hornstein).

[141] Crane, p. 63; Barron, p. 77.

[142] Guy's chief destination is indeed Jerusalem (7732–6). His actions are not tied to any specific political or military objectives: however, according to Powicke (p. 80), "it is not too much to say that the recovery of the Holy Land, whether as an ideal, a symbol or an immediate duty, pervaded the minds of men in the thirteenth century. It was inseparable from the air they breathed."

[143] *Gui*, 7574, 7581–9: "Guy started to think . . . how many men he had killed, how many castles and cities he had taken by force, and how much hardship he had endured in far-off foreign lands, all for the woman he loved, for whom he had endured so many pains. Yet never had he done so much for his Creator, who had done him such honour, never had he concerned himself with serving him." Auch. 21/6–10: "He thought with dreri mode Hou he hadde euer ben strong werrour, For Iesu loue, our saueour, Neuer no dede he gode. Mani man he hadde slayn with wrong." Cf. Urban II in Fulcher of Chartres, *Historia Hierosolymitana*, 828B: "Procedant contra infideles ad pugnam jam incipi dignam, trophæo explendam, qui abusive privatum certamen contra fideles consuescebant distendere quondam. . . . Nunc rite contra barbaros pugnent, qui olim contra fratres et consanguineos dimicabant." ("Let those who were once wastefully accustomed to swell civil discord among Christians, now enter a battle against the pagans which is honourable to undertake and which will bring them a

However, despite the gloss put on the renewal of Guy's adventures by these appeals to crusading ideology and to the model of St Alexis, it seems to me that the romance stresses the incompatibility of married life and adventure not in order to assert either a religious ideal or a basic hostility towards marriage, but simply to justify the hero's continued addiction to the courses of individual endeavour.

The appeal of this combination of elements can be gauged by the success of *Guy of Warwick*, which was immediate and substantial (in England at least). Three complete English versions survive in manuscript (the fourteenth-century Auchinleck text, and two fifteenth-century copies now at Cambridge), along with some fragments and early printings.[144] The story's popularity lasted well into the eighteenth century, and Guy is sometimes even numbered among the Nine Worthies.[145] For its populism *Guy of Warwick* has attracted the scorn of those with more sophisticated literary or religious tastes. It is one of the "romances of prys" ridiculed by Chaucer in *The Tale of Sir Thopas* (VII. 899). Churchmen condemned it for its frivolousness; and in 1805, Ellis announced that *"Guy of Warwick* is certainly one of the most antient and popular and no less certainly one of the dullest and most tedious of our early romances."[146] More recently, Charles W. Dunn has describes the romance as "repetitive and prolix".[147]

This is too harsh. In its headlong rush from one adventure to the next, the Middle English *Guy of Warwick* (as contained in Zupitza's edition of the Auchinleck and Caius manuscripts) lacks neither energy nor charm. As Andrea Hopkins says, "the poem's popularity has usually been accounted for by its multiplicity of adventures rather than by any literary merit".[148] However, she herself argues that, despite its apparent diffuseness, the poem was deliberately constructed according to a "didactic aim"; and that the poet utilized "the technique of repetition with variation" in order "to create

---

reward . . . Let those who once used to draw their swords upon their brothers and kinsmen fight justly against the pagans.") See also Keen, pp. 48–9.

[144] See Appendices. All of the Middle English versions are closely related to the Anglo-Norman *Gui*, as well as to each other. The relationship is especially close between Auch. and Caius. However, Caius (ff. 149v/25–175v/20) is more closely related to the ULC version (ff. 195v/4–242v/20) (Spahn, p. 90). Spahn argues that *Guy* is a literate rather than oral creation, although it stands "in einer Tradition, die auf mündliches Erzählen verweist" (p. 6). Barron remarks that, "though the various surviving manuscripts and early prints of *Guy of Warwick* preserve the substance of the Anglo-Norman original, they differ in completeness, in wording and in verse form to an extent which suggests the complex textual history of a perennial bestseller" (p. 76).

[145] Conlon, p. 13; Crane, 'Vogue'. Guy is named as one of the Worthies in *Love's Labour's Lost*, V. 1. 109.

[146] Hopkins, pp. 74–5. Ellis, *Specimens of Early English Romances* (London, 1805), p. 4, quoted by Legge, *ANL*, p. 167.

[147] Dunn, p. 31.

[148] Hopkins, p. 71.

significant contrasts".[149] Klausner also stresses the poem's didacticism –
indeed its "moral seriousness".[150] Yet the gesture of marital renunciation is
so appealing in romance as in hagiography precisely because it can seem so
flamboyantly irresponsible – in short, so consonant with the essential
egocentricity of the hero. Not only does Guy's refusal of the Emperor's
daughter, for example, prefigure his eventual rejection of married life: it is
also an index of the splendour of his marriage to Félice – a marriage which in
turn is sacrificed to his own impulsive resolution.[151] It is possible that Guy's
stated desire for a new kind of life is informed by something of the sensibility
of penance, as Hopkins and Klausner have stressed. However, Hopkins
admits that Guy's conversion in no way reflects the common practice of
penance in the Middle Ages. She suggests that it was modelled instead upon
the ceremony of contrition known as "Solemn Penance", which was
practised only rarely and by the great.[152] Even Guy's sudden self-abasement
therefore appears to be a prerogative to which he is entitled only because of
his nobility and exceptional prestige.

The Middle English *Guy of Warwick* is better seen, not as a didactic work,
but as a naïve one, popular precisely because it is so free of moral anxiety. Its
reflection of the legend of St Alexis cannot be taken as evidence of its didactic
intent. As Susan Crane has remarked, "piety enriches and broadens the
importance of heroic action, but in doing so it becomes in some ways merely
an attribute of secular heroism".[153] The author of the romance possibly
aspired to recreate the grand conflict between the ideals of social duty and
personal endeavour implicit in the Alexian motif of departure, but, in
borrowing the motif, he fundamentally transformed it. As in any romance,
Guy stresses the exceptionality of the hero by flattering him, exaggerating his
abilities and importance in comparison with other men. Thus, the
significance of the motif of marital rejection subtly shifts from an illustration
of the saint's unworldliness to an assertion of the hero's right to demonstrate
his worldly superiority without hindrance by social obligations. To some
extent this alteration might reflect the exigencies, not only of romance, but
also of a new era – one concerned much more urgently with an individual's
autonomy within the bonds of society.

It could be said that in hagiography the celebration of marriage is a point of
departure for the passage to another world and the locus for an expression of
contemptus mundi, while in secular romance the wedding-feast is often the
moment for the hero's return – indicating the completion of his *rite de passage*
and consequent re-identification with society.[154] However, this simple

---

[149] Hopkins, pp. 70–118, at p. 82.
[150] Klausner, 'Didacticism', p. 118.
[151] With some justice, Hopkins accuses Guy of boorish conduct (p. 98).
[152] Hopkins, pp. 45, 68–9.
[153] Crane, p. 93.
[154] For example, *King Horn*, 1439–504.

distinction between the sensibilities of romance and hagiography increasingly broke down as the Middle Ages progressed. Hagiographers grew ever less interested in remote, austere figures like the iconic St Alexis of the early medieval versions of his legend, and ever more concerned with emotional and social bonds strained by the demands of faith.[155] In its notion of the saint's power of intercession, even the *Chanson de Saint Alexis* demonstrates a consciousness of the wider demands of society which would have been incomprehensible to the authors of the earliest legends about the Man of God – although in this case such concerns are held in check by the poet's artistic intensity and deep religious fervour. Developing this process still further, medieval secular romances concentrate ever more on the individual, celebrating not so much social pre-eminence as their defiance of society. In this context, even when the protagonist is not a saint (as Guy is not), his renunciation of marriage can seem a bold and glamorous act, but it is a gesture no longer tinged with any genuine sense of contempt for marriage as such.

5. The Life of St Christina of Markyate

It seems likely that Christina of Markyate also responded powerfully to the example of St Alexis – although in an entirely individual way. She is associated with the *Chanson de Saint Alexis* by the *St Albans Psalter*, and her biography testifies to her imaginative engagement with hagiographic models. In order to convince her unwelcome suitor Burthred of the glory of chastity, Christina cites saintly precedents ("exempla . . . sanctorum"), and, in particular, the story of St Cecilia and her husband, Valerian.[156] Although this confrontation with Burthred is as suggestive of Alexis's wedding-night conversation with his bride as of Cecilia's with Valerian, Cecilia's story was more immediately suited to Christina's purposes. At this point in her career, she was still hoping to achieve a life of chastity through Burthred's acquiescence in a "spiritual" marriage.[157] This Cecilian ideal of a partnership in chastity is closely related to the Alexian motif of dramatic flight, as de Gaiffier has shown. The two motifs celebrate the same impulse. Indeed, paradoxical though it might seem, the legend of Alexis's flight depends for its impact on the sense that he remains spiritually and

---

[155] Uitti, p. 293. As Herlihy has remarked: "In their struggle to achieve sanctity, the saints break free from family entanglements, but not at all from familial sentiments" (p. 115).

[156] § 10, p. 50. Head argues (p. 84) that, as an Anglo-Saxon woman, Christina would have thought in terms of St Cecilia rather than St Alexis, whom he sees as belonging culturally to the world of the Anglo-Norman monks. It seems unnecessary to assume such a division between the two cultures: after all, Christina's friend, Abbot Geoffrey seems to have come from Le Mans.

[157] For a history of this phenomenon, see Elliott, *Spiritual Marriage*.

emotionally bonded to his bride. Such stories of flight from marriage do not exclude the possibility of an enduring moral and emotional link between their protagonists. Indeed, in the very absoluteness of the physical separations demanded by their ideals of chastity, their insistence upon the existence of what might be called a ''higher love'' appears all the more emphatic. In the *Chanson de Saint Alexis*, the husband's renunciation of married life on earth leads to the sublimation of the marital union as an eternally binding relationship in heaven. In Christina's case, the husband she rejects is unwilling to consider even the spiritualization of their marriage in terms of a chaste marriage, and she is free instead to create an intimate, even empathic, bond with her friend, Geoffrey, Abbot of St Albans – itself an ideal of the expression of love.

I have tried to show how the poet of the eleventh-century *Chanson de Saint Alexis* sought to resolve the conflict between the saint's desire for God and his duty to his wife by conceptually relocating their relationship in Paradise. Imagined as a parallel, yet eternal, realm of perfect justice, Paradise provides the poet with a way of expressing his strikingly absolute sense of the consequences of individual commitments. In the same way, a conviction of the universal resonance of personal intentions dominates the depiction of marriage in the *Life of St Christina of Markyate*.[158] The key to this author's understanding of the nature of marriage lies in his contrast between Christina's vow of chastity and her vow of espousal. We are told that one day she went to church where the priest was saying Mass:

> post evangelium accessit Christina ad altare et optulit unum denarium, dicens in corde suo: ''Domine Deus clemens et omnipotens, suscipe tu per manum sacerdotis tui meam oblationem. Tibi namque in resignatione mei ipsius denarium istum offero. Dignare queso candorem et integritatem virginitatis conferre michi, quo reformes in me ymaginem filii tui, qui tecum vivit et regnat in unitate spiritus sancti Deus per omnia secula seculorum. Amen.''
>
> Postquam autem venit Huntendoniam, Suenoni suo quid vovisset aperuit et ille, qui tanquam lucerna Dei in locis illis habebatur, votum virginis coram Deo confirmavit.[159]

Christina takes great pains to ensure that her intention of remaining a virgin is recorded among the heavenly statutes. The penny-donation might be seen

---

[158] Holdsworth, p. 198.

[159] § 4–5, p. 40: ''After the gospel Christina went up to the altar and offered a penny, saying in her heart: 'Lord God, merciful and omnipotent, accept my oblation through the hands of your priest. For I offer this penny as a token of my surrender of myself. I pray that you will honour me with purity and virginal integrity so that you can refashion me in the image of your Son: who with you lives and reigns in the unity of God the Holy Spirit for ever and ever. Amen.' However, after she returned to Huntingdon she revealed to Sueno what she had vowed, and he, who in that area was regarded as a lantern of God, confirmed the maiden's vow before God.''

as a kind of consideration – a basis for her contract with God.[160] The agency of the priest, the celebration of the Mass, and her presence at the altar are all designed to make her gesture of personal commitment as solemn as possible.[161] For precisely the same reason, the Church increasingly insisted upon these circumstances for the celebration of marriage. Christina's biographer presents this moment as being no less binding than if it had been a wedding-ceremony. The prayer which he depicts her as offering on the night previous to this is a further indication of the significance and consequences of her vow:

> Domine, ante te omne desiderium meum et gemitus meus a te non est absconditus. Quid enim michi est in celo et a te quid volui super terram? Defecit caro mea et cor meum: Deus cordis mei et pars mea Deus in eternum.[162]

She calls God to witness as her only judge, denying any distinction between justice on earth and in heaven: since God sees into hearts, he recognizes the intentions by which a spiritual commitment is formed. Even if a human being falters in its fulfilment on account of weakness (''Defecit caro . . . et cor''), it remains no less valid before God.

Christina momentarily wavers in her resolution to live in celibacy when, after months of pressure from her family and friends, she agrees to marry the nobleman, Burthred. It is, in Moule's words, ''a weak link'' in her story.[163] This is how Christina's biographer describes the incident:

> Postea vero quadam die congregati ad ecclesiam, aggressi sunt simul omnes ex improviso puellam. Quid multa? Nescio quomodo: scio quod nutu dei tot impinguentibus lingua concessit et eadem hora Burthredus illam in coniugem sibi desponsavit.[164]

The phrase ''nutu dei'', which Talbot translates ''by God's will'', here seems to suggest that, in letting wrong be done, God nods in sleep. The phrase ''lingua concessit'' implies, as Moule puts it, that the ''words of consent were a superficial external element which did not necessarily indicate the intention of the participants''. She points out that ''the issue of

[160] Head suggests (pp. 80–1) that Christina gives her penny in imitation of her parents' donation to St Alban – though this is not made explicit in the text.
[161] Cf. Head, p. 81; Brundage, 'Votive Obligations'; Dyan Elliott, pp. 159–63.
[162] § 4, p. 40: ''Lord, my desire is clear to you, and my groaning is not hidden from you. For what do I desire for myself in heaven or upon earth apart from you? My flesh and my heart are frail, but God is in my heart, God is my portion for ever.''
[163] Moule, p. 53, n. 19.
[164] § 7, p. 46: ''Afterwards, however, when they were assembled in the church one day, they suddenly put the girl under pressure. What else can I say? I don't know how it happened: only that by God's will, she was so harrassed that she gave way in word, and in that hour she was betrothed as Burthred's wife.''

qualitative assessment of consent was one which posed a particular problem for twelfth-century canon lawyers''. ''A dilemma was created,'' she goes on, ''for how was one to assess intention other than by reference to external manifestations such as the expression of a verbal formula?''[165] Peter Lombard, for example, seems to have faced this dilemma quite pragmatically. He argued that although a private vow of celibacy was indeed an impediment to marriage, it was invalidated by a subsequent public vow of marriage – ''since what is done in secret cannot be proved''.[166] The Lombard, however, is concerned with burden of proof in cases of dispute. Christina, by contrast, is serenely sure of her own desires, confident of God as her witness (''desiderium meum . . . non est absconditus''). From her perspective, the vow of chastity is the more binding, because it takes precedence, not only chronologically, but also qualitatively. It remains the more accurate reflection of her real intentions. As her biographer puts it:

> Ipsa tamen etsi desponsata perseverabat eodem animo quo prius, libere protestans collum suum nulla racione contaminandum fore carnalibus viri amplexibus.[167]

Moule argues that the vow to Burthred could not have been valid since ''if Christina had been pressurised into giving her agreement and had not in reality truly consented to the union, she could not surely be constrained to abide by it''.[168] However, although her biographer does attempt to discredit the motives and methods of those who arranged Christina's marriage, his case for its dissolution is not primarily based upon the fact of her intimidation. His descriptions of the attempts to flatter, bribe, beat, cajole or trick Christina into acquiescence only serve to emphasize the firmness of her conviction and to excuse her for the one occasion on which her resolve did weaken. He does not argue, as Moule suggests, that a vow should be set aside simply because of the circumstances under which it was taken: indeed, he argues the opposite – that a vow remains valid even if it were taken under circumstances that render it impossible to prove. He accepts that Christina's public acceptance of Burthred was a significant step in the creation of their marriage – ''eadem hora . . . illam . . . desponsavit''.[169] Through her weakness in not withholding her consent, Christina placed herself in a difficult position: she recognized that Burthred had some claim upon her, but she did not feel she could honour it, unless she could also honour her promise to devote herself in the first instance to God.

---

[165] Moule, pp. 54–5.

[166] *Sententiae*, IV, 39, PL 192. 934: ''quia probari non potest quod occulte factum est''.

[167] § 8, p. 46: ''Even though she was committed to marriage, she continued in her former beliefs, openly insisting that for no consideration would she submit herself to the physical embraces of any man.''

[168] Moule, p. 55.

[169] Cf. Head, p. 82.

The prior Fredebert tried to convince her of the justice of Burthred's case, declaring, "We know that the sacrament of marriage which is made sacred by divine institution cannot be dissolved."[170] Christina replies, with some disingenuousness, that she is ignorant of the "scripturae" to which he refers. She is quite aware that Fredebert's appeal to divine authority only glosses over the complexities of the issue. In denying the sacramentality of her marriage to Burthred by insisting that she did not consent to it at heart, she reflects the widespread use of "sacramentum" in canonical thought to denote a moment of individual spiritual significance:[171]

> Pater meus et mater mea, sicut audistis, perhibent michi testimonium, quod contra voluntatem meam suo compulsu celebratum est super me hoc quod dicis esse sacramentum.[172]

Since Fredebert denies the importance of individual consent, she rather wryly suggests that his conception of the sacramental ("quod dicis esse sacramentum") is clearly not the same as her own. Indeed, she probably regarded her vow of celibacy as being no less a sacrament than her vow of marriage, and therefore no more lightly dissoluble. To Fredebert she makes explicit her belief that, as long as her inner convictions are secure, their formal confirmation according to custom is of little importance:

> Quantocius scitote quod elegerim ab infancia castitatem et voverim Christo me permansuram virginem; et feci coram testibus qui etsi deessent adesset tamen consciencie mee testis michi Deus. . . . Quare diu hoc quantum licuit operibus ostendi.[173]

We are forced to admire Christina's confidence in her own conscience and her readiness to defy society for the love of God. Her stance before Fredebert is glamorized not only by the splendour of her vocation but also by the evocation of Christ, quite literally, as a suitor *par excellence*.

> Fredebertus . . . interrogavit eam dicens: "Quomodo probabis michi quod hec facis propter amorem Christi? - quia forsitan spretis Burhredi nupciis: diciores affectas."
> "Vere," inquid, "diciores. Quis namque Christo dicior?"

---

[170] § 15, p. 60: "Nos scimus sacramentum conjugii divina sanctum institucione non posse solvi."

[171] For example, Ivo of Chartres (see Moule, pp. 1-47); and Gratian (see Noonan, 'Power').

[172] § 16, p. 60: "Just as you have heard, my mother and father bear witness on my behalf that it was against my will and according to their compulsion that this that you call a sacrament was celebrated upon me."

[173] § 16, pp. 62-4: : "As often as you like, I'll affirm that I chose chastity from childhood and vowed to Christ that I would remain a virgin. I made this vow before witnesses. Even if they had been absent, God was present as a witness to my conscience. . . . And so for a long time I demonstrated this as much as I could by my actions."

Cui ille: "Non iocor," inquid, "sed serio tecum ago. Et si vis ut credamus tibi, satisfac nobis iureiurando quia non nuberes nec regis filio, etsi desponsata illi fuisses quemadmodum desponsata fuisti Burhredo."

Ad hanc vocem Christi virgo suspiciens in celum; hillari vultu respondit: "Non modo iureiurando, sed eciam calidum candensque ferrum hiis nudis portando manibus parata sum probare."[174]

Having sworn perpetual virginity she is already "married to Christ" and she does not feel able to commit herself to Burthred in any way that minimizes Christ's claims upon her.[175] As Head has remarked, Christina's sense of her relationship with Christ is remarkably "concrete": "being the bride of Christ was not a metaphorical expression of her spiritual intimacy with her savior, rather it was a contractual relationship involving mutual privileges and obligations which bound her to him – and him to her".[176] Although Fredebert takes it to be an absurdity, Christ's competition with earthly suitors is a recurring feature of female saints' lives and devotional literature for women.[177] In depicting Christina as being prepared to undergo trial by ordeal in order to demonstrate her devotion to her heavenly suitor, her biographer presents us with a heroic ideal of love. Her fidelity recalls the fidelity of Alexis's bride: in a sense, she is separated just as completely as the saint's abandoned wife from the husband to whom she feels herself legitimately bound.

However, there was at least potentially a solution to the conflict between Christina's two vows. Her attempt to persuade Burthred into accepting a spiritual marriage after the pattern of Cecilia and Valerian was the only course of action consistent with both her vows. By insisting on his conjugal rights, Burthred made the two vows irreconcilable. Christina therefore turned to the only other option available to her as a model in hagiography – that is, the Alexian model of secret flight.[178] In her resistance to social and

[174] § 17. p. 62: "Fredebertus asked her: 'How can you prove to me that you are doing this for the love of Christ? For perhaps you scorn marriage to Burthred because you prefer wealthier men?' 'Wealthier, certainly,' she replied. 'For who is richer than Christ?' 'I am not joking,' he replied. 'I am quite serious. And if you want us to believe you, satisfy us by swearing that you would not marry even a king's son, even if you were betrothed to him as you have been to Burthred.' At these words the maiden cast her eyes up to heaven and replied with a smile: 'Not only will I swear, but I even am prepared to prove it, by carrying hot and glowing iron in my bare hands.' "

[175] For example, in § 12, p. 54, a number of unfortunate occurrences obstruct the celebration of Christina's wedding to Burthred. Christ is described as thereby "watching over his own spouse's vow" ("respiciente votum sponse sue Christo").

[176] Head, p. 76.

[177] See Chapter Four; and Woolf, 'Christ'.

[178] Holdsworth suggests that Christina's adoption of a solitary religious life was "something of a second best" (p. 187; cf. Georgianna, p. 38; Dyan Elliott, p. 208) to profession in a convent – a possibility which would have required Burthred's acquiescence.

parental pressure, her devotion to chastity and her ultimate departure, her life plainly mirrors that of Alexis. Yet, the two stories differ in one important aspect. Unlike Alexis, Christina's relationship with the spouse she flees is not subsequently significant, either dramatically or spiritually. "There remains the question," as Beate Schmolke-Hasselmann puts it, "why the principle of marital fidelity appears to be so strongly emphasized in the text and illustrations of the *St Albans Psalter*. Was this significant to Christina as a nostalgic reminder of her own husband Burthred, who, unlike the bride of Alexis, neither understood her nor supported her in her desires?"[179] The reason, I think, is that despite her rejection of marriage, Christiana's *Life* shows her to have been deeply involved with the society in which she lived. It was precisely because of the failure of her relationship with Burthred that her social and emotional links with the people and institutions around her continued to be so important to her. An individual and to some extent selfish impulse thus enables her to exert an inspirational influence upon an entire community. In the *Chanson*, the agent of this process is the bride. Imperfect in her humanity, and therefore universally sympathetic, she is an intercessor between the audience and the saint's austere holiness. In a similar way, the *Life of St Christina of Markyate* is redeemed, both emotionally and devotionally, by the development of her close and loving relationship with Geoffrey, Abbot of St Albans.

It seems to me that one of the Life's purposes is to emphasize the links between Christina and this abbey. References to "our monastery" of St Albans are abundant, and the manuscript bears an inscription which tells us for certain that it originated there.[180] This text constitutes the abbey's claim to a share in Christina's luminous and vital spirituality. Its author describes her as St Alban's "partner" ("cooperatrix") in the work of developing his community on earth.[181] His panegyric presentation of the relationship between Christina and the Abbot must be regarded at least to some extent as one way of expressing his sense of her influence upon his institution:

> Illa vero preelegit nostrum monasterium . . . tum quia te super omnes sub Christo pastores in terra fortissime diligebat, sicut iugi experimento probasti.[182]

---

[179] Schmolke-Hasselmann, p. 312: "Es bleibt die Frage, warum in Text und Miniatur des Albanipsalters das Prinzip der ehelichen Treue so nachdrücklich betont erscheint. Sollte dies für Christina eine wehmütige Gemahnung an ihren eigenen Gatten [Burthred] bedeutet haben, der sie, anders als die Braut des Alexius, in ihrem Begehren weder verstand noch unterstützte?"

[180] Talbot, pp. 1–2.

[181] § 50, p. 126.

[182] § 50, p. 126: "But she picked out our monastery . . . because she loved you much more deeply than any other of Christ's shepherds, as you have learned by experience." The person to whom this apostrophe is addressed can only be Abbot Geoffrey. There is no reason to assume that he must still have been alive at the time this passage was written. The apostrophe could be rhetorical.

Christina's intimate, personal bond with the Abbot was no doubt the means by which her personality came to permeate the community of the Abbey. In her loving alliance with the father of the institution, its Abbot, she came to exert a motherly, spiritually nurturing influence upon it. In this way the author suggests a direct identification of this holy woman's spirit with the future interests of his Abbey.

Yet, even if Christina's biographer stressed her intimacy with Geoffrey because it was the most immediate aspect of her passionate link with the institution of which he was head, his depiction of their intimacy is also an ideal, an "ideal of emotional openness and tender sensibility".[183] He stresses not only their spiritual but also their emotional interdependence. To Christina, Abbot Geoffrey is "precordialis", "carissimus" and "dilectus". The portrayal of their relationship is an exaltation of human love as well as a model of partnership in faith and chastity. Christina's feelings for Geoffrey are presented as a profound affection and a wondrously pure love – "she cherished him with much affection, and loved him with a wonderful but pure love".[184] We are told that she was more solicitous for Geoffrey than for herself.[185] She had such an empathy with him that, not only did she know beforehand when he was coming to visit her, but she was also even aware of his thoughts.[186] She was the agent of the Abbot's conversion from headstrong worldliness to pious humility.[187] She was an unfailing source of consolation and inspiration.[188] The Abbot turned to her constantly for advice – and indeed she was not shy to rebuke him quite openly if she felt the need.[189] On three occasions, Geoffrey planned to make difficult and possibly dangerous business-trips to Rome, and on each of them Christina prayed successfully for the cancellation of his plans. The two were so intimate that before one of these projected journeys, Geoffrey could ask her to provide him with two under-garments "not out of salaciousness, but in order to relieve the hardship of his task".[190] Although these two holy people are united only in chastity, their relationship is nevertheless remarkably real, and even physical. As Dronke says, there is nothing quite like this depiction of a loving couple "in the realms of Christian *amicitia* or of real or imagined *hôhe minne*".[191]

It is hard not to read this section of Christina's Life as an idealization of a relationship which is at least analogous to marriage. Perhaps it is deliberately

---

[183] Dronke, 'Heloise's *Problemata*', p. 313.
[184] § 58, p. 138: "multo eum excoluit affectu, miroque sed sincero dilexit amore".
[185] § 58, p. 140: "amplius de ipso quam de se sollicita . . ."
[186] § 60, p. 142; § 58, p. 140. In § 65, Geoffrey is reduced to sleeplessness by worrying about how the maiden could know so much of his mind.
[187] § 65, p. 150. Cf. Dronke, 'Heloise's *Problemata*', p. 313.
[188] § 57, p. 138.
[189] § 58, p. 140.
[190] § 71, p. 160: "non ad voluptatem sed ad laboris relevandum sudorem".
[191] Dronke, 'Heloise's *Problemata*', p. 312.

contrasted with the carnal and economic contract with Burthred that Christina so narrowly escaped. As an ideal relationship it is strongly reminiscent, for example, of the divinely established pattern of marriage portrayed in the *Mystère d'Adam*. Important in both cases is mutuality, companionship, equality, and above all what the Adam-dramatist calls "conservage", a parallel dedication to God. We are told that, after receiving the Eucharist or during the celebration of the Mass, Christina was often so rapt in contemplation of the divine countenance that she was even unaware of the presence of the Abbot:

> Quo cognito, abbas in hoc aiebat: "Multa mea gloriacio si presenti mei oblita sibi me presentes, ob cuius presencie dulcedinem hic me presentem sentire non prevales."[192]

Such incidents illustrate the author's point that Christina's relationship with Geoffrey was subordinate to her bond with her heavenly "sponsus". Her love for the Abbot was a "shared love in Christ" ("mutua . . . in Christo dileccio"),[193] and not, as it might appear, a worldly idolatry. This phrase recalls Abelard's formula of address to Heloise, "my dearest in Christ" ("in Christo carissima").[194] Christina and Geoffrey were united by their shared love of Christ and not by the exclusive reciprocity of their love for one another. Their detractors were apparently not convinced of this:

> Hinc eam alii sompniatricem, alii animorum translatricem, alii quasi miciores secularium agendorum prudentem procuratricem appellabant – scilicet quod divini erat muneris seculari prudencie conantes imputare. Alii autem aliter loqui nescientes eidem abbati carnali devinctam amore summurmurabant.[195]

Christina's biographer anticipates such accusations in his depiction of the purity of her relationship with her earlier protector, the hermit Roger. Her dependence upon Roger in some ways prefigures her intimacy with Geoffrey. Roger, we are told, was reluctant even to look at Christina, but having inadvertently glanced at each other, both were kindled by "the fire that does not burn":[196]

---

[192] § 68, p. 154: "Aware of this, the abbot used to say: 'It is greatly to my honour that, even though you are forgetful of me while I am present, you present me to the one whose sweet presence makes you unable to recognise my own presence.''

[193] § 76, p. 177.

[194] 1 *Ad Heloissam*, 73/40.

[195] § 76, p. 172: "So some called her a dreamer, others a seducer of souls; others, pretending to be kinder, just called her a shrewd prosecutor of worldly concerns – that's to say they attributed to worldly cunning the accomplishments which were due to divine grace; but others who could think of nothing better to say whispered that she was attached to the abbot by carnal love." Cf. § 64, p. 148.

[196] The application of this image to sexual temperance amid temptation derives ultimately from Prov. 6:27–9, via Gregory the Great (*Ep.* 601). Gregory argues that continence

Nempe calor qui succensus fuit Dei spiritu ardebat in singulis; scintillas suas iaculatus est in corda ipsorum altrinsecus suo modo gracie mutue visionis, unde facti cor unum et anima una in caritate et in castitate in Christo non formidaverunt convivere in eodem habitaculo.[197]

This "heat" is implicitly contrasted with the fires of lust. The emphasis upon the effect of looking here recalls the Church Fathers' identification of the agency of the glance with the creation of desire, as well as the secularization of their argument by writers like Andreas Capellanus.[198] Sight ("visus") was the first of the conventional five stages of love ("gradus amoris").[199] Here, however, the pattern of desire is subverted in favour of an ideal of union ("cor unum et anima una"), which is presented as a spiritual alternative to the biblical formula of marriage ("non sunt duo sed una caro", Mt. 19:5).[200] Christina's biographer thus injects his account of an erotically suggestive moment with scriptural terminology in order to justify the spiritual alliance of a man and a woman even within the boundaries of religious commitment. Like the author of the *Chanson*, he is able to accommodate an ideal of loving mutual fidelity to the exaltation of chastity and unworldliness.

Christina's relationship with Geoffrey resembles in other ways some of the blueprints for marriage advocated by its theorists in the Church. In advising, inspiring and chiding him, she accepts the wife's responsibility for her husband's spiritual improvement – a duty strongly reminiscent of the obligation to good "conseil" laid upon Eve by the Figura of the *Mystère d'Adam*.[201] Christina's affectionate intimacy with Geoffrey is the channel through which she pours the invigorating influence of her faith. Again, we might compare the "love mutual but differing according to the sanctity of each" to Hugh of St Victor's argument in *De beatae Mariae virginitate* that the sacramentality of marriage lies in the differing needs of man and wife.[202] He suggests that the husband should love the wife because of her vulnerability

is more admirable in the face of opportunity. The phrase "qui in igne positur nescit ardore" became commonplace, but usually as an opportunity to express scepticism about the possibility of resisting sexual temptation. See Schnell, pp. 152–4; and for example, Andreas, *De amore*, I. 6, 476–7, pp. 180–2; the Archpoet, VII, str. 8, p. 48; and Nigel Wireker, *Speculum Stultorum* (Regenos, p. 114).

[197] § 38, p. 102: "Truly, the fire which had been kindled by the spirit of God burned in each of them; it threw its sparks into both their hearts by the grace of that mutual glance; and so they were made one heart and one soul in charity and chastity in Christ, and they were not afraid to live together in the same house."

[198] Bloch, *Medieval Misogyny*, p. 100; *De amore* I. 1, p. 32 ("Amor est passio . . . procedens ex visione . . ."); cf. e.g. 'Disputatio inter cor et oculum', *LPMap*, pp. 93–5.

[199] For example, CB 72, str. 2a; Alan of Lille, *Summa de arte praedicatoria* 210. 122; *Parson's Tale*, X. 851–64. See Friedman; Robertson, *Preface*, p. 407, n. 26.

[200] Cf. Mark 10:8; I Cor. 6:16; Eph. 5:31.

[201] See Farmer; Sheehan, 'Choice', pp. 24–5.

[202] § 58, p. 138: "amor mutuus. sed cuiusque pro modo sanctitatis"; Hugh of St Victor, *De beatae Mariae virginitate*, PL 176. 876C: "amor conjugalis . . . sacramentum est . . . propter naturam differentem".

"ex pietate", and she him for his protectiveness "ex necessitate". This strongly resembles the recurring formula by which Christina's biographer summarizes the nature of their partnership. He balances the practical dignity and power of Abbot against the unworldly authority of the holy woman:

> Abhinc enim virgo tua per abbatem ab exteriorum attenuacione: abbas iam tuus per virginem ab interiorum aggravacione levatur.[203]

> Illam ipse in exterioribus sustentabat. ipsum illa suis sanctis precibus attencius Deo commendabat.[204]

The ideal of intimacy expressed in the Life is closely parallel to those expressed in contemporary treatises on spiritual friendship, but not necessarily directly indebted to them, as Holdsworth suggests.[205] In this period the Church gradually endorsed the idea that the relationship between a man and a woman could be emotionally and intellectually uplifting as well as a sexual stopgap, a symbol, or a means of procreation, and the *Life of St Christina of Markyate* is part of this tendency.

The impact of the example of St Alexis upon Christina's life perhaps culminates in the visit paid to her by the mysterious pilgrim ("peregrinus quidam, ignotus quidem").[206] The spiritual significance of this event is underlined by the cycle of miniatures illustrating the story of Christ on the road to Emmaus which directly follows the *Chanson de Saint Alexis* in the *St Albans Psalter*.[207] According to Pächt, they "are the earliest example of a cyclical treatment of the Emmaus story", and they perhaps owe their existence to Christina's spiritual concerns.[208] However, to Christina, the pilgrim could possibly have signified not only Christ, but also Alexis. In this way, she might have been able to identify herself, not only with the saint who fled marriage as she did, but also with his lonely bride, to whom he eventually returns as a poor pilgrim ("pauper et peregrinus").[209] The appearance of this figure stands at the climax of Christina's biography, in its incomplete state. This is not unfitting. Just as it begins with a dramatic flight from a community whose values she rejected, so it concludes with the acceptance of the pilgrim by Christina's new community – her family of

---

[203] § 57, p. 138: "For in this way the abbot released your [God's] virgin from outward poverty, and the virgin lightened your abbot's inward burden."

[204] § 58, pp. 138-40: "He supported her materially: she commended him to God more carefully in her own prayers."

[205] Holdsworth, pp. 196-7.

[206] § 80. p. 182. The pilgrim's visits are narrated in § 80-81, pp. 182-8.

[207] Pächt, et al., Plates 38-40.

[208] Pächt, *Rise*, p. 38; Pächt et al., p. 73, nn. 4, 5.

[209] *Vita Sancti Alexii*, 5.43, Odenkirchen, p. 41. Although Alexis is not described as a pilgrim in the *CSA*, it is only natural to portray him as one, and several subsequent versions do exactly this (e.g. Laud, 232; Titus, 99). The biographer asks (§ 81, p. 188): "How else can we identify him but as the Lord Jesus or an angel?" ("Quem illum nisi Dominum Ihesum aut eius dicemus angelum?"). Cf. Holdsworth, p. 190.

fellow-devotees. In the intensity of her feelings for the pilgrim, Christina reflects the emotions of Alexis's bride – "Blessed and ever-grieving bride" ("O sponsa beata, semper gemebunda"), as the rubric to the St Albans miniature so paradoxically labels her. To Christina, Alexis's bride was perhaps a model for the ideal sensibility of the nun, who perpetually mourns the departure of her glorious bridegroom to another, better world.

6. Conclusion

In the earliest versions of the legend of St Alexis, the relationship between the saint and his bride illustrated only an ascetic contempt for marriage. In the *Chanson de Saint Alexis*, the relationship between the saint and his bride was redeemed by its sublimation. Its resonance derives from the inherent contradiction between the normal significance of marriage and the symbolic use to which the poet puts it. Although marriage is more naturally an image of an individual's social and sexual integration, both into the community and into the cycle of generations, in this case it is used to express a sense of the distance between this world and the next. On the one hand, the *Chanson de Saint Alexis* validates marriage as an absolute union. The saint is reunited with his bride even after their deaths. On the other, it undercuts it, by suggesting the impossibility of a perpetual and perfect bond on earth. The vignette of their wedding-night parting is thus implicitly dramatic. It is an emblem of the poem's essential theme, the tension between worldly and unworldly ideals. Thus, this poem's emotional impact depends upon a sense of the conflict between the earthly inadequacy of marriage and its absolute validity in heaven. In subsequent versions and in *Guy of Warwick*, the relationship between the protagonist and his bride was sentimentalized. In the course of this development, the demands of the individual become ever more insistent. In the earliest versions the saint almost completely transcends his identity. Later, his humility is no more than a posture: his selfish concentration upon his own spiritual ends is presented as a kind of romantic flamboyance – to the point at which the saint's identity was submerged in that of the popular hero, Guy of Warwick.

The *Chanson de Saint Alexis* was able to hold these contradictory impulses towards pious self-abnegation and sentimental individualism in tension only by referring the whole issue, as it were, to a metaphysical realm. This solution is perhaps typical of the era. In the *Mystère d'Adam*, for example, Eden is the location for a model of marriage. Similarly, Abelard and Heloise project the difficulties of their relationship upon what they saw in different ways as a deeper reality. Christina of Markyate testifies to a belief in the metaphysical force of personal commitments in her sense of the absolute validity before God of her unwitnessed vow of celibacy. Nevertheless, she balances her renunciation of earthly marriage with an ideal of a different kind of union: in her relationship with Abbot Geoffrey mutual physical attraction is sublimated, and becomes an almost empathic ideal of mental and emotional communion. Christina finds room for an ideal of human relationships within life, rather than beyond death – and this is entirely characteristic of Christina's disconcerting combination of piety, passion and pragmatism. Her personality still pervades what can only be regarded as a highly individual religious text. Even so, it is very likely that she was stimulated by the ancient precedent of St Alexis. She might have found in it both a justification for her own stubborn resistance to her parents' conception of marriage and a celebration of the power of the sentimental bond between two lovers separated physically by the desire for chastity. The very least one can say, in conclusion, is that all the texts which I have discussed in this chapter are rooted in a sense of the conflict between marriage and the various aspirations of the individual. In both the *Chanson de Saint Alexis* and the *Life of St Christina of Markyate*, this anxiety is expressed with remarkable intensity.

CHAPTER FOUR

Corpus Christi College Cambridge MS 402 and Oxford Bodley MS 34 (the 'AB-Group')

1. Introduction

In 1929, J.R.R. Tolkien demonstrated that the distinctive linguistic and orthographical features of the Corpus copy of the *Ancrene Wisse* are almost exactly reproduced in a Bodleian manuscript (Bodley MS 34) containing the *Sawles Warde*, *Hali Meithhad*, and the lives of three female saints, Juliana of Nicomedia, Margaret of Antioch and Katherine of Alexandria.[1] He suggested that all the works of the 'AB-Group' (as they are now called, after the respective sigla of the two manuscripts) were written in the same dialect, around the same time, and in the same, probably quite limited, area.[2] The coherence of these texts is also marked by their association in some other extant manuscripts. With the exception of the lives of Juliana and Margaret, all occur in the mid-thirteenth century collection, BL MS Cotton Titus D. 18, along with a unique copy of a prose meditation entitled 'The wohunge of ure lauerd'.[3] The 'Wohunge' is generally also assigned to the AB-Group, along with three similar meditations – 'On wel swuthe god ureisun of God almihti', 'On lofsong of ure lefdi', and 'On lofsong of ure louerde' – which are preserved, with another copy of *Ancrene Wisse*, in BL Cotton Nero A. 14.[4] There is an additional copy of the 'Lofsong of ure lefdi' in BL Royal MS 17 A. 27, where it is entitled 'The oreisun of seinte Marie'. This manuscript also contains *Sawles Warde* and the lives of the three virgin-saints.[5]

---

[1] Tolkien, '*Ancrene Wisse* and *Hali Meithhad*'. The Corpus copy has been described by E.J. Dobson as "a close copy of the author's own final and definitive version of his work" ('Affiliations', p. 163).

[2] Tolkien, p. 114. Dahood says (p. 12) that although Tolkien "overstated the similarity of language in Corpus and Bodley . . . the existence of the AB language may be taken as established". The most detailed analysis of the AB language is to be found in the appendices to d'Ardenne's edition of *SJ*.

[3] The language of the Titus MS has recently been analysed by Laing and McIntosh.

[4] There is another, incomplete copy of the 'Ureisun of God Almihti' in Lambeth Palace MS 487, edited by Thompson as 'On ureisun of ure louerde'. These short meditations are collectively known as the Wooing-Group.

[5] For the association of all these texts, see Mack, *SM*, pp. ix–xiv; Dobson, pp. 286–304; Dobson and d'Ardenne, *SK*, pp. xlix–liii; Watson and Savage, pp. 15, 29–32;

As well as coincidences of dialect and transmission, there are similarities of style, sentiment and purpose. All the texts in the group seem to have been designed for an audience of women leading a religious life. The first version of the *Ancrene Wisse* was apparently written for three sisters living together as recluses.[6] The Corpus manuscript tells us that this was the nucleus of a community which later grew to twenty or more.[7] *Hali Meithhad* is described by the Bodleian scribe as an "Epistel of meidenhad meidene froure" – "A letter on virginity for the consolation of virgins"; while the meditations of the Wooing-Group, as they are collectively known, were apparently written to reflect the perspective of a woman leading an anchoritic life.[8] All three saints are virgin-martyrs, whose lives would have had a particular relevance to dedicated women;[9] and indeed, the author of the *Ancrene Wisse* mentions that his charges were already reading an English life of St Margaret – presumably the very same text as the one which survives.[10] In *Sawles Warde*, the use of the metaphor of the human being as a house is perhaps particularly appropriate to the anchoritic experience.[11] The very choice of language might well indicate a female readership: if these texts had been written for men, it seems likely that they would have been written in Latin rather than English. In other words, it is probable that all of them were designed for use by female

Shepherd, *AW*, pp. xiii–xiv. The Royal copy of the life of St Juliana is very much shorter than the one in Bodley: Bella Millett ('Textual transmission') has recently suggested that the differences between the two texts can be explained by oral transmission of Royal.

[6] MWB, pp. xi–xii; Dobson, *Origins*, pp. 3–4. Even so, much of the first version does not appear to have been tailored specifically for these women: see Millett, 'Women', p. 93.

[7] Corpus MS, f. 69a/13–28, p. 130.

[8] For example, the feminine pronoun is used in *UL* (27) and *UGA* (31); in the *LLo*, the speaker asks to be able to "livien on eorthe with *meidhod*" (86–7); and in the *WL*, Christ promises to make the speaker "*lauedi* ouer all thine schaftes" (84–5). *WL* also seems to make a reference to anchoritic seclusion: "Mi bodi henge with thi bodi neiled o rode. sperred querfaste with inne fowr wahes & henge i wile with the & neauer mare of mi rode cume til thet i deie" (590–5). See Millett, 'Women', pp. 95–6. There is obviously no need to accept Einenkel's suggestion (Thompson, pp. xxiii–xxiv) that "the preponderance of enthusiasm and fantasy over thought" indicates that the meditations were written *by* a woman. Indeed there is some evidence to the contrary (Dobson, p. 154, n. 2; Watson and Savage, pp. 418–19, n. 1; Millett, 'Women', pp. 98–9).

[9] The author of *SM* says that maidens especially should heed his story (MWB, 44/25–6). Millett and Wogan-Browne describe *SM* as "a work with special relevance to virgins", suggesting that it "exemplifies the strength of will required to resist parental and social pressures towards marriage" (p. xxv), though they also argue that "the saints' lives, with their melodramatic action and flamboyantly rhythmical and alliterative style, were apparently intended in the first instance for public delivery to a general audience" (p. xiii).

[10] Corpus MS, 66a/19, p. 125; d'Ardenne, p. xliv; MWB, p. xiii. He also makes reference to some "writings" on the blisses of heaven (MWB, 128/30–1). These could well have been *Sawles Warde* and *HM*.

[11] MWB, pp. xxv–xxvi.

recluses. Perhaps together they once formed at least part of a collection written in order to answer the spiritual needs of a particular group of women. It is possible that they were all written by the same person, although this remains an open question.[12] The very least one can say is that they are "closely linked together in a way that invites us to study them as a whole, and allows us to use individual works in the group as an aid in the interpretation of the others".[13]

E.J. Dobson's detailed researches into the origins of the *Ancrene Wisse* led him to believe that the author was probably "a member of one of the independent Augustinian congregations".[14] He suggested that the scribal centre of the AB-language was the Victorine Abbey at Wigmore in Herefordshire (pp. 114–73), and that the community of female recluses was Limebrook Priory nearby (pp. 174–279). He dated the original version of *Ancrene Wisse* 1215–22, and the revision contained in the Corpus manuscript around 1230 (pp. 15–16). He and d'Ardenne suggested that, of the other works, *Seinte Margarete* and *Seinte Iuliene* were the earliest ("written in the last decade of the twelfth century or at the very beginning of the thirteenth"), followed by *Seinte Katerine* and *Sawles Warde* (1200–1210), and then by *Hali Meithhad* (1210–20).[15] More recently, Millett has argued for either Dominican or Premonstratensian authorship of the *Ancrene Wisse*.[16] She suggests that the original version was written after the arrival of the Friars in 1221 – perhaps several years after – and that it was revised some time after 1236.[17] The group as a whole may reasonably be placed in the first third of the thirteenth century.

In what follows, I am concerned with the function of marriage both as a symbol and as a representation of female experience in the world. Like the *Chanson de Saint Alexis*, the works of the AB-Group imaginatively project

[12] d'Ardenne, pp. xl–xlvii; Dobson, p. 154; MWB, pp. xii–xiii.

[13] Watson, p. 132: cf. d'Ardenne's assertion that "we are in the presence of a tradition, with one specially active and influential centre or school, rather than with one busy and universal provider of devotional literature".

[14] Dobson, *Origins*, pp. 16–113; here p. 170. He even suggested a name, Brian of Lingen.

[15] Dobson and d'Ardenne, *SK*, pp. xxxviii–xxxix; Dobson, *Origins*, pp. 156–66.

[16] Millett, 'Origins', pp. 209–19. To support this idea, she has to propose quite a complex, though not implausible, hypothesis: "assuming that the author *was* Premonstratensian or Dominican, how do we account for the linguistic evidence linking him and his work with a scribal centre which cannot have been a Premonstratensian or Dominican house? The simplest way round the difficulty would be to abandon the assumption that he must have belonged to that centre at the time when he wrote *AW*. It is reasonable to assume that he both had originally, and maintained, some kind of connection with the 'AB centre': his own written English seems to have been a form of 'language AB', and the centre must have had access to a revised fair copy of *AW* to produce the excellent Corpus text. But he may only have received his schooling there; or he may have been a member of the centre, but left it to join the order to which he belonged when he wrote *AW* . . ." (p. 215).

[17] Millett, 'Origins', p. 219.

marriage into heaven in order to be able to define its essence and its ideal. I shall focus on those aspects of the AB-Group's treatment of marriage which seem to me most distinctive or characteristic, and indicate, where I can, analogues and comparisons with other texts in the vast tradition of Christian virginity-literature. However, as Peter Dronke has warned, "it is clear that no one scholar can know intimately all the relevant primary sources for these themes, and that certain similar conceptions or modes of expression to those that seem unusual . . . may exist, after all, in other texts and other periods of the Christian world".[18] Despite the conventionality of theme and doctrine treated in the AB-Group, it can still be seen as the depiction of "a social and psychological landscape".[19] It exhibits a consistent and free-standing sensibility, sufficient for the definition of the symbolic and emotive function of marriage within it.

2. Wooing: *Ancrene Wisse*, Part VII

Although the AB-texts appear to have been written for at least a primary readership of female recluses – for women, that is, so absolutely withdrawn from the world as to live in the symbolic tomb of an anchorage – they nevertheless portray human society vividly and with a sympathetic comprehension of its ideals. As Linda Georgianna has argued of the *Ancrene Wisse*, the anchoress cuts herself off from the world "only so that she can withdraw into herself, where she will encounter the whole moral world in miniature". The question addressed by the author is "not how to become dead to the world but rather how to use human desires, memories, and experiences to one's spiritual advantage". It is, despite its avowedly unworldly aims, "an uncommonly worldly book".[20] The same is true of the other AB-texts. *Hali Meithhad*, for example, in the words of Millett and Wogan-Browne, "builds adroitly on the desires and fears of young women to persuade them of virginity's social and emotional advantages, not disdaining but using its audience's aspirations".[21] Thus, even though such devotional works might seem infertile ground for a literary analysis of medieval attitudes towards marriage, their concentration upon the exigencies and certainties of faith does not coldly remove them from the usual modes of human thought. Indeed, the ideals governing society's most valued structures are the very currency of their concerns. They represent society in an implicitly urgent and dramatic way: for they hold the social instincts of human beings in tension with a sense of the imminence of departure to another world.

[18] Dronke, 'Virgines', p. 101.
[19] Diamond, p. 149.
[20] Georgianna, *Solitary Self*, pp. 5, 7, 50; cf. Elizabeth Robertson, p. 46.
[21] MWB, p. xvii.

It is in keeping with the AB-Group's worldly immediacy that, in its use
of nuptial imagery as a metaphor for the union of the soul with Christ, the
accent falls not upon marriage – the completed union – but upon wooing –
the opportunity to choose. The AB-texts do not demand a sublimation of
the self in imitation of the heavenly soul-marriage to come: instead, they
present the anchoritic life as a continual process of individual decision.[22]
They do not expect their audience to have undergone, or to be undergoing,
a mystical transformation of the spirit.[23] They are designed to fortify the
women to whom they are addressed in the process of forming and
upholding a momentous commitment to a challenging way of life: but they
are addressed, nevertheless, to women of normal emotional stature, with
the same hopes and dreams as their peers in the world.[24] The AB-texts
attempt to confirm these women in their resolution by validating it in
worldly terms as well as in spiritual ones – by harmonizing, as it were, the
two systems of experience. In order to do so, they sympathetically
recognize the aspirations and ideals by which women living in the world
structure their lives. Rather than denying or sublimating these sentiments,
they engage directly with them, contrasting heavenly with earthly
experiences as if on the same plane of values.[25]

[22] It is because of this emphasis upon the personal determination of spiritual questions,
that the author questions the value of monastic obedience to a fixed rule. As
Georgianna argues, "the *Ancrene Wisse* author explicitly questions the value of
unhesitating obedience, whether to superiors or to the external rule itself", because he
is concerned with the "process by which an individual makes critical assessments", a
process antithetical to complete obedience to a rule (*Solitary Self*, pp. 8–31, at p. 27).

[23] Watson (p. 134) and Shepherd (*AW*, p. lvii) have pointed out the difficulty of applying
the word "mysticism" to the AB-texts. As Watson says, they are mystical in that they
are expressions of a "highly-elevated and demanding spirituality", but they have only
a marginal affinity with the "literary tradition which regards the ascent to God as
involving purgation, illumination and union". William James defines mystical
experience by four criteria: Ineffability, Noetic Quality, Transiency, and the Passivity
of the subject (pp. 380–2). By contrast, the AB-Group emphasizes the active
discrimination of the subject; it refers not to a transient intoxication of the spirit but to
a long-term sense of spiritual satisfaction; and, rather than invoking ineffability, it
freely accepts the challenge to describe with very specific and immediate imagery the
spiritual triumphs of the anchoritic life. As Georgianna says (*Solitary Self*, pp. 73–4),
"the *Wisse* author has been defined as a mystical writer primarily because he borrows
frequently from the mystical writings of St Bernard . . . but it must also be emphasized
that the author borrows selectively, ignoring and sometimes suppressing Bernard's
descriptions of mystical flight": he concentrates on what for Bernard is only the first
stage of loving God, the "carnal and worldly attraction to Christ as a man".

[24] Bolton has suggested (pp. 147–8) that the proliferation of female religious groups in the
thirteenth century can be explained at least partially by the increasingly lower status of
women in a secular society in which few could attain economic independence and in
which by no means all could marry.

[25] Elizabeth Robertson has sensed in this very concreteness an implicit disrespect for the
female intellect. "The very examples that have given the *Wisse* author a reputation for

Marriage is not the only emotional bond recognized by the AB-texts, though I would suggest that it is the most important – both because it was inevitably the social institution by which women's lives were most effectively defined, and because it was a powerful analogy for the ultimate resolution of the anchoress's relationship with Christ in heaven. Part VII of the *Ancrene Wisse* is an analysis of "luue", a term which the author uses to translate a cluster of words from the Vulgate – "pietas", "caritas", "dilectio" and "amor". He portrays love, not so much as an emotion, a physical effect, but as a bond, a spiritual and intellectual link between people – or between the individual and God. "It is said," he states, "that love binds."[26] He distinguishes as "cardinal loves" ("heaued-luuen") four types of affective bond in the world: between friends; between a man and a woman; between a woman and her child; and between the body and the soul. He demonstrates that Christ's love transcends ("ouergeath") them all, by casting the Redemption in each case as the gesture which supremely fulfils the demands of the relationship.

He deals rapidly with friendship, by saying that Christ gave a security to the Jews, as for a friend. In this case, the security which He offered was His life. "Never," says the author, "did a friend perform such a favour for his friend."[27] Then he turns to marriage. "There is often much love between a man and a woman", he says.[28] However, no man loves his wife so much that he would forgive her if she continually fornicated with other men: only Christ, he says, is merciful enough to forgive this. He fortifies the anchoress in her profession, not by denigrating the alternative lifestyle of marriage, but by establishing it as an ideal of mutual affection, which only Christ is loving enough to fulfil absolutely. The analogy of Christ with the husband loyal to a disloyal wife operates on two levels. Firstly, it depends upon the Old Testament identification of "Israel" as a faithless woman.[29] The image was applied by Christian thinkers to the commonwealth represented by the Church.[30] This historical association authorizes the second level of the analogy – that is, as an emotive human drama. Yet, it is not unimaginable that a loving man could in the real world forgive a woman's transgressions in this way, though the rarity of such gestures no doubt fittingly expresses the

psychological realism and acumen also can be seen as misogynist," she says (p. 57), "for through these images women are taught that they can never maintain the mystical heights available to men." I suspect that this adjustment on the part of the AB-texts has more to do with their authors' expectations about their audience's level of education than with hostility towards the intellectual activity of women.

[26] MWB, 128/12: "Me seith thet luue bindeth."
[27] MWB, 116/25–6: "Neauer fere ne dude swuch fordede for his fere." Cf. John 15:13. Abelard also exploits this idea: he suggests that Christ was Heloise's "verus . . . amicus" (2 *Ad Heloissam*, 30/15).
[28] MWB, 116/27: "Muche luue is ofte bitweone mon ant wummon".
[29] For example, Jer. 3:1–13; Ezek. 16; Hos. 2.
[30] Woolf, 'Christ', pp. 3–4.

rare price of Christ's mercy.[31] The scenario of forgiveness might be seen, in turn, as an *exemplum* of Christ's love, validating in human and affective terms, the grand conception of God's universal mercy. It is ironic that, in the *exemplum*, the Christ-figure forgives the woman for her failure in specifically the quality which devotional writing for women supremely exalts – chastity. The author is fully alive to this irony, and he derives from it a paradox which he ascribes to St Augustine: "a man's approaches make a maiden into a wife, but God makes a maiden out of a wife".[32]

The third cardinal love is the love binding a mother to her children. The author suggests that, if a child were so ill that it could only be cured by immersion in a bath of blood, the supreme demonstration of a mother's love would be to offer her own blood for her child. Christ, he says, made just such a sacrifice, in order to cleanse us of our sins. The striking image of blood-sacrifice is here used to validate maternal love, rather than, as in Hartmann von Aue's *Der arme Heinrich*, to demonstrate the redemptive possibilities of a woman's love for a man, or as in the romance of *Amis et Amiloun*, to dramatize the power of the bond of friendship. Again, analogy and allegory reinforce one another: not only is Christ's love cast as a paradigmatic version of a mother's love – in itself a powerful idea – but the status of motherhood is also dignified by its equation with Christ's heroic sacrifice on the Cross.[33] The fourth cardinal love, between the body and the soul, is demonstrated by their grief at parting. Like the first, that between friends, this one is quickly discussed and dismissed. The author thus places a much greater weight of emphasis upon the two kinds of love pre-eminent in the world in which women play an active role – that is, in marriage and in motherhood. Friendship, at least in the Aristotelian and Ciceronian tradition, was regarded as an distinctively masculine relationship, and it is often associated in medieval literature with antifeminism.[34] The body and soul are both abstract, non-gendered concepts. Of the worldly loves recognized by the author of the *Ancrene Wisse*, only the two which refer directly to female experience in the world are dramatically portrayed. The author's identification of the types of love cardinal on earth is thus part of his attempt to address his audience directly, in terms of their own patterns of experience.

The pattern to which Part VII of the *Ancrene Wisse* continually recurs, however, is that of love between a man and woman. Christ, we are told,

[31] Woolf suggests (p. 4) that "in the conventional patterns of characterization of medieval literature there was no room for the wronged but forgiving husband". It is true enough that medieval literature affords little respect to the cuckold. Perhaps it was felt that his unmanliness jeopardized the structure of house and inheritance upon which society depended.

[32] MWB, 118/6–7: "monnes neoleachunge maketh of meiden wif, ant Godd maketh of wif meiden". Cf. Osbert of Clare, *Ep.* 40, 139/29–31.

[33] For discussions of medieval attitudes towards motherhood, Bynum; Fellows, pp. 41–2; Herlihy, pp. 120–7.

[34] For example, Andreas, *De amore*, III, 288/9–290/12.

came like a suitor to a poor lady in a foreign land – "as a mon the woheth, as a king thet luuede a gentil poure leafdi of feorrene londe".[35] This analogy is transformed into a tale – "a hidden allegory" ("a wrihe forbisne").[36] Once, the author tells us, there was a lady who lived in a castle in a land laid waste; a king had fallen in love with her so that he constantly sent her gifts, messengers and supplies; but she was hard-hearted and did not give him her love, despite his beauty, wealth, power, and the great feats he performed; eventually he promised to rescue her even at the expense of his own life; he did so, was killed, and miraculously rose again. Although the presentation of Christ as a champion is not in itself original, this author makes it both immediate and memorable by using the story of the Passion as a fantasy of the absolute fulfilment of chivalric aspirations.[37] Moreover, in throwing the accent of the story upon the lady's responses, the author makes her the pivotal figure in the drama. The female reader or auditor for whom the lady stands is given the opportunity to test her own responses to this knightly paradigm. The force of the *exemplum* is thus not allegorical, but ontological.[38] It is a statement about the way in which the anchoress perceives her own existence in relation to Christ. His cosmic gesture is interpreted as a personal address to an individual woman. Here, the author concentrates, not on the idea of the lady's faithlessness, but on her hard-heartedness. In this, he plays consciously upon one of the conventions of secular love-poetry – that the lover requires a response from the lady he addresses.[39] "A lady should indeed be blamed," sang Bernart de Ventadorn, "when she goes on prevaricating to her lover."[40] The unresponsiveness of the lady in this case – her cold unwillingness even to recognize the extent of the knight's devotion to her – is presented as a "churlishness" of spirit ill-befitting a noble woman.[41]

[35] MWB, 112/26–7.

[36] MWB, 112/32.

[37] Cf. Osbert of Clare, *Ep.* 42, 164/24–8; Thomas of Hales, 'Luue-Ron', 103–4: "Mayde, to the He send his sonde/ And wilneth for to beo the cuth" ("Maiden, he is sending you his messenger, and wants to be acquainted with you"). See Woolf, 'Christ'; Shepherd, *AW*, pp. 55–6. Bugge suggests (p. 99) that, even as early in the Middle Ages as this, "one senses a twinge of nostalgia for a bygone age of chivalry", while Millett and Wogan-Browne speak of "the imaginary past of courtly romance" (p. xxxii; cf. Shepherd, p. 57). Even in the eleventh century, a poet could allude ironically to this romantic ideal: the redheaded man in the *Ruodlieb* reinforces his seduction of the young wife with a similar evocation of rescue by a gallant knight (VII. 65–79).

[38] This use of the image of the besieged lady can be contrasted with Langland's, for example (B. IX. 1–10, C. X. 127–135): he identifies the beleagured female figure not with a woman like the anchoritic reader but with an abstract concept, Anima; and the "proud prikere" stands not for Christ's gallantry but for the Devil's glamour.

[39] Hoffman, pp. 229–31.

[40] 'Can l'erba fresch' e'lh folha par . . .', lines 49–50, ed. Goldin, pp. 136–41: "Be deuri'om domna blasmar/ Can trop vai son amic tarzan."

[41] Cf. Woolf, 'Christ', p. 9.

Courtship by poetry is an effective analogy for the relationship of the enclosed woman with Christ, for a number of reasons. Firstly, it captures something of the urgency and passion which the author of the *Ancrene Wisse* was trying to communicate through his handbook.[42] Secondly, it is a way of translating the insubstantial bond between the anchoress and the object of her devotions into a system of readily comprehensible values. Thirdly, it provides a model for the practice of those devotions. Just as Christ-the-suitor had to woo continually, and to frame his desire in letters and messages, even out of his own heart's blood, so the anchoress has to urge her love continually upon God, and express it in her prayers and in her heartfelt commitment of self.[43] Finally, it places the anchoress, like the beloved lady, in a position of eminence. If Christ is like a bold knight in a tournament, a "kene cniht", then the anchoress is like a noble lady watching, proud in the prowess of her favoured knight. She is even, one might say, the prize. The whole scenario is structured so as to afford the lady, and by extension, the anchoress herself, a privileged role. Quite simply, the author flatters and reassures her by suggesting that she is loved by the best knight.[44]

After outlining the four cardinal loves, the author goes on immediately to specify Christ's wooing. Christ, he says, is the fairest of all suitors, the richest of kings, the most nobly-born, the wisest of the wise, the most courteous of men, and the most generous. To win a woman's love, Christ is prepared to offer the world – indeed, the universe:

> Sete feor o thi luue; thu ne schalt seggen se muchel thet Ich nule yeoue mare. Wult tu castles, kinedomes, wult tu wealden al the world? Ich chulle do the betere – makie the with al this cwen of heoueriche. Thu schalt te seolf beo seoueuald brihtre then the sunne. Nan uuel ne schal nahhi the, na wunne ne schal wonti the. Al thi wil schal beon iwraht in heouene ant ec in corthe – ye, ant yet in helle. Ne schal neauer heorte thenchen swuch selhthe thet Ich nule yeouen for thi luue unmeteliche, vnueuenliche, unendeliche mare. Al Creasuse weole, the wes kinge richest; Absalones schene wlite, the as ofte me euesede him, salde his euesunge – the her thet he kearf of – for twa hundret sicles of seoluer iweiet; Asaeles swiftschipe, the straf with heortes of urn; Samsones

[42] Georgianna (*Solitary Self*, p. 77) interprets the story as an exemplum against the hard-hearted religious apathy which could easily grow out from spiritual self-protectiveness of the anchoritic life.

[43] "[Christ] wrat with his ahne blod saluz to his leofmon, luue-gretunge for te wohin hire with ant hire luue wealden" (MWB, 112/30–32).

[44] For Elizabeth Robertson (p. 72), "the Christ-Knight allegory simply underscores the dependence and passivity assigned to women in Christianity. Like many courtly lyrics, this romance seems peculiarly male-oriented. We learn more about the man's desire than about the nature of the woman he adores. What we do learn about her is negative – she is haughty, disdainful, and unworthy of the worthiest of knights." The point of this passage is not so much the *passivity* of women as the *activity* of Christ, who here represents not masculinity, but the Word of God.

strengthe, the sloh a thusent of his fan al ed a time, ant ane bute fere; Cesares freolec; Alixandres hereword; Moysese heale – nalde a mon for an of theos yeouen al thet he ahte? Ant alle somet ayein mi bodi ne beoth nawt wurth a nelde.[45]

The suitor promises his 'lady' wealth, status, beauty, security and power. Yet, the woman achieves all this only because her ideal Husband excels all other men, and not in her own right. By defining her relationship with Christ as courtship, the author is able to express the dignity of her state in heaven, but he makes it the consequence of her dependence upon a masculine figure. The wooing is a fantasy, not of absolute freedom, but of a joyous subordination to an ideal man.[46] Even in his imaginary portrayal of female experience in heaven, the author retains marriage as a model of women's dependence upon men.

Geoffrey Shepherd has argued that this passage owes its structure to a traditional pattern of description of the rewards of the Blessed in heaven, which was popularized in the Middle Ages by St Anselm of Canterbury.[47] The Blessed possess seven corporal and seven spiritual Beautitudes, and Christ's seven virtues here, Shepherd argues, are based upon these. Indeed, as he says, "it would seem likely that a vernacular treatment of the beatific state deriving from Anselm's treatments should be considered one of the lost works of Middle English literature".[48] The association of particular legendary figures with worldly pre-eminence in certain virtues is also "a

---

[45] MWB, 120/17-32: "Set a price on your love: you can't ask so much that I wouldn't give much more. Do you want castles, kingdoms . . . Do you want to rule the whole world? I can do better for you than that – I can make you, as well as all this, the queen of heaven. You shall yourself be seven times brighter than the sun. No evil shall come near you, no joy will be lacking to you. Your wish will be entirely done on heaven and also on earth – yes, and even in hell. No heart can ever imagine such a joy that I won't give immeasurably, incomparably, infinitely more. All the wealth of Croesus, who was the richest of kings; the radiant loveliness of Absalom, who, as often as he had his hair cut, sold the clippings (the hair that he chopped off) for two hundred shekels of silver measured by the scales; the swiftness of Asael, who vied with the deer in running; the strength of Samson, who once slew a thousand of his foes single-handed; the generosity of Caesar; the fame of Alexander; the health of Moses – wouldn't a man give for just one of these gifts all that he had? Yet all together compared to my body are not worth a needle."

[46] Cf. Watson: "this anchoritic spirituality . . . employs fantasy, [but] it does not consist of fantasy; its roots are physical, existential" (p. 145). For St Bernard, as Shepherd points out "the sensitive affection for [Christ's] person is no more than an early stage upon the ladder of spiritual love" (AW, p. li). Even if, from a theological point of view this mode of argument is only such as would appeal to a "sentimental and intellectually unsophisticated" audience, from a literary perspective, the argument is one that demands from the author considerable deftness and sensitivity.

[47] Shepherd, 'All the wealth'.

[48] Shepherd, ibid., p. 163.

128

popular iconological convention'', and is probably related to the *Ubi sunt
. . .?* tradition.[49] In fact, both the schemata of virtues and their identification
with exemplary figures are conventions of great antiquity. They can be
traced back at least to Hellenistic rhetoric;[50] and they also belong to the
conventional rhetoric of romance.[51] They were used to embellish what was
ultimately a development of a topos relatively common in virginity-literature
from the fourth century A.D. onwards, in which the state of virginity is
dignified by a formulaic rejection of wealth and worldly advantage.[52] For
example, St Augustine, in his eighth sermon on the Gospel of St John, poses
the following question:

> Offerant homines quaelibet ornamenta terrarum, aurum, argentum,
> lapides pretiosos, equos, mancipia, fundos, praedia; numquid aliquis
> offeret sanguinem suum[?][53]

Similarly, St Ambrose, in his treatise, *De virginibus*, places this speech in the
mouth of a virtuous maiden:

> Sponsum offertis; meliorem reperi. Quaslibet exaggerate divitias,
> jactate nobilitatem, praedicate potentiam; habeo eum cui nemo
> comparet, divitem mundo, potentem imperio, nobilem coelo. Si talem
> habetis, non refuto optionem; si non reperitis, non providetis mihi,
> parentes, sed invidetis.[54]

What really motivates both St Augustine and St Ambrose is a scorn for all
material things. They describe supposedly highly desirable possessions in
curiously general terms – as if impatient even to think of such things. The
author of the *Ancrene Wisse*, by contrast, is far more appreciative of the riches
he describes, even to the point of sensuality. The reason for this difference of
tone is that, in the *Ancrene Wisse*, the topos is subtly adjusted so that worldly
riches are presented, not as the world's own offerings, but as a measure of
Christ's grace – even if a consciously inadequate one. Thus, where St
Augustine and St Ambrose say, as it were, ''worldly men may offer this, and

---

[49] Shepherd, ibid., pp. 164-6. In Thomas of Hales's 'Luue-Ron', Absalon is presented as
a paradigm of beauty and ''Henry vre kyng'' as a paradigm of wealth (81-6).

[50] Curtius, *European Literature*, p. 180.

[51] For example, *Erec et Enide*, 2209-14 (Hartmann, *Erec*, 2813-21).

[52] Millett, *HM*, p. xliii.

[53] *Tractatus in Joannis Evangelium VIII*, PL 35. 1452; quoted by Woolf, 'Christ', p. 3:
''Men may offer all kinds of earthly trappings – gold, silver, precious stones, horses,
slaves, lands, estates – but did any of them offer their own blood?''

[54] PL 16. 207; quoted Millett, *HM*, p. xliii: ''You offer me a husband but I have found a
better one. You can heap up his wealth as much as you like, throw his nobility before
me, lecture me about his power, but I have a man to whom no one may compare,
neither for his wealth in the world, nor for his power in sovereignty, nor for his nobility
in heaven. If you have one such as this, I would not reject that choice, but if you have
not found him, you are not providing for me, my parents, but envying me.''

it is nothing'', the *Ancrene Wisse* says, "worldly men may offer this, but Christ can offer more". The message is made more positive, more attractive and more reassuring. The topos follows the same path as the legend of St Alexis: it evolves from an illustration of the importance of rejecting the world, to an affirmation of the dignity of a spiritual bond.

Only at the end of His wooing-speech does Christ threaten the anchoress with the fires of Hell, and it does little to modify the impression of grand promises of great advantage ("muchele biheue"). Indeed, the author tells us that Christ is so much in love, that He makes the anchoress His equal, and indeed, His "master" – obeyed in all things.[55] It is hard not to read much of this as an attempt, quite simply, to make the anchoress feel good about her life. No doubt such assurances and injections of enthusiasm were necessary enough for women leading so harsh and dispiriting a life. Indeed the author lists "marvellous and joyful thoughts" ("thohtes . . . wunderfule ant gleadfule") among types of meditation legitimately helpful to the anchoress in resisting temptation – the others being those which inspire fear, wonder or sorrow. As an example of a joyful thought, the author asks the anchoress to imagine what it would be like "if you saw Jesus Christ and heard him ask you what – apart from your salvation and that of your dearest friends – would be most precious to you of things in this life and asked you to choose it (provided you resisted)".[56] Making people feel good is one of the functions of literature; and the concentrated glamorization of the anchoress's relationship with Christ attempted in Part VII of the *Ancrene Wisse* does not depart in essence from the methods of the romancers and hagiographers. They construct figures with whom Everyman may identify, but who have a greater capacity for dictating the agenda of their lives. A 'romantic' figure specifically orientated to an ideal of female piety is the bride of St Alexis. Her privileged role in the saint's self-sacrifice and subsequent exaltation could be closely compared to the anchoress's privileged relationship with Christ. Just as the *Chanson de Saint Alexis* evokes a tranquil image of marital perfection in the other world, so here, the anchoress's final rest and relief from trial is imagined as a supremely fortunate marriage – with heaven and all the world its dower.

---

[55] "Swa ouer-swithe he luueth luue thet he maketh hire his euening. Yet Ich dear segge mare: he maketh hire his meistre, ant deth al thet ha hat as thah he moste nede" (MWB, 128/5-7): "He loves love so inordinately that he makes her his equal. Indeed I dare say even more than this: he makes her his master, and does, as if compelled, all that she bids."

[56] Corpus MS, f. 65b/22-5, p. 124: "yef thu sehe iesu crist & herdest him easki the hwet te were leouest efter thi saluatiun & thine leoueste freond of thing o thisse liue & beode the cheosen with [thet] tu withstode".

3. Wooing: The Wooing-Group

I suggested earlier that the image of Christ's wooing provided a pattern of devotion for the anchoress: the Wooing-Group might be seen as an actualization of this pattern, the answer, as it were, to the "love-letters" of Christ referred to in Part VII of the *Ancrene Wisse*. The image of the love-letter recurs in the 'Wohunge of ure lauerd'. The piercing of Christ's side by Longinus is developed into a macabre and graphic image. Christ is pictured as "opening" his heart so that the anchoress might read within it "trewe luue lettres".[57] The anchoress figuratively "reads" the wounds for their burden of love by meditating upon the events and implications of Christ's self-sacrifice. In this sense, Christ's wooing is directly equated with the thoughts and feelings that arise in the anchoress's mind from thinking about His Passion. Just as it is expressed in love-letters, so the anchoress's meditations are made concrete in the imaginary "letters" of the Wooing-group.

They are, however, model letters rather than distillations of spontaneously overflowing emotion. Although Thompson emphasizes the "lyricism" of the group, arguing that "apparent sincerity and independent artistic merit give the 'Wooing-Group' the stamp of originality", there is in fact nothing distinctively personal about them.[58] They seem to have been tailored for use by female recluses, certainly, but not for the exclusive use of particular individuals. Although they are eloquent, and at times spirited, they are abstract, and in many ways conventional.[59] They concentrate, almost to the point of repetitiveness, on the events of Christ's life and and the dramatic details of the Passion. This is because they were designed to have a general utility as meditative aids. Rosemary Woolf has argued that the medieval religious lyric does not show "the poet meditating", but instead provides "versified meditations which others may use"; and the same distinction applies to the Wooing Group.[60] These prose-poems are eloquent and emotive enough for Thompson's description of them as "mystical rhapsodies" not to be misplaced, but they should be seen primarily as impersonal and exemplary texts. It seems likely that they were the direct products of a tradition. Elizabeth Salter has suggested that the Wooing Group is indebted to Marbod of Rennes, not only for the source the 'Lofsong of ure lefdi', but

---

[57] "A swete iesu thu oppnes me thin herte for to cnawe witerliche & in to reden trewe luue lettres. for ther i mai openliche seo hu muchel thu me luuedes" (*WL*, 546–551): "Ah, sweet Jesus, you opened your heart for [me] to know [your love] for sure and to read true love-letters; for I can see clearly there how much you love me." The image is perhaps a development of the "epistula . . . scripta . . . non in tabulis lapideis sed in tabulis cordis carnalibus" of II Cor. 3:2–3.

[58] Thompson, pp. xix, xxi.

[59] Salter argues that "these rhapsodies imitate, with great skill and inventiveness, the Latin literature of affective devotion which had been developing since the eleventh century, first on the continent, and then in England too" (p. 73).

[60] Woolf, *English Religious Lyric*, pp. 5–6.

131

also for the stylistic guidance of his rhetorical treatise, *De ornamentis verborum*.[61] Yet, the attempt to address universal concerns by writing in a formal style for an abstract persona can be just as revealing in some ways as writing in a more directly individual fashion. In the case of the Wooing-Group, the depiction of the anchoress's relationship with Christ in terms of the urgency and intimacy of absolute love is not simply the expression of one woman's longings, but a deliberate statement about the very structure and nature of the anchoritic vocation.[62]

The 'Wohunge of ure lauerde' uses the idea of choosing a husband, as in the *exemplum* of the hard-hearted lady in the *Ancrene Wisse*, to express a sense of the dignity and privilege of determining this vocation. Christ is explicitly presented as a competitor with other men for the love of His lady. As with the four cardinal loves, Christ proves himself superlative in each of the seven criteria upon which women are said to give their love to men:

> thu with thi fairnesse, thu with richesce, thu with largesce, thu with wit
> and wisdom. thu with maht and strengthe, thu with noblesce and
> hendeleic, thu with meknesse and mildschipe and mikel debornairte, thu
> with sibnesse, thu with alle the thinges thet man mai luue with bugge,
> haues mi luue chepet.[63]

Men are often beloved for their beauty (13–16), says the author: yet Christ is so beautiful that the angels only want to look at His face (37–40), and a view of it would outweigh even the pains of Hell (40–5). Men are often beloved for their material possessions, their "gold and Gersum and ahte" (16–19), but who is richer than the one who rules in heaven (60–2)? Each of the seven criteria is treated in this way, and the section is structured by the use of a refrain: "A iesu mi swete iesu leue thet te luue of the beo almi likinge" ("Jesus, sweet Jesus, believe that my only desire is to love you"). At no point does the author attempt to invalidate any of these criteria: he simply argues that it is Christ who meets all of them most fully. In doing so Christ becomes a paradigm of the ideal husband: the life shared in heaven with him is imagined as the supreme dignity of a matchless marriage. The anchoress is expected to support her belief in this ideal marriage, not by a selective blindness to any of the values important on earth, but by a celebration of all the things which might make marriage attractive to women.

---

[61] Salter, p. 73.

[62] Cf. Leclercq on letters about the monastic vocation (*Love*, p. 179).

[63] *WL*, 253–62: "You have purchased my love with all the things with which a man could buy love – with beauty, wealth, generosity, intelligence and wisdom, power and strength, birth and nobility, meekness, gentleness and marvellous grace, and with kinship." That these criteria are seven in number suggests the influence of the Anselmian tradition of the Beatitudes of the Blessed (Shepherd, 'All the wealth', pp. 161–4).

Thompson suggested that this "mystical marriage is symbolical; but whether, in any particular instance, the *Himmelsbraut* is a particular woman, or man (the soul in either sex being feminine), or humanity as a whole, or Holy Church, or the world, or any complex of these, is often very difficult to decide".[64] By contrast, Watson and Savage have pointed out that this treatment of the nuptial theme is markedly less abstract than St Bernard's: "where Bernard is always conscious that the idea of the soul's marriage to Christ is a metaphor, the reader of the 'Wooing' is encouraged to choose Christ as a lover in a literal, one might even say a physical, way, and to argue over his suitability as a husband as though this is exactly what he is, or is to become".[65] As in Christina's biography, the anchoress's relationship with Christ is strikingly "concrete".[66] Bugge has suggested that the Wooing-Group "presents the passionate union with Christ inconsistently, that is, neither as fully allegorical nor as fully literal, but somewhere between. It thus represents an imperfect literary adaptation of an authentic mystical impulse."[67] It seems to me that the appeal of the group, in both literary and mystical terms, derives from the fact that it does not set out to authorize a particular set of ideas, but rather to depict and direct the psychological drama of an individual's determination of faith. This drama is portrayed in realistic terms as the exercise of choice between suitors.

The rhetorical gambits of the imaginary suitor in the *Ancrene Wisse* and the 'Wohunge of ure lauerd' represent the fortification of individual resolution within a system of potent ideals, a process which is the necessary preliminary to the recognition of a calling. To communicate these ideals and convince his audience that devotion to Christ represents a privileged and fulfilling emotional union, the author borrows the system of ideals governing earthly marriage, and translates them into heavenly terms. In equating the anchoritic life with the experience of being wooed by an ideal suitor, the Group suggests that the woman who decides to marry embarks upon a vocation just as much as the woman who decides to retire from the world. What is most striking about this approach to anchoritic spirituality is its stress upon what Bynum calls "the interior and choosing self" in the drama of ideas which leads to conviction.[68] That courtship and marriage are the predominant symbol in their explication of this drama, suggests that for most

---

[64] Thompson, pp. xxii–xxiii.

[65] Watson and Savage, p. 246; e.g. Bernard, *Ep.* 113, *Ad Sophiam*. Sophia is here perhaps a personification of 'Wisdom'. Speaking of this letter, Leclercq has said that "it is the nuptial theme which guarantees the coherence of the whole message, centered as it is on personal loving union with Christ the King. Everything to do with this union must be interior and profound in contrast with all that is exterior, apparent and superficial in human relations." It is a "an invitation to interiority" (*Women*, pp. 74, 76).

[66] Head, p. 76.

[67] Bugge, p. 137.

[68] Bynum, p. 107.

people they formed the most obvious point at which the individual was forced to test his or her emotions and resolve them in acceptance of a social duty.

The author of the 'Wohunge' seems to accept that the anchoress will never wholly relinquish at heart all the things she valued in this world, and he does his best to adapt them into a means to enlightenment. In the 'Lofsong of ure Louerde', the speaker describes herself as one that "has so much heartfelt regret for the loss of earthly things".[69] The author or authors of the Group have to steer a delicate course between, on the one hand, so sympathetic an attitude towards the values of earthly marriage that the anchoress never properly focuses her mind on the heavenly union, and, on the other, so intransigent a hostility towards an institution which she is accustomed to respect, that she dismisses the Group's message as repellently extreme. The problem is solved in the Wooing-Group, and indeed throughout the AB-Group, by the contention that the marital ideal is too beautiful to be realized on earth. Disappointment on earth is inevitable, but in heaven, impossible. This separation of marriage into the real and the ideal, as I have argued already, is one of the characteristic ways in which the literature of this period addresses marriage and the issues surrounding it. The Wooing-Group captures both the bitterness and nostalgia of disillusionment. The 'Lofsong of ure Louerde' suggests that worldly ties are, as it were, a trap:

> nu ich understonde hu soth hit is thet seint austin seith in his boc: "Unseli is thet is with luue to eni eorthlich thing iteied, uor euer bith thet swete abouht mid twofold of bittre . . ."[70]

The idea that earthly sweets are mixed with bitterness recurs in the 'Ureisun of ure Louerde':

> nis nan blisse sothes inan thing thet is utewith, thet ne beo to bitter aboht, thet huni ther in beoth liked of thornes . . ."[71]

Here, the author speaks of "outward things", rather than of "earthly things", though clearly they correspond. The heavenly and ideal experience which these texts continually distinguish from the earthly and real represents an intellectual and imaginative process. The opposition between worlds represents a deliberate withdrawal into oneself, and an attempt to satisfy the heart not with real achievements or possessions, but with ideas alone.

In the 'Lofsong of ure louerde', the speaker says that men have "betrayed" her in her dependence upon them for support – "behold, high

---

[69] *Llo*, 71–2: "uor eorthliche luren so muche mislicunge habbe in mine heorte".

[70] *LLo*, 152–6: "Now I understand how true it is what St Augustine says in his book: miserable is the person tied by love to any earthly thing, for each such sweetness is purchased with twofold bitterness." Cf. *HM*, 24/20–2; Augustine, *Confessions*, IV. 6. 11.

[71] *UL*, 29–31: "there is no true bliss in anything that is outward. It is too bitterly bought; and its honey is licked off thorns".

Lord, how I am let down by man's support".[72] Henceforth, she will depend upon Christ, she says, for he has allowed her to be deprived of men's support only so that he can give her his own.[73] This is what Abelard argues Heloise should do, and why he pleads that his love for her was lust not love ("concupiscentia, non amor"): "I slaked my wretched pleasures in you, and this was all that I loved."[74] In the 'Lofsong', the allusion to men's faithlessness is not so specific. The charge evokes not only the cynicism of sexual desire, but also the inevitable disappointments of life on earth – and of marriage in particular.[75] "Betrayal" is a powerful idea by which to express this sense of the world's fickleness. Yet the anchoress's withdrawal is presented as a direct consequence of men's deceit. She seems to have been able to enter a religious life only because she has been failed by those she depended upon. She speaks of herself as being abandoned by the world, rather than abandoning it.[76] Perhaps the "world" referred to here is the marriage-market which determined the destinies of well-born women. By "fulst of monne" the speaker means the patronage of fathers, brothers and husbands necessary to thrive within the marital system. She may have been deprived of this patronage in widowhood; or perhaps she is a spinster sidelined by deformity or dynastic politics. The author recognizes in this passage that events beyond her control may have played a large part her adoption of a religious life, but he tries to present it as a positive decision – "Lord, I believe it and love and shall love you all the more, lord, because of this hardship than ever I should have done before in all my happiness".[77] Perhaps only in the failure of dependence was the anchoress freely able to choose a religious life. This would always have been the best option – "had I done so earlier, things would stand better with me than they do now, that's for sure".[78] Yet, even if this passage is specifically shaped to take into account the anchoress's likely sense of having been marginalized by the marital system, it is so abstract that it remains relevant to women in a wide range of circumstances.

---

[72] *LLo*, 89–90: "bihold heie louerd hu monnes help truketh me".

[73] *LLo*, 103–4: "thu hauest binume me fulst of monne. uor thu wult thin yeouen me".

[74] 2 *Ad Heloisam*, 92/18–9: "miseras in te meas voluptates implebam, et hoc erat totum quod amabam".

[75] Cf. Osbert of Clare, *Ep.* 40, 136/7–9: "Magna differentia est inter caelestes nuptias et terrenas. carnales enim nuptiae a gaudio incipiunt sed in maerore terminantur, a risu inchoant sed in luctu consummantur" ("there's a great difference between heavenly and earthly marriage. Marriage in the flesh begins with joy but ends in lamentation, begins with laughter but finishes with sorrow").

[76] *LLo*, 139–41: "The world haueth for let me & godd haweth underfo me": "the world has abandoned me, and God has received me".

[77] *LLo*, 107–110: "louerd ich ileue hit & luuie & wulle luuien the more louerd thurh this wondred then er in al min weole".

[78] *LLo*, 92–3: "hefdich yare so idon me stode betere then me deth ich hit wot to sothe".

The Virgin Mary has a special place in the Wooing-Group – as model and as mediator. We are told that Christ will do whatever she wants. In the 'Ureisun of God almihti', the poet tells her that Christ is "so much in your power that he wants your will to be done everywhere: to show this he stretched his right arm forth, as he stood upon the cross".[79] She is thus honoured as the woman most able to intercede for women. She is also a model for the ideal of motherhood by which the anchoress's relationship with Christ is so strikingly expressed in the ('Ureisun of ure louerde', 43–4). Most importantly, she authorizes the very presence of women before Christ, both literally and imaginatively, in their sympathetic apprehension of his story. Where she stands near the Cross is the perspective from which the anchoress "sees" the Passion.[80] Her grief, like the love-letters of Christ's side, is another imaginative model for the anchoress's contemplation. As a female role-model, she reassures the anchoress of the dignity of her own relationship to Christ. In the same way, the Wooing-Group uses the *sponsa Christi* motif, not only to define an affective method of contemplation, but also to affirm the privileged status of the woman practising it.

Like the *Ancrene Wisse*, the Wooing-Group employs the scenario of the lady beset with foes who is rescued by a generous suitor. At the end of the 'Wohunge of ure lauerd', the speaker addresses Christ with the words:

> Iesu swete iesu thus tu faht for me ayaines mine sawle fan; thu me derendes with like and makedes of me wrecche thi leofmon and spus. Broht tu haues me fra the world to bur of thi burthe, steked me i chaumbre. I mai ther the swa sweteli kissen and cluppen and of thi luue haue gastli likinge . . .[81]

This passage is permeated with the influence of the Song of Songs, it vibrates also with an immediate sense of relief, security and the comforts of perfect intimacy. "What can I give in return for this?" asks the speaker, and her suggested response, to suffer fastened between four walls as Christ suffered on the Cross, casts her anchoritic experience as a direct participation in the glory of His sacrifice.[82] The effect, once again, is to exalt the status of the anchoress. Just as marriage is the emotional link which binds the bride of Alexis to her husband in his sacrifice, so marriage here is the image for the

---

[79] *UGA*, 144–7: "so abaundune thet he wule thet thine wille oueral beo i uorthed: for to scheawen us this, he streccheth thene ritht erm uorth, ase he stont orode". Cf. *UL*, 118–20.

[80] Cf. Abelard, 2 *Ad Heloisam*, p. 91: "Esto de populo et mulieribus quae plangebant et lamentabantur eum": "Be among the people and the women, grieving and lamenting for him."

[81] *WL*, 568–77: "Jesus, sweet Jesus, thus you fought for me against my soul's foes. You vindicated me with your body, and made of me, a wretch, your lover and your spouse. You have taken me from the world to the bower of your birth; and locked me in your chamber. There can I so sweetly kiss and embrace you and enjoy your love in spirit."

[82] *WL*, 580–90.

emotional relationship which associates the anchoress with Christ's triumphal gesture. The implication is that marriage is such a powerful bond that it provides a channel even for the greatest of spiritual benefits. Recalling the *Ancrene Wisse* almost word for word, the 'Wohunge' concludes by affirming Christ's generosity once again:

> yette yif thet imi luue bede for to selle and sette feor ther upon swa hehe swa ich eauer wile, yette thu wult hit habbe and teken al thet tu haues yiuen, wil tu eke mare . . .[83]

Amid the urgent assertions of the absoluteness of Christ's love, the impression these lines give is that the anchoress herself is "priceless", an impression only little modified by the reminder that all that she is is what God has given her. "If only I love you truly", the speaker concludes, "you will crown me in heaven, to rule beside you for ever and ever."[84] These lines recall the promise made to his lady by Guilhem IX: "All the joys of the world will be ours, if we love each other."[85]

Despite their audience's abandonment of marriage, the *Ancrene Wisse* and the Wooing-Group recognize its value in two ways: both as a symbol of the anchoress's communion with Christ; and as a beautiful ideal, sadly unrealizable on earth, and now placed deliberately out of reach there by her adoption of a religious life. These texts exploit the idea of marriage not only for its connotations of wealth, status, power and security in the world, but also as a model both of the emotional bond between individuals and of a vocation requiring a total sense of duty and commitment. In equating the anchoritic life with courtship, they present it as a process of continual decision, which seems a privilege because the choice available is so attractive. These texts emphasize and exalt the role of the anchoress as a discriminating and responsible individual. In this way, they confirm and reassure her in her calling, without asking her to change radically her perceptions of society, or of the duties of women within it.

4. Wooing: The *Lives* of Juliana, Margaret and Katherine

The three virgin-saints are also wooed, and their suitors promise to fulfil several of the criteria for loving a man listed in the 'Wohunge of ure lauerd'. Margaret's persecutor, Olibrius, promises her dignity and power in marriage: "if you trust in me, you will be my lover and my wedded wife, and

[83] *WL*, 625–31: "No matter how much I ask to sell my love, how ever high a price I wish to set upon it, yet you will have it, and besides all that you've given [already], give even more."

[84] *WL*, 632–4: "yif i the riht luuie, [tu] wilt me crune in heuene with the self to rixlen werld in to werlde".

[85] 'Farai chansoneta . . .', 27–8: quoted in Chapter One.

govern as lady all that I have in the world and everything of which I am lord''.[86] There is nothing dishonourable about this promise, and indeed, it strongly resembles Christ's promise in the Wooing-Group that the anchoress will be crowned his lady and wield power in his realm. It also recalls a phrase used by Chrétien's Enide: she affirms her loyalty to Erec by saying that she was equally his wife and his lover.[87] Olibrius's promise is devalued because it is tied to savage threats, and because it depends upon Margaret's apostasy. The predatory nature of his desire is metaphorically laid bare when he commands that she be stripped before being tortured.[88] Yet Margaret does not dispute Olibrius's sincerity: " 'I believe your promises,' she said.''[89] She challenges neither the value of what he offers nor the likelihood that he will deliver it. Instead, like Christina of Markyate, she argues that she is already irrevocably contracted to Christ. In Margaret's Life, as in Christina's, the vow of chastity is presented as a decisive moment of absolute commitment. When Margaret was fifteen, "she chose him as her love and her lover, and commended to his hands the honour of her maidenhood, her heart and her deeds, and everything that she had in the world to keep and use, and all of herself besides''.[90] The ceremoniousness of these words, reinforced by alliteration, expresses a sense of the indissolubility of the vow. In worldly terms, it is to be interpreted as a betrothal. In that sense, Olibrius's attempt to impose marriage upon Margaret is an infringement, not of her liberty, but of Christ's rights over her. She refuses Olibrius's hand in order to assert not her independence, but her dependence upon the 'husband' of her choice.

Juliana's suitor/persecutor, Eleusius, is initially presented as an attractive and honourable man. He is one of the favourites of the Emperor, Maximian, "of noble descent, ample lands and youthful years''.[91] Seeing Juliana often, he is "wounded by love" for her, and does her the particular honour that "without long discussion he himself went to her father Africanus, rather than sending a messenger, and eagerly begged that he would give her to him; and [promised] that he would honour her with everything he owned as the thing that he loved most in the world''.[92] Though Eleusius's desire soon reveals itself to be a possessive and egotistical obsession and ultimately the pathological motivation for his sadism, at this stage there is nothing

---

[86] *SM*, (ed. MWB), 50/26–8: "yif thu wult leue me, thu schalt beon mi leofmon ant min iweddede wif, ant welden ase lefdi al thet Ich i wald hah ant am of lauerd''.

[87] *Erec et Enide*, 4649–50.

[88] *SM*, 52/6–8; cf. *SJ*, p. 15; *SM*, 564–5.

[89] *SM*, 50/29: " 'Ich ileue the,' quod ha, 'wel of thine beheaste' .''

[90] *SM*, 46/9–12: "ha ches him [Christ] to luue ant to lefmon, ant bitahte in his hond the menske of hire meithhad, hire wil ant hire werc, ant al thet heo eauer i the world i wald hahte, to witen ant to welden with al hireseoluen''.

[91] *SJ*, p. 5: "akennet of heh cun, ant swithe riche of rente, ant yung mon of yeres''.

[92] *SJ*, p. 5: "withute long steuene wes himseolf sonde to Affrican hire feader, ant bisohte him yeorne thet he hire yeue him; ant he hire walde menskin with al thet he mahte as the thing i the world thet he meast luuede''.

intrinsically evil either in his courtship or in the promises he makes in its course.[93] Like the Christ-figure in the *Ancrene Wisse*'s fable of the besieged lady, he does her the honour of being his own messenger, and offers "to make her queen of all he ruled".[94] There, the lady's refusal is presented as a wonder of pride and hard-heartedness: here her determination in rejecting Eleusius's offer of marriage is held up as a model of faith and fortitude. Juliana's role approaches that of the romantic heroine in another way. Just as Félice's rejections of Guy of Warwick were the spur to his achievements in the world, so here the saint becomes the catalyst for the advancement of Eleusius. She attempts "for a while to keep herself from him" by refusing to marry him until he is "the most important man in Rome after Maximian, that is High Sheriff".[95] Maximian, however, promptly grants him this honour, and Juliana reneges on her promise.[96] The incident seems to be designed to remind the audience of its expectations of the role of the romantic heroine as an inspiration to worldly honours, only to defeat them with Juliana's sudden change of attitude.

Like Margaret, Juliana rejects marriage because she is already married to Christ. Recalling the 'Lofsong of ure louerde' (86–7), she prays for guidance in preserving a life of virginity: "praying urgently with sorrowful tears that he would show her how she could preserve her virginity intact from man's transactions".[97] She tells Africanus, her father, "I want him to understand

---

[93] Wogan-Browne argues that the "conventional iconography of feeling in the suitor" is in *Seinte Iuliene* "disturbingly extended" (Price, '*Liflade*', pp. 39–44). While I agree with her that Eleusius's inability to take Juliana's wishes into account shows that he is no true "courtois", I am not wholly convinced that the author's purpose was to "discredit" a "model of desire" (p. 42). Literature often portrays symptoms of love-sickness in extreme ways – often with no other end than melodrama. The romance *Aucassin et Nicolette*, for example, portrays extremes of behaviour in love, not to discredit it (as Clark and Wasserman have argued), but as a whimsical recognition that exactly such extravagance of feeling is essential to love. I would argue that Eleusius's emotional commitment is attractive even at this stage. This makes the transformation of his desire into hatred seem even more sudden and disturbing. See also the discussion of Eleusius's "courtliness" by Elizabeth Robertson, pp. 117–21.

[94] MWB, 114/7–8: "to makien hire cwen of al thet he ahte"; cf. Watson, p. 139.

[95] *SJ*, p. 7: "for te werien hire with him summe hwile . . . under Maximien hehest i Rome, thet is heh reue".

[96] *SJ*, p. 9.

[97] *SJ*, p. 7: "biddinde yeorne with reowfule reames thet he wissede hire o hwuche wise ha mahte witen hire meithhad from monnes man unwemmet". Elizabeth Robertson's argument that the centrality of sexual temptation to all three of the AB-Group's saint's lives "reflects the prevalent view of women as bound by their fundamentally guilty sexual natures" (p. 95) is true to some extent, but her case should be balanced by the fact that each of the saints in question here clearly states and finally realizes her intention to live without sex. Despite the challenge posed to them by their own sexual natures, they ultimately assert their freedom to control their own bodies.

clearly, and you too, that I am plighted to one that I shall remain true to and honestly love, one who is unlike him and all men in the world. And never will I ever deceive or leave him for any weal or wealth, woe or hardship which they cause me.''[98] Like the prior Fredebert questioning Christina, Africanus demands to know the identity of this mysterious "other man": "But what is he, this man you're married to? – this man to whom you've gone so far as to grant your love without my leave, caring little for all those you should love? For I am not aware that I have ever been acquainted with him!"[99] His uncomprehending reponse is either a sarcasm or, as Jocelyn Wogan-Browne puts it, a "hagiographical joke" on him.[100] In either case, as she says, it "effectively highlights the way in which Juliana and her opponents share terms but not meanings".[101]

Seinte Katerine does not begin with a wooing-scene like those of its companion-pieces. It recognizes and challenges the same social ideals in slightly different ways. In *Seinte Iuliene*, the importance of marriage in preserving dynastic continuity is underlined by the "collusion" of the saint's father with her suitor.[102] In *Seinte Katerine*, by contrast, the heroine is a woman of independent means, yet willingly bound by a sense of duty to the administration of her family's possessions and the interests of those dependent upon them:

> Theos meiden wes bathe feaderles ant moderles of hire childhade, ah
> thah ha yunge were, ha heold hire ealdrene hird wisliche ant warliche i
> the eritage ant i the eard thet com hire of burde: nawt forthi thet hire
> thuhte god in hire heorte to habbe monie under hire ant beon icleopet
> leafdi, thet feole telleth wel to, ah ba ha wes offearet of scheome ant of
> sunne yef theo weren todreauet other misferden thet hire forthfeadres
> hefden iuostret; for hire seolf ne kepte ha nawt of the worlde.[103]

[98] *SJ*, p. 13: "ich chulle thet he [Eleusius] wite hit ful wel, ant tu eke mid al, ich am to an iweddet thet ich chulle treowliche to halden ant withute leas luuien, thet is unlich him ant all worltliche men. Ne nulle ich neauer mare him lihen ne leauen for weole ne for wunne, for wa ne for wontreathe they ye me mahen wurchen."

[99] *SJ*, p. 13: "Me hwet is he, thes were thet tu art to iweddet, thet tu hauest withute me se forth thi luue ilenet, thet tu letest lutel of al thet tu schuldest luuien? Ne ich nes neauer thet ich wite yet with him icnawen!" Cf. *LCM*, § 17, p. 62.

[100] Price, 'Liflade', p. 48. Cf. Curtius (*Literature*, p. 428): "Humoristic elements are part of the style of the medieval *vita sancti*. They were present in the material itself, but we may be sure that the public expected them as well."

[101] Price, p. 48.

[102] Price, p. 49.

[103] *SK*, 27–34: "This maiden had been both fatherless and motherless since her childhood, and, although she was young, she governed her parents' servants wisely and carefully in the fiefs and the house which she had inherited – not because she took any pleasure in her heart from having in authority over so many and being called lady, which many value so highly, but because she was afraid that it would be a shame or a sin if everything which her ancestors had fostered was dissipated or abused. For herself, she did not care at all about worldly matters."

The saint's acceptance of the role of feudal *domina* is here presented not as a spiritual weakness, but as an attractively modest recognition of worldly responsibility. Like her colleagues, Katherine is wooed by her persecutor – though, in her case, only once she has already demonstrated her intellectual and spiritual vigour by vanquishing the fifty scholars. In the Latin "Vulgate" version upon which *Seinte Katerine* is based, the Emperor, Maxentius, offers to make Katherine "second to the queen in my palace".[104] He insists, however, that he will not allow their relationship to undermine the marital rights of his wife: "In this one matter, the queen's status will differ from yours: in the royal bed, the woman joined to me in lawful matrimony will not be defrauded; otherwise you will be governor and controller both of imperial policies and of provincial decrees."[105] In the English version, by contrast, the Emperor offers to make Katherine his concubine as well as his counsellor – the *domina* of his realm in all but name:

> O mihti meiden! O witti wummon, wurthmunt ant alle wurthschipe
> wurthe! O schene nebschaft ant schape se swithe semlich, thet schulde
> beo se prudeliche ischrud ant iprud ba with pel and with purpre![106] Nim
> yeme of thi yuhethe, areow thi wlite and tac read, seli meiden, to the
> seoluen. Ga ant gret ure godes the thu igremet hauest, ant tu schalt,
> efter the cwen, eauer the other beon in halle ant i bure, ant al ich
> chulle dihten the deden of mi kinedom efter thet tu demest.[107]

The phrase "in halle ant i bure" recalls the legal tag denoting married cohabitation, "at board and bed" ("mensa et thorus");[108] and it certainly suggests that, even though some of the dignity of the Empress is reserved, Katherine is being offered the right to usurp many of her prerogatives in marriage. The Emperor's disrespect for the bond of marriage undermines the very credibility of his promises. What he offers Katherine is devalued by his unwillingness to honour his commitment to his wife. It is fitting that, having been betrayed by her husband in his offers to Katherine, the Empress becomes one of her converts. Even the honours which Maxentius withholds from Katherine are thus ultimately rejected by her protégée.

---

[104] *Passio Sancte Katerine*, 571, pp. 144–203: "secunda post reginam in palatio meo".

[105] *Passio*, 577–9: "In hoc uno a te distat regina, quod regio thoro, iuncta legali matrimonio, non fraudabitur; ceterum tu imperialibus consiliis, tu prouincialibus edictis, princeps et moderatrix eris."

[106] Cf. Esth. 1:6; 8:15; Prov. 31:22.

[107] *SK*, 528–35; cf. *SM*, 50/5–7: "O virtuous maiden! O wise woman! – worthy of all honour and reverence! Such a bright countenance and such a lovely figure, which should be so proudly adorned, and decorated with costly and purple fabric! Remember your youth; have pity on your own beauty; and accept the advice, blessed maiden, which is in your own interest! Go and hail our gods whom you've offended, and then you'll be second after the queen in public and in private, and I shall manage the business of my kingdom just as you decide."

[108] Parmisano, p. 95; Brundage *Law*, p. 543; Kelly, *LMAC*, p. 111; Stone, pp. 46–7; cf. *O&N*, line 1579.

As if to compensate for the fact that Katherine will not be his queen, he promises to erect in the city a golden image of her as crowned queen ("as cwen icrunet"). This phrase is used throughout the AB-Group to denote the dignity of the *sponsa Christi* in heaven,[109] and its use here is plainly a parody of that spiritual marriage. Katherine replies by asserting the indissolubility of her bond with Christ. In the Latin version, she asserts, "Christ has chosen me as his spouse, and I have committed myself as a bride to Christ by an indissoluble bond."[110] The English author elaborates this metaphor into a striking image of marriage, in which the outward token of the bond, ("the ring") is wholly matched by its inner fulfilment ("the knot"):

> Bihat al thet tu wult, threp threfter inoh, ant threate thet tu beo weri; ne mei me wunne ne weole ne na worldes wurthschipe, ne mei me nowther teone ne tintreohe, turnen from mi leofmones luue thet ich on leue. He haueth iweddet him to mi meithhad with the ring of rihte bileaue, ant ich habbe to him treowliche itake me. Swa wit beoth iuestnet ant iteiet in an, ant swa the cnotte is icnut bituhhen us tweien, thet ne mei hit liste, ne luther ne strengthe nowther, of na liuiende mon lowsin ne leothien.[111]

Katherine's assertion of her previous contract to Christ becomes the occasion for the affirmation of a sense that the outer and inner states of marriage, the social and emotional, are parallel aspects of the same indestructible tie.

It seems odd at first that courtship and marriage can be employed both positively, to illustrate the anchoress's relationship with Christ, and negatively, to illustrate the seductive flatteries of the world. Similarity of terms, as Wogan-Browne points out, does not necessarily preclude difference of meaning. As I suggested above, the idealization of Christ as a suitor is only an extension of the patristic topos in which worldly suitors are scorned. Yet, it seems to me that the audience would have been expected to enjoy the vicarious experience of being wooed as much in the saints' lives as in the *Ancrene Wisse* and the Wooing-Group – even if the glorious promises are made not by the finest of all suitors, but by men soon to become cruel torturers. All three of the virgin-saints recognize that their suitors' promises are flattery, but these promises still illustrate some of the

---

[109] For example, *SK*, 585, 782, 890, 913; *HM*, 6/8. It is a conventional feature of writing on virginity: cf. e.g., Osbert of Clare, *Ep.* 40, 135/20; Bernard of Clairvaux, *Ep.* 113, p. 288, lines 25–6.

[110] *Passio Sancte Katerine*, 625–6: "Christus me sibi sponsam adoptauit, ego me Christo sponsam indissociabili federe coaptaui".

[111] *SK*, 549–557: "You can promise all you like, and nag on afterwards, and make threats until you're weary; but never will either wealth, fortune or worldly honour, either anger or torment, turn me away from loving the dear one that I believe in. He has pledged himself to my maidenhood with the ring of true faith, and I have faithfully committed myself to him. Thus we are bound and fastened in one mind, and thus the knot is tied between us two, so that it can never be loosened or untied by a mortal man either by malice or by force."

ways in which the world can seem sweet – a sweetness which the AB-texts always recognize, even while they emphasize that it is treacherous and short-lived. Whether the idea of courtship functions as an index of Christ's love or of the seductiveness of the world, it makes the same statement about the nature of the anchoress's spiritual role, her rights and responsibilities.

Just as the idea of Christ's courtship is an affirmation of the individual dignity and value of the individual woman, so even the solicitude of evil men suggests that the female reader or auditor who identifies with the virgin-saint has a special destiny and a special place in the universe. The privilege suggested by the wooing-promises is that of having a choice, not the possession of what is chosen. The tyrannical suitors of the saints' lives are also vivid examples of the other men implied as competitors to Christ in the 'Wohunge of ure lauerde'; and they provide opportunities of stating in a similar way the pre-eminence of Christ as a claimant upon the lady's soul. The suits of Olibrius, Eleusius and Maxentius are direct challenges to Christ's, and they allow the virgin-saints to demonstrate in practice the imaginary process of discrimination outlined in the 'Wohunge of ure lauerde'. St Margaret uses her rejection of Olibrius as an opportunity to assert the superiority of Christ in loyalty, wisdom, power and beauty:

> Ant unwurth, thet wite thu, me beoth thine wordes; for him ane Ich luuie ant habbe to bileue the weld ant wisseth with his wit windes and wederes, ant al thet biset is with se ant with sunne. Buuen ba ant bineothen, al buheth to him ant beieth. Ant to-eke this, thet he is se mihti ant se meinful, he is leoflukest lif for to lokin upon ant swotest to smellen; ne his swote sauour ne his almihti mihte ne his makelese lufsumlec neuer mare he mei lutli ne aliggen, for he ne alith neuer, ah liueth a in are, ant al thet in him lith lesteth a mare.[112]

Although its hyperbole gives this passage an unworldly feel, the actual criteria on which Christ is judged superior are curiously physical and worldly. As in the Wooing-Group, what lies behind this image of the heavenly bridegroom, is an image of the ideal husband within the world. In order to convince the maidens of their desirability as suitors, Olibrius and Eleusius in particular try to present themselves as images of this ideal, even though we know that they cannot fulfil it. Indeed, the persecutors soon

---

[112] *SM*, 50/15–22: "Your words are worthless to me, be sure of that. For the only one I love and trust is the one who in his wisdom rules and controls the winds and storms, and everything embraced by the sea and the sun. Both above and below, everything bows to him and does him homage. And as well as being so mighty and so powerful, he is the most lovely creature to look upon and the sweetest to smell. Never can his sweet fragrance or his almighty strength or his matchless beauty ever diminish or fail, for he never dies, but lives forever in glory, and everything that is part of him will last forever."

identify themselves with the predatory circle of foes, like ravening wolves ("o wude wulues wise"), alluded to in the 'Wohunge of ure lauerd'.[113]

Whoever the suitors, the image of courtship represents in a striking way the anchoress's spiritual prerogatives. She is not asked to submit herself to a sense of fatalism or rapture, nor to blur in mysticism the boundaries of her own individuality, but, rather, to remain fully aware of her own capacity of choice. The promises of the earthly and heavenly suitors represent the responsibility to choose between different ideals, which is of the essence in establishing any sense of vocation.[114] The analogy depends on the idea that, whether the decision is the acceptance of the suitor or the continued practice of an anchoritic lifestyle, an equivalent sense of absolute personal commitment is required – a concept for which, in terms of marriage, the canon lawyers used the word *consensus*. The saints' lives distinctly suggest that the persecutors demonstrate their inhumanity by setting their own desires before the maidens' right to exercise a choice. We are told, for example, that Juliana's father gave her to Eleusius "even though it was against her will", a phrase which subtly implies the baseness of the transaction.[115] Maxentius's offers are devalued, in the English version, by the casual way in which he treats his wife. These female saints suffer torture in order to preserve, not only their physical and spiritual integrity, but also their emotional integrity. Their struggle for the liberty to make their own marital choices is a process parallel to the trials suffered by the protagonists of romance; and exactly as in romance, the audience is expected to feel that the obstruction of an individual's free will in love is a crime against the dignity of mankind.[116]

The virgin-saints are projections of the anchoress's own spiritual persona, but they are also exemplary and even iconic figures. In their superhuman courage and indeflectible resolution they personify the spiritual grandeur to which the anchoress aspires. Just as the Wooing-Group and the *Ancrene Wisse* attempt to assure her of the dignity of her calling by imaginatively crowning her Queen of Heaven, so the saints' lives project her experience of temptation and trial into an arena where she (or at least, her representatives) cannot fail.

---

[113] *WL*, 290, 383: "like ravening wolves". Maxentius is described as "wed wulf" (678) and as "awariede wulf" (741); Margaret addresses Olibrius as "heathene hund" (54/5; cf. 56/4) and "luthere liun" (54/9); Eleusius becomes "wod ut of his witte" (Royal, line 216, p. 26).

[114] Wogan-Browne has drawn attention to the richly resonant way in which the word "lahe" is used in the Life of St Juliana (Price, '*Liflade*', pp. 49–50). She suggests that for the author law denotes "areas of moral choice": "The notion of a binding and defining consuetudinal, ethical or religious system is, in the *Liflade*, inseparable from the notion of an individual's movement into or out of it." In a similar way, St Jerome (*Ep.* 22. 5, p. 62) speaks of the process of moral choice in terms of a conflict between the "law" of the body ("lex . . . in membris") with the "law" of the will ("lex mentis"), and the possibility of enslavement by the "law" of sin ("lex peccati").

[115] *SJ*, p. 7: "thah hit hire unwil were".

[116] For example, *Aucassin et Nicolette*; *Floris et Blauncheflur*.

These female saints are strident to the point of being brutal.[117] This is because they exude a confidence in their own spiritual invulnerability which the anchoress is implicitly urged to share.[118] They live out the rhetorical topos of glorying in the rejection of worldly husbands, wealth and power. In doing so they triumphantly enact a process of resistance to worldly desires, which for the anchoress in her cell must have been a continual and difficult fight. Just as the product of St Alexis's struggle is the "charter" of his life, so these lives of female saints become talismans in the anchoress's attempt to overcome the glamour of the world:

> Ich iseh hwer ha feaht with the ferliche feond, ant hire bonen that ha bed wrat o boc-felle, ant hire liflade al lette don o leaue, ant sende hit sothliche iwriten wide yont te worlde. . . . Alle theo the this iherd heorteliche habbeth, in ower beoden blitheluker munneth this meiden, thet ha with the ilke bone thet ha bed on eorthe bidde yet for ow i the blisse of heouene . . .[119]

5. Virginity and Marriage: *Hali Meithhad*

In Part VII of the *Ancrene Wisse*, the Wooing-Group, and the saints' lives, marriage is only ever presented as a token of honour. It stands both for the superficial and transient dignity of women's lives in the world, and for the profound and everlasting dignity of spiritual intimacy with Christ. Only in *Hali Meithhad* does marriage ever become less than a flattering ideal. Here an uncompromisingly critical view of earthly marriage as an obscene and humiliating drudgery balances both the author's awareness of the ways in which it might seem attractive to young women and his idealization of the virgin's experience as Christ's bride. It could be said that *Hali Meithhad* is less directly concerned with "virginity" ("meithhad") than with the contrast between these different perspectives upon marriage.[120] The author clearly feels that he can best advocate virginity to women only by taking into account the pattern of life which poses the most serious challenge to it. To do this, he

---

[117] Cf. Bugge, p. 101, 123; Wilson, p. 118. In *SM*, the author speaks of martyrs, both men and women, who "as icudde kempen, ouercomen ant akeasten hare threo cunne uan" (44/4–5). Osbert of Clare even addresses the nun, Ida, as "splendida et clara virgo, immo de viro Christo virilis et incorrupta virago" (*Ep.* 40, 136/4–5).

[118] For the iconographical currency of the *mulier fortis*, see Emerson Brown.

[119] *SM*, 82/30–2, 84/3–5: "I saw where she fought the dreadful fiend, and wrote down upon parchment the prayers which she spoke; I had her whole life set down in a book, and sent it correctly copied throughout the wide world . . . All those who have listened to this and taken it to heart, remember this maiden the more cheerfully in your prayers, so that with the same prayer she once prayed on earth, she will still pray for you in the bliss of heaven." Margaret's own prayer is then quoted (84/6–13).

[120] Even the prayer with which the work ends (42/19–26) speaks in terms of happiness in marriage – in this case, the heavenly marriage.

145

draws polarized images of marriage. Its 'best' aspects are symbolically absorbed into the model of virginity through the imagery of the heavenly marriage; and its 'worst' are absolutely dissociated from the idealized tranquillity of a life of chastity.

The coordination of these multiple perspectives demands clarity of thought and breadth of imagination. *Hali Meithhad* has both to a remarkable degree. It is often criticized, however, for the harshness of its attitude towards marriage and sexuality. George Sampson, for example, has said that it presents "ideals of chastity with a crudeness likely to provoke hostility in the modern reader".[121] Alfred Baugh has suggested that its "vehemence and strong conviction make up for the absence of any logical plan"; and that its "uncompromising attitude" makes it a lesser text than the *Ancrene Wisse*.[122] *Hali Meithhad*'s orthodoxy has been doubted by John Bugge. He describes it as "grossly encratistic"; and "rather more reminiscent of Tatian than even Jerome". He explains what appears to be its "crabbed and mordant spirit" as a late survival of the Gnostic strain in Christian thought.[123] More forcefully still, Basil Cottle has described it as "a strident mockery of God's arrangements for continuing human-kind".[124] Even partisans of the AB-Group like S.R.T.O. d'Ardenne and E.J. Dobson have tended to diminish its spirituality.[125] The implication seems to be that *Hali Meithhad* is narrow-minded and mean-spirited – the work of a fanatic, isolated by his learning and preoccupations from the sensibility of the women he addressed.

There are a number of ways of refuting such a suggestion. Nicholas Watson has argued that the text is "an exercise written for those who have already repudiated sexual activity and family ties, intended to confirm them in a sense of the rightness of their action, and to fortify them for the future. Its extremism is deliberate and strategic . . . It was not intended to be seen by anyone who was not already in agreement with its premises and who was not vowed to celibacy and committed to solitude."[126] It is quite possible, as Watson suggests, that many of those addressed by the author already shared his convictions, but the charge of extremism is hardly answered by the argument that the message was preached to the converted. As Millett and Wogan-Browne point out, *Hali Meithhad* would have been suitable not only to those already leading a life of virginity, but also to those "facing the choice of marrying or consecrating themselves to Christ, since, "in so far as it presents

---

[121] Sampson, p. 31.

[122] Baugh, *Middle Ages*, p. 125. Far from lacking "any logical plan", *Hali Meithhad* reveals a distinct quadripartite structure (MWB, p. xviii).

[123] Bugge, pp. 111, 115.

[124] Cottle, p. 137.

[125] d'Ardenne, *SJ*, p. xlvi: "It has little elevation or spirituality"; cf. Dobson, *Origins*, pp. 155–6.

[126] Watson, pp. 138–9; cf. Elizabeth Robertson, p. 77.

the meaning of virginity as an ideal, it can be received by a variety of audiences''.[127]

Bella Millett has also emphasized the extent of *Hali Meithhad*'s debt to previous literature. "Almost everything in it," she says, "has a direct source or at least a precedent in earlier and contemporary Latin writings.''[128] Answering Bugge's charge of heterodoxy, she argues that "the author's theological position seems to have been within the limits of contemporary Christian orthodoxy", explaining "the occasional inconsistencies in *Hali Meithhad*" as "the result of its author's rhetorical overstatement of an essentially orthodox position''.[129] Yet, whether or not the author's thinking was essentially orthodox, and whether or not the perversity of rhetorical caricature can be adduced as an excuse, these "occasional inconsistencies" certainly do seem to overstep the boundaries of legitimate Christian feeling. *Hali Meithhad*'s sometimes hysterical denunciations of marriage and sexuality undoubtedly reveal more than the author's rhetorical intransigence. It is tempting to a modern reader to interpret his obsession with the grotesque aspects of marriage and sexuality as a neurosis. Yet it seems to me that, not only does *Hali Meithhad* reflect a genuine sense of the way in which married life can be a disillusionment, but also that it must have struck a chord with the women it addressed. Rather than simply parroting the well-worn theme of *contemptus mundi*, the author attempts to tap its wellsprings with an appeal to the personal disappointments of every individual in his audience. These disappointments need not have been marital ones, for the woes of marriage are here only an imaginative paradigm of all the world's miseries. The author's extremism may be justified as an evocation of the bitterness of human experience, tailored for the use of women by its orientation to marriage. The purpose of the treatise is the substitution for worldly ambitions of an ideal of peace – within walls and within hearts.

The quotation with which *Hali Meithhad* begins, "Listen, my daughter, and look, and incline your ear; and forget your people and your father's house" ("Audi, filia, et uide, et inclina aurem tuam; et obliuiscere populum tuum et domum patris tui''), is drawn from the epithalamic Psalm 45, and it was originally a statement of the bride's exclusive responsibility to her new husband's family. Jerome used it at the beginning of his 22nd Letter, *Ad Eustochium*, in order to stress the absoluteness of the virgin's responsibility to her vocation: "After grasping the plough it is not right to look back or to return home; nor after wearing Christ's tunic is it right to descend from the roof to pick up another garment.''[130] The immediate source for the author of

---

[127] MWB, p. xx.

[128] MWB, p. xv; Millett, *HM*, pp. xlv–lii.

[129] Millett, pp. xxx, xxxiii.

[130] Jerome, *Ep*. 22, p. 54: "Non expedit adprehenso aratro respicere post tergum nec de agro reverti domum nec post Christi tunicam ad tollendum aliud vestimentum tecta descendere''.

Hali Meithhad was Alan of Lille's *Summa de arte praedicatoria*, whose allegorical interpretation he adopts in identifying the bride's "populum" with "the accumulation of lustful thoughts within you" ("the gederunge inwith the of fleschliche thonkes") and with "Babylon's people, the army of the Devil of Hell" ("Babilones folc, the deofles here of helle").[131] This use of a statement about marital commitment as an opportunity to identify parental concern for their daughter's marriage with the interests of lust and the Devil is indeed highly disturbing, but the responsiblity for this transformation lies not with our author but with Jerome and Alan. The English author shows in the way he develops this rhetorical strategy that he was also thinking of marriage in quite literal terms. He imagines that the young woman's family, as he puts it, "eggs you on to marriage and a husband's embrace, telling you how delightful it is, what ease and splendour is enjoyed by married ladies, and how much good may come about through your children".[132] These hypothetical advocates of marriage have the same unthinking confidence in the world as the fathers of the saints Alexis and Juliana. The author's reproach is that they give no warning of the troubles that inevitably lie ahead: they hide "all that bitter torment that lurks underneath [these promises], and all the great loss which arises [from them]".[133] The allegorical reading he borrows from Alan is balanced by a sense of the tragedy of disappointment in marriage, which he makes universally representative of women's experiences in the world.

The high tower of Jerusalem, "Syon", is introduced as an image of the eminence of virginity with respect to the lives of married women or widows, but it also has a deeper resonance as a metaphor of the serenity of heavenly freedom. The author's strategy is to trade on the virgin's self-respect, comparing the "high" state of her inner confidence and security with the "low" state of the woman who lives among outward things. The heavenly marriage stands for a state of spiritual self-sufficiency. It makes a sanctuary of the woman's own individuality. As the Bride of Christ, she is loved and cared for, unchallengeable in dignity, and in command of her own destiny, while in the world, she can neither guarantee her fate nor escape dependence upon a man who may not respect her as an individual. As the author puts it, the woman dedicated to God is:

> Godes spuse, Iesu Cristes brude, the Lauerdes leofmon thet alle thinges
> buheth, of al the worlt leafdi, as he is of al lauerd; ilich him in halschipe,
> vnwemmet as he is, ant thet eadi meiden his deorrewurthe moder; ilich

---

[131] *HM*, 2/15-16, 24. Alan of Lille, *Summa de arte praedicatoria*, cap. 47, PL 210. 195; see Millett, *HM*, n. to 1/1-2.

[132] *HM*, 2/17-20: "eggith the to brudlac ant to weres cluppunge, ant makieth the to thenchen hwuch delit were thrin, hwuch eise i the richedom thet theos leafdis habbeth, hu muche god mahte of inker streon awakenin".

[133] *HM*, 2/21-2: "al thet bittre bale thet ter lith under, ant al thet muchele lure thet terof ariseth".

his hali engles ant his heste halhen; se freo of hireseoluen thet ha nawiht ne thearf of other thing thenchen bute ane of hire leofmon with treowe luue cwemen, for he wule carie for hire thet ha haueth itake to of al thet hire bihoueth, hwil ha riht luueth him with sothe bileaue.[134]

The author stresses the woman's independence – she is "se freo of hireseoluen". Her relationship to Christ is no more restrictive a bond than it would be in a honeymoon. By contrast, earthly marriage is portrayed exclusively in its mundane troubles and annoyances. A woman in the world "commits herself to drudgery, to caring for the house and the servants, and to so many trials; to looking after so many things; to suffering irritation and annoyance, and sometimes shame; and to enduring so many miseries for such feeble wages as the world always pays in the end".[135]

In keeping with this definition of virginity as a psychological state rather than merely a promise of heavenly honour, the author insists that its rewards can also be realized in this world:

Ne mei na thing wonti the the berest him thet al wealt inwith i thi breoste. Ant swuche swettnesse thu schalt ifinden in his luue ant in his seruise, ant habbe se muche murhthe throf ant licunge i thin heorte, thet tu naldest changin thet stat thet tu liuest in for te beo cwen icrunet. . . . This ure Lauerd yeueth ham her as on earnesse of the eche mede thet schal cume threfter. Thus habbeth Godes freond al the frut of this worlt thet ha forsaken habbeth, o wunderliche wise, ant heouene ed ten ende.[136]

This use of the image of the "cwen icrunet" is oddly reminiscent of Heloise's willingness not to be an Empress ("imperatrix") as long as she can be Abelard's whore ("meretrix").[137] This is because it is not only an allusion to the *sponsa Christi*, but also, as for Heloise, a hyperbole of self-respect. The social eminence of royalty in both cases represents the privilege of an inviolate individuality. In the same passage, the phrase "ed ten ende"

[134] *HM*, 4/13–19: "God's spouse, Jesus Christ's bride, the lover of the Lord to whom all things do homage, lady of all the world, as he is lord of it all; [she is] like him in integrity, spotless as he is, and that blessed virgin his dear mother; [she is] like his holy angels and his highest saints; so at liberty with herself that she need not think of anything except pleasing her lover with true love, for the one she has chosen will provide for all her needs, as long as she loves him properly with true faith."

[135] *HM* 4/28–32: "deth hire into drecchunge, to dihten hus ant hinen, ant to se monie earmthen, to carien for se feole thing, teonen tholien ant gromen, ant scheomen umbe stunde, drehen se moni wa for se wac hure as the worlt foryelt eauer ed ten ende".

[136] *HM*, 6/4–8; 6/13–6: "You can feel no want when you bear the ruler of all within your breast. And such sweetness will you find in his love and in his service, and so much joy in it and pleasure in your heart, that you would not change the state in which you live to be a crowned queen. . . . This Our Lord gives them here, as a pledge of the eternal reward which comes afterwards. Thus, in a marvellous way, God's friends enjoy all the fruit of the world they've forsaken and heaven in the end."

[137] 1 *Ad Abaelardum*, 71/10–14.

stresses the parallelism between the duplication of ills in earthly marriage (all that trouble, and then so poor a reward) and the duplication of joys in the divine equivalent (spiritual integrity in this life, and then boundless glory in the next). Yet this is something of a rhetorical chicane. The "pleasure and sweetness" of mortal devotion to Christ is entirely dependent upon an imaginative anticipation of the immortal relationship to come. As the author says, the virtue of virginity is "the only one in this mortal life that prefigures the state of immortal bliss in that blessed land where bride does not take groom, nor groom bride; in her lifestyle here it teaches her the lifestyle of heaven; and in this world that is called the 'land of unlikeness' preserves her nature in likeness of heavenly nature, even though it is exiled from there and in a body of clay".[138] Thus, though *Hali Meithhad* stresses that virginity is immediately rewarded in the world, it makes this reward conditional upon an imaginative commitment to a distant image of marriage in heaven.

In order to coordinate these opposite senses of marriage, both as an earthly drama inevitably ending in disappointment, and as an inspirational heavenly ideal, the author resorts to a scale of values based on the traditional distinction between the three estates of female experience – marriage, widowhood and virginity. These three estates were conventionally associated with the three rates of return in the parable of the sower (Mt. 13:3-23) – respectively, thirty-, sixty- and a hundredfold.[139] The woman who marries in the world is seen as clinging, almost desperately, to a kind of spiritual respectability. She is on the lowest rung of virtue, and beneath her stretches the abyss (20/26-8). *Hali Meithhad* implicitly evokes the struggle of a well-born woman who marries beneath her to sustain the minimum social standards of her nobility in the more constrained circumstances of her adopted household. Indeed, the author states clearly that in his society, as in the French aristocracy analysed by Georges Duby, it was normal for women to marry downwards in rank.[140] In this way the author dramatizes his message that worldly marriage is only just within the pale. The right of salvation is implicitly compared to the privilege of blood. The virgin, by

---

[138] *HM*, 10/25-30: "thet an thet i this deadliche lif schaweth in hire an estat of the blisse undeadlich i thet eadi lond as brude ne nimeth gume ne brudgume brude; ant teacheth her on eorthe in hire liflade the liflade of heouene; ant i this worlt thet is icleopet 'lond of unlicnesse' edhalt hire burde in licnesse of heouenlich cunde, thah ha beo utlahe throf ant i licome of lam". Cf. Mt. 22:30; Luke 20:34-6; Mark 12:25; "land of unlikeness" is a Neoplatonic phrase, reaching *Hali Meithhad* through St Bernard of Clairvaux (*Sermo 27 in Cantica*, PL 183. 916, § 6): see Millett, p. 32; Courcelle.

[139] For example, *Speculum Virginum*, VII (pp. 190-220). Bloomfield, '*Piers Plowman*', pp. 230-1; Millett, *HM*, pp. xxxviii-xxxix; Bugge, pp. 67-9; Brown, *Body*, p. 359; for *ad status* sermons, d'Avray and Tausche. The doctrine of the three estates is conventionally outlined at *HM*, 20/17-29.

[140] *HM*, 8/2-5; Duby, *Knight*, p. 221. It is also possible that virginity was implicitly seen as an attribute of rank: Jeay has observed that, in the later Middle Ages, pre-marital virginity validated a bride's social status (pp. 333b-334a).

contrast, is seen as having married so well that, as long as she stays loyal to her new house – as long as she forgets "her people and the house of her father" – she need never fear for the debasement of her nobility.

It is against the background of this appeal to the woman's self-respect, both as an individual and as a lady of rank, that his description of married people as "beasts of burden" ("eaueres", 12/4–7) should be considered. It was conventional to identify such animals with the lecherous;[141] but here it represents not so much the "grind" of sexual desire as the means of its containment, marriage. With this comparison the author suggests that earthly marriage is a shared humiliation and a back-breaking trial. Once again it is presented as a submission to indignity an unworthy of the woman addressed:

> Lo nu, hu this vntheaw ne eueneth the . . . to witlese beastes, dumbe ant broke-rugget, ibuhe towart eorthe – thu thet art i wit iwraht to Godes ilicnesse, ant iriht ba bodi up ant heaued towart heouene, forthi thet tu schuldest thin heorte heouen thiderwart as thin eritage is, ant eorthe forhohien . . .[142]

The word "eritage" here represents not only the woman's sense of her own nobility both within society and as Christ's bride, but also her intellectual heritage, the human privilege of reason. To enslave oneself to sexuality is to forgo the definitive human capacity of "discrimination . . . both of good and evil, proper and improper".[143] It is in keeping with this emphasis upon the rights and duties of reason that *Hali Meithhad* sets such a high premium upon a woman's own ability to discriminate between worldly and heavenly ideals. In this, it stands apart from the rest of the *de virginitate* tradition. While other texts tend to view virginity "from outside" – by comparing remote images of feminine purity with grotesque caricatures of the physical effects of pregnancy and age – *Hali Meithhad* sees the issue "from inside", as a matter for every woman to decide for herself.

It is in the centrepiece of the work – its systematic critique of the state of marriage in the world – that the fundamental differences between *Hali Meithhad* and its intellectual inheritances can be most clearly demonstrated.[144] The troubles of marriage are a commonplace of Christian teaching on female virginity – the inevitable legacy of women as the lesser and tainted sex.[145] The

---

[141] d'Avray and Tausche, p. 82.

[142] *HM*, 22/22–27: "Now look how this vice reduces you to the level of insentient animals, dumb and hunchbacked, bowing down towards the earth – you who are created to be rational in the likeness of God, and erect with body and head towards heaven, so that you should turn your heart towards heaven where your heritage is, and scorn the earth."

[143] *HM*, 22/16–17: "tweire schad . . . ba of god ant of vuel, of kumelich ant vnkumelich".

[144] That is, *HM*, 20/30–36/19.

[145] Hansen, 'Molestiae nuptiarum'; Millett, *HM*, p. xxxiv; Owst, pp. 379–80.

author's citation of St Paul's description of the "tribulaciones carnis" (I Cor. 7:28) is itself borrowed from Hildebert of Lavardin.[146] However, the motif of the "tribulaciones carnis" ran two separate courses throughout antiquity and the early Middle Ages.[147] One strand was implicitly masculine and misogynist, and oriented towards a philosphical ideal of intellectual self-fulfilment.[148] The other was closely tied to the *de virginitate* tradition. It presented the "tribulaciones" as the punishment for femininity itself, a punishment which the female individual could only escape by wonderfully surpassing, in the discipline of virginity, the moral and intellectual frailty of her sex.[149]

Medieval authors found the blueprints for both strands of anti-matrimonialism in the works of St Jerome. His 22nd Letter, *Ad Eustochium*, was an influential model for the *de virginitate* tradition, while his treatise, *Adversus Jovinianum*, was a cornerstone of misogynistic writing in the Middle Ages.[150] It is striking that, while *Ad Eustochium* is a product of Jerome's intimate relationship with his circle of admiring Roman noblewomen, the *Adversus Jovinianum* to some extent depends on the neurotic belief that men's minds and morals may be insidiously corrupted by contact with women.[151] As David Wiesen has said, "inconsistency is characteristic of Jerome"; and he was not "an honest debater".[152] Nevertheless, medieval authors did not seek to resolve his contradictions. Peter of Blois, for example, practised both forms of anti-matrimonial rhetoric.[153] In his *Liber Decem Capitulorum*, III and IV, Marbod of Rennes followed a hysterical denunciation of women's capacity for evil with a eulogy of their usefulness to men. Andreas's *De amore* follows the Ovidian pattern of two books on the arts of seduction and the conservation of love, followed by a third palinodally condemning the exercise of desire and the immorality of women.

The practice of balancing positive with negative images of women in different literary modes persisted throughout the Middle Ages.[154] Yet neither

---

[146] *HM*, 32/26–8; cf. Hildebert of Lavardin, *Ep.* 1. 21, PL 171. 195.

[147] Cf. Leclercq, *Women*, p. 156.

[148] Delhaye, 'Dossier'; Foucault, *Care*, pp. 39–68.

[149] For example, Peter of Blois (*Ep.* 55): "Filiae hujus saeculi filiae Babylonis, quae de carnis immunditia sibi destinant successores, in peccato concipiunt, in dolore pariunt, in timore nutriunt, de viventibus semper sollicitae sunt, de morientibus inconsolabiliter affliguntur." ("The daughters of this world are the daughters of Babylon. By means of the filth of the flesh they appoint their successors, conceiving in sin, giving birth in pain, and bringing up their children in fear. They are constantly worried about the surviving ones: and the dead cause them inconsolable grief.") Peter then goes on to a grotesque evocation of the pains of childbirth.

[150] Mann, *Geoffrey Chaucer*, p. 55: see Schmitt; Delhaye, 'Dossier'.

[151] Wiesen, p. 159; Brown, p. 377.

[152] Wiesen, pp. 149–50.

[153] *Ep.* 79 is a plagiaristic and misogynistic letter; *Epp.* 35, 36, 55, 234 are exhortations to virginity.

[154] Mann, *Geoffrey Chaucer*, pp. 1–3, 49–50.

the eulogy of the virgin nor the satire of the wife affords women any sympathetic perspective from which to view their own femininity. The men who wrote about female virginity evoked images of woman beyond sexuality not so much in order to provide a programme for the women they addressed, as to affirm their own desire for purity; and the men who exalted the philosophical ideal of intellectual self-sufficiency excluded women from their ideal world because they saw them as a distraction and a threat. As Howard Bloch has stressed, it is the very essentialization of Woman, whether in negative or positive terms, which most effectively disempowers women.[155] By limiting women to these polar categories, these masculine discourses denied them the dignity of individuality.

By contrast, *Hali Meithhad*'s analysis of the disadvantages of marriage for women depends upon the conflation of these two traditions. It presents the issue not as a woman's choice between two polarized and unrealistic images of herself – angel or whore – but rather, as a rational process designed to safeguard her own intellectual and spiritual well-being. This method and its aims reflect the "philosophical" tradition of antimatrimonialism, which had previously only served men. As Bugge observes, "it is interesting that arguments once employed as negative evidence over the question 'utrum vir sapiens uxorem ducat' appear in the twelfth-century *Hali Meidenhad* in support of the liberated woman".[156] The author of *Hali Meithhad* appeals directly to the discretion of women as intelligent individuals. His rhetorical method is governed by a sense that a woman's resolution to virginity is more valuable if she really believes that it is the best option for her to take, both for practical and personal reasons, as well as in order to fulfil a doctrinal ideal. Hence he sees a woman's abandonment of chastity as a double guilt ("o twa half", 30/26). She sins not only against God, but against herself. Though the author's opposition to marriage is certainly trenchant, and at times grotesque (e.g. 20/33–22/8), it is should be seen as the expression of his desire for thoroughness in leaving no argument in its favour unrefuted. He never presents his audience's acceptance of his argument as a foregone conclusion. His respect for the process of choice may be seen in the way this central section of the treatise is structured almost as a debate:

> "Nai," thu wilt seggen, "for thet fulthe nis hit nawt; ah monnes elne is muche wurth, ant me bihoueth his help to fluttunge ant te fode. Of wif ant weres gederunge worldes weole awakeneth, ant streon of feire children the gleadieth muchel the ealdren."[157]

---

[155] Bloch, *Medieval Misogyny*, p. 6.

[156] Bugge, p. 88.

[157] *HM*, 22/33–24/1: " 'No,' you'll say, 'that indecency isn't worth considering; but a man's support is very valuable, and I need his help for provisions and food. From the union of a man and a woman springs worldly fortune, and the generation of fine children to delight their parents.' "

He recognizes the sense of the practical, family and personal considerations which motivate young women to marry. These structure his criticisms of marriage – "Thu seist", "Thus speke thruppe", "Ant hwet yef . . .?" Indeed, it is only by a sympathetic recognition of the possible reasons for desiring marriage that he can achieve his stated aims. He imagines that society predisposes young women towards marriage, and his treatise is intended to redress this by challenging his charges' expectations about marriage:

> for nu Ich habbe ihalden min biheaste thruppe, thet Ich walde schawin
> with falschipe ismethet thet te moni an seith – ant thuncheth thet hit soth
> beo – of the selhthe ant te sy thet te iweddede habbeth; thet hit ne feareth
> nawt swa as weneth thet sith utewith, ah feareth al otherweis, of poure
> ba ant riche, of lathe ant ec of leouie, thet te weane ihwer passeth the
> wunne, ant te lure oueral the biyete.[158]

This dialogic structure enables the author to demonstrate an attractive breadth of understanding.[159] On this account, his advocation of virginity seems less like a programme for the confinement of the spiritually weaker sex, than a disinterested, philosophical discussion of a generally familiar human experience. It lays claim, in other words, to a respect for argument far more characteristic of the 'masculine' academic *dissuasio* than of the 'feminine' exhortation to virginity. This section of *Hali Meithhad* is very reminiscent, for example, of the passage devoted to marriage in Hugh of St Victor's *De vanitate mundi*. This work is a dialogue between two abstract figures, D[ocens] and I[nterrogens]. As in *Hali Meithhad*, the teacher has to address an idealistic view of marriage:

> Magna laetitia ibi est, magnus ornatus, et apparatus multus, et (ut quod
> mihi videtur non taceam) hoc opus idcirco caeteris operibus hominum
> beatius judico, quoniam ipsum praecipue est, quod per dilectionis
> vinculum pacem et concordiam parit animorum. Hoc societatem
> commendat, amorem sanctificat, amicitiam servat. Hinc fructus prolis
> oritur, hinc generis nostri propago dilatatur, hinc mortis dirae necessitas
> resistitur, et damna patrum in filiis reparantur.[160]

---

[158] *HM*, 34/15-21: "for now I have kept my promise above that I would show that what many people say to you – and themselves believe true – about the happiness and prosperity of married people is glossed over with falsehood; that all does not go on as might appear to an outward observer, but in fact completely differently; that, for both rich and poor, in hatred and in love, everywhere the misery exceeds the joy, and the loss exceeds the profit".

[159] The *Speculum Virginum* is also a dialogue, but there is no sense of any tension between the positions of the two speakers. The female speaker asks questions of her teacher: she does not support a point of view.

[160] Hugh of St Victor, PL 176. 708: "[In marriage] is great joy, honour, and magnificence, and (this I feel I have to say) it on this account I regard it as more blessed than any of the other works of mankind, since it is the particular means by

To this Docens replies that marriage is a matter for grief rather than laughter ("certe in nuptiis magis flendum quam ridendum"). His distinction recalls the AB-author's apology for mentioning "silly things" ("vnwurthliche thinges") – "Though it might seem ridiculous, . . . those who try it don't think it so."[161] As in *Hali Meithhad*, Docens refers to the difficulties of parenthood:

> quis dicere potest, nisi qui expertus est, quantus labor, quanta molestia sit infantes excipere, et praeter caeteras miserias, quae magis tacendae sunt, lactare, educare, nutrire, pueros instruere, disciplina pariter et scientia informare, et ad legitimum usque aetatem perducere?[162]

Though the author of *Hali Meithhad* mirrors Hugh in his use of a dialectical structure, his deployment of the ancient Christian and classical motif of the troubles of marriage far surpasses any of his models in sympathy and force of imagination.[163]

Hali Meithhad's critique of marriage transforms the traditional "list of trivial bourgeois inconveniences" into a portrait of a lifestyle entailing a comprehensive erosion of spirit and self-respect.[164] It resuscitates the conventional depictions of the *tribulaciones* with a grainy realism that makes the experience of marriage both immediate and touching:

> Ant hwet yef Ich easki yet, thah hit thunche egede, hu thet wif stonde, the ihereth hwen ha kimeth in hire bearn schreamen, sith the cat et te fliche ant ed te hude the hund, hire cake bearnen o the stan ant hire kelf suken, the crohe eornen i the fur – ant te cheorl chideth?[165]

Hali Meithhad characteristically portrays such scenes not as abstract tableaux but as dramatic predicaments directly involving the projected persona of the

which the bond of love creates peace and spiritual concord. It ennobles companionship, sanctifies love and serves friendship. It is the cradle of generation, the seedbed of dynasty, a shield against the inevitability of horrible death, and the means by which sons repair the injuries of their fathers."

[161] *HM*, 34/3, 34/9–11: "Thah hit beo egede i sahe . . . nawt ne thuncheth hit hire egede thet hit fondeth."

[162] *De vanitate mundi*, 709: "Who can say, unless they've experienced it, what hard work and what trouble it is to bring up children – leaving aside those miseries which are best left unmentioned – to nurse, train, feed, and educate children, to teach them both manners and knowledge, and to bring them to maturity?" Cf. *HM*, MWB, 32/18–34/5.

[163] Cf. Elizabeth Robertson, pp. 84–5.

[164] Wiesen, p. 119.

[165] *HM*, 34/6–9: "And what if I ask as well – though it might seem ridiculous – how it is with that wife who, when she comes in, hears her kid screaming, the cat at the flitch and the dog at the hide, her loaf burning on the hearthstone, her calf sucking [the milk?] and the pot boiling over into the fire – while the churl chides her?" Owst argues that such "half-comic, half-tragic" vignettes became a conventional theme for preachers (p. 377).

woman it addresses. For example, it considerably expands the description of the troubles of pregnancy in the Latin tradition, emphazing not so much its disfiguring effects as the woman's own sensations – dizziness, headache, swelling, stomach-ache, stitches, backache, discomfort of the breasts and nausea.[166] It concludes its analysis of the distresses of childbirth with an evocation of the young woman's shame before the midwives.[167] Similarly, it censures sex not only as a physical indecency but also as a psychological trial:

> Hwuch schal beo the sompnunge bituhen ow i bedde? Me, theo the best luuieth ham tobeoreth ofte thrin, thah ha throf na semblant ne makien ine marhen; ant ofte of moni nohtunge, ne luuien ha ham neauer swa, bitterliche bi hamseolf teonith either other. Heo schal his wil muchel hire unwil drehen, ne luuie ha him neauer swa wel, with muche weane ofte; alle his fulitoheschipes ant his unhende gomenes, ne beon ha neauer swa with fulthe bifunden, nomeliche i bedde ha schal, wulle ha, nulle ha, tholien ham alle.[168]

The author's emphasis is always upon the immediate experience of marriage and the mental stress of a woman trapped within it. Her subordination in marriage is presented as an encroachment upon her own mental space and individuality. The image with which it is contrasted, the heavenly marriage, becomes an ideal of liberty, wisdom, nobility and selfhood. In this way, *Hali Meithhad*, shows how virginity can be more than a physical and spiritual state, a duty imposed upon women by the legacy of Eve and the hostility of men towards female sexuality. Virginity can also be an uplifting way of life, a woman's means to preserve health, rank and self-respect. In short, it can be a vocation.

Hali Meithhad thus recognizes the various anxieties and aspirations, often contradictory ones, with which women approached marriage. It deploys its appeals to them so sensitively and emotively that I think it unfair to treat it simply as a work of Christian propaganda. It is a work of great literary sophistication, and as such it reveals a great deal of the sensibility of its age. In addressing women as choosing individuals, rather than icons; in

---

[166] *HM*, 30/31–32/7; cf. Hildebert of Lavardin, *Ep.* 1. 21, PL 171. 194–5: "Vultum pallor, inficit, caput vertigine fatigatur, renum dolor assiduus, stomachi frequens indignatio."

[167] *HM*, 32/10–13: but cf. *Vita S. Domitillae, ASS*, May 12, III, pp. 7–13 at I. 4, p. 7D: this evokes the shame of exposure, not only to the female midwife, but also to the male doctor.

[168] *HM*, 28/8–15: "What will it be like when you are together in bed? Even those who love each other often differ there, although they show no signs in the morning; and often, no matter how much they love each other, because of trivial things they manage to annoy each other by themselves. However much they love each other, she has to suffer his wishes unwillingly, often in great unhappiness; particularly in bed she has to suffer all his indecencies and ignoble games, no matter how filthily devised, whether she likes it or not."

comparing marriage and virginity equivalently as vocations to which the maiden binds herself by will; in setting marriage against an ideal of inward and unearthly tranquillity; and in doubting the possibility of fulfilling personal, spiritual needs within marriage – in all these ways, *Hali Meithhad*'s treatment of marriage exemplifies the deepening response to it which I think distinctive of the period. As an evaluation of marriage from a feminine perspective (albeit one probably written by a man), it is perhaps a valuable correlative to male-oriented texts like *Erec et Enide* and the *Chanson de Saint Alexis*.[169]

Though *Hali Meithhad* draws heavily on the ancient, clerical tradition of writing about virginity for many of its themes and motifs, it animates this rigid and inert framework with a rich awareness of the drama of human experience. It shows how the venerable tissue of ideas about virginity – such as the *sponsa Christi* and *molestiae nuptiarum* motifs – could be renovated and made relevant in each age. It is not the work of a narrow-minded fanatic. Rather, it demonstrates the author's profound sensitivity to the resonance of ancient themes and their relationship to the patterns of human experience. He employed them to make the call to virginity seem more immediate and more real to the women he addressed in their own tongue. In a similar vein, Peter Dronke has drawn attention to the physical immediacy and imaginative daring of a text which also shows a creative commitment to these ancient themes, the sequence, *Virgines caste*. To explain its combination of the vivid and the traditional, he suggests that "in different cultures, a high contemplative mode, solemn and austere, may have a more joyous popular mode existing alongside it, sharing and expressing in its own way some of the basic conceptions of the human and divine". He speculates that "in the West in the early Middle Ages a more popular, more sensual mysticism may have co-existed with that *de virginitate* tradition which is so richly documented by the Fathers and by monastic theologians".[170] The existence of such a popular substratum of sensibility is, as he admits, impossible to prove. Yet, as I argued of the legend of St Alexis, it is not necessary to draw a distinction between popular and conservative spiritualities. What texts like *Hali Meithhad* and *Virgines caste* reveal is not a division between high and low cultures, but the emotional resonance and imaginative potential of even the most commonplace of religious metaphors.

In other words, I would argue that it might be possible, without minimizing *Hali Meithhad*'s uncompromising didacticism or its pessimistic evaluation of human life on earth, to regard it as a consciously tragic work. In Barbara Hardy's definition, for example, "tragic art is the attempt to make sense out of the pain of being human; it is speculative, never simply

---

[169] Another such contribution might be found in the evocative and enigmatic Occitan lyric, 'Na Carenza, al bel cors avinen . . .'.

[170] Dronke, 'Virgines', p. 111.

sensational"[171] Christian consolation posits pain, and to that extent it does not exclude a response to pain which is essentially tragic – as long, that is, as that response is neither trite nor insensitive. Even while *Hali Meithhad* is rooted in a sense of life's darkness which seems alien and rebarbative to a modern reader, it is nevertheless profoundly engaged with the impulses of pain, and subtle to the point of ingenuity in its attempt to sublimate suffering as tragedy. Above all, even within its traditional antimatrimonial and antifeminist agenda, it sustains an ideal of the dignity both of human relationships and of female individuals. Such a reading is open to the charge of a certain romanticism on my own part, but it is, I would insist, wholly consistent within the framework of the text. Moreover this positive reading avoids the contradiction inherent in much of the recent critical attention to it as a vernacular text designed for women: that is, if *Hali Meithhad* has no literary or human value, if it is simply a recreation in the vernacular of a discourse which for women is only oppressive and disempowering, and if it makes no valid representation of the condition or attitudes of the women it supposedly addressed, then what justification is there for paying any respect to it now? Indeed, if *Hali Meithhad* is regarded as a fundamentally unsympathetic and cynical work, then we are surely forced to set a lower valuation upon the whole programme of vernacularization to which all the AB-texts apparently belonged, including the now highly respected *Ancrene Wisse*. I prefer not to do so, and I think that I am justified in regarding these texts as the expressions of a significant spiritual and literary movement.

6. Conclusion

Throughout antiquity and the Middle Ages, questions about the nature of marital commitment and the evaluation of married life were normally orientated much more directly towards women than towards men. While men were distinguished by their fields of endeavour, women continued to be defined in terms of marriage even after they had embraced celibacy – as the texts discussed in this chapter demonstrate. Wogan-Browne remarks that, "though practising a wide range of actual occupations and skills, twelfth- and thirteenth-century women are often conceptualised and addressed by their marital status (*either* wives and mothers *or* brides of Christ), so that much of what is addressed to women, perceived in terms of either kind of marriage, is of relevance to its obverse".[172] Just as Abelard tried to reconcile Heloise to the end of their earthly relationship by evoking the dignity of Christ's Bride, so the authors (or author) of the AB-texts sought to sublimate the aspirations of their charges into a system of ideals which they located imaginatively in the

[171] Hardy, p. 1.
[172] Wogan-Browne. 'Clerc', p. 65.

next world. Like the *Chanson de Saint Alexis*, the AB-texts reconcile the contradictory social, sexual and spiritual impulses of humanity only by projecting these anxieties onto a backdrop of paradisal serenity. In this sense, *Seinte Katerine*'s description of heaven is no digression. Indeed, it derives its emotional impact only from the tensions of identity and ideal which the saint's life attempts to resolve:

> Constu bulden a bur[h] inwith [i] thin heorte, al abute bitrumet with a deore[w]urthe wal, schininde ant schen[e] . . .? For ther is a liht ant leitinde leome, ne niht nis ther neauer, ne neauer na n[o]wcin; ne eileth ther na mon nowther sorhe ne sar, nowther heate ne chele, nowther hunger ne thurst, ne nan ofthuncunge.[173]

The pun on "burh" ('city') and "bur" ('bower' or 'heart') was perhaps a deliberate one, stressing the correspondence between the other world and the inner world.[174]

In attempting to confirm women in their religious vocation by adapting their marital aspirations into a symbolism based on marriage, the AB-Group extended rather than weakened its audiences' idealistic engagement with marriage. Here the *sponsa Christi*-motif is much more than a rhetorical metaphor for spiritual union: it is used to evoke a psychological process. The ancient symbolism provides an occasion for an attempt to understand the inner dialogue by which an individual comes to recognize a sense of vocation. By modelling the determination of religious commitment upon the movement of consent towards marriage, the AB-texts present it as a relationship between two people, between the anchoress and Christ, and as such something active and evolving – a true drama of feeling. It enriches even the lonely anchoritic calling with at least the fiction of companionship. Yet the symbolism of marriage could only do so much if these authors shared with their audiences an awareness of the inward as well as the outward realities of marriage. Indeed, they make marriage a paradigm of emotional commitment, and, in particular, of the union of individuals to which it ideally tends. It is, finally, a quite remarkable paradox that, although the AB-Group is devoted to the celebration of a way of life specifically opposed to marriage, it nonetheless testifies to some of the the ideological pressures upon it which ultimately resulted in the heightened dignity of marriage within the medieval model of society.

---

[173] *SK*, lines 602–4, 614–17: "Can you build a city inwardly in your heart, entirely surrounded by a precious wall, shining bright . . .? For there is a light and a gleaming radiance; there's no night there, nor ever any hardship; there's neither pain or sorrow there, neither heat nor cold, neither hunger or thirst, nor any regret."

[174] Bodley "bur"; Royal "abur"; Titus "aburh". d'Ardenne and Dobson reject the Bodley/Royal reading, suggesting that the interpretation "bower" "only explains the error; it does not justify the reading" (p. 255).

CHAPTER FIVE

Jesus College Oxford MS 29
and BL MS Cotton Caligula A. 9

1. Introduction

The ten pieces common to the two late thirteenth-century manuscripts, Jesus College, Oxford 29 and BL Cotton Caligula A. 9, constitute a neat miscellany of early vernacular literature.[1] The group contains two long debate-poems in English and Anglo-Norman – respectively, *The Owl and the Nightingale* and the *Petit Plet*. It also includes two Anglo-Norman hagiographical texts ascribed to a certain "Chardri" and clearly designed to appeal to lay as well as religious audiences; and, in addition, six short and grimly moralistic English lyrics. Disparate though these pieces appear at first sight, they are nonetheless linked by certain affinities of style and theme, as well as by their context. It is tempting to follow the precedent of the AB-Group and label them by their sigla as the 'CJ-Group'.[2]

The CJ-text most often read today is *The Owl and the Nightingale*. According to R.M. Wilson, "all students of mediæval literature have . . . united in praise of the *The Owl and the Nightingale*".[3] The critical consensus has long been that the poem was written between 1189 and 1216, but it is more likely to belong to the middle of the thirteenth century (and possibly even to the 1270s).[4] The poem is an account of a vehement debate between

---

[1] Jesus 29 is actually two separate manuscripts, the first part being an unrelated Latin chronicle (Ker, pp. xi, xx). For simplicity's sake, whenever I refer to "Jesus", it will be to the second part.

[2] Reichl's tabulation (pp. 64–5) of the contents of 18 vernacular miscellanies from this period clearly demonstrates the various links between them. Cotton Caligula A. 9 is also one of the two surviving manuscripts of Laȝamon's *Brut* (see Roberts).

[3] Wilson, *EMEL*, p. 149.

[4] Eric Stanley accepted the dating 1189–1216 in his edition of the poem (p. 19), but see my article 'The Date of *The Owl and the Nightingale*'. Onions assumes that the poem was written in a south-eastern dialect. The poet refers with familiarity to Portesham in Dorset, and we know that in 1400 two copies existed at Titchfield Abbey only 60 miles away (Wilson, 'Medieval Library'). The language of the Jesus manuscript has been placed near Ledbury, about ten miles east of Hereford (McIntosh et al., *A Linguistic Atlas*, LP 7440). For its subsequent history, see Hill, 'History' and 'Oxford'.

the two birds of the title, ranging across matters as diverse as the propriety of their nesting-sites, their songs and their chicks' toilet-habits; the possibility of foreknowledge; and the quality of women's experience in marriage. Along the way they allude tantalizingly to all kinds of topical events and concerns. In its abundance of colour and detail, confident craftsmanship, humour and flexibility of tone, it is an almost unique survival from its era, and it is little wonder that scholars have been moved to speak of its preservation as a miracle.[5] Yet, partly as a result, they have tended to foster the assumption that *The Owl and the Nightingale* was produced in a cultural vacuum.[6] Its relationship with the other texts which I am calling the 'CJ-group' belies this impression. Indeed, as Derek Pearsall has said, *The Owl and the Nightingale* "is often treated by English scholars as if it were some kind of freak, [but] perhaps no poem demonstrates more sharply how inexplicable early Middle English poetry is if it is not related to its multilingual background".[7]

The other long debate-poem in the group is *Le Petit Plet*.[8] Although it is written in the Anglo-Norman dialect of Old French, its author was probably an Englishman.[9] He does not name himself, but his editors have identified him with the "Chardri" who wrote the two hagiographical works also belonging to this group – *Les Set Dormanz* and *La Vie de Seint Josaphaz*.[10] The *Petit Plet* is an outstandingly attractive work in its own right, and it is odd that it has been so little studied, especially given its close contextual relationship to *The Owl and the Nightingale*.[11] The two poems are

---

[5] W.P. Ker, for example, described the poem as "the most miraculous piece of writing, or if that is too strong a term, the most contrary to all pre-conceived opinion, among the medieval English books" (*English Literature: Medieval*, p. 181).

[6] Wilson speaks of "the poverty of contemporary literature" (*EMEL*, p. 149); and Atkins of "a barren period of our literature" (p. xi). Wells said that the author was "endowed with astonishing poetical gifts for his time and environment" (p. 420), while Utley suggested that the poem's "occasional roughnesses" might be excused by "its lack of a sophisticated milieu" ('Dialogues', p. 720). More recently, John Frankis has suggested that the poem is "outstandingly anomalous" in its context (p. 180). Overlooking the presence of Chardri's works, and in particular the *Petit Plet*, he argues that the *O&N* is too witty and urbane to belong among the texts with which it survives. Finally, Thomas L. Reed, jr, has referred to the *O&N* as "this masterful anachronism" (*Middle English Debate Poetry*, p. 219).

[7] Pearsall, *OEMEP*, p. 94. Cf. Salter, pp. 4, 37–45; Conlee, 'Owl', p. 57; Ziolkowski, *Talking Animals*, pp. 134–5.

[8] The *PP* is also preserved in a third manuscript, Vatican MS Reg. lat. 1659.

[9] For the author's English patriotism, lines 1255–84.

[10] In the *PP*, the author does not name himself, but Merrilees (p. xxix) and Koch both argue that the three poems are the work of a single hand. Chardri was possibly a "Richard" who reversed the syllables of his name in imitation of Tristram's pseudonym, "Tramtris".

[11] For Chardri, see Legge, *ANL*, pp. 192–201. She describes him as "a skilful and agreeable narrator . . . a true poet" (p. 201).

closely comparable in style, scale, metre and matter.[12] They share, as Elizabeth Salter has said, "an unusual flexibility of approach to the themes of their choice".[13] Marriage is one of the topics treated in both poems, and they devote similar amounts of space to it.[14] Yet they treat it very differently. The protagonists of the *Petit Plet* are both male, and they evaluate marriage by contrasting an ideal of the loyal wife with a misogynistic critique of female behaviour. Just as the poem is polarized in its attitude towards women, so it presents a polarized view of marriage, as on the one hand a profound joy and on the other a purgatory of mundane troubles. By contrast, the Owl and the Nightingale are unanimous in their sympathy for women both inside and outside marriage. Though they regard marriage as part of the natural order – and defend it as such – they turn a critical eye upon the way it determines the nature of women's lives.

Like the texts discussed in Chapter Four, these two debate-poems tend to use marriage as a means of distinguishing between different styles of life. They are secular poems in the sense that their speakers are not clerks and are clearly concerned with marriage as the normal prerogative of their class. Unlike nearly all the texts treated so far in this book, they address marriage not as an ideal but as a fact: they examine the impact of the conjugal bond upon an individual's quality of life. It seems natural that, at a time when marriage was being contrasted ever more sharply with other models of social engagement, and enriched ever more profoundly as a symbol, its effect upon the lives of those whose lives it circumscribed should also be discussed. However, even such assured and self-sufficient works as the *Petit Plet* and *The Owl and the Nightingale* tend to portray marriage in rather schematic ways – in terms of typical personalities and scenarios. I hope to demonstrate this by adducing relevant analogues. That these authors shared common ideals and images of marriage with others does not necessarily indicate lack of imagination or originality: for indeed the treatment of marriage is often deepened by the appeal to certain universally recognizable types.

The Jesus and Cotton manuscripts have sometimes been described as "Friars' Miscellanies", on the assumption that their blend of religious and secular material in the vernacular is best explained by reference to the didactic methods of the friars.[15] The evidence for the association in this case is extremely tenuous, and, as Reichl says, the idea can be "no more than a

---

[12] The two poems use the same word for the debates they contain – Anglo-Norman "plet"; English "plait" (*O&N*, 5). The *PP* is 1780 lines long; *O&N* 1794 lines. Both are in octosyllabic couplets. Both make extensive use of proverbs – what the *PP* calls "verraiz respiz/ De ben assiz e de bonz diz" (15–16).

[13] Salter, p. 39.

[14] *PP*, 1175–34; *O&N*, 1331–602.

[15] Robbins, 'Authors'; Pfander, *Popular Sermon*; Pearsall, *OEMEP*, pp. 94–100; Jeffrey, *Early English Lyric*; Jeffrey and Levy, intro.; Burton, *Monastic and Religious Orders*, pp. 206–7.

conjecture – one possibility among many".[16] I think it significant that nowhere in Humphreys's recent catalogue of manuscripts known to have been owned by the friars during the Middle Ages is there a single one bearing any resemblance to miscellanies like Jesus or Cotton. Another plausible but equally unprovable hypothesis is that the Jesus manuscript was designed for privileged, cloistered women.[17] Among the texts in Jesus (although not Cotton) is the 'Luue-Ron' by the Franciscan, Thomas of Hales, which was written specifically for a girl dedicated to God ("ad instanciam cuiusdam puelle deo dicate");[18] and it also contains several Marian pieces (items 8, 9, 10 and 19). The Jesus-manuscript's use of the vernacular for a work like the 'Passion of Our Lord' could perhaps have been addressed to the needs of a specifically female religious group. The interest in marriage which unites the *Petit Plet* and *The Owl and the Nightingale* might also be taken as an indication that Jesus, at least, was designed for women. However, there is no evidence to support such a notion. Indeed the only firm evidence which we have for the circulation of the CJ-texts suggests some sort of association with a group of male religious – the Premonstratensian canons of Titchfield Abbey in Hampshire. So many of the texts now preserved in Jesus and Cotton apparently existed in manuscripts which were present at Titchfield in 1400 (and listed in its catalogue that year), that there must have been some sort of relationship between the surviving manuscripts and the ones now lost – although the precise nature of this relationship is difficult to determine.[19] In short, since the exact nature of the milieu in which Jesus and Cotton were compiled remains unclear, it would be unwise to base any reading of the CJ-texts upon assumptions about the users of the manuscripts.

2. The Middle English Lyrics

Before looking at the two long debate-poems, *The Owl and the Nightingale* and the *Petit Plet*, I should like to introduce six short religious poems in English which also belong to the group. They are, to use Ker's titles, 'Death's Wither-clench', 'An Orison to Our Lady', 'Doomsday', 'The Last Day', 'The Ten Abuses' and 'A Lutel Soth Sermun'.[20] It seems likely that Cotton's

[16] Reichl, p. 72: "nicht mehr als Vermutung sein, eine von vielen Möglichkeiten". See also Frankis, pp. 179–80.

[17] Barratt has argued that "*The Owl and the Nightingale* was written in the early thirteenth century, for or by a religious community of women, specifically the Benedictine abbey of Shaftesbury" (p. 471).

[18] See Hill, '*Luue-ron*'.

[19] Reichl, p. 69; Hill, 'History', p. 103. Millett ('Origins') has recently revived the possibility that the Premonstratensians were involved in the production of another set of Middle English texts – the AB-Group.

[20] 'An Orison to Our Lady' is also preserved in Trinity College, Cambridge, MS 323 and Royal MS 2. F. 8. 'Doomsday' and 'The Last Day' also appear together in Digby MS

'Will and Wit', also once existed in Jesus, and that its absence may be explained by the loss of a bifolium at f. 180. Both manuscripts preserve all these poems in the same order.[21] As Baugh has said, they are "unusually interesting, treating familiar themes in a lively and fresh spirit, in verse that shows considerable metrical skill".[22] The first four are meditations upon the inevitability and indignity of death, the pains of hell and the necessity of repentance. In 'Death's Wither-clench', for example, life is seen as a kind of illusion – "deth the sal dun throwen/ Thar thu wenest heye ste" (38–9). Death often comes suddenly, and no one can escape it:

> Waylaway, nys king ne quene
> That ne schal drynke of dethes drench.
> Mon er thu falle of thi bench,
> Thyne sunne thu aquench.[23]

'The Last Day' is related to the body-and-soul debate-tradition.[24] It depicts the Soul's bitter reproaches to the Body on its death-bed, since the Soul will suffer eternally for the Body's sins:

> Nv thu schalt by-leuen
> And ich mot fare nede.
> For alle thine gultes
> Fongen i schal mede,
> That is hunger and chele
> And fur-bernynde glede.
> And so me wule sathanas
> Ful atelyche brede.[25]

'Will and Wit' dramatizes a similar psychomachia, though in a more gnomic fashion: unless the Will is restrained by the Wit, sorrow will inevitably follow. Pearsall has spoken of 'The Last Day' in terms of its "grim strength and imaginative limitation"; and Woolf in terms of its "tone of grim and personal ferocity".[26] Both these formulations could apply equally well to all

86. In Trinity MS 323, they form a composite poem. Reichl suggests that the two poems belonged together from the first (p. 415).

[21] Carleton Brown, pp. xxii–xxv. Dobson suggests that two of them, 'An Orison to Our Lady', and 'Death's Wither-clench', are likely to have shared the same melody (Dobson and Harrison, p. 123).

[22] Baugh, *Middle Ages*, p. 121.

[23] Morris (Jesus), 7–10: "Alas, there's neither king nor queen that won't drink death's drink. Man, before you drop off your bench, make sure your sin is extinguished." Cf. *Pardoner's Tale*, VI. 672–4.

[24] Conlee, *Middle English Debate Poetry*, pp. xxiv–xxvii, 2–62. He sees the soul's monologue as an early stage in this tradition.

[25] Jesus (Morris), 193–200: "Now you have to remain, and I must put up with the consequences. For all your sins I'll receive the reward – hunger and cold, and the consuming coals. And thus will Satan horribly roast me."

[26] Pearsall, *OEMEP*, p. 96; Woolf, p. 96.

the Middle English lyrics in the group. Even the 'Orison to Our Lady' invokes the Virgin's aid only in terms of the pains of hell: "Heo gon vs bote brynge/ Of helle pyne that is strong."[27] She is addressed not as an agent of compassion and grace, but as an icon against the evils of the world. As such, she is contrasted starkly with her ante-type, Eve:

> Thu brouhtest day and Eue Nyht;
> He brouhte wo thu brouhtest ryht;
> Thu almesse and heo sunne.[28]

Equally minatory is 'The Ten Abuses'. If people behave in ways contrary to nature and the duties of their estates, says the poet, disaster will be sure to follow: "Al so seyde Bede, 'Wo there theode.' "[29]

'A Lutel Soth Sermun' is no less apocalyptic in perspective, but it is the liveliest of the lyrics – if only because its criticisms are so specific. The author consigns to hell not only backbiters, robbers, thieves, murderers, lechers and whoremongers, but also dishonest merchants, bakers and brewers. There will be no salvation, he goes on, for "preostes wives" (49):

> Ne theos prude yongemen
> That luuyeth Malekyn,
> And theos prude maydenes
> That luuyeth Janekyn.
> At chireche and at chepyng,
> Hwanne heo to-gadere come,
> Heo runeth to-gaderes
> And speketh of derne luue.[30]

The familiar, rustic names make this critique of society seem, for all its fervour, rather a homely one. The preacher complains that, when young men and women are in church, they are so preoccupied with flirting that they pay no attention to the services. Moreover, he tells them a cautionary tale in order to warn them of the consequences of their behaviour:

> Robyn wule Gilothe
> Leden to than ale,
> And sitten ther to-gederes
> And tellen heore tale.
> He may quyten hire ale
> And seoththe don that gome,

---

[27] Jesus (Morris), 4–5: "She will bring us a remedy for the terrible pains of hell."

[28] Jesus (Morris), 15–17: "You brought Day, and Eve Night. You brought aid, and she sin."

[29] Jesus (Morris), 13–14: "So says Bede, woe to that people."

[30] Lines 53–60: "Nor those proud bachelors who love Malkyn; or those proud maidens who love Jankyn. When they meet at the church or at the fair, they rush together and speak of secret love."

An eue to go myd him –
Ne thincheth hire no schome.
Hire syre and hire dame
Threteth hire to bete
Nule heo fur-go Robyn.
For al heore threte
Euer heo wule hire skere.
N[u] com hire no mon neyh,[31]
Forte that hire wombe
Up aryse an heyh.
Godemen for godes luue,
Bi-leueth óure sunne.[32]

Having so far only presented hell as the inevitable reward for the sinful, the preacher now suggests that pregnancy out of wedlock is itself a terrible enough fate for foolish young maidens. His phrasing emphasizes the physical immediacy and momentousness of the disaster. Indeed, Gilothe's plight stands at the climax of the "sermun". The preacher only adds that "godemen" should avoid sin, and commends himself to the Virgin Mary. The parable of extra-marital pregnancy was perhaps designed to illustrate the importance of regulating sexual relationships by public marriage. Attachments formed in the tavern, the preacher suggests, are sinfully slight. However, he lays all the responsibility for the disaster on the woman – in having been so lightly seduced by the man's patter (the "tale"); in disrespectfully ignoring her parents' warnings; and in believing that there is no shame in sex – that it was a "gome". The cynicism of the man involved here is clearly more of a premise than a point of protest.[33] The preacher's message that it is not good to enter a sexual relationship without the protection afforded by a public contract is directed primarily at women, for it is only the female figure who is troubled by the outcome of the liaison. In other words, the fact that the evidence for fornication is expressed only in the girl's body is here used to reinforce a double standard: sexual morality and marriage are placed in a specifically female dimension of concern.

---

[31] MSS: ne.
[32] Lines 73–90: "Robyn presses Gilot to go with him to the alehouse, where they sit together, and he chats her up. He might pay for her ale, and afterwards play that 'game', so that she goes with him in the evening, nor does she see any disgrace in it. Her mother and father threaten to beat her unless she gives Robyn up, but for all her threats, she still wants to be free. Now no man comes near her, because her stomach has swollen up. Good people, for the love of God, remain above sin."
[33] Robert Mannyng warns women specifically against men who swear oaths only in order to seduce them:

> A werse spyce yyt men holdes,
> To begyle a womman with wordys;
> To gyue here trouthe but lyghtly
> For no thyng but for lygge here by. (lines 8393–6)

3. Chardri: *Le Petit Plet*

Although Chardri's *Petit Plet* is very much lighter in tone than the four Middle English meditations upon death and judgement, it clearly owes a debt to the sombre, didactic tradition which they represent.[34] Chardri tells us how a young man (the "Enfant") went out one day to amuse himself by a pleasant spring, and there met an old man (the "Veillard"), who reproached him for his frivolity.[35] Life is uncertain and humanity frail (164–7), he says: no man can predict the hour of his death (171–7), and so it is better to repent now, before it is too late.[36] The Enfant replies that there is no point in grieving more than is necessary ("de trop duleir", 137). The Veillard sets out to prove to him the importance of living in sadness, rather than enjoyment – "En tristur plus ke en enveisure" (254). His method of persuasion is to recount each of his own fears and afflictions, as if to present his own experience as an *exemplum* of the eventual misery of life. He says that he is afraid to die, especially far from home, prematurely or without friends, and that he is afflicted with poverty and ill-health. He mourns successively the deaths of his children, his wife and, finally, his friend.[37] The implication is that such burdens are the universal condition of human experience, but the poem does not follow the course we might expect from reading the Middle English lyrics. Here, *joie de vivre* triumphs over morbid piety. The failure of the apocalyptic vision in this case is intimated by Chardri's application of the word "enveisure" to the poem itself ("amusement", 2). By successfully consoling the Veillard for each of his griefs in turn, the Enfant forces to him acknowledge that the younger is the wiser man in this case.[38]

Unlike *The Owl and the Nightingale*, Chardri's *Le Petit Plet* has a direct source. It is an elaboration of the *De remediis fortuitorum* traditionally ascribed to the younger Seneca. The extant version of this work is certainly no more than an epitome of Seneca's work, and I think that it is more likely to belong entirely to the Middle Ages (albeit with a strongly stoical cast).[39] As it stands, the work is a dialogue between "Ratio" and "Sensus" illustrating the moral, "Death, exile, grief and sorrow are not punishments, but the fees of life."[40]

[34] As Burrow says (*Ages*, p. 169), the poem seems "as if uneasily balanced between the new cult of youth and an older morbidity".

[35] Cf. 'Phebus libram perlustrabat . . .', str. 2.

[36] The Enfant's immediate reaction to this argument is that "Tant avez la lange pleine/ Des diz le preste al dimeine" (185–6). A similar comparison is made by the Owl of the Nightingale – "Thu chaterest so doth on Irish prost" (322).

[37] The Veillard thus evokes all four of the bonds discussed in Part VII of the *Ancrene Wisse* – friendship, parenthood, marriage and the link between body and soul (see Chapter Four).

[38] The Enfant is a striking example of the "puer senex" motif: see Curtius, *European Literature*, pp. 98–101.

[39] The *De remediis* was first printed in 1470 (Flodr, pp. 281–2).

[40] Palmer, p. 64: "Mors, exilium, luctus, dolor, non sunt supplicia, sed tributa viuendi."

The Enfant takes the place of Ratio – that is, humanity's rational and intellectual capacity: the Veillard is a development of Sensus – its physical and affective aspect. It is interesting to note, however, that this psychological division is very similar to those I have pointed out in two of the Middle English lyrics in the group, 'Will and Wit' and 'The Last Day'. The nature and order of the Veillard's griefs are exactly those of Seneca's Sensus, with the exception that Chardri makes the friend's death, rather than the wife's, the Veillard's ultimate complaint. In placing the friend foremost, Chardri perhaps consciously reflects the preference for *amicitia* in medieval texts with aspirations to the ideal of philosophical detachment.

Yet, although the cynical Enfant is credited with the victory in debate, Chardri never gives us the impression that he endorses his position. The eloquence and fluency of the Enfant are balanced by the intensity and dignity of the feelings Veillard expresses for his wife. He describes her death as "the greatest grief in the world" ("la greinnur dolur del mund", 1179-80), for she was both a sweet lover and a loyal wife:

> jo ai perdue ma duce amie
> Ke me leale espuse esteit;
> De ceo doler en ai grant dreit.[41]

Noble, loyal and beautiful (1185-8), she surpassed all other women "as sapphire does the gravel" ("cum saphir fet la gravele", 1192). The Enfant's response to this moving elegy is completely inept. Though he admits that the Veillard is in much need of consolation ("de beau solaz e de cunfort", 1207), he begins:

> Ore me entendez, fet il, beau pere:
> Quant tant pleinnez vostre amie,
> N'est pas merveille, si fous se i fie . . .[42]

He goes on to argue that all women tend to the bad (1215-16). Their sweet looks ("beau semblant") are so deceptive that they can make black white, and folly wisdom (1217-24). If a woman wishes to do a man harm, she can do it, for women have many tricks (1229-33). In short, a woman is only to be trusted "when she openly reveals her evil disposition" ("Quant felunesse vus ert en apert", 1238). All of this is an expansion of Seneca's "every inexperienced man [sets] his heart entirely upon a deceitful woman".[43] The expression of such sentiments is the final product of the *De remediis*, but here the Veillard's personal conviction that he has lost a good woman in his wife challenges the Enfant's appeal to the proverbial image of the *mulier mala*.

[41] *PP*, 1182-4: "I have lost my sweet lover. She was my loyal wife. It is only right that I grieve for her."

[42] *PP*, 1212-14: " 'Now listen to me, good father', he said, 'However much you grieve for your beloved, it's no marvel if fools trust them . . .' ".

[43] Palmer, p. 62: "Omnium imperitorum animus quidem maxime in lubrica muliere."

The Enfant admits that not all women are so malicious – "Ne sunt pas tutes si demaleires" (1243) – and wishes more of them to be amenable and good ("debonaires", 1244–54). He asserts that more of such women are to be found in England than in France (1255–6). Indeed, England surpasses all other lands in the charm and nobility of its ladies (1261–5). Its knights, similarly, are worthy, courteous and liberal ("pruz, gentils e francs adés", 1270). Their splendid way of life ("lur bele vie") is only marred by their love of drinking (1271–2). This marvellously frivolous digression reminds us that the *Petit Plet* is in the first instance a light-hearted entertainment ("enveisure"), despite the occasion provided by the Veillard's misfortunes. The Enfant's extravagant nationalistic loyalty towards English knights and ladies is amusing in itself, and his jolly criticism of Englishmen's facility with drink might be taken as a back-handed compliment. The Enfant concludes by praising the Veillard for speaking so highly of his wife, and quotes a proverb which suits exactly his Hotspur-like posture of bluff and manly Englishness:

> Ore sai jeo ben par vostre dit
> Ke vus l'amastes de grant affit.
> Por ceo dist li Engleis trop ben:
> Tant cum l'amez, luez tun chen
> E ta femme e tun cheval.[44]

The remark is absurd in itself; and what it reveals about the nature of the Enfant's understanding of affection ("affit") is no credit to him.

The Veillard simply replies by insisting ("a estrus") upon his wife's irreproachability (1286–90). The Enfant is forced to adopt a new tack from Seneca. He argues that it was only because the Veillard's wife had been forestalled by death that she had never shown any of the bad qualities generic to women:

> Si ele fu franche e deboneire,
> La mort li ad recopé sun eire
> Ke ele ne changast sun quor avant,
> Cum feverer tredze covenant.[45]

Again directly echoing Seneca, he asserts that there is nothing on earth more changeable than the heart of a woman (1304–6). The Veillard accuses the Enfant of simply not understanding his point of view – "Mes vus ne entendez mun espeir" (1312). His wife was loyal ("leale") – indeed the joy of his life. He suggests that there are so many bad women that the good are not

---

[44] *PP*, 1277–81: "Now I understand well by what you say that you loved your wife with great affection. The English have a good saying about this: You should show your love for your dog or your wife or your horse, by praising it."

[45] *PP*, 1295–8: "Even if she was noble and courteous, death has cut short her career, so that she could not afterwards change her heart like February of the thirteen moods."

acknowledged ("Ke les bones crewes ne sunt", 1320). He is adamant that the woman he loved would never have changed for the worse – "Because I would have been as sure of her as of myself, that's the truth" ("Car ausi seur fu jo de li/ Cum de mei memes, sachez de fi", 1335–6). In this exchange, the Veillard's robust confidence in the particular qualities of his wife is far more impressive than the Enfant's indiscriminate cynicism.

"Are you sure," the Enfant now asks, "that she loved you as you loved her?" (1344–5). He says that he has never heard of a woman who fully returned a man's love (1348–51).[46] This is perhaps a playful allusion to the testimony of medieval love-poets, who conventionally "sing about desire rather than its accomplishment".[47] Once a woman realizes that she is loved, asserts the Enfant, she becomes malicious and bad-tempered (1353–6). He says that every woman puts on a sweet appearance before her marriage (1365–6), but while she swears her love, she is only plotting in her heart to make a fool of her husband: it is impossible to guarantee that a woman will not turn out badly (1379–82).[48] Like Seneca's Ratio, the Enfant asserts that many women, including even chaste and loyal wives ("chaste epuse e leale"), have become sluts (1387–92). He goes on to accuse women of maliciously bringing their husbands into disrepute:

> Les plus devorz ke unt esté
> Firent femmes par mauvesté.
> Si ren i ad ke lur desplet,
> Enz en chapitres moevent lur plet.
> L'une dist ke le soen mari
> Est lere fort, si n'est par li.
> L'autre dist ke le soen est un chevre,
> L'espus a l'autre est felun e enrevre.
> Icele dist ke ele ad grant dreit
> Ke cil ne li fet ke fere deit.
> Issi se peine por un curuz
> Chescune hunir sun ami duz.[49]

[46] Cf. Andreas Capellanus, *De amore*, III. 65, p. 306: "Amorem namque mutuum, quem in femina quaeris, invenire non poteris. Non enim aliqua unquam dilexit femina virum nec amanti mutuo se novit amoris vinculo colligare." ("You could not find the reciprocal love which you seek for in a woman. For no woman has ever loved her husband or been able to bind herself to a lover by the mutual bond of love.")

[47] Payen, 'Mise', pp. 222–3: "chantent le désir et non son accomplissement".

[48] The Wife of Bath admits being less keen to please her husband once she has married him (*Wife of Bath's Prologue*, III. 209–14). Cf. Theophrastus, in Jerome, *Adv. Jov*, I. 47; *Le Roman de la Rose*, 8661–86. The idea is not an exclusively misogynistic one: in the *Vita S. Domitillae*, husbands are accused of doing the same (*ASS*, May 12, III, pp. 7–13 at I. 3, p. 7C).

[49] *PP*, 1393–1404: "Most of the dissensions there ever were have been caused by women's malice. If there is anything that causes them displeasure, they present their complaints before their assemblies. One says that her husband is a dreadful scoundrel, and not because of her. Another says that hers is an old goat [i.e. lecher]. The husband

We are perhaps meant to imagine the women making allegations against their husbands as plaintiffs in a court of law. The phrase "moevent lur plet" might be translated "they bring an action". "Devorz" might stand for the Latin 'divortium', which could refer specifically to divorce as well as separation in a more general sense. The word "chapitres" suggests the ecclesiastical courts which dealt with marital cases. Sense can be made of the apparently vague allegation "Ke cil ne li fet ke fere deit" if it is interpreted as an action for separation on the grounds of the husband's inability to pay the marital debt. However, it seems to me that what Chardri is really portraying is a gathering of gossips. The Wife of Bath tells us that she revealed her husband's "conseil every deel" to her friends, so as to make "his face often reed and hot".[30] Such meetings are frequently depicted in medieval debate-poetry. Women meet conventionally, not only to compare men, as in the *de clerico et milite* tradition, but also to criticize them – especially as husbands.[51] Several of the medieval *chansons de malmariée* are cast in this way:

> Trois dames trovai parlant
>   Et disant
> Que trop sunt ennuieus
> Lor mari et trop gaitant.[52]

The Enfant's tone is hostile and uneasy because he adopts the perspective of the innocent husband – the "fond lover" ("ami duz"), as he calls him – whose peace and honour are blighted by these malicious assemblies. The legal atmosphere is evoked in order to make these gatherings of women seem all the more threatening. The Enfant underlines their sinister exclusivity by using the intensifier "enz" ("inside") along with "en chapitres". According to his misogynistic point of view, women are motivated to complain against their husbands only by wanton seditiousness and the desire to justify their adulterous lusts:

> Unc n'i vi femme itant amer
> Ne tant cherir sun bacheler,
> Si ele veist un plus beals de li,
> Ke ele nel coveitast, sachez de fi.[53]

of another is said to be a malicious villain; while another says that she has good cause for complaint, since he does not do with her what he is obliged to do. Thus each one strains to cause a row by bringing shame upon her sweet lover."

[30] *Wife of Bath's Prologue*, III. 529–42.
[51] Conlee, *Middle English Debate-Poetry*, pp. xvii–xviii. For the debates *de clerico et milite*, see Oulmont; Raby, II, 290–7.
[52] 'Deduisant com fins amourous . . .', 3–6: "I found three ladies chatting, and saying that their husbands were too tiresome and too vigilant."
[53] *PP*, 1409–12: "I've never seen a woman who loved and cherished her husband so much that if she saw a man more attractive than him, she wouldn't desire him, be sure of that."

This is possibly an allusion to the longings for a better lover which the *chansons de malmariée* conventionally and so frankly express.[54]

The Veillard warns his opponent that he should moderate his criticism of women, and insists, as before, that his wife was peerless. The Enfant replies that he will be able to find another one equally good – especially if he looks for the same qualities in her as in the first. This argument and the advice on choosing a wife to which it gives rise are drawn from the *De remediis*, though Chardri expands Seneca's three sentences on the subject to eighty lines. Above all, says the Enfant, a man must be careful not to be blinded by a prospective bride's wealth – "since possessions [can be] a veil, so that he [does] not recognise her nature" ("Car le chatel si fu visere/ Ke ne fu coneue sa manere", 1453-4). A poor woman, as long as she is pretty and well brought-up, is better than a rich one, who will be haughty (1455-9). A wealthy bride is expensive to support (1459-68), and if her unfortunate husband does not keep her in the manner to which she is accustomed, she will threaten him with the anger of her kinsmen (1470-6). While she lives in splendour, he is reduced to rags (1477-88). If she sees her neighbour going better dressed:

> sanz fin
> Vus criera sur e tost e tart
> E si dirra: "La male hart
> Vus pende, mauveis putre vilein,
> Quel ke ceo seit ui e demain,
> Car vus me hunissez entre gent
> Ke vus mei vestez si povrement.[55]

This outburst recalls the satirical vignette from the "Golden Book" of Theophrastus, which Jerome copied into his *Adversus Jovinanum*:

> Deinde per noctes totas garrulae conquestiones. Illa ornatior procedit in publicum: haec honoratur ab omnibus, ego in conventu feminarum despicior.[56]

Theophrastus also contrasts rich and poor brides, but he is content with neither – "it is difficult to feed a poor one", he says, "a torment, to endure a rich one".[57] His argument was quoted verbatim in a number of Latin works

---

[54] See below, part 7.

[55] *PP*, 1492-8: "Remorselessly, she will cry against you, all the time. She'll say: 'The cursed noose hang you, you evil stinking rascal, whatever happens, for you make me ashamed in public, because you clothe me so poorly.' "

[56] Jerome, *Adv. Jov.* I. 47, PL 23. 276C-D: "Then there are the ceaseless interrogations every night. 'That woman went better-dressed in public: this one is admired by everyone, and I am despised among women.' "

[57] Jerome, *Adv. Jov.* I. 47, PL 23. 277A: "pauperem alere, difficile est: divitem ferre, tormentum".

throughout the twelfth century, beginning with Abelard's *Theologia Christiana* in around 1124.[58] If Chardri did utilize it, he was one of the first writers to do so in the vernacular. However, the coincidences are not so extensive as necessarily to suggest a direct debt. The Anglo-Norman writer's lively caricature of a nagging wife could also be seen as the product of a broad tradition of antimatrimonial satire in the Middle Ages.

Finally, the Enfant exhorts the Veillard to be manly in his grief:

> Lessez ester vostre doleir,
> Si pensez ben ke vus estes humme,
> Ne devez pas por chescune pumme
> Plurer cum enfant mesaffeité.[59]

The Veillard admits that the Enfant's arguments have greatly fortified him in his grief – ''Because in this matter, which was very difficult, you have greatly reassured me'' (''Car en cest cas, ki fu mult dur,/ Mult me avez fet ben asseur'', 1539–40). He now turns to lament the death of his friend. The Veillard's sudden capitulation does not mean that Chardri expected his audience to be convinced by the Enfant's arguments. It is simply a device which permits a change of topic. Chardri gives the impression that the Enfant is so infinitely well-armed in the strategies of argument that surrender is the only escape. Yet the Enfant is fluent in his rhetoric only because he is so indiscriminate in its use. His tendentious intellectualization of the common emotional events of our lives leads to some extravagant perspectives – not least, his extreme antifeminism. Chardri revels in the audacity of adopting positions which so transgress the normal evaluations of human experience. The Enfant's method of argument provides an opportunity for the play of wit, not of conviction. Like many medieval debates, the *Petit Plet* exploits the discrepancy between 'reason' – in the sense of a balanced and proportionate view of the world – and 'Reason' – the brutal logic of polemical rhetoric. The Veillard represents Everyman: not only in the universal applicability of his experiences, but also in the normality of his reactions to them. His repeated insistence on the qualities of his wife have an almost refrain-like quality about them. Despite the arid stoicism of its source, the *Petit Plet* is a fundamentally humane poem. The Enfant's ingenious cynicism about marriage is ultimately discredited by the assurance we can find in the character of the Veillard that marital love is a powerful emotion and a natural part of human experience.

---

[58] Schmitt, p. 262; Delhaye, 'Dossier', p. 71.
[59] *PP*, 1528–31: ''Leave off your grieving. Remember that you are a man. You should not weep like a sulky child for some apple.''

4. *The Owl and the Nightingale*: Introduction

Discussion of marriage forms a substantial part of *The Owl and the Nightingale*, but in none of the interpretations so far developed by its critics has this theme been properly integrated. The poem is very often treated as if it possessed a single, monolithic significance. Wilson, for example, argued that "obviously the dispute between the two birds is allegorical, but the exact significance of the allegory is more difficult to determine".[60] It has been variously suggested that the conflict between the birds represents a contrast between different styles of preaching;[61] of poetry and music;[62] of rhetoric;[63] or of monastic observance.[64] Their significance has also been sought in folklore;[65] in astrology;[66] in biblical exegesis;[67] in social commentary;[68] and in their resemblance to contemporary political and intellectual figures.[69] Various moral, religious and philosophical truths have been extracted from the text of their confrontation, yet none has ever proved wholly convincing.[70] Scholarly thinking about the poem has been dominated by the notion that there must be a "key" to its interpretation.[71] This is a chimera, for the poem is too complex to be the coded expression of a single idea.

[60] Wilson, *EMEL*, pp. 160–1.

[61] Owst, p. 22.

[62] Atkins sees the poem as contrasting traditional religious and didactic poetry with "the new poetry with its love-motive" (edn, p. lvii; cf. *English Literary Criticism*, pp. 143–4). Bennett suggests (p. 2) that it captures "the conflict between traditional native mores and the French culture that was represented by a new poetic and that gave a new sweetness to love". Allen emphasizes the role of music in the poem and concludes that the poem is "formulated upon a contrast between old and new in literary styles" (p. 58). Wilson also opts for the idea that the poem is a contrast of styles of poetry (*EMEL*, p. 161). Ker (p. 135) sees it as contrasting Art with Philosophy. Finally, Swanton describes the theme of the poem as "the relationship of literature to life itself" (p. 262).

[63] Carson.

[64] Coleman, pp. 549–54.

[65] Hinckley, 'Date, Author'.

[66] Cawley.

[67] Donovan; Peterson.

[68] Schlauch (p. 161) sees the poem as a contrast between clergy and nobility; the poet, she says, preferred both to the "brutish ignorance" of "the masses".

[69] Baldwin, 'Henry II'. Coleman suggests that the poet makes allusions to "well-known contrasting features of Cistercians and Cluniacs, Bernard [of Clairvaux] and Abelard" in order to heighten the contrast between the birds (p. 566).

[70] For example, Moran argues that, while "the theological nature of the poem is not immediately apparent", "the 'delightful nature poem' obviously disguises a serious debate which deals with love, nature, Providence and Original Sin and Grace" (p. 162). Sampson's opinion is that the Nightingale represents "the world" and the Owl "the cloister" (p. 33). Olsson argues that the poem's comedy is a means to turn "our vision from the birds to truth", by which he seems to mean religious enlightenment (n. 24, p. 368).

[71] It is remarkable how often the image of the key is used in criticism of the *O&N*: e.g. Coleman, p. 517; Hume, p. 56; Moran, pp. 162, 171; Gellinek-Schellekens, p. 121.

Hume's interpretation of the poem is one of the most persuasive so far presented. She suggests that the poem is an illustration of how "quarrelling may result in death".[72] To her, it is a "burlesque-satire on human contentiousness" designed to show up "the pointlessness and ugly results of quarrelling".[73] In the course of the poem, each of the speakers describes the death of an individual of the other's kind (lines 1061-6; 1165-8). Hume suggests that the reason why the issues of adultery and prophecy "receive more attention than we might anticipate . . . is that they are responsible for the birds' deaths".[74] Yet, even if the birds' deaths are the consequence of the issues in dispute, they are not the consequence of the dispute itself. Their fate does not undermine – any more than the result of any other *Streitgedicht* – the medieval love of debate to which the popularity of the genre bears witness.[75] In any case, we are left to assume at the end of the poem, firstly, that both birds are alive and well, and secondly, that the wise Nicholas of Guildford will be able to reconcile them.[76]

Alfred Baugh argues that "there is no necessity for seeing in the poem anything more than a lively altercation between two birds, with the poet's skill sufficiently revealed in the matching of wits, the thrust and parry of the opponents, the shrewd observation and homely wisdom for which the argument gives constant occasion".[77] It is certainly simpler to see the poem as a piece written purely for entertainment, with no political, religious or literary significance. Hume's objection that "it is difficult to believe that a poem of such length and quality should be merely a *jeu d'esprit*" is hardly valid when authors like Rabelais, Sterne and Byron have produced much longer and no lesser such *jeux*.[78] Baugh's characterization, however, is a critical dead-end. It stops uncourageously short of suggesting circumstantial reasons for any of the poem's features. With his dismissive formula, "no necessity for seeing . . . anything more than", he implies that the poem is poor in content. This is an implication which the intelligent and sensitive debate on marital issues patently resists.

It seems to me that the primary *raison d'être* of the poem is the expression of the poet's fascination with the dramatic contrast of ideas. The inconsistency of the two birds' arguments is the result, not of an attempt at psychological

---

[72] Hume, p. 98.

[73] Hume, pp. 100, 117. Mehl, by constrast, suggests that the poem is almost a celebration of eloquence ("fast wie eine Verherrlichung der Beredsamkeit", p. 79).

[74] Hume, p. 109.

[75] See Bossy, introduction.

[76] The poem could hardly have been written to further Nicholas's career, if only because the Owl's allegations of corruption and nepotism among his superiors (1769–78) would hardly have helped his cause. It seems most likely that Nicholas was the author and that the adulation he receives in the poem is a whimsical joke: see Peter Dronke, 'Peter of Blois', p. 214, n. 70.

[77] Baugh, *Middle Ages*, p. 155.

[78] Hume, p. 51; cf. Peterson, p. 13.

verisimilitude, but of the movement of the poem from one confrontation of ideas to the next. As each new issue comes into the field, the birds' opinions are adjusted to form a new point of contrast. Thus, the characterization of the two birds which emerges is only an incidental product of the dynamics of debate. The attempts of some scholars to present either bird with the prize for victory are, as Elizabeth Salter has said, "a wasteful business".[79] The interest of the poem lies, not in the relative coherence of the protagonists' cases, but in the dramatic opposition of certain concepts. There is no embracing allegorical or didactic framework governing the poet's choice of material. The traditional and natural characteristics of the two birds provide suggestions for confrontation both directly in the small details of avian behaviour, and indirectly in their conventional literary and mythical associations. As John Burrow says, the poet writes "as if no fact about either bird could possibly be irrelevant"; their natural qualities are God-given, and their moral significance is thus inexhaustible.[80] Though we can hardly reconstruct the precise range of traditions which might have been available to the author, the Nightingale's association with love was ubiquitous in medieval literature.[81] In medieval lyric, for example, the nightingale's song is conventionally a metonym for the joyous sexual liberation of springtime. Nightingales, along with other birds, play active roles in some songs as the allies, messengers and confidants of the lovers.[82] Moreover, there is a precedent for some of the Owl's criticism of the Nightingale in terms of her musical characteristics in the parody of 'Aurea personet lira . . .' printed by Karl Strecker with the Cambridge Songs – 'Aurea frequenter lingua . . .'. This poem reproaches the Nightingale for the interminability of her song, its tinny, jangling sound, her inflated self-esteem, her diminutive stature, and her habit of not singing when she breeds. In any case, the English poet limits his field of reference to a specific story – that of the husband who kills a nightingale because of his suspicion of its complicity in his wife's adultery.[83]

The poet's choice to extend the subsequent debate on marital issues for nearly three hundred lines was the consequence not only of birds' traditional sympathy for lovers, but also of his depiction of the Owl and the Nightingale as female. They discuss marriage at length because they are representatives or even projections of women.[84] As such, it is their natural prerogative to

---

[79] Salter, p. 44. For example, Hall, II, 567; Atkins, p. 58; Stanley pp. 1, 22; Wilson, *EMEL*, p. 164; Pearsall, *OEMEP*, p. 94; Shippey, p. 60.

[80] Burrow, *Medieval Writers*, p. 98.

[81] Some indication of the "wealth" and "variability" of the traditional associations of the Nightingale is given by Gellinek-Schellekens, pp. 1–28; and Pfeffer, *Change*.

[82] For example, Marcabrun, 'Estornel, cueill . . .' and 'Ges l'estornels . . .'; Peire d'Alvernhe, 'Rossinhol el seu repaire . . .'; 'Iuvenilis lascivia . . .'; and the late medieval *chanson de malmariée*, 'Je ne le seré de .VII. ans . . .', str. 6.

[83] See below, 'The Death of the Nightingale'.

[84] According to Stanley, "The words *owl* and *nightingale* are historically fem[inine]"

scrutinize the social institution which so much circumscribed women's lives. Perhaps the poet imagined them gossiping about the troubles and scandals of marriage like women gathered "en chapitres", described by Chardri's Enfant. The forms in which the poet contrasts the experiences of women probably reflects distinctions conventionally made in genres orientated towards women. Resonances of devotional material for women, like the AB-texts I discussed in Chapter Four, can be found in both birds' arguments.[85] More importantly the very structure of their discussion, which develops into a contrast between maidens and wives, is founded upon the address to women in terms of their marital "estates", which is especially characteristic of treatises and sermons. These 'grades' of female experience are made more resonant by reference to their dramatic stylizations in contemporary lyric. The exploited girl and the ill-married wife – la fille délaissée and la malmariée – are types common in medieval song.[86]

What is most striking about this poem's treatment of marriage is its perspective. The two birds compete in their sympathy for women. Throughout the poem, they behave as if feminine loyalty were the first of principles – even though they are otherwise quite prepared to be unscrupulous and even dishonest in their rhetorical strategies against each other. A sense of the inconsistency of their arguments is perhaps the inevitable result of the priority of matter over character which is in the nature of the fictional debate. Yet, so extravagantly partisan is the birds' support for women that one sometimes suspects the poet of irony. Nevertheless, the cynicism of men is a premise of both the scenarios which the birds invoke – the battered wife and the abandoned girl – and the truculence of their sympathy for women is the natural and justifiable response to male injustice.

(p. 105). Hinckley argues that, in the case of nightingale, this was not necessarily so, and suggests that the author deliberately imagined his birds as "scolding women" ('Science', p. 312). Gottschalk declares that, "One is constantly aware that the Owl and the Nightingale seem to be women as well as birds" (p. 662), and makes this the basis of her argument that the poem was "intended to give moral instruction to a mixed popular audience living in the world" (p. 657; cf. Coleman, p. 544). Mertens-Fonck points out (p. 190) that "the poet's strategy in adapting his sources in matters of love and marriage consists in systematically turning ideas to the advantage and exculpation of women".

[85] I am not suggesting that the O&N-poet knew the AB-texts directly, but there is perhaps some justification in regarding the AB-texts as surviving representatives of what must have been once an even broader tradition (Millett, 'Women', p. 97).
[86] Bec, Lyrique, pp. 57–90.

5. The Death of the Nightingale

The origins of the birds' discussion of female experiences inside and outside marriage lie in the Owl's allegation that when the Nightingale sits near people's houses – near the privy, as the she prefers to put it (584–90) – she incites them to carnal lust ("fleses luste", 894–6). The Nightingale replies, rather superciliously, that it is her proper place ("righte stede") to sit and sing wherever a gentleman has his beloved in bed ("Thar louerd haueth his loue ibedde", 955–68). She declares that "it is my right, it is my nature, that I am drawn to the highest".[87] The Owl supports her allegation that her opponent incites women to commit adultery by referring to the story of the nightingale who was executed by an angry husband for just this crime (1049–62). She presents it as if it were a historical event – "Once, as I know well" ("Enes . . . – ic wod wel ware"). Several medieval versions of this story still survive and it was perhaps widely current, but even the extant medieval versions permit widely differing constructions of the Nightingale's role in the lady's infidelity.[88]

Marie de France's 'Laüstic' is almost lyrical in its brevity.[89] She represents the bird as a tragic victim of circumstance, for he has no independent motivation.[90] The lady has been getting up to gaze at her lover from her window. She hides this by telling her husband that she has been listening to the nightingale sing. The bird itself has no responsibility either for the woman's wish to commit adultery or for concealing it. To the lady, the bird's song perhaps only evokes the sweetness of her unattainable love. Yet her description of her feelings is equivocal, for it could refer as easily to the lover as to the song: "He delights me so much, and I want him so much that I can get no sleep at all."[91] The nightingale thus both represents and *is* the lady's beloved. The *lai* might well be alluding to an episode in the Tristran-cycle in which the hero indicated his return to

---

[87] *O&N*, 968–70: "Hit is mi right, hit is mi lawe/ That to the hexst ich me drawe". The notion of 'kind' – the natural order of things – recurs throughout the poem (Bennett, pp. 4–5).

[88] Marie de France, 'Laüstic'; Alexander Neckam: *De Naturis Rerum*, I. 51, pp. 102–3; *Gesta Romanorum*, no. 121, ed. Oesterley, pp. 470–2; ME version, ed. Herrtage, pp. 60–3; *Renart le Contrefait*, II, 233–5 (see Flinn, pp. 364–441). All these versions are discussed by Stanley (pp. 165–6) and Reinhold Köhler (Warnke, pp. cxxvi–cxxxiii), who also prints and discusses a late medieval analogue, 'On doit bien aymer . . .'. Cf. Boccaccio, *Decameron*, V. 4, in which the nightingale's association with illicit love provides the opportunity for a bawdy joke.

[89] Bullock-Davies regards abbreviation as a distinctive and deliberate aspect of Marie's style (pp. 95–6); Stevens argues that Marie "distils or represents, scarcely ever discusses or analyses, feeling" (p. 4).

[90] The Nightingale is grammatically masculine in Old French.

[91] 'Laüstic', 89–90: "Tant me delit'e tant le voil/ Que jeo ne puis dormir de l'oil."

Iseult by imitating bird-song.[92] Similarly, in *Aucassin et Nicolette* the nightingale's presence in the garden reminds the heroine of her beloved, and inspires her to flee her prison: "One night, Nicolette was lying in her bed, and she saw the moon shining brightly through the window, and heard the nightingale singing in the garden. This reminded her of Aucassin her beloved whom she loved so dearly . . . and so she decided that she wouldn't stay there anymore . . .".[93] These literary parallels might seem to justify the husband's suspicions to some extent, but in Marie's tale the nightingale's association with the lover is only symbolic, and there is no suggestion that the bird will inspire her to take any action. In his inability to make more than a literal identification of the nightingale with the lover, the husband reveals the fundamental harshness of his soul. Marie reinforces the impression that his cruelty is extravagantly disproportionate by her pathetic description of the nightingale's fragile little body ("cors petit"). The contrast between the majesty of the song and the tiny, drab corpse stands for the gulf between the beauty of the lady's aspiring love and the meagreness of reality. We feel that the husband's callousness in some ways justifies the lady's desire to be free of him. As she puts it, "Anyone who has not heard the nightingale sing has had no joy in this world."[94]

The husband is thus identified with a brutal and joyless realism. As an individual he is cold-hearted: as a type, he stands between women and the joys of youthful liberty, love and courtship. The contrast between the two knights, the lover and the husband, perhaps represents two stages in the lady's life. The lover is the spirit of her youth: her husband stands for the mundane constrictions of her married life. In contrasting these figures, the *lai* evokes the passing of time. The beauty of the song enclosed in the Nightingale's frail body is an image for the transience of youthful happiness. Marie's version of the tale thus hardly permits the Owl's inference of her opponent's personal responsibility for "wicked love" ("uuel luue"). Indeed it actually supports the Nightingale's claim to a special empathy with the processes of nature.

---

[92] Cf. *Le Donnei des Amants*, 493–6:

> Entre ses braz le rei la tent,
> Tristan dehors e chante e gient
> Cum russinol que pret congé
> En fin d'esté od grant pité.

("The king holds her in his arms, while outside Tristan sings and plays, like a nightingale sorrowfully taking its leave at the end of the summer.") Other stories based on Tristan's Return are told by Marie de France ('Chevrefoil') and in the two *Folies Tristan*: Weiss, p. xviii.

[93] *Aucassin*, XII. 5–7, 9–10: "Nicolete jut une nuit en son lit, si vit la lune luire cler par une fenestre et si oï le lorseilnol center en garding, se li sovint d'Aucassin sen ami qu'ele tant amoit . . . si sc pcnsa qu'ele ne remanroit plus ilec . . .".

[94] 'Laüstic', 84–5: "Il nen ad joië en cest mund,/ Ki n'ot le laüstic chanter."

The Owl emphasizes an element of the story which is absent from Marie's version. She tells us that the nightingale was sentenced to a judicial punishment for its role in the lady's adultery: "The only judgment you received was the condemnation to be torn apart by wild horses."[95] She implies that the nightingale's death was not merely the cruel whim of a jealous husband but a publicly ratified, and therefore deserved, sentence. This kind of execution also appears in the version of the tale referred to by Alexander Neckam in the *De naturis rerum*, but he uses the story as the basis for a lively burlesque:

> Sed o dedecus! quid meruit nobilis volucrum praecentrix, instar Hippolyti Thesidae, equis diripi? Miles enim quidam nimis zelotes philomenam quatuor equis distrahi praecepit, eo quod secundum ipsius assertionem animum uxoris suae nimis demulcens, eam ad illiciti amoris compulisset illecebras. Sed quid? O zelotypia excandescens, et in saevitiam tyrannidis transiens! Nonne unicus equus protervae improbitati voluntatis tuae in aviculam, sed et innocentem, sed et gratiae singulorum reconciliatricem, posset suffecisse? Sed quid? Animum excaecatum ruere cogit in praeceps impetus habenis moder-aminis non coercitus, et sibi male blandiens commen[d]atrix mendax est voluntas inhonesta.[96]

The epithet for the Nightingale – "image of Hippolytus, Theseus's son" – and the formula – "would not *one* horse have been enough . . .?" – are clearly preposterous, while the depiction of the husband as a slavering tyrant invests the bird with a suffering saintliness she hardly deserves. The elaborate execution of such a tiny creature – by wild horses no less – is comical. In his posture of moral outrage, Neckam simply plays upon the absurdity of the situation.

His presentation of the fable as an *exemplum* of the folly of impetuousness suggests that he was familiar with a version in which the jealous husband is punished for his "voluntas inhonesta". In the *Gesta Romanorum*, the lover treats the bird's murder as an intimation of the husband's vengeance, and forestalls it by arming himself and killing him. In *Renart le Contrefait* the

---

[95] *O&N*, 1061-2: "Thu naddest non other dom ne lawe/ Bute mid wilde horse were todrawe."

[96] "But what a disgrace! How did that noble precentor of birds, the very image of Theseus's son Hippolytus, deserve to be torn apart by horses? For a certain over-jealous knight once ordered that a nightingale be drawn apart by four horses, because he said that, by softening his wife's spirit, the bird drove her towards the traps of illicit love. But why? Such burning jealousy, expressed as a tyrant's savagery! Would not one horse have satisfied the depravity of your arrogant hatred for this little bird – this innocent, in whom every aspect of grace is assembled? Why? This headlong assault, unrestrained by the reins of caution, only drove his blinded mind to ruin, for the will to dishonesty deceitfully flatters and commends itself." For "commendatrix", Wright prints "commentatrix".

story is used as an illustration of the way in which people bring disaster upon themselves.[97] By murdering the nightingale in spite of his wife's pleas, the husband only prompts her rebellion: "Because now she sees clearly that he really despises her".[98] It is this tradition to which the Nightingale resorts in attempting to manipulate the tale to her own advantage: "What, are you saying this to shame me? The knight suffered harm because of this".[99] Her part in the drama, she argues, was simply to console the lady out of pity (''milse an ore'') for her husband's cruelty in locking her up. It was malice (''nithe'') that motivated the husband's actions against her, she says, and it led directly to his punishment at the hands of the king (1091).

Since it is clear even from the extant versions of the story that a number of different constructions could be placed upon it, it seems likely that the poet introduced it as an *exemplum* precisely because it was susceptible to such different readings. The Owl's attempt to fix its significance as an illustration of the Nightingale's association with adultery is balanced by the Nightingale's interpretation of her role as the victim of reprehensible jealousy. The poet himself resorts to such material only in order to *extend* the significant possibilities of the protagonists. The effect is to make a narrow identification of the two birds in terms of allegory almost impossible. Indeed, it is only as long as their moral significance remains in doubt that their discussion of moral issues can be entertainingly sustained. The task which so many critics have set themselves – the identification and evaluation of the birds' allegorical meaning – is frustrated by the very workings of the poem. The Owl and the Nightingale resist allegorical identification, just as the issues which they discuss militate against resolution. The poet uses their personae to balance ideas, not confine them.

6. The Nightingale's Defence – lines 1331–1416

> Thah sum wif beo of nesche mode –
> For wummon beoth of softe blode –
> That heo, for sum sottes lore
> The yeorne bit & siketh sore,
> Misrempe & misdo summe stunde,
> Schal ich tharuore beon ibunde?[100]

---

[97] Flinn, p. 432. Cf. *Castia Gilós*, 44–5.

[98] *Renart*, p. 234b: "Car or voit elle fermement/ Qu'il la despise voirement."

[99] *O&N*, 1075–6: "Wat! seistu this for mine shome? The louerd hadde herof grame."

[100] *O&N*, 1349–54: "Though sometimes a woman has such a delicate temperament (for women are made of soft material), that she goes astray and does wrong sometimes, on account of some idiot flattering her and urgently beseeching her with pitiful sighs, should I be held responsible for that?"

The Nightingale's argument for her lack of responsibility perhaps deliberately parallels the Owl's that she is an observer and not an agent of men's fortunes (1235-50). In suggesting that her song is, like money or weapons, good in itself, whether it be turned to good or ill (1363-76), the Nightingale tries to associate herself with "Love" as an impersonal and universal power in nature.[101] She even implies that, when the the Owl maligns her, she maligns Love. "Ah you wretch, do you dare to accuse love?" she demands reproachfully;[102] and, still posing as Love's mouthpiece, she launches into a pugnacious defence of love within marriage:

> Bo wuch ho bo, vich luue is fele
> Bitweone wepmon and wimmane;
> Ah yef heo is atbroide, thenne
> He is unfele and forbrode.
> Wroth wurthe heom the holi rode,
> The rihte ikunde swo forbreideth![103]

This tirade is less ethical than it appears to be. Her initial assertion, that any marital relationship is proper, no matter how conducted, is far removed from the medieval Church's actual teaching on the practice of sexual love in marriage, as Chaucer's Parson remarks – "and for that many man weneth that he may nat synne for no likerousnesse that he dooth with his wyf, certes, that opinion is fals".[104] While Christian thinkers did appeal to such a concept as "rihte ikunde" ("natural law"),[105] the Nightingale's understanding of it is obviously extremely limited, for her morality is always in accord with self-interested pragmatism – "whoever goes outside her nest to breed," she declares, "is mad" ("heo beoth wode/ The bute nest goth to brode", 1385-6).

Throughout this section the Nightingale praises marriage but emphasizes and defends the weakness of women. However, her support for women takes priority over her sense of the fitness of marriage. She remains sympathetic even to those women who offend the natural order which she sees expressed in marriage:

---

[101] Pearsall, *OEMEP*, p. 91: "in the treatment of love and sexuality there are faint echoes of Alan de Lille and the school of Chartres as well as hints of goliardic irreverence".

[102] *O&N*, line 1377: "Ah schaltu, wrecch, luue tele?"

[103] *O&N*, 1378-83: "Whatever kind it is, any love is proper between a husband and wife; but if the woman is snatched away, it becomes bad and corrupted. Whoever so corrupts the natural order, may they earn [or: they will earn] the wrath of the Holy Cross!"

[104] *Parson's Tale*, X. 858. Decretists and canon lawyers could not agree how to distinguish between mortal, venial and sinless sex in marriage (Kelly, *LMAC*, pp. 262-85). They placed many restrictions upon the practice of marital sex (Brundage, *Law*, pp. 197-9, 278-88).

[105] Brundage, *Law*, pp. 235, 279.

Ne beoth heo notht alle forlore
That stumpeth at the flesches more,
For moni wummon haueth misdo
That arist op of the slo.[106]

She seems to be referring to the doctrine that any sin is pardonable if the
sinner repents, but the only substantiation of her case which she offers – at
least at first – is the assertion that "flesches gult" is less grave than the sins of
the spirit. The division of the sins into these two categories dates back to
Cassian and Gregory.[107] However, as Stanley points out, "it is unusual in the
Middle Ages to regard the sins of the flesh as less than those of the spirit" –
although there are texts which treat carnal sins as being, while no less serious,
more easily remediable than those of the spirit.[108] The Nightingale's
argument perhaps depends upon a confused version of the idea that pride is
the first of the sins.[109] Alternatively, she may be referring specifically to the
principle often applied to virginity that bodily continence is devalued by
psychological impurity – as, for example in Peter Lombard's formulation
"Virginity of the mind is better than that of the flesh."[110] To this principle
Heloise also appealed: "purity of the flesh is a virtue of the mind, not of the
body".[111] Such formulations were naturally common in devotional literature
addressed to women. In *Hali Meithhad*, for example, we find the warning:

Ah thah thu, meiden, beo with unbruche of thi bodi, ant tu habbe
prude, onde other wreaththe, yisceunge other wac wil inwith i thin
heorte, thu forhorest te with the unwiht of helle, ant he streoneth on the
the team thet tu temest.[112]

---

[106] *O&N*, 1391–4: "If she trips over the root of the flesh, she's not completely lost, for
many women have done wrong, and afterwards arisen from the mire."

[107] Bloomfield, pp. 145–8, at p. 146: "He [*sic*: meaning the Nightingale] then refers to the
sins of the body and those of the spirit, a division which immediately informs us that
the poet is thinking of the chief sins in the well-known classification made by Cassian
and Gregory."

[108] Stanley, p.146, n. to line 1410.

[109] Bloomfield, pp. 73–5, also n. 56, p. 359; McNeill and Gamer, p. 19. The
Nightingale's argument here might be compared with Lady Mede's equally
unsubstantiated assertion that lechery is "synne of the sevene sonnest relessed" (*Piers
Plowman*, B III. 58, C III. 62).

[110] Peter Lombard, *Sententiae*, IV, 33, PL 192. 926: "Melior est autem virginitas mentis
quam carnis."

[111] 2 *Ad Abaelardum*, 81/20: "munditia carnis . . . non [est] corporis, sed animi virtus."
Coleman (p. 521) suggests that the *O&N*-poet is alluding here to Abelardian ethics.

[112] *HM*, 36/20–23: "But, maiden, although your body remains unblemished, if you are
proud, envious, irascible, covetous or weak-willed at heart, you prostitute yourself to
the Devil of Hell, and he fathers on you the progeny you bear." Cf. St Augustine, *De
sanctae virginitate*, cap. 46, PL 40. 423–4; Aldhelm, (prose) *De Virginitate*, 67.X–
70.XIII; *Speculum Virginum*, VII. 615–41 (pp. 211–12). The *Speculum* even uses the
phrase "uterus mentis" (VII. 53, p. 191).

However, neither Heloise nor the author of *Hali Meiðhad* are attempting to provide excuses for sexual misconduct. Their stress upon mental purity depends upon an assumption of the importance of physical integrity. The Nightingale is understandably reluctant to develop what is in this context a tenuous argument. Instead, by defining the sins of the spirit as malice and envy ("nithe an onde"), *Schadenfreude*, callousness and pride (1401-6), she merely insinuates that these are her opponent's faults: "She's a fine one to make accusations of folly, who sings worse because of pride."[113]

7. Maidens and Wives – lines 1417-1602

At line 1417, the Nightingale abruptly switches from the theme of the susceptibility of women in general to the proposition that the sexual misdemeanours of maidens are more forgiveable than those of married women. If she could induce love, she says, she would far rather that maidens loved "derneliche" – secretly – than wives (1417-22). The phrase "derne luue" also occurs in 'A Lutel Soth Sermun'. There its disastrous consequences are heavily underlined. The Nightingale has apparently drifted from a eulogy of marriage to a defence of women for their waywardness. In order not to appear to condone adultery and thus justify the Owl's charges, she sets up a new point of contrast. From this point on, neither of the birds is immediately concerned with the Nightingale's role in adultery, and the contrast between wives and maidens becomes the new focus of the poem. Indeed, in putting the case of unfaithful wives, the Owl herself condones adultery. According to Moran, "Some scholars have been puzzled and thought that the Owl is justifying adultery, but this would be completely in contrast with her doctrine and what she represents."[114] Moran is drawn into this view by her belief that the birds' discussion of pre-marital sex and adultery is only an occasion for them to air their views on sin. However, it strikes me as very Procrustean to say that the Owl cannot mean what she says – and she undoubtedly does come to condone adultery – because of a prejudice about what she represents. Moreover, her interpretation of line 1570 – the Owl's wish that the *malmariée* will get a "betere ibedde" – would be unconvincing even if she had not also mistranslated "ibedde". She argues that "naturally a better bed means a convent" (p. 202), but "ibedde" actually means "bedfellow" not "bed". In fact, by the time that the Owl has reached this position, both birds have "forgotten" that the condonement of adultery was ever at issue. This is the consequence not of their dishonesty as speakers, but of the demands of the

---

[113] *O&N*, 1415-16: "Swuch he may telen of golnesse/ That sunegeth wurse i modinesse." Bloomfield (pp. 146-8) argues that the Nightingale's list can be assimilated to the tradition of the Seven Deadly Sins.
[114] Moran, n. 106, p. 202.

genre – for a debate-poem of this length requires a steady flow of different topics to sustain the interest of its audience.

"If a maiden loves secretly", says the Nightingale, she commits only a minor fault, a mistake both reparable ("heo stumpeth") and natural ("heo . . . falth icundeliche"): the measure of its gravity is the ease with which it can be mended:

> For thah heo sum hwile pleie
> Heo nis nout feor ut of the weie;
> Heo mai hire guld atwende
> A rihte weie thurth chirche bende,
> An mai eft habbe to make
> Hire leofmon withute sake,
> An go to him bi daies lihte
> That er stal to bi theostre nihte.[115]

Janet Coleman has argued that the Nightingale here alludes to canonical teaching on marriage.[116] Though the affair which the Nightingale describes is both secret and illicit, by a strict interpretation of the law it might already be deemed a binding marriage. Therefore the Nightingale argues that the girl's "guld" is not a serious matter like adultery or fornication, but the peccadillo of not publicizing the liaison – despite the insistence by the Church on the necessity of banns and celebrations *in facie ecclesie*. "In effect", says Coleman, "the Nightingale argues that the girl who has chosen her partner secretly can render this lightly sinful position corrected by the Church's bond."[117]

Some idea of the confusion and abuses to which the Church's recognition of clandestine marriages gave rise can be gained from the thirteenth- and fourteenth-century consistory court records studied by Sheehan, Helmholz and Kelly.[118] The court records bear witness to "the tenacity of the belief that people could regulate their own matrimonial affairs, without the assistance or interference of the Church".[119] The most common marital action in these records was "the petition which asserted the existence of a marriage contract and asked the court to enforce it by a declaration of validity and by an order,

---

[115] *O&N*, 1425–32: "For though she plays around for a while, she isn't far off course; through the Church's bonds she can turn away from guilt onto the right track. Then she can have her lover without any argument, and go to him by the light of day, rather than creeping to him in the dead of night." Cf. Wolfram von Eschenbach's 'Der helden minne . . .', lines 11–15: "Swer pfliget oder ie gepflac/ daz er bî lieben wîbe lac/ den merkern unverborgen,/ der darf niht durch den morgen/ dannen streben" ("Whoever is or has ever been accustomed to lie beside his beloved wife without having to hide from anyone, he need not force himself to go away from there because of the morning")

[116] Coleman, pp. 537–44.

[117] Coleman, p. 537.

[118] Sheehan, 'Formation'; Helmholz, *Marriage Litigation*; Kelly, *LMAC*, pp. 169–72.

[119] Helmholz, p. 32.

in most dioceses, that it should be solemnized *in facie ecclesie*".[120] By insisting upon the validity of even the most tentative of contracts, the Church not only justified such informal arrangements, but also fostered the resort to litigation in the case of the inevitable misunderstandings – usually resulting in an action asserting "pre-contract". Such an action is perhaps what the Nightingale means by "sake" ('contention'): she might be suggesting that by publicizing her liaison the maiden will save herself from immersion in such a tangle.[121]

The highly anomalous situation in which the Church fulminated against unpublicized marriages but accepted them to be valid, arose out of a contradiction of beliefs: on the one hand, that marriage is a public matter, the means by which children are legitimized and social morality upheld; on the other, that it is an entirely private matter, the expression of two people's desire for their own unique and indissoluble union. Perhaps medieval preachers often had to remind their flocks of the social and spiritual advantages of regulating their relationships according to the Church's law. However, even if ecclesiastical teaching on marriage was the model for the Nightingale's argument, she distorts it. Churchmen emphasized the convenience and guiltlessness of marriage in order to encourage people to formalize their relationships not privately, at home, but publicly, in church. They were concerned that, where the intention of the two parties to contract a permanent and exclusive union existed (with or without parental approval), they should be brought to church where the union could be publicly sanctified. Relationships conducted secretly precisely because the parties had no marital intention were fornicatory and the decretists did not seek to offer excuses for them. The jurist, Rufinus, for example, taught that, in cases of clandestine marriage, the onus was upon the couple to prove that they had in fact contracted a marriage.[122] Some fourteenth-century consistory courts recognized clandestine unions, but had the parties to them whipped.[123]

By contrast, the Nightingale seems to be arguing that even had there been no matrimonial intention, the Church's bonds would nevertheless absolve the hypothetical maiden of any guilt. It is quite possible that this woman has formed her sexual relationship without any intention of making it a preliminary to marriage. What the Nightingale might mean by the girl being not "feor ut of the weie" is that, if she becomes pregnant or is discovered and dishonoured in some other way, she can use the marriage to absolve herself of the consequences. She suggests that the Church's arguments in favour of the public legitimization of common-law relationships can be used by women as a kind of social insurance policy allowing them to indulge securely in secret

---

[120] Helmholz, p. 25.
[121] Coleman, pp. 538–9.
[122] Brundage, *Law*, p. 276. Similarly, Hugh of St Victor pointed out that "concealed agreements" might not be "marriages but adulterous cohabitations or defilements" (*De sacramentis*, II. 11, cap. 6).
[123] Kelly, *LMAC*, pp. 170–2.

and temporary liaisons. Rather conveniently, she thinks that the law of marriage was flexible enough to admit even promiscuous young maidens into the fold of respectability.

She justifies her assertion that it is natural for young girls to "fall" is justified by saying that they are ignorant and that their biological urges, "yunge blod", are responsible for their transgressions. In this, she closely echoes (perhaps deliberately) the Owl's defence of her chicks' toilet-habits (635–6), also on the grounds of natural necessity and ignorance. Underlying these arguments is probably a proverbial idea widely current in medieval literature – "Necessity knows no law" ("Necessitas non habet legem"/ "Necessité n'a loy").[124] As before, the Nightingale argues that if a maiden slips, the man is to blame:

> An sum sot mon hit tihth tharto
> Mid alle than that he mai do:
> He cometh & fareth, & beoth & bid,
> An heo bistant & ouersid,
> An [heo] bisehth ilome & longe.
> Hwat mai that chil thah hit misfonge?[125]

This argument also appears in one of the lyrics of the Vernon manuscript, 'This World's Weal comes from Women':

> Wimmen wroughte neuer no wrong
> But thorw Monnes entysement.
> Men secheth wimmen so strong,
> And sei in Bale thei mote be brent,
> And ligge aboute hem so long,
> To bringen hem til heore a-sent;
> And thus thorw monnes false song,
> Ofte wymmen hath be schent.[126]

The insistent suitor is a character with a long literary history – going back at least to Ovid – but the joviality of the Nightingale's references to him suggests that the type was not only still vivid, but also a specifically comic one.[127] Both she and the Vernon-poet turn a cynical eye upon the lover's persistence and his rhetoric. It was perhaps in a similar way that the preacher

[124] Whiting, N 51; Schnell, p. 102.
[125] *O&N*, 1435–40: "And some foolish man entices her, as best as he can: he comes and goes, pleads and demands, harrasses and besets her, and beseeches her often and at length. How is a young girl to blame if she does wrong?" Both the C and J MSS omit "heo" in line 1436; Stanley's edition reads "An [h]i sehth".
[126] Lines 49–56: "Women never did wrong, except through a man's enticement. Men pursue women so fiercely, and swear upon the fires of hell, and beset them so long, until they can get them to consent: and thus because of men's deceitful song, women often suffer disaster."
[127] It might be said that Ovid adopted the pose of a cynical seducer in the *Amores* and illustrated the consequences in the *Heroides*. Cf. Andreas, *De amore*, II. 6, 9, p. 240.

187

of 'A Lutel Soth Sermun' imagined Robin's "tale". There is a relish and rapidity about the Nightingale's repeated use of the word "sot" which suggests the ubiquity of such men.

The Nightingale also argues that a young girl might be susceptible to a lover's importunities on account of her curiosity – her desire to "wite iwis hwuch beo the gome/ That of so wilde maketh tome" (1443-4). Her strange way of alluding to love's power may only be a reminder of her animal-perspective and a further attempt to identify herself with love's natural authority, but there is also a slight air of fashionable hyperbole in the phrase, as if the Nightingale momentarily pretends to sound knowledgeable about the kind of things said in courtly love-poetry.[128] The word "gome" also recalls the maiden's foolish attitude in 'A Lutel Soth Sermun'. Yet, having evoked the idea of love as a mesmerizing power, the Nightingale immediately goes on to speak of its transience – specifically in terms of the fragility and brevity of her own sweet song:

> Ich teache heom bi mine songe
> That swucch luue ne lest noght longe;
> For mi song lutle hwile ileste,
> An luue ne deth noght bute rest
> On swuch childre, & sone ageth,
> An falth adun the hote breth.
> Ich singe mid heom one throwe,
> Biginne on heh & endi lawe,
> An lete mine songes falle
> An lutle wile adun mid alle.
> That maide wot, hwanne ich swike,
> That luue is mine songes iliche:
> For hit nis bute a lutel breth
> That sone kumeth & sone geth.
> That child bi me hit understond,
> An his unred to red vvend,
> An iseyth wel bi min songe
> That dusi luue ne last noght longe.[129]

For all love's intoxication of the young, it inevitably marks their passage to the responsibilities of maturity. Like Marie de France, the poet uses the

---

[128] Compare, for example, Guilhem IX, 'Mout jauzens . . .', 25-30.

[129] *O&N*, 1449-66: "I show them by my song that such love does not last long; for my song only goes on for a little while, and love scarcely rests upon such children, and soon goes, and the warm breath fades away. I sing for them a while, begin high, and end low, and let my song fade away altogether after a while. This maiden knows by my labour that love is like my song, for it's but a little breath that soon comes and soon goes. She understands this because of me and changes her unwise course to wisdom, seeing clearly in my song that dizzy love doesn't last long." In its description of the Nightingale's song as breath and the emphasis on its rise and fall, this passage recalls Pliny, *Natural History*, vol. 3, Book X, c. XLIII, p. 344.

Nightingale's song as an emblem of time. In terms of her battle with the Owl, the Nightingale uses this idea to suggest that her song is not a stimulus to love, but a demonstration of its intangibility. She is simply a sympathetic spectator, whose song might be taken as an image, in its beauty and delicacy, of the splendour and transience of youth. It is remarkable that in this passage the Nightingale strikes what is perhaps the key-note of all the English pieces in the CJ-Group.[130] They characteristically attempt to stimulate devotion and repentance by stressing the impermanence of life's joys. Two of the most beautiful early Middle English poems upon this theme, Thomas of Hales's 'Luue-Ron' and the 'Poema Morale', appear in the Jesus manuscript.[131] The similarity of sentiment between the Nightingale's speech and these even extend to verbal echoes.[132] Young women are also urged to think about the transience of men's love in devotional literature for women. An example is the Vernon lyric, 'Of Clene Maydenhod':

> For monnes love, yif thou beo-holde,
> Hit lasteth but a luytel res . . .[133]

Comparison could also be made with the process of disillusionment which the AB-Group refers to in terms of the treachery of men – "behold, high Lord, how man's support betrays me" ("bihold heie louerd hu monnes help truketh me", *LLo*, 89–90).

It is possible that the Nightingale's evocation of the transience of a young woman's joys is underpinned by a consciousness of the social calamitousness

---

[130] Even the *PP* might also be seen as a meditation upon the theme of the transience of life.

[131] Millett has recently suggested that the 'Luue-Ron' was written for a female recluse ('Women', p. 97).

[132] For example:

> Vve wilneth after worldes ayhte, that longe ne may
>   ileste
>   ['Poema Morale', 313; cf. *O&N*, 1450]

> And lutle hwile he her ilest
>   ['Luue-Ron', 22; cf. *O&N*, ibid.]

> Mayde, her thu myht biholde
> This worldes luue nys bute o res
>   ['Luue-Ron', 9–10; cf. *O&N*, 1459–62]

> Monnes luue nys buten o stunde
> Nv he luueth, nv he is sad,
> Nu he cumeth, nv wile he funde,
> Nv he is wroth, nv he is gled.
>   ['Luue-Ron', 49; cf. *O&N*, 1455–8]

[133] Lines 25–6, Furnivall, *Minor Poems*, pp. 464–8: "Man's love, if you look at it, only lasts a moment . . .".

of pregnancy out of wedlock similar to that of the 'Lutel Soth Sermon'.[134] The strained face ("tohte ilete", 1446) brought on by love might be interpreted as the "pallor" of pregnancy conventionally described in devotional literature[135] – or more simply as a token of the distress caused by her deceitful lover. The Nightingale certainly does not explicitly justify a reading in terms of an unwanted pregnancy. More decorously, she focuses instead upon a universal sense of feminine vulnerability to the disillusionments of love. The measure of her sympathy for young women is that she finds something essentially tragic in their susceptibility to love and the inevitability of their disappointment. Despite the emotiveness of her argument, it is also a strategy. It enables her simultaneously to support her assertion that young girls are too much the victims of their innocence to be held responsible for their actions, and to dissociate her song from the impetus to love.

As the Owl recognizes (1512-14), this is her opponent at her most persuasive, but, in the rest of the Nightingale's speech, in which she attacks adultery, the limitations of her essentially pragmatic, avian outlook reassert themselves. Her initial argument against women's adultery is that they should follow her own example in not singing when she breeds (1469-70). In other words, marriage is like breeding; it has nothing to do with love: and therefore married women should not concern themselves with adultery. However, in all the medieval lyrics which adduce this natural characteristic, the nightingale's example is discredited by the accusation that she is wanton and irresponsible.[136] Moreover, our Nightingale makes no suggestion that wives should refrain from adultery out of love for their husbands or out of respect for the dignity of matrimony as an institution. She goes on to say that she cannot understand why any man would want to have an affair with a married woman. A husband may be either worthy ("wurthful & aht") or unworthy ("forwurde . . . unorne"). In the former case, the husband will avenge himself by causing the lover a serious injury ("grame") and even, as she graphically suggests, castrate him. She says that it is also a wrong and a great folly ("unright & gret sothede") to come between a good man and his spouse – a phrase by which the Nightingale seems to mean an offence to the social rather than the moral order. If the husband is unworthy, on the other hand, the lover dishonours himself by association with his wife, and is deprived of any pleasure in the affair by the recollection of the "cheorl" to whom the lady belongs (1505-10). There is a hint here of that misogynistic

---

[134] A fourteenth-century preacher quoted by Wenzel (*Preachers*, pp. 238-9) explicitly compares a maiden whose irresponsible conduct leads to pregnancy out of wedlock with the nightingale, who sings so sweetly before mating, but then turns her song to sorrow.

[135] For example, Hildebert of Lavardin, *Ep.* 1. 21, PL 171. 194-5.

[136] Långfors, nos 86, 100 and 106; 'Aurea frequenter lingua . . .', str. 15; for other examples, Pfeffer, 'When the Nightingale'. In the sermon quoted by Wenzel, pp. 238-9, this habit is explicity moralized as a warning against pre-marital promiscuity.

repulsion for female sexuality which is found in works like the *Epistola Valerii*, but, at the simplest level, the Nightingale only seems to be saying that it is too shamefully easy to accede to the desires of such women. All they can offer, she implies, is what is "left over" from their husbands. In her view of the matter, the lover of a married woman must choose between harm and dishonour – "that on his aren, that other schonde" (1498).

The Nightingale's argument strongly resembles Alan of Lille's 'Vix nodosum valeo . . .', not only in its line of thought, but also in its graphic explication:

> Iam naturam Veneris nimis denaturat,
> De complexu coniugis cuius cura curat,
> Quam flagello mentule rusticus triturat,
> Que sub tantis ictibus inconcussa durat.
> Nullus qui sit sapiens talem ludum temptat,
> Tali gaudet gaudio, timor quem fermentat,
> Metus horror gemitus ubi se presentat,
> Vbi se securitas penitus absentat.
> Vbi sepe sompnio mortis soporatur
> Mechus, dum mechanice cum mecha mechatur,
> Vbi sepe mentule bursa sincopatur,
> Vbi sepe geminus frater decollatur.[137]

Like the Nightingale, Alan suggests that an affair with a married woman is undesirable because of the possibility of the cuckolded husband's violent revenge – and in particular by castration. He also alludes to a peasant ("rusticus"), who clearly corresponds to the "cheorl" so despised by the Nightingale. Alan's style is so terse that the "rusticus" does not unambiguously emerge as the woman's husband, but his line of thought is clearly illuminated by the English poem. 'Vix nodosum valeo . . .' is an unpleasantly masculine piece, written very much in celebration of the exploitability of women by men. The resemblance between its arguments and the Nightingale's suggests that, long before Chaucer, the author of *The Owl and the Nightingale* had hit upon the device of creating a dramatic and disorientating tension in the voice of a female character by having her manipulate distinctively antifeminist ideas.[138]

---

[137] 'Vix nodosum . . .', 113–24: "For he goes too far in perverting Nature's nature, who concerns himself with embracing a married woman, a woman threshed by the flail of a peasant's manhood, who lies unshaken under so many blows. No wise man would attempt such sport, rejoice in a joy brewed with fear, where dread, horror and moaning stand by, where security is wholly absent, where a fornicator is often drugged in a mortal sleep, as he fornicates mechanically with his whore, where the purse of manhood is often cut off and a twin-brother beheaded."

[138] Cf. Mann, *Geoffrey Chaucer*, p. 51. The Nightingale is not, of course, a woman, but a female bird; nor is what she says strictly satirical of women in general. However, while her sympathies and outlook are entirely feminine, her argument is "masculine".

However, the Nightingale makes no suggestion that adultery is immoral in itself. She seems to have forgotten the ideal of married love which she evoked at the very beginning of the debate on marriage, for she does not adduce it as a reason for lovers to steer clear. Perhaps she feels that the violence of the "worthy" husband is the woman's protection, while, in his very feebleness, the "cheorl" has failed in his duties to her. This figure is plainly conceived as a *senex amans*.[139] The Nightingale's vocabulary suggests age as well as weakness ("unorne", "forwurde"); low rank as well as uncultivation ("cheorl"); and physical unattractiveness, especially in bed (the great stomach, "buc"). Why should the wife of such a man be unworthy of a lover's suit? Is it because the Nightingale assumes that she could only have consented to a dishonourable match for materialistic reasons – as the Wife of Bath did to her old husbands? Or because she was too pusillanimous to resist her parents' wishes? Or simply because a woman in that situation is seen as being desperate to have an affair and therefore embarrassingly unfussy about her lovers? Whatever the Nightingale's rationale, her pretensions to the moral high ground disintegrate in this final part of her case.

The Owl replies by transforming the Nightingale's image of the bad husband, feckless and pitiful, into one much worse – a selfish tyrant.[140] This sort of man spends so much of what he has upon his mistress that he leaves his "righte spuse" in a desolate and empty house ("wowes weste & lere huse"), ill-clad, ill-shod and without "mete & clothe" (1523–30). When he does come home his wife dare not speak to him, for he brings nothing but chiding and complaint, like a madman ("swuch he beo wod", 1531–3). Everything she says or does he takes amiss, and often, even when she is innocent ("hwan heo noght ne misdeth"), he punches her in the face (1535–8). All this is extremely reminiscent of the portrait of the cruel husband in *Hali Meithhad*. There again we find references to the wife's economic hardship – she is described as "godles inwith westi wahes" (26/30–1); he shouts and rails at her – "chit te ant cheoweth the" (28/3–4); she is scared even if he looks at her – "his lokunge on ageasteth the" (28/2–3); and he beats her up – "beateth the ant busteth the as his ibohte threl ant his ethele theowe" (28/5–6). The Owl's description of the wife's unhappiness in terms of his behaviour both out of the house and within it is parallel to *Hali Meithhad*'s:

> Hwen he bith ute, hauest ayein his hamcume sar care ant eie. Hwil he bith et hame, alle thine wide wanes thuncheth the to nearewe.[141]

Thus, as in the other cases cited by Mann, "speaker and speech are thus set at odds with each other in an ironic relationship".

[139] See Burrow, pp. 156–62; Micha.

[140] It was not until the Council of Westminster in 1285 that English law recognized the possibility of an action for separation brought on the grounds of cruelty (Coleman, p. 543).

[141] *HM*, 26/36–28/2: "When he is out, you are filled with anxiety and fear of his homecoming. While he is at home, all your wide halls seem to you too narrow."

Hali Meithhad in turn reflects the influence of the Latin tradition of virginity-literature. This passage occurs in a letter by Osbert of Clare:

> de custodibus quid dicam qui super uxores nobilium virorum tyrannidem exhibent effrenatam? si oculum fortuitu ad aliquem levaverit, si vel semel risum fecerit, statim iudicatur ut fatua, condemnatur ut adultera, nec tam verbis quam verberibus affligitur, et ad odium coniugis pravis accusatoribus incitatur. ita fit ut caritas coniugalis quae in sponsalibus ad invicem servanda promittitur pessimis instigatoribus violetur, dumque vir uxorem habet suspectam et uxor contra maritum gestat discordiam, procedente tempore divortium nascitur et moechus aut moecha in alterutro reputatur.[142]

A similar passage can be found in an *ad status* sermon by Jacques de Vitry:

> Perfidi enim reputari debent et proditores, qui splendide volunt vivere, et uxores suas fame cruciari permittunt, qui a mane usque ad vesperam vinum in tabernis bibunt, et uxores eorum in domo remanentes non nisi aquam bibunt; et insuper, dum ebrii redeunt, uxores sine causa verberant, et male tractant; unde quandoque ex tristitia et desperatione maritos relinqunt et alienis viris commiscentur, et licet non excusentur a peccato, maritus qui occasionem prebuit non reputabitur immunis.[143]

Although Osbert, Jacques and the Owl all argue that marriages can be damaged by husbands' mistreatment of their wives, the two churchmen are considerably more careful than the Owl not to provide an excuse for infidelity. Her outraged sympathy for bullied wives extends even a defence of adultery:

> Nis nan mon that ne mai ibringe
> His wif amis mid swucche thinge;

[142] Osbert of Clare, *Ep*. 40, 137/1–11: "What shall I say about those watchmen who display unbridled tyranny over the wives of noble men? If she happens to raise her eye to anyone, or if she smiles for a moment, immediately she is judged a foolish woman, condemned as an adulterer, punished not only verbally but also by beating, and made loathsome to her husband by her malicious accusers. Thus it happens that the conjugal love which each partner vowed to preserve is blighted by evil trouble-makers: then the man suspects his wife, and the wife nurses mutiny against her husband, and eventually divorce is born, each thinking the other a lecher or a whore."

[143] BN lat. 17509, f. 135va, quoted by d'Avray and Tausche, p. 106, n. 70: "Those men should be judged faithless traitors, who want to live splendidly, while they allow their wives to be tormented by hunger, who from morning till night are drinking wine in the taverns, while they wives stay at home with only water to drink; worse still, when they come home drunk, they beat their wives for no reason, and mistreat them: because of this sometimes in sadness and desperation they abandon their husbands and mingle with other men, and even though this does not excuse them for their sin, the husband who gives them occasion should not be reckoned free from responsibility."

> Me hire so ofte misbeode
> That heo do wule hire ahene neode.
> La, Godd hit wot! heo nah iweld,
> Thah heo hine makie kukeweld.[144]

Often, she says, a wife is delicate and gentle, beautiful and well brought-up, but even then a man will go off and spend his substance on a woman much less worthy (1545–50). Other men are oppressively jealous of their wives. They suspect them of harbouring adulterous thoughts if they see them so much as look at other men or speak nicely to them (1554–6). This is an idea which also appears in *Hali Meithhad*: "If you are pretty, and address everybody nicely with a cheerful manner, you won't be able to protect yourself from slander or wicked accusations."[145] Jealous men sometimes even lock their wives up, the Owl goes on:

> Tharthurh is spusing ofte tobroke,
> For yef heo is tharto ibroht
> He deth that heo nadde ear ithoht.[146]

This idea is to some extent a traditional one. In the collection known as the 'Proverbs of Prophets, Poets and Saints', Solomon's "Non sis zelotes, hoc est dictu: non zeles mulierem sinus tui" is rendered into English as:

> Yif thou haue a feir wyf
> And wolt that heo be trewe of lyf,
> Repreue her for no Cumpaygnye
> Of no mon for gelesye;
> Him to loue so thou maight make hire bolde
> On whom to-fore heo nolde be-holde.[147]

The female voices of the *chansons de malmariée* also portray their husbands as jealous, violent or inadequate – in this case, in order to justify their claims to sexual independence. In 'L'autrier tout seus chevauchoie mon chemin . . .', for example, the hero encounters a beautiful lady in a garden on the way out of Paris, who argues that "a woman does no wrong to take a lover if she has a bad husband" ("Dame qui a mal mari,/ S'el fet ami,/ N'en fet pas a blasmer"). She tells us:

---

[144] *O&N*, 1539–44: "Any man can drive his wife astray by behaving like this. He might abuse her so often, that she will satisfy her own needs. Oh, God knows, she is not responsible, even if she makes him a cuckold."

[145] *HM*, 28/22–4: "Yef thu art feier, ant with gleade chere bicleopest alle feire, ne schalt tu o nane wise wite the with unword ne with uuel blame."

[146] *O&N*, 1558–60: "In this way, marriages are often violated, for if she's driven that far, she'll do what she would never previously have considered."

[147] Furnivall, ed., *Minor Poems*, p. 537: "If you have a fair wife, and you want her to live chastely, don't tell her off for seeing any man, because of your jealousy; you might only encourage her to love a man she'd never looked at before."

> A un vilain m'ont donee mi parent,
> Qui ne fet aüner fors or et argent,
> Et me fet d'ennui morir assez sovent,
> Qu'il ne me let joer.[148]

The purpose of this reference to the husband's wealth and avarice is to discredit her parents' marital policy as financial exploitation. The last two lines imply the claim that, in her youth and beauty, she has a right to "play" – a right which has been unnaturally and selfishly abrogated by others. The *chanson* presents the case of the woman married to a "cheorl", of whom the Nightingale was so scornful. The woman's emphasis on the cynicism of the interests involved in her marriage is an attempt to justify the corresponding cynicism of her own willingness to break her conjugal vows. As in the Owl's speech, the husband's own oppressive jealousy is cited as the cause of his cuckolding. Yet in the French poem the woman's credibility is undermined by her willingness to do what the lover wishes there and then (28–31) on the grounds that she is too worried about her reputation to elope. However, were she truly careful of her honour, she would hardly indulge in such casual adultery: and if she truly despised her marriage, she would take the chance to escape it. It seems that as long as she can take her pleasure wherever she chooses she is quite happy to keep the material comforts of marriage to a rich man. It is perhaps these she means by "honeur" – for her parents' concern with money was perhaps not the selfish exploitation she claims it to be but a perfectly reasonable intention to see her supported in comfort and security. A comparable feminine pragmatism perhaps reasserts itself in the Owl's rather profane suggestion that Christ's grace to an unhappy wife should extend to the provision of a better man in bed ("betere ibedde", 1570), as she so bluntly puts it. The *chansons de malmariée* were apparently popular enough, in English as well as in French, for a late thirteenth-century preacher to refute their attitude to marriage with an affirmation of its sanctity:[149]

> Contra matrimonium [faciunt], quia maritis multum detrahitur quibus dicitur:
>
> > *Pur mun barun, fi!*
> > *Vn plus bel me at choisi.*
>
> Et Anglice dicitur:
>
> > *Of my husband giu I noht,*
> > *Another hauet my luue ybohit,*

---

[148] Lines 15–18: "My parents gave me to a churl. All he did was gather gold and silver. He often made me die of frustration because he would not let me play."

[149] Dublin, Trinity College, MS 347, f.199v: ed. Wenzel, *Preachers*, pp. 216–17 and p. 217, n. 29. Wenzel says that "this passage is taken verbatim from Peraldus' *Summa de vitiis*, into which several vernacular verses have been set" (p. 216), and he cites Peraldus, *Summa*, III. iv. 3 (ed. Lyons, 1668, p. 39).

For tuo gloues wyht ynoht.
If Hic him luue, Y naue no woht.

Multi eciam incitantur ad faciendum contra matrimonii fidem. Aperte vero contra legem matrimonii predicatur cum cantatur quod pro pravo viro uxor dimittere non debeat quin amicum faciat. Unde:

Lete the cukewald syte at hom
And chese the another lefmon.
Lete the chorl site at hom and pile,
And thu salt don wat thu wile –
God hit wot hit nys no skile!

Cum secundum legem Dei eciam leprosum dimittere non debeat, quin loco et tempore debitum ei reddat si ipse voluerit.[150]

At line 1571 of *The Owl and the Nightingale*, the focus of the debate shifts slightly. So far the Owl has evoked women's miseries in marriage, specifically in order to excuse their adulteries. Now she emphasizes the sadness of the female experience of marriage in a more general way. The issue of adultery which initiated this section of the birds' debate has now been almost totally submerged by the contrast between wives and maidens. The Owl is also perhaps keen to show that her empathy with women is as extensive as the Nightingale's. She asserts that husbands and wives can love one another:

Moni chapmen & moni cniht
Luueth & hald his wif ariht,
An swa deth moni bondeman.
That gode wif deth after than,
An serueth him to bedde & to borde
Mid faire dede & faire worde . . .[151]

Yet a woman can be wounded in marriage on account of her very love. Husbands, both merchants and knights (1575), are obliged to go away on business. Even when he goes "on thare beire nede" a wife grieves in his absence (1584–6). The problems raised when a lover journeys abroad

---

[150] "Their behaviour is not suitable to marriage, because it is a great discredit to their husbands when they sing: 'Fie upon my husband: I have chosen myself a much nicer man.' Or in English: 'I don't care about my husband. Another's bought my love for two white gloves. If I love him, I won't regret it.' Indeed many are encouraged to act against marital fidelity. For clearly it's an attack upon marriage, if someone sings that a wife should not hesitate to take a lover in place of a bad husband. Thus: 'Let the cuckold sit at home, and choose another lover. Let the churl sit at home and grow bald, and you can do what you want – God knows there's no trickery in it!' According to divine law, a woman cannot relinquish even a leper, but must render him the debt wherever and whenever he so desires." The predicament of marriage to a leper is dramatized in the Latin lyric, 'In me, dei crudeles nimium . . .'.

[151] *O&N*, 1575–80: "Many a merchant or knight loves and looks after his wife properly, and many a peasant too. Then his good wife serves him accordingly, and serves him in bed and at board, with good deeds and fair words . . .".

("''ultramarina coamans expeditione''") are discussed among the decretals of the *De amore*.[152] Like the Owl, Andreas's adjudicator (the Countess of Champagne) emphasizes that the woman's partner is absent only for their mutual advantage. She decrees that a lady should not desert her lover with no better justification than his absence. The Owl tries to evoke the anxiety of the abandoned wife – her cares by day and sleepless nights ("daies kare & nightes wake"). Every step her husband has to take seems a mile to her (1590–2). This line of thought – that even a happy marriage brings unhappiness in the inevitability of parting – can again be paralleled in devotional literature for women. The author of *Hali Meithhad*, for example, argues that "always, the more joy they had together, the deeper their sorrow at parting''.[153] The Owl claims to share the lonely wife's burden of sorrow by sitting outside her window and harmonizing her song to the lady's misery (1593–9). Not only is she a companion to such women: she helps them to stay on the "straight and narrow":

> Forthan ich am hire wel welcume:
> Ich hire helpe hwat i mai,
> For hogheth thane rehte wai.[154]

The Owl seems to imply in this last phrase that even a loving wife may be tempted to stray if her husband leaves her alone for a while. The Owl, like the Nightingale, has a low opinion of women's capacity to be faithful. However, both birds are careful to argue that their generous sympathy for women is balanced by a critical awareness of the moral aspects of their conduct. The birds argue that they express this awareness in their songs.

The deepest inconsistencies in the birds' discussion of love and marriage are the result of the poem's shift of focus – from the Nightingale's defence against the allegation of inciting adultery (1331–416) to the contrast between maidens and married women (1417–602). The second develops smoothly from the first, but it forces the Owl to make a complete *volte-face*. Initially, she accuses the Nightingale of condoning adultery; but then she condones it herself. The poet's choice of the contrast of wives and maidens was deliberate enough for him to sacrifice the Owl's consistency of viewpoint. It is possible that the contrast is simply a development of the opposition of youth and age implied in the way the two birds are first introduced in the poem – the Nightingale on a blossomy bough (15–16) and the Owl on an old, ivy-grown tree-stump (25–8). Alternatively, the poet may have absorbed the idea of the

---

[152] *De amore*, II. 7. 31–4, p. 262; cf. also I. 6. 551–6, pp. 204–6. See also, Brundage, 'Crusader'.

[153] *HM*, 24/19–20: "eauer, se hare murhthe wes mare togederes, se the sorhe is sarre ed te twinnunge". The author of *HM* is probably thinking of death rather than separation.

[154] *O&N*, 1600–02: "And therefore she's pleased to hear me. I help her as best I can, to be mindful of her proper course."

grades or estates of womanhood – perhaps directly from devotional literature. The literature of misogyny often portrays women in terms of species, and it seems very likely that the poet owed at least the Nightingale's portrayal of the adulterous wife to antifeminist literature. This is ironic in the light of the birds' overt partisanship for women, but it is one that the poet presumably meant us to relish. One need not look so far, perhaps, since marriage naturally marked a boundary-line in female experience. I also think that this part of *The Owl and the Nightingale* is likely to have been deliberately shaped as a contrast between two of the stereotypical scenarios dramatically exploited in the medieval lyric – those of the abandoned and sometimes exploited maiden, and the battered and often rebellious wife.

I have argued that the inconsistencies in the birds' arguments do not undermine their credibility as speakers. A little dishonesty of argument is in any case quite realistic in a quarrel between two such absolutely antagonistic personalities. The variations in their perspectives are the effects of different literary strategies. Sometimes the birds adopt the cynicism of satire or the earthiness of beast-fables; sometimes they appeal to the idealism of romance or the sentimentality of lyric. What makes this author's approach particularly clever is that he deliberately subverts what is in itself a feature of a literary strategy, the silence of women in debates about women, by having the birds, whose sympathies are so absolutely feminine, speak on their behalf.[155] As in Tom Stoppard's ingenious play, *Rosencrantz and Guildenstern are Dead* – a version of *Hamlet* from the point of view of its two most minor characters – the effect is to have the furniture come suddenly alive and voice its opinion. It is perhaps with some similar sense of daring to speak for the conventionally unspeaking and spoken-of that the Wife of Bath demands, "Who peyntede the leon, tel me who?" (III. 692). If the discussion of love and marriage in *The Owl and the Nightingale* is sharpened by the speakers' dramatic marginality of perspective *as women*, it could also be the case that the author's choice of birds as commentators upon human affairs was dictated by their marginality *as birds*. Not only do both of them sit in their trees at the margins of human settlements, as the poem tells us, observing, commenting and taking sides, but birds also sit quite literally in the margins of illuminated manuscripts where they are drawn as decorations.[156] Although *The Owl and the Nightingale* is not a simple poem, concerned with any single issue or making any specific case, as far as the voices of the two birds can be characterized in any way, it is

---

[155] In the 'Vix nodosum . . .', Alan of Lille clearly marks the conventionality of his theme, a connoisseurial evaluation of young women and married ones from the point of view of their utility to men (37–44). Cf. 'Quam velim virginum . . .'; Richard de Fournival, 'Chascuns qui de bien amer . . .'; the poetic exchange between Bertran de Preissac, Jausbert de Puicibot and one "Audebert" (a *tenso* and two *sirventes*); but also the female-voiced 'Bele mere, ke frai? . . .'.

[156] The owl is commonly drawn in such circumstances: the less distinctive nightingale occurs much more rarely (Yapp, pp. 35–43, 64–5).

by their obliqueness. They are licensed to take new and surprising views of mankind's behaviour by their tangential relationship to it.

8. Conclusion

The Owl and the Nightingale and the texts related to it are in many ways less revealing about marriage than the avowedly ascetic material which I discussed in Chapters Three and Four. Even though these secularly orientated texts pretend to address marriage as a reality rather than as an ideal, they are in fact almost equally abstract. They tend to depict married life only in terms of conventional personae – the abandoned girl, the flattering seducer, the lonely wife, the flirt and the cuckold. The impression of debate is an effect only of the confrontation between different kinds of literary discourse – devotional, satirical, misogynistic, sentimental and lyrical. As a result, paradoxically, these texts appear to be less seriously engaged with the ideological and sentimental significance of marriage than the devotional texts addressed to celibates.

Yet it seems to me that the consciously literary way in which the *Petit Plet* and *The Owl and the Nightingale* play with different experiences of marriage does not preclude a genuine compassion. The grief of the Veillard for his wife is impressive – and I think that Chardri meant it to be so. It is not discredited by the extremes of morbidity to which the old man sometimes tends. Similarly, the respective sympathies of the Owl and the Nightingale for the ill-treated wife and the exploited maiden are not invalidated by the birds' casuistry or by their patent partisanship for women. These are points at which the poem is meant to be both serious and emotive. Indeed, the very prevalence of such scenarios in literature probably reinforced their credibility. Preachers apparently used them as a form of anecdotal evidence for moral abuses. Similarly, the author of 'A Lutel Soth Sermun' illustrated the folly of pre-marital sex by appealing to the stereotypical scenario of the peasant-girl's seduction. The persistence of such literary depictions of exploited girls possibly testifies to continuing anxiety about the potential for uncertainty in the formation of marriage, which was implicit in the canon law definition of marriage as a purely consensual matter. Similarly, the recurring depictions of abused wives might be taken to reflect an awareness of the domestic tensions and tragedies consequent upon the Church's renunciation of divorce and separation. Moreover, as much as the Owl and the Nightingale compete for superiority over each other, the female figures which they deploy compete for our sympathy towards them in their plights. In this way, the poet makes us highly aware, not only of the importance of the marital system for women, but also of its inadequacies – and in particular, of the potentially dire consequences for women whom marriage did not protect.

General Conclusion

Modern evaluations of the place of marriage in medieval society have too long been overshadowed by a belief in the literal existence of a kind of courtly metacosm, which supposedly enshrined a particular set of values and practices and provided an arena for literary creativity, but which stood apart from the ideology and ethics of medieval society as a whole. An imaginary court like Wolfram von Eschenbach's Munsalvæsche, where the Holy Grail is found in *Parzifal*, is certainly a powerful vehicle for the expression of certain ideas, but it is not a realistic image of medieval society – nor even of medieval conceptions of utopia. As A.T. Hatto points out, "without some powerful moral influence emanating from the Gral which Wolfram fails to mention, Gral Society even in his bare description would not last a week".[1] In modern models of the medieval world, marriage has been marginalized because critics have tended to accept the images painted by literature simply at face-value, without attempting to understand the ideological dynamics which motivate them. What has impressed me in my reading of the literature of the twelfth and thirteenth centuries is the rigour and persistence with which authors tried to grasp the essence of the idea of marriage. This intensity of thinking is perhaps all the more impressive for its distance from the confusion and uncertainty in custom and practice. At a time when a legal and social system based on written records was still embryonic, medieval writers perhaps discussed marriage in such absolute terms as an assertion of the need for order and regulation in human relationships. While this rigid intensity undoubtedly justified clumsy responses to practical problems (such as the Church's recognition of clandestine marriage) it also enabled medieval people to enunciate principles that are still held sacrosanct in western society today. Among these are the rejection of concubinage and the indispensability to marriage of the partners' free and equal consent.

The treatment of marriage in early medieval literature can be characterized, firstly, by its ambitious attempts to coordinate it with other claims upon the mind and heart. Marriage is a point at which romances (both secular and hagiographical) characteristically assert the individuality of the protagonist, because it represents a junction between the realms of the personal and the social. They contrast marriage with the demands made by chivalry (for example, Chrétien's *Erec*, *Guy of Warwick*), dynastic responsibilities (*Ruodlieb*) and religion (*Chanson de Saint Alexis*, *The Life of Christina of Markyate*). Other

[1] *Parzifal*, p. 417.

200

types of texts deal with the challenges to marriage posed by the impulses to study (the letters of Abelard and Heloise) and to define one's own inner space (the AB-texts). Medieval literature is also characteristically concerned with determining the moment in which marriage was created, as well as the conditions essential to its creation. By seeking to define marriage as a contract between individuals, medieval literature (along with law and theology) came to find the meaning of marriage in the feelings of individuals; and to identify the delicate equilibrium of personal resolution with an indestructible metaphysical bond. Literature in particular tended to sublimate ideals of marriage – to define it as a significant link between individuals only by the construction of a kind of counter-reality in another world – in Heaven, perhaps, or in an earthly Paradise. This sublimation was a tendency which might be interpreted as the means by which the new ideology of marriage coped with, and adapted for itself, the antique values of asceticism. It made possible the combination of sexual anxiety with a belief in the perfectability of marriage. This in turn expressed itself as a rejection of concubinage, divorce and remarriage.

Finally, medieval literature often adopts marriage as a structural principle. The AB-Group, for example, characteristically discusses the devotional experiences of the women it addressed in terms both of their actual marital circumstances and of their imaginative progress towards mystical marriage with Christ. In this way, literature emphasized the fundamental place of marriage within the social order. Several of the texts I have discussed are specifically concerned with the experience of marriage by women (whether real or hypothetical). *The Owl and the Nightingale*, for example, develops a contrast between the experiences of women vulnerable to exploitation by men (trapped, as it were, outside marriage), and those subject to the unhappiness caused by the cruelty or absence of their husbands (and thus trapped inside it). This weighting towards women can be explained at least partly by the fact that I have given particular attention to vernacular texts, and these are much more likely than Latin ones to cater for female patrons. Though these texts do not preclude compassion, they are perhaps surprisingly dependent upon stereotypical depictions of women inside or outside marriage, which are often closely related to the grotesque distortions of comic modes like antifeminist satire and *fabliaux*. Yet even these stylized images of marriage betray what I can only describe as a sense of the brittleness of the individual – in this case, the female individual – within the action of the marital system. Critical concern with the failures of marriage was perhaps a natural development from marital idealism. In sum, all the texts which I have treated in this dissertation testify to their sense of marriage as a field of experience and ideology shaping and shaped by the inward responses of individuals.

201

Bibliography

1. Reference Works

Bell, David N., *The Libraries of the Cistercians, Gilbertines and Premonstratensians*, Corpus of British Medieval Library Catalogues 3 (London, 1992)

Biblia Sacra Vulgata, ed. B. Fischer et al. (3rd edn, Stuttgart, 1983)

Brown, Carleton and Rossell Hope Robbins, eds, *The Index of Middle English Verse* (New York, 1943)

Buchwald, W., A. Hohlweg, and O. Prinz, eds, *Tusculum-Lexikon: griechischer und lateinischer Autoren des Altertums und des Mittelalters* (Munich, 1982)

Drabble, Margaret, ed., *The Oxford Companion to English Literature* (5th edn, Oxford, 1985)

Flodr, Miroslav, *Incunabula Classicorum* (Amsterdam, 1973)

Godefroy, Frédéric, ed. with J. Bonnard and A. Salmon, *Lexique de l'Ancien Français* (Paris, 1990)

Humphreys, K.W., *The Friars' Libraries*, Corpus of British Medieval Library Catalogues 1 (London, 1990)

Krueger, Paul, ed., *Digest*, as *Corpus Iuris Civilis*, vol. I (Berlin, 1964)

Laing, Margaret, *Catalogue of Sources for a Linguistic Atlas of Early Medieval English* (Cambridge, 1993)

Linker, Robert White, *A Bibliography of Old French Lyrics*, Romance Monographs 31 (University of Mississippi, 1979)

McIntosh, Angus, Michael L. Samuels and Michael Benskin, *A Linguistic Atlas of Late Mediæval English*, 4 vols (Aberdeen, 1986)

Oguro, Shoichi and Tetsuo Kimura, *A Concordance to 'The Owl and the Nightingale'* (Tokyo, 1991)

Pillet, Alfred, and Henry Carstens, eds, *Bibliographie der Troubadours*, Schriften der Königsberger Gelehrten Gesellschaft, Sonderreihe 3 (Halle, 1933)

Robbins, R.H., and J.L. Cutler, *Supplement to the Index of Middle English Verse* (Lexington, 1965)

Sadie, Stanley, ed., *New Grove Dictionary of Music and Musicians*, 6th edn, 20 vols (London, 1980)

Severs, J. Burke, and Albert E. Hartung, eds, *A Manual of the Writings in Middle English 1050–1400*, 9 vols (New Haven, 1967–93)

Smith, W., and S. Cheetham, eds, *A Dictionary of Christian Antiquities*, 2 vols (London, 1908)

Spanke, Hans, ed., *G. Raynauds Bibliographie des altfranzösischen Liedes* (Leiden, 1980)

Storey, Christopher, *An Annotated Bibliography and Guide to Alexis Studies: (La Vie de Saint Alexis)*, Histoire des idées et critique littéraire 251 (Geneva, 1987)

Thompson, Stith, *Motif-Index of Folk-Literature* (Copenhagen, 1955)

Vacent, A., E. Mangenot, and E. Amann, eds, *Dictionnaire de théologie catholique*, 15 vols (Paris, 1903–50)
Walther, Hans, ed., *Initia carminum ac versuum medii aevi posterioris Latinorum: Alphabetisches Verzeichnis der Versanfänge mittellateinischer Dichtungen* (Göttingen, 1959)
Ward, H.L.D., *Catalogue of Romances in the Department of Manuscripts in the British Museum*, 3 vols (London, 1883)
Wells, John E., *A Manual of the Writings in Middle English 1050–1400* (New Haven and London, 1916)
Whiting, Bartlett Jere, and Helen Wescott, *Proverbs, Sentences, and Proverbial Phrases from English Writings Mainly Before 1500* (London and Cambridge MA, 1968)

2. Anthologies of Primary Sources

Adcock, Fleur, ed. and trans., *The Virgin and the Nightingale* (Newcastle, 1983, rpt. 1988)
Axton, Richard and John Stevens, trans. *Medieval French Plays* (Oxford, 1971)
Bate, Keith, ed., *Three Latin Comedies [Geta, Babio, Pamphilus]*, Toronto Medieval Latin Texts (Toronto, 1976)
Bec, Pierre, ed., *Burlesque et Obscénité chez les Troubadours: Pour une approche du contre-texte médiéval* (Paris, 1984)
Bennett, J.A.W., and G.V. Smithers, eds, *Early Middle English Verse and Prose* (2nd edn, Oxford, 1968)
Bevington, David, ed. and trans., *Medieval Drama* (Chicago, 1975)
Blamires, Alcuin, trans., *Woman Defamed and Woman Defended: An Anthology of Medieval Texts* (Oxford, 1992)
Bogin, Meg, ed. and trans., *The Women Troubadours* (New York, London and Ontario, 1976)
Bolandus, J., et al., *Acta Sanctorum . . .*, 62 vols (Paris, [1863]–75)
Bossy, Michel-André, ed. and trans., *Medieval Debate-Poetry: Vernacular Works*, Garland Library of Medieval Literature, Series A, vol. 52 (New York and London, 1987)
Brown, Carleton, ed., *English Lyrics of the XIIIth Century* (Oxford, 1932)
Conlee, John W., ed., *Middle English Debate Poetry: A Critical Anthology* (East Lansing, 1991)
Davies, R.T., ed., *Medieval English Lyrics* (London, 1963, rpt. 1987)
Dickens, Bruce and R.M. Wilson, eds, *Early Middle English Texts* (London, 1952)
Dobson, E.J. and F. Ll. Harrison, *Medieval English Songs* (London and Boston, 1979)
Dufournet, Jean, ed., *Anthologie de la poésie lyrique française des XIIe et XIIIe siècles* (Paris, 1989)
Elliott, Alison Goddard, ed. and trans., *Seven Medieval Latin Comedies*, Garland Library of Medieval Literature 20 (New York and London, 1984)
Furnivall, F.J., ed., *Adam Davy's 5 Dreams about Edward II, etc., from Bodleian Laud MS, Laud 622*, EETS OS 69 (London, 1878)

Furnivall, F.J., ed., *The Minor Poems of the Vernon MS*, Vol. II, EETS OS 117 (London, 1901)

Goldin, Frederick, ed. and trans., *Lyrics of the Troubadours and Trouvères: An Anthology and a History* (Gloucester MA, 1983)

Greene, Richard Leighton, ed., *The Early English Carols* (2nd edn, Oxford, 1977)

Hall, Joseph, ed., *Selections from Early Middle English: 1130–1250*, 2 vols (Oxford, 1920)

Haug, Walther and Benedikt Konrad Vollmann, ed. and German trans., *Frühe Deutsche Literatur und Lateinische Literatur in Deutschland: 800–1150*, Bibliothek des Mittelalters, vol. 1 (Frankfurt a. M., 1991)

Jeffrey, David L. and Brian J. Levy, eds, *The Anglo-Norman Lyric: An Anthology* (Toronto, 1990)

Kinsley, James, ed., *The Oxford Book of Ballads* (Oxford, 1982)

Långfors, A., et al., eds, *Receuil général de jeux-partis français* (Paris, 1926)

Levy, B.J., and C.E. Pickford, eds, *Selected Fabliaux* (Hull, 1978)

McDonough, C.J., ed., *The Oxford Lyrics of Hugh Primas and the Arundel Lyrics*, Toronto Medieval Latin Texts 15 (Toronto, 1984)

McNeill, J.T., and H.M. Gamer, trans., *Medieval Handbooks of Penance* (New York, 1938, repr. 1990)

Migne, J., ed., *Patrologiae cursus completus . . .*, 221 vols (Paris, 1844–64)

Millett, Bella, and Jocelyn Wogan-Browne, ed. and trans., *Medieval English Prose for Women* (Oxford, 1990)

Mills, Maldwyn, ed. *Six Middle English Romances* [*The Sege of Melayne, Emaré, Sir Isumbras, Sir Gowther, Sir Amadace*] (London, 1973, rpt. 1988)

Morris, Richard, ed. *An Old English Miscellany: containing a Bestiary, Kentish Sermons, Proverbs of Alfred, Religious Poems of the thirteenth century*, EETS OS 49 (London, 1872)

Neumann, F., and M.E. Meurer, ed. and German trans., *Deutscher Minnesang* (Stuttgart, 1978)

Oulmont, Charles, ed., *Les débats du clerc et du chevalier dans la littérature poétique du moyen-age* (Paris, 1911)

Perceval, Henry R., ed. *The Seven Ecumenical Councils of the Unilateral Church*, in *A Select Library of Nicene and Post-Nicene Fathers of the Christian Church*, vol. 14 (Oxford and New York, 1900)

Press, A.R., ed. and trans., *An Anthology of Troubadour Lyric Poetry* (Edinburgh, 1985)

Reardon, B.P., trans., *Collected Ancient Greek Novels* (Berkeley, 1989)

Rieger, Angelika, ed., *Trobairitz: Der Beitrag der Frau in der altokzitanischen höfischen Lyrik: Edition der Gesamtkorpus*, Beihefte zur Zeitschrift für romanische Philologie 233 (Tübingen, 1991)

Riquer, Martín de, ed., *Los Trovadores: Historia literaria y textos*, 3 vols (Barcelona, 1975, new edn, 1983)

Rivière, Jean-Claude, ed., *Pastourelles*, 3 vols (Geneva, 1974–6)

Sands, Donald B., ed., *Middle English Verse Romances* (Exeter, 1966, new edn, 1986)

Schultz, O., ed., *Die provenzalischen Dichterinnen* (Leipzig, 1888; rpt. Geneva, 1975)

Silverstein, Theodore, ed., *English Lyrics before 1500* (York, 1971, rpt. 1988)

Weiss, Judith, trans., *The Birth of Romance: An Anthology: Four twelfth-century Anglo-Norman romances* (London, 1992)

Wright, Thomas, ed., *The Latin Poems commonly attributed to Walter Mapes* (London, 1841)

3. Primary Sources

Where several editions of a single text are listed, I have used an asterisk to indicate the edition from which my quotations are taken.

Abelard: see Peter Abelard

AB-Group: *Anchoritic Spirituality: 'Ancrene Wisse' and Associated Works*, trans. Anne Savage and Nicholas Watson (New York and Mahwah NJ, 1991); see also *Ancrene Wisse, Hali Meithhad, Sawles Warde, Seinte Iuliene, Seinte Katerine, Seinte Margarete, Wooing Group*

St Adalbert of Prague: *Homilia in Natale S. Alexii Confessoris*, *PL 73. 897–900; *ASS*, July 17, pp. 257–8

Adam de la Halle, *Le Jeu de la Feuillée*, ed. J. Dufournet (Ghent, 1977)

Adam de la Halle, *Le Jeu de Robin et de Marion*, ed. Kenneth Varty (London, 1960)

Adam: *Le Mystère d'Adam: (Ordo representacionis Ade)*, ed. *Paul Aebischer, TLF (Geneva and Paris, 1963, rpt. 1964); Bevington, pp. 80–121

Aithiopika: Reardon, pp. 349–588

Alan of Lille, *Summa de Arte Praedicatoria*, PL 210. 109–98

Alan of Lille, *The Plaint of Nature*, trans. James J. Sheridan, Mediaeval Sources in Translation 26 (Toronto, 1980)

Alan of Lille: 'The poem *Vix nodosum* by Alan of Lille', ed. N.M. Häring and trans. James J. Sheridan, *Medioevo, Rivista di storia della filosofia medievale* 3 (1978) 165–85

St Aldhelm, *De Virginitate*, trans. Michael Lapidge in Michael Lapidge and Michael Herren, eds, *Aldhelm: The Prose Works* (Ipswich, Cambridge and Totowa NJ, 1979)

St Alexis: Amiaud, Arthur, Fr. trans., *La légende syriaque de Saint Alexis, l'homme de Dieu*, Bibliothèque de l'Ecole des Hautes Etudes, 79 (Paris, 1889)

St Alexis: Aßmann, Erwin, ed., 'Ein rhythmisches Gedicht auf den heiligen Alexius', in *Festschrift Adolf Hofmeister zum 70. Geburtstage*, pp. 31–8 (Halle, 1955)

St Alexis: *La Chanson de Saint Alexis*: see *Storey, Odenkirchen, Paris

St Alexis: Elliott, Alison Goddard, ed., *The Vie de Saint Alexis in the twelfth and thirteenth centuries: an edition and commentary*, UNCS 221 (Chapel Hill NC, 1983)

St Alexis: Hemming, T.D., ed., *La Vie de saint Alexis: texte du manuscrit A (BN nouv. acq. fr. 4503)* (Exeter, 1994)

St Alexis: Horstmann, Carl, 'Alexiuslieder', *Archiv* 59 (1878) 71–106

St Alexis: Horstmann, Carl, ed., *Altenglische Legenden* (Heilbronn, 1881)

St Alexis: Horstmann, Carl, 'Leben des h. Alexius nach MS Laud 108', *Archiv* 51 (1873) 101–110

St Alexis: Horstmann, Carl, 'Zwei Alexiuslieder', *Archiv* 56 (1876) 391–416

St Alexis: see also under **Marbod of Rennes**

St Alexis: Maßmann, H.F., ed., *Sanct Alexius Leben in acht gereimten mittelhochdeutschen Behandlungen, nebst geschichtlicher Einleitung, so wie deutschen, griechischen und lateinischen Anhangen*, Bibliotek der gesammten deutschen National-Literatur 9 (Quedlinburg and Leipzig, 1843)

St Alexis: Mölk, Ulrich, ed., 'Die älteste lateinische Alexiusvita: Kritischer Text und Kommentar', *Romanistisches Jahrbuch* 27 (1976) 293–315

St Alexis: Odenkirchen, Carl J., ed. and trans., *The Life of St Alexius* (Brookline MA and Leyden, 1978)

St Alexis: Paris, Gaston and Léopold Pannier, eds, *La Vie de Saint Alexis, poème du XIe siècle et renouvellements des XIIe, XIIIe et XIVe, siècles publiées avec préfaces, variantes, notes et glossaire*, Bibliothèque de l'Ecole des Hautes Etudes 7 (Paris, 1872)

St Alexis: Paris, Gaston, 'La Vie de Saint Alexi en vers octosyllabiques', *Romania* 8 (1879) 163–80

St Alexis: Schipper, J., *Englische Alexiuslegenden aus dem XIV. und XV. Jahrhundert*, vol. 1, Quellen und Forschungen zur Sprach- und Culturgeschichte der germanischen Völker 20 (Strasbourg and London, 1877)

St Alexis: Schipper, J., *Die zweite Version der mittelenglischen Alexiuslegenden* (Vienna, 1887)

St Alexis: Storey, Christopher, ed., *La Vie de S. Alexis*, TLF (Geneva, 1968)

St Alexis: *Vita S. Alexii*: BHL 286; *ASS* July 17, pp. 251–3; ed. and trans. *Odenkirchen, pp. 34–51

St Alexis: Wagner, Fritz, ed., 'Die metrische Alexius-vita "Eufemianus erat, ceu lectio sacra revelat . . ." ', *MlJh* 2 (1965) 145–64

St Alexis: Wagner, Fritz, ed., 'Die Verslegende von hl. Alexius *Duxit Romanus vir nobilis Eufemianus . . .*', *MlJh* 1 (1964) 78–99

St Alexis: see also *Northern Homily Cycle*; *Scottish Legendary Collection*

St Ambrose, *De viduis liber unus*, PL 16. 265–302; trans. H. de Romestin, in *A Select Library of Nicene and Post-Nicene Fathers of the Christian Church*, vol. X, *St Ambrose. Select Works and Letters* (Oxford and New York, 1896), pp. 391–407

St Ambrose, *De virginibus ad Marcellinam sororem suam libri tres*, PL 16. 187–232; trans. H. de Romestin, ibid., pp. 363–87

St Ambrose, *De virginitate liber unus*, PL 16. 265–302

Amis and Amiloun, ed. MacEdward Leach, EETS OS 203 (London, 1937)

Ami e Amile, ed. P. Dembowski, CFMA (Paris, 1969)

Amys e Amylloun, ed. Hideka Fukui, ANTS Plain Texts Series 7 (London, 1990); trans. Judith Weiss, *The Birth of Romance*, pp. 159–78

St Anastasia: *ASS*, March 2, pp. 40–1

Ancrene Wisse: Guide for Anchoresses, trans. Hugh White (Harmondsworth, 1993)

Ancrene Wisse: *The English Text of the Ancrene Riwle: Ancrene Wisse, Corpus Christi College, Cambridge, MS 402*, ed. J.R.R. Tolkien, EETS OS 249 (London, 1960)

Ancrene Wisse, Parts 7 and 8: ed. and trans. *Millett and Wogan-Browne, pp. 110–48

Ancrene Wisse, Parts 6 and 7: ed. Geoffrey Shepherd (Manchester and New York, 1959, rpt. 1972)

Andreas Capellanus, *De Amore*, ed. and trans. P. G. Walsh, as *On Love* (London, 1982)

Apollonius: trans. Reardon, pp. 736–772

Aucassin et Nicolette, ed. and Fr. trans. J. Dufournet (Paris, 1984)

St Augustine of Hippo, *De bono conjugali liber unus*, PL 40. 373–396

St Augustine of Hippo, *De sancta virginitate liber unus*, PL 40. 397–428

St Augustine of Hippo, *Tractatus in Joannis Evangelium*, VIII, PL 35. 1450–8

'Aurea frequenter lingua . . .': ed. Strecker, *Carmina Cantabrigiensia*, App. 1, pp. 111–3, str. 15; trans. Adcock, pp. 30–5

Aurigena, *Facetus* ["'Moribus et vita . . .'"]: ed. A. Morel-Fatio in 'Mélanges de Littérature catalane', *Romania* 15 (1886) 224–9; ed. and trans. *Alison Goddard Elliott as 'The *Facetus*, or Art of Courtly Living', *Allegorica* 2/2 (1977) 27–57

St Bernard of Clairvaux, *Epistolae* 113–7, in *S. Bernardi Opera: Vol. VII.: Epistolae I*, ed. J. Leclercq and H. Rochais (Rome, 1974)

Bernard Silvestris *Cosmographia*, ed. Peter Dronke (Leiden, 1978)

Bertran de Born: *The Poems of the troubadour Bertran de Born*, ed. William D. Paden, jr, Tilde Sankovitch and Patricia H. Stablein (Berkeley, 1986)

Bertran de Preissac, Jausbert de Puicibot, "Audebert": 'Les jeunes femmes et les vielles: une *tenso* (PC 88.2 = 173.5) et un échange de *sirventes* (PC 173.1a + 88.1)', ed. and Fr. trans. J.H. Marshall, *FS Pierre Bec*, pp. 325–38

Boccaccio, Giovanni, *The Decameron*, trans. Guido Waldman (Oxford, 1993)

'Borgoise d'Orliens': 'De la borgoise d'Orliens', ed. Levy and Pickford, pp. 19–27

Burchard of Worms, *Decretorum libri viginti*, PL 140. 537–1058

Carmina Burana: *Die Lieder der Benediktbeurer Handschrift: Zweisprachige Ausgabe*, ed. and German trans. B. Bischoff et al. (Munich, 1979)

Carmina Cantabrigiensia: *Die Cambridger Lieder*, ed. Karl Strecker, MGH 40 (Berlin, 1926; rpt. Munich, 1978)

Chaereas and Callirhöe: Reardon, pp. 17–124

Chardri, *La Vie des Set Dormanz*, ed. Brian S. Merrilees, ANTS 35 (London, 1977)

Chardri, *Le Petit Plet*, ed. Brian S. Merrilees, ANTS 20 (Oxford, 1970)

Chardri: *Chardry's Josaphaz, Set Dormanz und Petit Plet: Dichtungen in der anglo-normannischen Mundart des XIII. Jahrhunderts*, ed. John Koch, Altfranzösische Bibliothek 1 (Heilbronn, 1879)

Chaucer, Geoffrey: *Complete Works*, ed. F.N. Robinson (2nd edn, London, 1957); *The Riverside Chaucer*, ed. *Larry D. Benson (3rd edn, Oxford, 1992)

Chrétien de Troyes: *Les Romans de Chrétien de Troyes*, CFMA: vol. 1, *Erec et Enide*, ed. Mario Roques (Paris, 1990); vol. 2, *Cligés*, ed. Alexandre Micha (Paris, 1957); vol. 3, *Le Chevalier de la Charrette* [*Lancelot*], ed. Mario Roques (Paris, 1958); vol. 4, *Le Chevalier au Lion* [*Yvain*], ed. Mario Roques (Paris, 1982)

Chrétien de Troyes: *Arthurian Romances*, trans. D.D.R. Owen (London, 1988)

St Christina of Markyate: *The Life of St Christina of Markyate: A Twelfth-Century Recluse*, ed. and trans. C.H. Talbot, Oxford Medieval Texts (Oxford, 1959, rpt. 1987)

Cicero: *De Senectute, De Amicitia, De Divinatione*, ed. and trans. W.A. Falconer, LCL (London and Cambridge MA, 1946)

'Consultatio sacerdotum' [inc. "Clerus et presbyteri nuper consedere . . ."]: ed. Thomas Wright, *LPMap*, pp. 174–9

'De concubinis sacerdotum' [inc. "Prisciani regula penitus cassantur . . ."]: ed. Thomas Wright, *LPMap*, pp. 171–3

'De convocatione sacerdotum' [inc. "Rumor novus Angliae partes pergiravit . . ."]: ed. Thomas Wright, *LPMap*, pp. 174–9

De non ducenda uxore: ed. and trans. A.G. Rigg, as *Gawain on Marriage* (Toronto, 1986); *LPMap*, pp. 77–85

St Domitilla: *Vita S. Domitillae, ASS*, May 12th, vol. III, pp. 7–13

Donnei des Amants: *Le Donnei des Amants*, ed. Gaston Paris, *Romania* 25 (1896) 497–541

Egbert of Schönau, *Sermones contra Catharos*, PL 195. 1–93

Epistolae duorum amantium: ed. Eugen Könsgen, as *Epistolae duorum amantium: Briefe Abaelards und Heloises?*, Mittellateinisches Studien und Texte 8 (Leiden, 1974)

Eructavit . . .: ed. T. Atkinson Jenkins, Gesellschaft für romanische Literatur 20 (Dresden, 1909)

St Euphrosine: *La Vie de Sainte Euphrosine*, ed. R.T. Hill, *RR* 10 (1919) 191–232

Flamenca: *The Romance of Flamenca*, ed. and trans. M.J. Hubert and M.E. Porter (Princeton, 1962)

Folie Tristan: *La Folie Tristan d'Oxford*, trans. Judith Weiss, *The Birth of Romance*, pp. 121–40

Fournival, Richard de: *L'Oeuvre lyrique de Richard de Fournival*, ed. Yvan G. Lepage (Ottawa, 1981)

Fulcher of Chartres, *Historia Hierosolymitana* PL 155. 821–940

Gawain: see *De non ducenda uxore*

Gereint: see *Mabinogion*

Gesta Romanorum: ed. Hermann Oesterley (Berlin, 1871; rpt. Hildesheim, 1963); selected edn and German trans. Rainer Nickel (Stuttgart, 1991); *The Early English Versions of the Gesta Romanorum*, ed. Sidney J.H. Herrtage, EETS ES 33 (London, 1879)

Gratian, *Concordia discordantium canonum* [*Decretum*], PL 187; ed. Emil Friedberg and Emil Ludwig Richter, *Corpus iuris canonici*, 2 vols (Leipzig, 1879; rpt. Graz, 1959), vol. 1

Guilhem or **Guillaume IX of Aquitaine**: *Les chansons de Guillaume IX, duc d'Aquitaine, 1071–1127*, ed. A. Jeanroy (Paris, 1927); *The Poetry of William VII, Count of Poitiers and IX Duke of Aquitaine*, ed. and trans. *Gerald A. Bond, Garland Library of Medieval Literature, ser. A, vol. 4 (New York and London, 1982)

Guillaume de Lorris and Jean de Meun, *Le Roman de la Rose*, ed. D. Poirion (Paris, 1974); *The Romance of the Rose* trans. Charles Dahlberg (Hanover NE and London, 1971; 2nd edn, 1983)

Guy of Warwick: *Fragments of an early fourteenth-century Guy of Warwick*, ed. Maldwyn Mills and Daniel Huws, Medium Aevum Monographs NS 4 (Oxford, 1974)

Guy of Warwick: *Gui de Warewic*, ed. E. Ewert, CFMA, 2 vols (Paris, 1932–3)

Guy of Warwick: *Guy of Warwick: A Knight of Britain . . .*, [a French version

printed by François Regnault (Paris, 1525) and trans. Caroline Clive (1821)],
ed. William B. Todd (Austin, 1968)

Guy of Warwick: *Le Rommant de Guy de Warwik et de Herolt d'Ardenne*, ed. D.J.
Conlon, UNCS 102 (Chapel Hill NC, 1971)

Guy of Warwick: *The Romance of Guy of Warwick edited from Ms. Ff.2.38 in the
University Library, Cambridge*, ed. Julius Zupitza, EETS ES 25–26 (London,
1875–6)

Guy of Warwick: *The Romance of Guy of Warwick edited from the Auchinleck Ms. in the
Advocates' Library, Edinburgh and from Ms.107 in Caius College, Cambridge*, ed.
Julius Zupitza, EETS ES 42, 49, 59, 3 vols (London, 1883, 1887, 1891)

Hali Meithhad ed. Bella Millett, EETS OS 284 (London, 1982); ed. and trans.
*Millett and Wogan-Browne, pp. 2–43

Harley Lyrics: ed. G.L. Brook, *The Middle English Lyrics of MS Harley 2253*
(Manchester, 1948); *Facsimile of British Museum MS Harley 2253*, ed. N.R. Ker,
EETS 255 (London, 1965)

Hartmann von Aue, *Der Arme Heinrich*, ed. and German trans. H. Henne
(Frankfurt a. M., 1985); *Der Arme Heinrich*, trans. F. Tobin *Allegorica* 1/2
(1976) 5–77

Hartmann von Aue, *Erec*, ed. and German trans. Thomas Cramer (Frankfurt a.
M., 1972, rpt. 1990)

Havelok: *Havelok the Dane*, ed. Donald B. Sands, *Middle English Romances*, pp. 55–
129; *Lai d'Haveloc*, trans. Judith Weiss, *The Birth of Romance*, pp. 141–58

Heloise: see Peter Abelard

Hildebert of Lavardin, *Ep.* 1. 21, PL 171. 193–7

Honorius Augustodunensis, *Speculum Ecclesie*, PL 172. 807–1104

Honorius Augustodunensis, *Imago Mundi*, ed. V.I.J. Flint, *Archives* 49 (1982)
7–153

Horn: see **Thomas**; and **King Horn**

Hugh of Fouilloy (de Folieto), *De nuptiis libri duo*, PL 176. 1201–18

Hugh of St Victor, *De Amore Sponsi ad Sponsum*, PL 176. 987–994

Hugh of St Victor, *De beatae Mariae virginitate libri tres*, PL 176. 857–76

Hugh of St Victor, *De sacramentis Christianae fidei*, PL 176. 173–618; trans. Roy J.
Deferrari, *Hugh of St Victor on the Sacraments of the Christian Faith* Medieval
Academy of America, Publication 58 (Cambridge MA, 1951)

Hugh of St Victor, *De vanitate mundi et rerum transeuntium usu libri quattuor*, PL 176.
703–40

'Interludium de clerico et puella': ed. Bennett and Smithers, *EMEV*, pp. 196–200

St Ivo of Chartres: *Epistolae*, PL 162. 11–296; *Epistolae 1–70*, ed. Jean Leclercq,
Yves de Chartres: Correspondance, vol. 1 (Paris, 1949)

St Ivo of Chartres, *Decretum*, PL 161. 47–1022

Jacobus de Voragine: *The Golden Legend of Jacobus de Voragine*, trans. Granger
Ryan and Helmut Ripperger (1941, rpt., New York, 1969)

Jean de Meun: 'La prima lettera d'Eloisa ad Abelardo nella traduzione di Jean
de Meun', ed. Fabrizio Beggiato, *Cultura Neolatina* 32/2–3 (1972) 211–29; see
also Guillaume de Lorris

Jean Renart, *Le Roman de la Rose: ou de: Guillaume de Dole*, ed. Félix Lecoy, SATF
(Paris, 1979); trans. Patricia Terry and Nancy Vine Durling, *The Romance of
the Rose: or: Guillaume de Dole* (Philadelphia, 1993)

'Je ne le seré de .VII. ans . . .': ed. Paul Aebischer, 'Une chanson de "mal mariée" dans un manuscrit fribourgeois du XVe siècle', *Romania* 54 (1928) 492–503

St Jerome, *Adversus Jovinianum* in PL 23. 211–388, trans. W.H. Fremantle, in *A Selection of Nicene and Post-Nicene Fathers of the Christian Church*, vol. 6, ed. H. Wace and P. Schaff (Oxford, 1893)

St Jerome, *Select Letters* ed. and trans. F.A. Wright, LCL (Cambridge MA, 1933, rpt. 1991)

St John Chrysostom, *On Marriage and Family Life*, selected works, trans. Catharine P. Roth and David Anderson (New York, 1986)

John of Salisbury: *Ioannis Saresberiensis Episcopi Carnotensis Policratici: sive, De nugis curialium et vestigiis philosophorum libri VIII*, ed. Clemens C.I. Webb, 2 vols (Oxford, 1909); abridged trans. Cary J. Nederman, *John of Salisbury: Policraticus: Of the Frivolities of Courtiers and the Footprints of Philosophers*, Cambridge Texts in the History of Political Thought (Cambridge, 1990)

Seinte Iuliene: *The Liflade ant te Passiun of Seinte Iuliene*, ed. and trans. S.R.T.O. d'Ardenne, EETS OS 248 (London, 1961)

Justinian: *Codex Justinianus*, ed. Paul Krüger, in *Corpus Iuris Civilis*, vol. 2 (Berlin, 1959)

Juvenalis, Decimus Junius, *Satires: Juvenal and Persius*, ed. and trans. G.G. Ramsay, LCL (Cambridge MA and London, 1940, rpt. 1990)

St Katherine: *Passio Sancte Katerine virginis et martyris*: ed. Dobson and d'Ardenne, *Seinte Katerine*, pp. 144–203)

Seinte Katerine: *Re-Edited from MS Bodley 34 and the other Manuscripts*, ed. S.R.T.O. d'Ardenne and E.J. Dobson, EETS SS 7 (London, 1981)

King Horn: ed. Donald B. Sands, *Middle English Romances*, pp. 15–54

Laʒamon: *Brut*, ed. G.L. Brook and R.F. Leslie, EETS OS 250, 277, 2 vols (London, 1963, 1978); trans. Rosamund Allen, *Lawman: Brut* (London, 1992, rpt. 1993)

Langland, William: *The Vision of Piers Plowman: A Complete Edition of the B-Text*, ed. A.V.C. Schmidt (London, 1978, rpt. 1982); *Piers Plowman: the C-text*, ed. Derek Pearsall (York, 1978, rpt., Exeter, 1994)

'Laüstic': Marie de France, *Lais*, ed. Ewert, pp. 97–101; ed. Warnke, pp. 146–51

Lucan, *The Civil War [Pharsalia]* ed. and trans. J.D. Duff, LCL 220 (Cambridge MA and London, 1988)

Lydgate, John: *The Minor Poems of John Lydgate: Part II: Secular Poems*, ed. Henry Noble MacCracken, EETS OS 192 (London, 1934)

Mabinogion: *The Mabinogion*, trans. Gwyn Jones and Thomas Jones (London, 1949, rpt. 1994)

Malory, Sir Thomas, *Works*, ed. Eugène Vinaver (Oxford, 2nd edn, 1971, rpt. 1991)

Mannyng, Robert: *Robert of Brunne's "Handlyng Synne", AD 1303: with those parts of the Anglo-French Treatise on which it is founded, William of Wadington's "Manual des Pechiez"*, ed. Frederick J. Furnivall, EETS OS 119, 123 (London, 1901, 1903)

Map, Walter: *Walter Map. De Nugis Curialium*, ed. and trans. M.R. James, R.A.B. Mynors and C.N.L. Brooke, Oxford Medieval Texts 14 (Oxford, 1983)

Map, Walter: *Epistola Valerii* = *De Nugis Curialium*, dist. iv, c. 3, pp. 288–313

Marbod of Rennes, *Vita Sancti Alexii* [metrical: inc. "Praestans magnatis, summae vir nobilitatis . . ."], *ASS* July 17th, pp. 254–6

Marbod of Rennes, *Liber Decem Capitulorum*, ed. R. Leotta (Rome, 1984); PL 171. 1693–1716

Marbod of Rennes, *Vita Sancti Licinii*, PL 171. 1493–1504

Marbod of Rennes, *De ornamentis verborum*, PL 171. 1687–92

St Maria Meretrix: *Vita S. Mariae Meretricis*: PL 73. 654–660

Marie de France, *Lais*: *Die Lais der Marie de France*, ed. Karl Warnke, Bibliotheca Normannica 3 (Halle, 1885; 2nd edn, 1900); *Les Lais de Marie de France*, ed. *A. Ewert (Oxford, 1952); *The Lais of Marie de France*, trans. Glyn S. Burgess and Keith Busby (Harmondsworth, 1986, rpt. 1988)

Seinte Margarete: ed. Frances M. Mack, EETS OS 193 (London, 1934, rpt. 1958); ed. and trans. *Millet and Wogan-Browne, pp. 44–84

'Na Carenza, al bel cors avinens . . .': ed. Schultz, p. 28; ed. and Fr. trans. Pierre Bec, 'Avoir des enfants ou rester vierge? Une tenson occitane du XIIIe siècle entre femmes', *FS Erich Köhler* pp. 21–30; ed. and trans. Bogin, pp. 144–5, 178–9; ed. and trans. *Dronke, *Women Writers*, pp. 101–3, 300–302; ed. and German trans. Rieger, pp. 155–6

Neckam, Alexander: *Alexandri Neckam, De Naturis Rerum, Libri Duo*, ed. Thomas Wright, Rolls Series 34 (London, 1863)

Nigel Longchamps or **Wireker**, *Speculum Stultorum*, trans. G.W. Regenos as *The Book of Daun Burnel the Ass* (Austin, Texas, 1959)

Norman Anonymous [Anonymous of Rouen or York], *De sancta uirginitate et de sacerdotum matrimonio*, ed. Karl Pellens, *Die Texte des Normannischen Anonymus*, Veröffentlichungen des Instituts für europäischen Geschichte Mainz 42 (Wiesbaden, 1966)

Northern Homily Cycle: ed. C. Hörstmann, *Altenglische Legenden* (Heilbronn, 1881) [= NHC]

'On doit bien aymer l'oysellet . . .', ed. Gaston Paris, *Chansons du XVe siècle*, SATF (Paris, 1875), no. 109

Osbert of Clare: *The Letters of Osbert of Clare, Prior of Westminster*, ed. E.W. Williamson (London, 1929)

Ovid, *Heroides and Amores*, ed. and trans. Grant Showerman, LCL (2nd edn, Cambridge MA and London, 1986)

Ovid: *P. Ovidi Nasonis: Amores, Medicamina faciei femineae, Ars amatoria, Remedia amoris*, ed. E.J. Kenney (Oxford, 1961, rpt. 1986)

The Owl and the Nightingale: [*IMEV* 1384] ed. J.H.G. Grattan and G.F.H. Sykes, EETS ES 119 (London, 1935); ed. J.W.H. Atkins (Cambridge, 1922, rpt. New York, 1971); ed. *Eric Gerald Stanley (1960, rpt., Manchester, 1981); *The Owl and the Nightingale: Facsimile of the Jesus and Cotton Manuscripts*, ed. N.R. Ker, EETS OS 251 (London, 1963); ed. A. Bravo, F. Garcia and S. Fernandez-Corugedo (Oviedo, 1991)

Peire d'Alvernhe: *Peire d'Alvernhe: Liriche*, ed. Alberto del Monte (Turin, 1955)

Peter Abelard and Heloise: 'The Personal Letters Between Abelard and Heloise', ed. J.T. Muckle, *MS* 15 (1953) 47–94; 'The letters of Heloise on Religious Life and Abelard's First Reply', *MS* 17 (1955) 240–81; 'Abelard's

Rule for Religious Women', MS 18 (1956) 241–92; *The Letters of Abelard and Heloise*, trans. Betty Radice (Harmondsworth, 1974)

Peter Abelard and Heloise: *Problemata Heloissae*, PL 178. 677–730

Peter Abelard: *Ethics*, ed. and trans. David E. Luscombe (Oxford, 1971)

Peter Abelard: 'Abelard's Letter of Consolation to a Friend (*Historia Calamitatum*)', ed. *J.T. Muckle, MS* 12 (1950) 163–213; *Historia Calamitatum*, ed. J. Monfrin (2nd edn, Paris, 1962)

Peter Abelard: *Carmen ad Astralabium*, PL 178. 1759–66; ed. J.M.A. Rubingh-Bosscher (Groningen, 1987)

Peter Abelard: *Planctus Dinae filiae Jacob*, PL 178. 1817; ed. Peter Dronke, *Poetic Individuality*, p. 146

Peter Abelard: *Theologia Christiana*, in *Petri Abaelardi opera theologica*, ed. E.M. Buytaert, CCCM 12 (Turnhout, 1969), pp. 69–372

St Peter Damian, *Sermo Sancti Alexii Confessoris*, no, 28, in *Sancti Petri Damiani Sermones*, ed. J. *Lucchesi, CCCM 57 (Turnhout, 1983), pp. 162–70; also PL 144. 652–660

Peter Lombard, *Sententiarum libri quatuor*, PL 192. 965–1112

Peter of Blois: *Ep.* 35 [Ad Anselma sanctimonialem], PL 207. 113–4; *Ep.* 55 [Ad Adelitiam monialem], PL 207. 166–8; *Ep.* 79 [Dilecto amico suo R.], PL 207. 243–247

Peter the Venerable: *The Letters of Peter the Venerable*, ed. Giles Constable (Cambridge MA, 1967); Letter 115 (Ad Eloysam Abbatissam), also in *Cluny Studies*, pp. 23–27

Pliny, *Natural History*, ed. and trans. H. Rackham, LCL, 10 vols (Cambridge MA and London, 1947)

'Poema Morale': ed. Morris, *An Old English Miscellany*, pp. 58–71

Rabelais, François, *Gargantua and Pantagruel*, trans. J.M. Cohen (Harmondsworth, 1955, rpt, n.d. [after 1989])

Raimon Vidal de Besalú, *Castia Gilós*, trans. Alison Goddard Elliott as '*The Punishment of the Jealous*', *Allegorica* 1/2 (1976) 103–30

Renart le Contrefait: *Le Roman de Renart le Contrefait*, ed. Gaston Raynaud and Henri Lemaitre, 2 vols (Paris, 1914)

Richard de Fournival: *L'Oeuvre lyrique de Richard de Fournival*, ed. Yves G. Lepage (Ottawa, 1981)

Robert of Flamborough: *Liber Poenitentialis*, ed. J.J. Francis Firth (Toronto, 1971)

Roscelin of Compiègne, *Ad Abaelardum*, ed. J. Reiners, *Der Nominalismus in der Frühscholistik: Ein Beitrag zur Geschichte der Universalienfrage im Mittelalter: Nebst einer neuen Textausgabe des Briefes Roscelins an Abälard*, Beiträge zur Geschichte der Philosophie des Mittelalters 8/5 (Münster, 1910), pp. 63–80

Ruodlieb: *Faksimile-Ausgabe der Codex Latinus Monacensis 19486 der Bayerische Staatsbibliothek und der Fragmente von St Florian*, vol. I, with intro. by Walther Haug (Wiesbaden, 1974); vol. II, critical edition by Konrad Vollman (Wiesbaden, 1985); C.W. Grocock, ed. and trans., *The Ruodlieb* (Warminster, 1985); Dennis M. Kratz, ed. and trans., in '*Waltharius*' and '*Ruodlieb*', Garland Library of Medieval Literature 13 (New York and London, 1984); *Haug and Vollmann, *Frühe Deutsche Literatur und Lateinische Literatur . . .*, with German trans., pp. 388–551

Sauvage d'Arras (d. 1305), *Doctrinal Sauvage*, ed. Aimo Sakari, Studia Philologica Jyväskyläensia 3 (Jyväskylä, 1967)

Sawles Warde, ed. and trans. Millet and Wogan-Browne, pp. 86–108

Scottish Legendary Collection: ed. W. Metcalfe, as *Legends of the Saints*, Scottish Text Society, 3 vols (Edinburgh, 1896) [= SLC]

Seneca, Lucius Annaeus (?), *De remediis fortuitorum*, ed. Ralph Graham Palmer in *Seneca's 'De remediis fortvitorum' and the Elizabethans*, Institute of Elizabethan Studies, Publication 1 (Chicago, 1953), with the translation by Robert Whyttynton (London, 1547)

Speculum virginum, ed. Jutta Seyfarth, CCCM 5 (Turnhout, 1990)

Thomas of Chobham, *Thomae de Chobham, Summa confessorum*, ed. F. Broomfield, Analecta Namurcensia (Louvain, 1968)

Thomas of Hales, 'Luue-Ron': *IMEV* 66; ed. Morris, *An Old English Miscellany*, pp. 93–100; ed. *Dickins and Wilson, pp. 104–9

Thomas, *Le Roman de Horn* ed. Mildred K. Pope, ANTS, 9, 10, 12, 13, 2 vols (Oxford, 1955, 1964); trans. Judith Weiss, *The Birth of Romance*, pp. 1–120

Waltharius: ed. and trans. Dennis M. Kratz, *'Waltharius' and 'Ruodlieb'*, Garland Library of Medieval Literature 13 (New York and London, 1984); ed. and German trans. Haug and Vollmann, *Frühe Deutsche Literatur und Lateinische Literatur*, pp. 164–259

William IX of Aquitaine: see Guilhem IX

Wolfram von Eschenbach: *Der helden minne ir klage . . .*, ed. Neumann, pp. 88–9

Wolfram von Eschenbach, *Parzifal*, trans. A.T. Hatto (Harmondsworth, 1980)

Wolfram von Eschenbach, *Willehalm*, trans. M.E. Gibbs and S.M. Johnson (Harmondsworth, 1984)

Wooing Group: *The Wohunge of ure Lauerd*, ed. W. Meredith Thompson, EETS OS 241 (London, 1958)

Ywain and Gawain, ed. Albert B. Friedman and Norman T. Harrington, EETS OS 254 (London, 1964, rpt. 1982)

4. Secondary Studies

Aertsen, H., and A.A. MacDonald, eds, *Companion to Middle English Romances* (Amsterdam, 1990)

Alexander, Flora, 'Women as lovers in early English romance', in Meale, pp. 24–40

Alexiou, M., and Peter Dronke, 'The lament of Jephtha's Daughter: Themes, Traditions, Originality', *Sm*, 3rd Series, 12 (1971) 819–863; *IPMA*, pp. 345–388

Allen, Richard E., 'The Voices of *The Owl and the Nightingale*', *Studies in Medieval Culture* 3 (1970) 52–8

Altman, Charles F., 'Two Types of Opposition and the Structure of Latin Saints' Lives', *MeH* NS 6 (1975) 1–11

Anson, John, 'The Female Transvestite in Early Monasticism: The Origin and Development of a Motif', *Viator* 5 (1947) 1–32

Archibald, Elizabeth, 'Women and Romance', in Aertsen and MacDonald, pp. 171–87

Ashley, Kathleen, 'Voice and Audience: The Emotional World of the *cantigas de amigo*', *VF*, pp. 35–45

Atkins, J.W.H., *English Literary Criticism: The Medieval Phase* (Cambridge, 1943; London, 1952)

Atkinson, C.W., 'Precious Balsam in a Fragile Glass: The Ideology of Virginity in the Later Middle Ages', *Journal of Family History* 8 (1983) 131–43

Auerbach, Erich, *Mimesis: The Representation of Reality in Western Literature*, trans. Willard R. Trask (German, 1946; trans., Princeton, 1953, rpt. 1991)

Axton, Richard, *European Drama of the Early Middle Ages* (London, 1974)

Baker, J.H., *An Introduction to English Legal History* (2nd edn, London, 1979)

Baldwin, Anne W., 'Henry II and *The Owl and the Nightingale*', *JEGP* 66 (1967) 207–29

Baldwin, John W., *The Language of Sex: Five Voices from Northern France around 1200* (Chicago and London, 1994)

Barratt, Alexandra, 'Flying in the Face of Tradition: A New View of *The Owl and the Nightingale*', *University of Toronto Quarterly* 56 (1987) 471–85

Barron, W.R.J., *English Medieval Romance* (London and New York, 1987, rpt. 1990)

Baugh, Albert C. and Kemp Malone, *The Middle Ages*, vol. 1 of *A Literary History of England*, ed. Albert C. Baugh (2nd edn, London, 1967, rpt. 1980)

Baugh, Albert C., 'Improvisation in the Middle English Romance', *Proceedings of the American Philosophical Society* 103 (1959) 418–54

Bec, Pierre, *La lyrique française au moyen-age (XIIe–XIIIe siècles): Contribution à une typologie des genres poétiques médiévaux*, Publications du Centre d'Etudes Supérieures du Civilisation Médiévale de l'Université de Poitiers 6–7, 2 vols (Paris, 1977)

Bec, Pierre: *Il miglior fabbro . . . : Mélange de langue et littérature occitanes en hommage à Pierre Bec . . .* (Poitiers, 1991)

Bender, K.-H., 'Beauté et mariage selon Chrétien de Troyes: un défi lancé à la tradition', *FS Erich Köhler*, pp. 31–42

Bennett, J.A.W., 'Gower's "Honeste Love" ', in Lawlor, pp. 107–121

Bennett, J.A.W., *Middle English Literature*, ed. Douglas Gray (Oxford, 1986)

Benson, Robert L. and Giles Constable, eds, *Renaissance and Renewal in the Twelfth Century* [proceedings of a conference at Harvard, 26–9/11/77] (Oxford, 1982)

Benton, John F., 'A Reconsideration of the Authenticity of the Correspondence of Abelard and Heloise', in *Trier Studies*, pp. 41–52

Benton, John F., 'Clio and Venus: An Historical View of Medieval Love', in *MCL*, pp. 19–42

Benton, John F., 'Collaborative Approaches to Fantasy and Reality in the Literature of Champagne', *Court and Poet*, pp. 43–57

Benton, John F., 'Fraud, Fiction and Borrowing in the Correspondence of Abelard and Heloise', *Cluny Studies*, pp. 469–511

Benton, John F., 'Philology's Search for Abelard in the *Metamorphosis Goliae*', *Speculum* 50 (1975) 199–217

Benton, John F., 'The Court of Champagne as a Literary Center', *Speculum* 36 (1961) 551–91

Benton, John F., 'Trotula, Women's Problems and the Professionalization of Medicine in the Middle Ages', *Bulletin of the History of Medicine* 59 (1985) 30–53

Bezzola, Reto R.,'Guillaume IX et les origines de l'amour courtois', *Romania* 66 (1940–1) 145–237

Biller, P.P.A., 'Birth-Control in the West in the Thirteenth and Early Fourteenth Centuries', *Past & Present* 94 (1982) 3–26

Bischoff, Bernhard, *Latin Palaeography: Antiquity and the Middle Ages*, trans. Dáibhí Ó Cróinín and David Ganz ([German] Berlin, 1979; Cambridge, 1990)

Blangez, G. *'Dissuasio Valerii* ou la dissuasion de mariage de Gautier Map', in *Mélanges d'études anciennes offerts à Maurice Lebel* (Quebec, 1980) pp. 385–394

Bliss, A.J., 'Notes on the Auchinleck MS', *Speculum* 26 (1951) 652–8

Bloch, R. Howard, ' "Mieux vaut jamais que tard": Romance, Philology and Old French Letters', *Representations* 36 (1991) 64–86

Bloch, R. Howard, 'Medieval Misogyny', *Representations* 20 (1987) 1–24

Bloch, R. Howard, 'The Medieval Text – *Guigemar* – As a Provocation to Medieval Studies', in Brownlee and Nichols, pp. 99–112

Bloch, R. Howard, *Medieval Misogyny and the Invention of Western Romantic Love* (Chicago and London, 1991)

Bloomfield, Morton W., *'Piers Plowman* and the three Grades of Chastity', *Anglia* 76 (1958) 227–253

Bloomfield, Morton W., *The Seven Deadly Sins: An Introduction to the History of a Religious Concept, with Special Reference to Medieval English Literature* (Michigan, 1952)

Boase, Roger, *The Origin and Meaning of Courtly Love: A critical study of European scholarship* (Manchester, 1977)

Boffey, Julia, 'Women authors and women's literacy in fourteenth- and fifteenth-century England', in Meale, pp. 159–82

Bogdanow, Fanni, 'The Tradition of the Troubadour Lyrics and the Treatment of the Love Theme in Chrétien de Troyes' *Erec et Enide'*, in *Court and Poet*, pp. 79–92

Bolton, Brenda M., 'Mulieres Sanctae', in Stuard, pp. 141–58

Bowden, Betsy, 'The Art of Courtly Copulation', *MeH* NS 9 (1979) 67–85

Breier, Willi, *'Eule und Nachtigall': Eine Untersuchung der Überlieferung und der Sprache, der örtlichen und der zeitlichen Entstehung des me. Gedichts*, Studien zur englischen Philologie 39 (Halle, 1910)

Brewer, Derek, *Symbolic Stories: Traditional narratives of the family drama in English literature* (Cambridge, 1980)

Briffault, Robert, *The Troubadours* (Bloomington, 1965)

Brogyanyi, Gabriel John, 'Motivation in *Erec et Enide*: An Interpretation of the Romance', *Kentucky Romance Quarterly* 19 (1972) 407–31

Bronson, Bernard H., Eric Sams and Nicholas Temperley, 'Pastourelle', *NGDMM*, II, 70–6

Brooke, Christopher N.L., *The Medieval Idea of Marriage* (Oxford, 1989, rpt. 1991)

Brooke, Christopher N.L., 'Marriage and Society in the Central Middle Ages', in *Marriage and Society: Studies in the Social History of Marriage*, ed. R.B. Outhwaite (London, 1981)

Brown, Emerson, jr, 'Biblical Women in the *Merchant's Tale*: Feminism, Antifeminism, and Beyond', *Viator* 5 (1974) 387–412

Brown, Peter, *The Body and Society: Men, Women and Sexual Renunciation in Early Christianity* (New York, 1988; London, 1989)

Brownlee, Marina S., Kevin Brownlee and Stephen G. Nichols, eds, *The New Medievalism* (Baltimore and London, 1991)

Brundage, James A., 'Concubinage and Marriage in Medieval Canon Law', *JMH* 1 (1975) 1–17

Brundage, James A., 'The Crusader's Wife Revisited', *SG* 14 (1967) 241–51

Brundage, James A., 'The Crusader's Wife: a Canonistic Quandary', *SG* 12 (1967) 425–41

Brundage, James A., *Law, Sex and Medieval Society in Christian Europe* (Chicago and London, 1987)

Brundage, James, A., 'The Votive Obligations of Crusaders: The Development of a Canonistic Doctrine', *Traditio* 24 (1968) 77–118

Bugge, John, *Virginitas: an Essay in the History of a Medieval Ideal*, International Archives of the History of Ideas, Series Minor 17 (The Hague, 1975)

Bullington, Rachel, *The 'Alexis' in the Saint Albans Psalter: A Look into the Heart of the Matter*, Garland Studies in Medieval Literature 4 (New York and London, 1991)

Bullock-Davies, Constance, 'Marie de France: A Reassessment of her Narrative Technique in the *Lais*', *Court and Poet*, pp. 93–9

Bullough, Vern L., 'Medieval Medical and Scientific Views of Women', *MMA*, pp. 485–501

Burgess, Glyn S., *Court and Poet: Selected Proceedings of the Third Congress of the International Courtly Literature Society*, ARCA, Classical and Medieval Texts, Papers and Monographs 5 (Liverpool, 1981)

Burrow, John A., *Medieval Writers and Their Work: Middle English Literature and its Background 1100–1500* (Oxford, 1982, rpt. 1990)

Burrow, John A., *The Ages of Man: A Study in Medieval Writing and Thought* (Oxford, 1986)

Burton, Janet, *Monastic and Religious Orders in Britain, 1000–1300* (Cambridge, 1994)

Buytaert, E.M., ed., *Peter Abelard: Proceedings of the International Conference. (Louvain, May 10–12, 1971)* (Leuven and The Hague, 1974) [= *Leuven Studies*]

Bynum, Caroline Walker, *Jesus as Mother: Studies in the Spirituality of the High Middle Ages*, Publications of the Centre for Medieval and Renaissance Studies, UCLA, 16 (Berkeley, Los Angeles and London, 1982)

Cadden, Joan, 'Medieval Scientific and Medical Views of Sexuality: Questions of Propriety', *MeH* NS 14 (1986) 157–71

Calin, William, 'Defense and Illustration of *Fin'amor*: Some Polemical Comments on the Robertsonian Approach', in Smith and Snow, pp. 32–48

Campbell, Joseph, *The Masks of God*: 4 vols, especially: vol. 3, *Occidental Mythology* (New York, 1964, rpt., Harmondsworth, 1976); vol. 4, *Creative Mythology* (New York, 1968, rpt., Harmondsworth, 1987)

Cannon, Christopher, 'The style and authorship of the Otho revision of Laȝamon's *Brut*', *MÆ* 62/2 (1993) 187–209

Carlson, David, 'Religion and Romance: The Languages of Love in the Treatises of Gerard of Liège and the Case of Andreas Capellanus', in Lazar and Lacy, pp. 81–92

Carson, M. Angela, 'Rhetorical Structure in *The Owl and the Nightingale*', *Speculum* 42 (1967) 92–103

Cartlidge, Neil, 'The Date of *The Owl and the Nightingale*', *MÆ*, forthcoming

Cave, Terence, *Recognitions: A Study in Poetics* (Oxford, 1988)

Cawley, A.C., 'Astrology in *The O & N*', *MLR* 66 (1951) 161–74

Cherchi, P., 'New uses of Andreas' *De amore*', in *Mittelalterbilder*, pp. 22–30

Clanchy, Michael T., *From Memory to Written Record: England 1066–1307* (Oxford and Cambridge MA, 1979; 2nd edn, 1993)

Clark, Elizabeth A., ' "Adam's Only Companion": Augustine and the Early Christian Debate on Marriage', in Edwards and Spector, pp. 15–31

Clark, S.L. and J. Wasserman, 'Wisdom Buildeth a Hut: *Aucassin et Nicolette* as Christian Comedy', *Allegorica* 1/1 (1976) 250–68

Coghill, N.K., 'Love and "Foul Delight": some contrasted attitudes', in Lawlor, pp. 141–56

Coghlan, Maura, 'The Flaw in Enide's Character: A Study of Chrétien de Troyes' *Erec*', *Reading Medieval Studies* 5 (1979)

Coleman, Emily, 'Infanticide in the Early Middle Ages', in Stuard, pp. 47–70

Coleman, Janet, '*The Owl and the Nightingale* and Papal Theories of Marriage', *Journal of Ecclesiastical History* 38 (1987) 517–568

Colgrave, B., '*The Owl and the Nightingale* and the "Good Man from Rome"', *English Language Notes* 4 (1966) 1–4

Conlee, John W., 'The *Owl and the Nightingale* and Latin Debate Tradition', *The Comparatist* 4 (1980) 57–67

Constable, Giles, 'Renewal and Reform in Religious Life: Concepts and Realities', *RRTC*, pp. 37–68

Constable, Giles, *Letters and Letter-Collections*, Typologie des Sources du Moyen Age Occidental (Turnhout, 1976)

Coppin, Joseph, *Amour et mariage dans la littérature française du nord au moyen-âge* (Paris, 1961)

Cottle, Basil, review of Bella Millett, *Hali Meithhad*: *MÆ* 54/1 (1985) 136–7

Coulton, G.G., *Medieval Panorama: The English Scene from Conquest to Reformation* (Cambridge, 1945)

Courcelle, Pierre, 'Tradition néo-platonicienne et traditions chrétiennes de la "région de dissemblance"', *Archives* 24 (1957) 5–33

Crane, R.S., 'The Vogue of Guy of Warwick', *PMLA* 30 NS 23 (1915) 125–94

Crane, Susan, *Insular Romance: Politics, Faith, and Culture in Anglo-Norman and Middle English Literature* (Berkeley, Los Angeles and London, 1986)

Curtius, E.R., 'Zur Interpretation des Alexiuslieds', *ZFRP* 56 (1936) 113–37

Curtius, E.R., *European Literature and the Latin Middle Ages*, trans. Willard R. Trask (Princeton, 1967)

d'Ardenne, Simonne R.T.O., 'Ine so gode kinges londe', *English Studies* 30 (1949) 157–64

d'Ardenne, Simonne R.T.O., 'The Editing of Middle English Texts', in *English Studies Today*, ed. C.L. Wrenn and G. Bullough (Oxford, 1951), pp. 74–84

d'Avray, D.L. and M. Tausche, 'Marriage sermons in *ad status* collections of the Central Middle Ages', *Archives* 47 (1980) 71–119

Dahood, Roger, '*Ancrene Wisse*, the Katherine Group, and the *Wohunge* Group', in *Middle English Prose: A Critical Guide to Major Authors and Genres*, ed. A.S.G. Edwards (New Brunswick NJ, 1984) 1–33

Davis, Norman, review of Sundby: *MÆ* 20 (1951) 64–70

de Gaiffier, B. 'Intactam sponsam relinquens. A propos de la Vie de S.Alexis', *Analecta Bollandiana* 65 (1947) 157–95

de La Torre Bueno, Lillian, 'A Note on the Date of *The Owl and the Nightingale*', *Anglia* 58 (1934) 122–30

de Rougemont, Denis, *Love in the Western World*, trans. M. Belgion (Princeton, 1983)

Delehaye, Hippolyte, *The Legends of the Saints* (1905, 4th edn, Brussels, 1955); trans. Donald Attwater (London, 1962)

Delhaye, Philippe, 'Le dossier antimatrimonial de l'*Adversus Jovinianum* et son influence sur quelques écrits latins au XIIe siècle', *MS* 13 (1951) 65–86

Delhaye, Philippe, 'The Development of the Medieval Church's Teaching on Marriage', *Concilium* 5/6 (May, 1970) 83–8

Diamond, A., 'Revelations and Reevaluations: Medieval Women', *MeH* NS 19 (1993) 147–58

Dobson, E.J., 'The Affiliations of the Manuscripts of *Ancrene Wisse*,' in *English and Medieval Studies: Presented to J.R.R. Tolkien on the Occasion of his Seventieth Birthday*, ed. Norman Davis and C.L. Wrenn (London, 1962), pp. 128–63

Dobson, E.J., 'A New Edition of "The Owl and the Nightingale"' [review of Stanley, *The Owl and the Nightingale*], *N&Q* 206 (1961) 373–8, 405–11, 444–8

Dobson, E.J., *The Origins of the 'Ancrene Wisse'* (Oxford, 1976)

Donaldson, E.T. 'The Myth of Courtly Love', (1965; rpt. *Speaking of Chaucer*, London, 1970), pp. 154–63

Donovan, Mortimer, J., 'The Owl as Religious Altruist in *The Owl and the Nightingale*', *MS* 18 (1956) 207–14

Dronke, Peter and Jill Mann, 'Chaucer and the Medieval Latin Poets', in Derek Brewer, ed., *Writers and their Backgrounds: Geoffrey Chaucer* (London, 1974), pp. 154–83

Dronke, Peter and M. Alexiou: see Alexiou

Dronke, Peter, 'Abelard and Heloise in Medieval Testimonies', 26th W.P. Ker Memorial Lecture (Glasgow, 1976); *IPME*, pp. 247–294

Dronke, Peter, 'A Critical Note on Schumann's Dating of the Codex Buranus', *Beiträge zur Geschichte der deutschen Sprache und Literatur* 84 (1962) 173–83

Dronke, Peter, 'A Note on *Pamphilus*', *JWCI* 42 (1979) 225–30; *LVMA*, cap. II

Dronke, Peter, 'Andreas Capellanus', *Journal of Medieval Latin* 4 (1994) 51–63

Dronke, Peter, 'Bernard Silvestris, Natura and Personification', *JWCI* 43 (1980) 16–31; *IPME*, pp. 41–61

Dronke, Peter, 'Dido's Lament: From Medieval Latin Lyric to Chaucer', in *Kontinuität und Wandel: Lateinische Poesie von Naevius bis Baudelaire: Franco Munari zum 65. Geburtstag*, ed. U.J. Stache et al. (Hildesheim, 1986), pp. 364–90; *IPME*, pp. 431–56

Dronke, Peter, 'Francesca and Heloise', *Comparative Literature* 26/2 (1975) 113–35; *MPHW*, pp. 359–85

Dronke, Peter, 'Guillaume IX and Courtoisie', *RF* 73 (1961) 328–30; *MPHW*, pp. 237–47

Dronke, Peter, 'Heloise's *Problemata* and Letters: some questions of form and content', *Trier Studies*, pp. 53–73

Dronke, Peter, 'Heloise, Abelard, and some recent discussions', in *IPME*, pp. 323–42

Dronke, Peter, 'Laments of the Maries: From the Beginnings to the Mystery Plays', in *Idee, Gestalt, Geschichte – Festschrift Klaus von See*, ed. G.W. Weber (Odense, 1988), pp. 89–116; *IPME*, pp. 457–89

Dronke, Peter, 'Learned Lyric and Popular Ballad in the Early Middle Ages', *Sm*, 3rd Series, 17 (1976) 1–40; *MPHW*, pp. 167–207

Dronke, Peter, 'Narrative and Dialogue in Medieval Secular Drama', in *Literature in Fourteenth-Century England*, ed. Piero Boitani and Anna Torti, Tübinger Beiträge zur Anglistik 5 (Tübingen, 1983) pp. 99–120; *LVMA*, cap. IV

Dronke, Peter, 'Peter of Blois and Poetry at the Court of Henry II', *MS* 28 (1976) 185–235; *MPHW*, pp. 281–339

Dronke, Peter, 'Poetic Meaning in the *Carmina Burana*', *MlJb* 10 (1975) 116–37; *MPHW*, pp. 249–79

Dronke, Peter, 'Profane Elements in Literature', *RRTC*, pp. 569–92

Dronke, Peter, 'Pseudo-Ovid, *Facetus* and the Arts of Love', *MlJb* 11 (1976) 126–131; *LVMA*, cap. III

Dronke, Peter, 'The Conclusion of *Troilus and Criseyde*', *MÆ* 33 (1964) 47–52

Dronke, Peter, 'The Rise of the Medieval Fabliau: Latin and Vernacular Evidence', *RF* 85 (1973) 275–97

Dronke, Peter, 'Virgines caste', in *Lateinische Dichtungen des X. und XI. Jahrhunderts: Festgabe für Walther Bulst zum 80. Geburtstag* (Heidelberg, 1981) pp. 93–117; *LVMA*, cap. VI

Dronke, Peter, review of C. Buridant, trans., *André le Chapelain: Traité de l'amour courtois*: in *MÆ* 45 (1976) 317–21

Dronke, Peter, review of Felix Schlösser, *Andreas Capellanus: seine Minnelehre und das christliche Weltbild um 1200* (Bonn, 1960): *MÆ* 32 (1963) 56–60

Dronke, Peter, *Intellectuals and Poets in Medieval Europe* (Rome, 1992)

Dronke, Peter, *Latin and Vernacular Poets of the Middle Ages* (London, 1991)

Dronke, Peter, *Medieval Latin and the Rise of the European Love-Lyric*, 2 vols (2nd edn, Oxford, 1968)

Dronke, Peter, *Poetic Individuality in the Middle Ages: New Departures in Poetry 1000–1150* (2nd edn, London, 1986)

Dronke, Peter, *The Medieval Lyric* (London, 1968; 2nd edn, London and New York, 1977)

Dronke, Peter, *The Medieval Poet and his World* (Rome, 1984)

Dronke, Peter, *Women Writers of the Middle Ages: A Critical Study of Texts from Perpetua († 203) to Marguerite Porete († 1310)* (Cambridge, 1984)

Duby, Georges, 'Dans la France du Nord Ouest au XIIe siècle: les jeunes dans la société aristocratique', *Annales. Economies, sociétés, civilisations* 19 (1964), pp. 835–46, rpt. *Hommes et structures du Moyen Age* (Paris and The Hague, 1973)

Duby, Georges, 'Le mariage dans la société du haut moyen âge', *Spoleto Studies*, pp. 15–39

Duby, Georges, ed., *A History of Private Life: Revelations of the Medieval World*, trans. Arthur Goldhammer, vol. 2 of *A History of Private Life*, ed. Philippe Ariès and Georges Duby (Cambridge MA and London, 1988)

Duby, Georges, *Medieval Marriage: Two Models from Twelfth-Century France*, trans. Elborg Forster (Baltimore and London, 1978, rpt., 1991)

Duby, Georges, *The Knight, the Lady and the Priest: The Making of Marriage in Medieval France*, trans. Barbara Bray (New York, 1983)

Dumitrescu, 'Les premiers troubadours connus et les origines de la poésie provençale: (Contribution à l'étude du problème)', *CCM* 9 (1966) 345–54

Dunn, Charles, W., 'Romances derived from English legends', *Manual*, I, 17–37

Durling, Nancy Vine, 'Hagiography and Lineage: The Example of the Old French *Vie de Saint Alexis*' *RP* 40/4 (1987) 451–69

Dworkin, Ronald, *Law's Empire* (London, 1986)

Earnshaw, Doris, *The Female Voice in Medieval Romance Lyric*, American University Studies, Series II, Romance Languages and Literatures 68 (New York, Berne, Frankfurt a. M. and Paris, 1988)

Edwards, Robert R., and Stephen Spector, eds, *The Old Daunce: Love, Friendship, Sex and Marriage in the Medieval World* (New York, 1991)

Eis, Gerhard, ' "Alexiuslied" und christliche Askese', *ZFSL* 59 (1934) 232–6

Elliott, Alison Goddard, *Roads to Paradise: Reading the Lives of the Early Saints* (Hanover NE and London, 1987)

Elliott, Dyan, *Spiritual Marriage: Sexual Abstinence in Medieval Wedlock* (Princeton NJ, 1993)

Engels, Friedrich, *The Origin of the Family, Private Property and the State*, trans. in *Karl Marx and Frederick Engels: Selected Works* (Moscow, London and New York, 1968, rpt. 1973), pp. 449–583

Evans, Dafydd, 'Wishfulfilment: the Social Function and Classification of Old French Romances', *Court and Poet*, pp. 129–34

Fälschungen im Mittelalter: Internationaler Kongress der Monumenta Germaniae Historica: Munich, 1986 vol. 5: *Fingierte Briefe, Frömmigkeit und Fälschung, Realienfälschungen*, MGH Schriften 33 (Hanover, 1988)

Farmer, Sharon, 'Persuasive Voices: Clerical Images of Medieval Wives', *Speculum* 61/3 (1986) 517–43

Fellows, Jennifer, 'Mothers in Middle English romance', in Meale, pp. 41–60

Festugière, A.J., 'Lieux communs littéraires et thèmes de folk-lore dans l'Hagiographie primitive', *Wiener Studien: Zeitschrift für klassische Philologie* 73 (1960) 123–52

Flinn, John, *Le Roman de Renart dans la littérature française et dans les littératures étrangères au moyen âge* (Toronto, 1963)

Foster, Idris Llewellyn, '*Gereint, Owein* and *Peredur*', in *ALMA*, pp. 192–205

Fotitch, Tatiana, 'The mystery of "Les renges d'espethe"', *Romania* 79 (1958) 495–507

Foucault, Michel, *The History of Sexuality*, trans. Robert Hurley: vol. I, *An Introduction* (1976, rpt. Harmondsworth, 1990); vol. II, *The Use of Pleasure* (1984, rpt. Harmondsworth, 1988); vol. III, *The Care of the Self* (1984, Harmondsworth, 1990)

Foulet, Alfred, review of Paul Aebischer, *Le Mystère d'Adam*: *RP* 19 (1965–6) 121–2

Fraioli, Deborah, 'The Importance of Satire in Jerome's *Adversus Jovinianum* as an Argument Against the Authenticity of the *Historia calamitatum*', in *Fälschungen*, pp. 167–200

Frank, Roberta, 'Marriage in Twelfth and Thirteenth-Century Iceland', *MMA*, 473–84

Frankis, John, 'The Social Context of Vernacular Writing in Thirteenth Century England: the Evidence of the Manuscripts', in *Thirteenth Century England I: Proceedings of the Newcastle upon Tyne Conference 1985*, ed. P.R. Coss and S.D. Lloyd (Woodbridge, 1986), pp. 175–84

Frappier, Jean, 'Chrétien de Troyes', in *ALMA*, pp. 157–91

Friedman, Lionel J., 'Gradus Amoris', *RP* 19 (1965–6) 167–77

Gally, Michèle, 'Disputer d'amour: les Arrageois et le jeu-parti', *Romania* 107 (1986) 55–76

Garrigues, Marie-Odile, 'Quelques recherches sur l'oeuvre d'Honorius Augustodunensis', *Revue d'histoire ecclésiastique* 70 (1975) 388–425

Gaudemet, Jean, 'La définition romano-canonique du mariage', *Speculum Iuris et Ecclesiarum: Festschrift für Willibald M. Plöchl zum 60. Geburtstag* (Vienna, 1967) pp. 107–114; rpt. in *Eglise et société en Occident au Moyen Age* (London, 1984) cap. XIV

Gaudemet, Jean, 'Le célibat ecclésiastique: Le droit et la practique du XIe au XIIIe siècles', *Zeitschrift der Sauvigny-Stiftung für Rechtsgeschichte: kanonische Abteilung* 68 (1982) 1–31; rpt. in *Eglise et société en Occident au Moyen Age* (London, 1984) cap. XV

Gaunt, Simon B., 'Marginal Men, Marcabru and Orthodoxy: The Early Troubadours and Adultery', *MÆ* 59/1 (1990) 55–72

Gellinek, Christian, 'Marriage by Consent in Literary Sources of Medieval Germany', *SG* 12 (1967) 555–79

Gellinek-Schellekens, Josepha E., *The Voice of the Nightingale in Middle English Poems and Bird Debates* (New York, 1984)

Georgianna, Linda, 'Any Corner of Heaven: Heloise's Critique of Monasticism', *MS* 49 (1987) 221–53

Georgianna, Linda, *The Solitary Self: Individuality in the 'Ancrene Wisse'* (Cambridge MA and London, 1981)

Gieysztor, Alexander, 'Pauper et peregrinus sum: La légende de saint Alexis en occident: Un idéal du pauvreté', in *Etudes sur l'histoire du pauvreté (Moyen âge – XVIe siècle)*, ed. M. Mollat (Paris, 1974), pp. 125–35

Gilbert, Jane Louise, 'Comparing Like with Like: Identity, Identicalness and Difference in Selected Medieval French and English Narratives' (unpub. Ph.D. diss., Cambridge, 1993, no. 18432)

Gillespie, G., 'Origins of Romance Lyrics: A Review of Research', *Yearbook of Comparative and General Literature* 16 (1967) 16–32

Gilson, Etienne, *Heloise and Abelard* (University of Michigan, 1960, rpt. 1992)

Glasser, Marc, 'Marriage in Medieval Hagiography', *SMRH* NS 4 (OS 14) (1981) 1–34

Gnädinger, Louise, *Eremetica: Studien zur altfranzösischen Heiligenvita des 12. und 13. Jahrhunderts*, Beihefte zur Zeitschrift für romanische Philologie 130 (Tübingen, 1972)

Goetinck, Glenys W., 'Chrétien's Welsh Inheritance', in *Gallica: Essays presented to J. Heywood Thomas by colleagues, pupils and friends* (Cardiff, 1969)

Goldberg, Jeremy, *Women, Work and Life Cycle in a Medieval Economy* (Oxford, 1992)

Goody, Jack, *The development of the family and marriage in Europe* (Cambridge, 1983)

Goosse, A., 'La *Vie de Saint Alexis*', *Les Lettres Romanes* 14 (1960) 62–5

Gottschalk, Jane, '*The Owl and the Nightingale*: Lay Preachers to a Lay Audience', *PQ* 45 (1966) 657–67

Gravdal, Kathryn, 'Camouflaging Rape: The Rhetoric of Sexual Violence in the Medieval Pastourelle', *RR* 76 (1985) 361–73

Gravdal, Kathryn, 'Chrétien de Troyes, Gratian and the Medieval Romance of Sexual Violence', *Signs* 17/3 (1992) 558–85

Green, D.H., review of W. Braun, *Studien zum 'Ruodlieb': Ritterideal, Erzählstruktur und Darstellungsstil* (Berlin, 1962): *MÆ* 32 (1963) 53–6

Hamilton, Bernard, 'The Monastery of S. Alessio and the Religious and Intellectual Renaissance in Twelfth-Century Rome', *SMRH* 2 (1965) 265–310

Hanawalt, Barbara A., *The Ties that Bound: Peasant Families in Medieval Europe* (New York, 1986)

Hansen, G.C., 'Molestiae Nuptiarum', *Wissenschaftliche Zeitschrift der Universität Rostock, Gesellschafts- und Sprachwissenschaften* 12 (1963) 215–19

Häring, Nikolaus M., 'Abelard Yesterday and Today', *Cluny Studies*, pp. 341–403

Haskell, A.S. 'The Paston Women on Marriage in the Fifteenth Century', *MMA*, pp. 459–72

Hatcher, A.G., 'The Old French Poem *St Alexis*: A Mathematical Demonstration', *Traditio* 8 (1952) 111–58

Hatzfeld, Helmut A., 'Esthetic Criticism Applied to Medieval Romance Literature', *RP* 1 (1947–8) 305–27

Head, Thomas, 'The Marriages of Christina of Markyate', *Viator* 21 (1990) 75–101

Heiserman, Arthur, *The Novel before the Novel* (Chicago, 1977)

Heller, B., 'L'épée, symbole et gardien de la chasteté', *Romania* 36 (1907) 36–49

Helmholz, Richard H., *Marriage Litigation in Medieval England*, Cambridge Studies in English Legal History (Cambridge, 1974)

Herlihy, David, *Medieval Households* (Cambridge MA, 1985)

Higuchi, Masayuki, 'On the Language of *The Owl and the Nightingale*: How Language Becomes a Weapon for a Verbal Duel', *Poetica* 25–6 (1987) 73–92

Hill, Betty, 'British Library MS Egerton 613', *N&Q* 223 (1978) 394–409, 492–501

Hill, Betty, 'Oxford, Jesus College MS 29: Addenda on Donation, Acquisition, Dating and Relevance of the ''Broaken Leafe'' note to *The Owl and the Nightingale*', *NQ* 220 (1975) 98–105

Hill, Betty, 'The History of Jesus College, Oxford, MS. 29', *MÆ* 32 (1963) 203–13

Hill, Betty, 'The *Luue-ron* and Thomas de Hales', *MLR* 59 (1964) 321–30

Hinckley, Henry B., 'Science and Folk-Lore in *The Owl and the Nightingale*', *PMLA* 47 (1932) 303–14

Hinckley, Henry B., 'The Date, Author and Source of *The Owl and the Nightingale*', *PMLA* 44 (1929) 329–34

Hinckley, Henry B., 'The Date of *The Owl and the Nightingale*', *MP* 17 (1919) 63–74

Hinckley, Henry B., 'The Date of *The Owl and the Nightingale*. Vivian's Legation', *PQ* 12 (1933) 339–49

Hoepffner, E., ' ''Matière et sens'' dans le roman d'*Erec et Enide*', *Archivum Romanicum* 18 (1934) 433–50

Hoffman, Ruth Cassel, 'The Lady in the Poem: A Shadow Voice', in *Poetics of Love in the Middle Ages: Texts and Contexts*, in Lazar and Lacy, pp. 227–35

Holdsworth, Christopher J., 'Christina of Markyate', in *Medieval Women: dedicated and presented to Rosalind M. T. Hill on the occasion of her seventieth birthday*, ed. Derek Baker, Studies in Church History: Subsidia 1 (Oxford, 1978) pp. 185–204

Holmes, Urban T., jr, 'The Idea of a Twelfth Century Renaissance', *Speculum* 26 (1951) 643–51

Hopkins, Andrea, *The Sinful Knights: A Study of Middle English Penitential Romance* (Oxford, 1990)

Hornstein, Lillian Herlands, 'Eustace-Constance-Florence-Griselda Legends', *Manual*, I, 120–32

Huganir, Kathryn, *The Owl and the Nightingale: Sources, Date and Author* (Philadelphia, 1931)

Huganir, Kathryn, 'Further Notes on the Date of *The Owl and the Nightingale*', *Anglia* 63 (1939) 113–34

Huizinga, Johan, *The Waning of the Middle Ages: A study of the forms of life, thought and art in France and the Netherlands in the fourteenth and fifteenth centuries*, trans. F. Hopman (1924, trans. Harmondsworth, 1955)

Hume, Kathryn, *The Owl and the Nightingale: The Poem and its Critics* (Toronto and Buffalo, 1975)

Hürsch, Melitta, 'Alexiuslied und christliche Askese', *ZFSL* 58 (1934) 414–8

Il matrimonio nella società altomedievale: 22–28 aprile 1976, Settimane di studio del centro italiano di studi sull' alto medioevo 24, 2 vols (Spoleto, 1979)

Jackson, William T.H., 'The *De amore* of Andreas Capellanus and the Practice of Love at Court', *RR* 49 (1958) 243–51

Jackson, William T.H., 'The Medieval Pastourelle as a Satirical Genre', *PQ* 31 (1952) 156–70

Jacobs, Nicolas, '*The Owl and the Nightingale* and the Bishops', in *Medieval Literature and Antiquities: Studies in honour of Basil Cottle*, ed. Myra Stokes and T.L. Burton (Cambridge, 1987)

James, William, *The Varieties of Religious Experience: A Study in Human Nature* (1902; new edn, Harmondsworth, 1982, rpt., 1985)

Jeanroy, Alfred, *La Poésie lyrique des Troubadours*, 2 vols (Toulouse and Paris, 1934)

Jeanroy, Alfred, *Les origines de la poésie lyrique en France au moyen age* (3rd edn, Paris, 1925)

Jeanroy, Alfred, *Poésie lyrique en France au moyen âge* (3rd edn, Paris, 1925)

Jeay, Madeleine, 'Sexuality and Family in Fifteenth-Century France: Are Literary Sources a Mask or a Mirror?', *JFH* 4 (1979) 328–45

Jeffrey, David L., *The Early English Lyric and Franciscan Spirituality* (Lincoln, 1975)

Jones, William Powell, *The Pastourelle: A Study of the Origins of a Lyric Type* (Cambridge MA, 1931)

Kamuf, Peggy, *Fictions of Feminine Desire: Disclosures of Heloise* (Lincoln, Nebraska, and London, 1982) pp. xi–43

Karnein, Alfred, 'Amor est Passio – A Definition of Courtly Love?', *Court and Poet*, pp. 215–21

Karnein, Alfred, 'La réception du *De Amore* d'André Le Chapelain au XIIIe siècle', *Romania* 102 (1981) 324–51, 501–42

Keen, Maurice, *Chivalry* (New Haven, 1984)

Kelly, Douglas, 'Courtly Love in Perspective: The Hierarchy of Love in Andreas Capellanus', *Traditio* 24 (1968) 119–47

Kelly, Douglas, 'La forme et le sens de la quête dans l'*Erec et Enide* de Chrétien de Troyes', *Romania* 92 (1971) 326–58

Kelly, Henry Ansgar, 'Clandestine Marriage and Chaucer's *Troilus*', *Viator* 4 (1973) 435–57

Kelly, Henry Ansgar, 'Medieval Relations, Marital and Other', *MeH* NS 19 (1993) 133–46

Kelly, Henry Ansgar, *Love and Marriage in the Age of Chaucer* (Ithaca and London, 1975)

Ker, W.P., *Medieval English Literature* (1912, rpt., London, 1969)

Klausner, David N., 'Didacticism and Drama in *Guy of Warwick*', *MeH* NS 6 (1975) 103–119

Klausner, David N., *The Nature and Origins of Didacticism in some Middle English Romances* (unpub. Ph. D. diss, Cambridge, 1967, no. 6085)

Kooper, Erik, 'Love and Marriage in Middle English Romances', in Aertsen and MacDonald, pp. 171–87

Kooper, Erik, 'Loving the Unequal Equal: Medieval Theologians and Marital Affection', in Edwards and Spector, pp. 44–56

Krauss, H. and D. Rieger, eds, *Mittelalterstudien: Erich Köhler zum Gedenken* (Heidelberg, 1984)

Küchler, Walther, 'Über den sentimentalen Gehalt der Haupthandlung in Crestiens *Erec* und *Ivain*', *ZFRP* 40 (1920) 83–99

Ladner, Gerhardt B., 'Homo Viator: Medieval Ideas on Alienation and Order', *Speculum* 42/2 (1967) 233–59

Laing, Margaret, and Angus McIntosh, 'The Language of the *Ancrene Riwle*, the Katherine Group Texts and *Þe Wohunge of ure Lauerd* in BL Cotton Titus D. xviii', *Neuphilologische Mitteilungen*, 96 (1995) 235–63

Laing, Margaret, 'A Linguistic Atlas of Early Middle English: the value of texts surviving in more than one version', in *A History of Englishes: New Methods and Interpretations in Historical Linguistics*, Topics in English Linguistics 10 (Berlin and New York, 1992)

Laing, Margaret, 'Anchor Texts and Literary Manuscripts in Early Middle English', in Riddy, pp. 27–52

Laing, Margaret, 'The linguistic analysis of medieval vernacular texts: Two projects at Edinburgh', in *Corpora across the Centuries: Proceedings of the First International Colloquium on English Diachronic Corpora*, ed. Merja Kytö, Matti Rissanen and Susan Wright (Amsterdam, 1994)

Laurie, Helen C.R., '*Cligés* and the legend of Abelard and Heloise', *ZFRP* 107/3-4 (1991) 324–42

Lausberg, Heinrich, 'Das Proömium (Strophen 1–3) des altfranzösischen Alexiusliedes', *ASNS* 192 (9156) 33–58

Lawlor, John, ed., *Patterns of Love and Courtesy: Essays in Memory of C.S. Lewis* (London, 1966)

Lawson, Lise, 'La Structure du récit dans les *Lais* de Marie de France', in *Court and Poet*, pp. 233–40

Lazar, Moshé, 'Carmina Erotica, Carmina Iocosa: The Body and the Bawdy in Medieval Love Songs', in Lazar and Lacy, pp. 249–76

Lazar, Moshé, *Amour courtois et "fin'amors"*, Bibliothèque française et romane, Etudes littéraires 8 (Paris, 1964)

Lazar, Moshé, and Norris J. Lacy, *Poetics of Love in the Middle Ages: Texts and Contexts* (Fairfax, Virginia, 1989)

Le Bras, Gabriel, 'La doctrine du mariage chez les théologiens et les canonistes depuis l'an mille', *DTC*, IX, 2123–2317

Le Bras, Gabriel, 'Le mariage dans la théologie et le droit de l'Eglise du XIe au XIIIe siècle', *CCM* 11 (1968) 191–202

Le Roy Ladurie, E., *Montaillou* (Paris, 1975), trans. Barbara Bray (London, 1978)

Leclercq, Jean, 'L'amitié dans les lettres au Moyen Age', *RMAL* 1 (1945) 391–410

Leclercq, Jean, 'L'amour le mariage vus par des clercs et religieux, spécialement au XIIe siècle', in Van Hoecke and Welkenhuysen, pp. 102–115

Leclercq, Jean, 'Modern Psychology and the Interpretation of Medieval Texts', *Speculum* 48 (1973) 476–90

Leclercq, Jean, *Monks and Love in Twelfth-Century France: Psycho-Historical Essays* (Oxford, 1979)

Leclercq, Jean, *Monks on Marriage: A Twelfth-Century View* (New York, 1982)

Leclercq, Jean, *The Love of Learning and the Desire for God: A Study of Monastic Culture*, trans. Catharine Misrahi (Paris, 1957; trans. New York, 1961, rpt. 1993)

Leclercq, Jean, *Women and Saint Bernard of Clairvaux*, trans. Marie-Bernard Saïd, Cistercian Studies 144 (Kalamazoo, 1989)

Lefèvre, Yves, 'La Femme du moyen âge en France, dans la vie littéraire et spirituelle', in *Histoire mondiale de la femme*, ed. Pierre Grimal, 4 vols (Paris, 1965–74), vol. II, *L'Occident, des Celtes à la Renaissance*, pp. 79–134

Legge, M. Dominica, 'Anglo-Norman Hagiography and the Romances', *MeH* NS 6 (1975) 41–9

Legge, M. Dominica, 'Archaism and the Conquest', *MLR* 51 (1956) 227–9

Legge, M. Dominica, 'La Précocité de la littérature anglo-normande', *CCM* 8 (1965) 327–49

Legge, M. Dominica, 'Les renges de s'epethe', *Romania* 77 (1956) 88–93

Legge, M. Dominica, *Anglo-Norman Literature and its Background* (Oxford, 1963)

Lewis, C.S., *The Allegory of Love: A Study in Medieval Tradition* (Oxford, 1936, rpt. 1992)

Lewis, C.S., *The Discarded Image: An Introduction to Medieval and Renaissance Literature* (Cambridge, 1964)

Leyerle, John, ed., 'Marriage in the Middle Ages', *Viator* 4 (1973) 413–501

Loomis, Roger Sherman, ed., *Arthurian Literature in the Middle Ages: A Collaborative History* (Oxford, 1959)

Loomis, Roger Sherman, *The Development of Arthurian Romance* (London, 1963)

Lucas, A.M., *Women in the Middle Ages: Religion, Marriage and Letters* (Brighton, 1987)

Lumiansky, R.M., 'Concerning *The Owl and the Nightingale*', *PQ* 32 (1953) 411–7

Luscombe, David E., 'From Paris to the Paraclete: The Correspondence of Abelard and Heloise,' *PBA* 74 (1989) 247–83

Luscombe, David E., *Peter Abelard*, Historical Association pamphlet, General Series, G. 95 (London, 1979)

Luscombe, David E., *The School of Peter Abelard: The Influence of Abelard's Thought in the Early Scholastic Period* (Cambridge, 1969)

Makowski, E.M., 'The conjugal debt and medieval canon law', *JMH* 3/2 (1977) 99–114

Malone, Kemp, 'Two English *Frauenlieder*', *Studies in Old English Literature in Honor of Arthur G. Brodeur* (University of Oregon, 1963), pp. 106–117

Mann, Jill, *Chaucer and Medieval Estates Satire: The Literature of Social Classes and the 'General Prologue' to the 'Canterbury Tales'* (Cambridge, 1973)

Mann, Jill, *Geoffrey Chaucer: Feminist Readings* (Hemel Hempstead, 1990)

Markale, Jean, *L'amour courtois: ou le couple infernal* (Paris, 1987)

Mathew, Gervase, 'Ideals of Friendship', in Lawlor, pp. 45–53

Mathew, Gervase, 'Marriage and "Amour Courtois" in Late-Fourteenth-Century England', in *Essays Presented to Charles Williams* (Oxford, 1947), pp. 128–35

Mathews, W., 'The Wife of Bath and All her Sect', *Viator* 5 (1947) 413–443

McCulloch, F., 'Saint Euphrosine, Saint Alexis and the Turtledove', *Romania* 98 (1977) 168–185

McIntosh, Angus, M.L. Samuels and Margaret Laing, *Middle English Dialectology: essays on some principles and problems*, ed. and intro. Margaret Laing (Aberdeen, 1989)

McLaughlin, Mary M., 'Peter Abelard and the Dignity of Women: Twelfth Century "Feminism" in Theory and Practice', *Cluny Studies*, pp. 287–333

McLaughlin, Mary, M., 'Abelard as Autobiographer: The Motives and Meanings of his "Story of Calamities" ', *Speculum* 42 (1967) 463–88

McLaughlin, T.P., 'The formation of the Marriage Bond According to the *Summa Parisiensis*', *MS* 15 (1953) 208–212

Meale, Carol M., ed., *Women and Literature in Britain: 1150–1500*, Cambridge Studies in Medieval Literature 17 (Cambridge, 1993)

Mehl, Dieter, '*The Owl and the Nightingale*: Mündlichkeit und Schriftlichkeit im Streitgespräch', in *Mündlichkeit und Schriftlichkeit im englischen Mittelalter*, ed. Willi Erzgräber and Sabine Volk, ScriptOralia 5 (Tübingen, 1988)

Mélange de langue et littérature occitanes en hommage à Pierre Bec . . . (Poitiers, 1991)

Ménage, René, 'Erec et Enide: quelques pièces du dossier', in *Mélanges de langue et littérature française du moyen age et de la renaissance offerts à Charles Foulon*, Vol. 2, Marche romane: Mediaevalia 83 (Liège, 1980), pp. 203–21

Ménard, Philippe, 'Sens, contresens, non-sens, réflexions sur la pièce *Farai un vers de dreyt nien . . .* de Guillaume IX', *FS Pierre Bec*, pp. 326–48

Mertens-Fonck, Paula, 'Tradition and Feminism in Middle English Literature: Source-hunting in the Wife of Bath's Portrait and in *The Owl and the Nightingale*', in *Multiple Worlds, Multiple Words: Essays in Honour of Irène Simon*, ed. Hena Maes-Jelinek, Pierre Michel and Paulette Michel-Michot (Liège, 1988)

Metz, René, 'Recherches sur la condition de la Femme selon Gratien', *SG* 12 (1967) 377–96

Mews, Constance, 'On dating the works of Peter Abelard', *Archives* 52 (1985) 73–134

Meyer, H. 'Die Eheschliessung im *Ruodlieb* und das Eheswert', *Zeitschrift der Sauvigny-Stiftung für Rechtsgeschichte: Germanische Abteilung* 52 (1932) 276–93

Micha, A. 'Le mari jaloux dans la littéraire romanesque des XIIe et XIIIe siècles', *Sm* NS 17 (1951) 303–20

Miller, B.D.H., 'The Early History of Bodleian MS Digby 86', *Annuale Mediaevale* 4 (1963) 23–56

Millett, Bella, 'The Origins of *Ancrene Wisse*: new answers, new questions', *MÆ* 61 (1992) 206–28

Millett, Bella, 'The textual transmission of *Seinte Iuliene*', *MÆ* 59 (1990) 41–54

Millett, Bella, 'Women in No Man's Land: English recluses and the development of vernacular literature in the twelfth and thirteenth centuries', Meale, pp. 86–103

Moi, Toril, 'Desire in Language: Andreas Capellanus and the Controversy of Courtly Love', in *Medieval Literature: Criticism, Ideology and History*, ed. David Aers (Brighton, 1986), pp. 11–33

Molin, Jean-Baptiste and Protais Mutembe, *Le rituel du mariage en France du XIIe au XVIe siècle* (Paris, 1974)

Mölk, Ulrich, 'Saint Alexis et son épouse dans la légende latine et la première chanson française', in Van Hoecke and Welkenhuysen, pp. 162–170

Monfrin, J. 'Le problème de l'authenticité de la correspondance d'Abélard et d'Héloïse', *Cluny Studies*, pp. 409–424

Monson, Donald A., '*Auctoritas* and Intertextuality in Andreas Capellanus' *De Amore*', in Lazar and Lacy, pp. 69–79

Moore, John C., 'Love in Twelfth-Century France: A Failure in Synthesis', *Traditio* 24 (1968) 429–43

Moran, Irene, '*The Owl and the Nightingale*: An Interpretation', *Filologia Germanica (Istituto Universitario Orientale, Annali, Sezione Germanica)* 20 (1977) 157–212

Morris, Colin, *The Discovery of the Individual 1050–1200* (1972, rpt. Toronto, Buffalo and London, 1991)

Moule, Carolyn Janet, 'Entry into Marriage in the Late Eleventh and Twelfth Centuries, c. 1090–1191' (unpublished Ph.D. diss, Cambridge, 1983, no. 13018)

Murphy, James J., *Rhetoric in the Middle Ages: A History of Rhetorical Theory from Saint Augustine to the Renaissance* (Berkeley, 1974)

Murphy, Margueritte S., 'The Allegory of "Joie" in Chrétien's *Erec et Enide*', in *Allegory, Myth and Symbol*, ed. Morton W. Bloomfield, Harvard English Studies 9 (Cambridge MA and London, 1981), pp. 109–27

Newman, Barbara, 'Authority, authenticity and the repression of Heloise', *JMRS* 22/2 (1992) 121–157

Newman, F.X., ed., *The Meaning of Courtly Love*, (Albany NY, 1968) [= *MCL*]

Newstead, Helaine, 'Isolt of the White Hands and Tristan's Marriage', *RP* 19 (1965–6) 155–66

Nichols, Stephen G., 'An Intellectual Anthropology of Marriage in the Middle Ages', in Brownlee and Nichols, pp. 70–95

Nitze, William Albert, 'Eric's Treatment of Enide', *RR* 10 (1919) 26–37

Nitze, William Albert, 'Sans et Matière dans les oeuvres de Chrétien de Troyes', *Romania* 45 (1915–7) 14–36

Nitze, William Albert, 'The Romance of Erec, Son of Lac', *MP* 11 (1913/14) 445–489

Noble, Peter S., *Love and Marriage in Chrétien de Troyes* (Cardiff, 1982)

Noonan, John T., 'Marital Affection in the Canonists', *SG* 12 (1967) 459-509

Noonan, John T., 'Power to Choose', *Viator* 4 (1973) 419-34

Northcott, Kenneth J., 'Some Functions of "Love" in the "Carmina Burana" ', *Deutsche Beiträge zur geistigen Überlieferung* 6 (1970) 11-25

Nykrog, Per, 'The Rise of Literary Fiction', *RRTC*, pp. 593-612

Olsson, Kurt, 'Character and Truth in *The Owl and the Nightingale*', *Chaucer Review* 11/4 (1977) 351-68

Onions, C.T., 'An Experiment in Textual Reconstruction', *E&S* 22 (1936) 86-102

Örsy, Ladislas, S.J., *Marriage in Canon Law: Texts and Comments: Reflections and Questions* (Dublin and Leominster, 1988)

Owst, G.R., *Literature and Pulpit in Medieval England* (2nd edn, Oxford, 1961)

Pächt, O., C.R. Dodwell and F. Wormald, *The St Albans Psalter*, Studies of the Warburg and Courtauld Institutes 28 (London, 1960)

Pächt, Otto, *The Rise of Pictorial Narrative in Twelfth Century England* (Oxford, 1962)

Paden, William D., jr, 'Rape in the Pastourelle', *Romanic Review* 80/3 (1989) 331-49

Page, Christopher, *The Owl and the Nightingale: Musical Life and Ideas in France 1100-1300* (London, 1989)

Pagels, Elaine, *Adam, Eve, and the Serpent* (London, 1988)

Paget, Violet [alias Vernon Lee], 'Medieval Love', in *Euphorion, being studies of the Antique and the medieval in the Renaissance*, 2 vols (London, 1884), II, 123-217

Paris, Gaston, 'Etudes sur le roman de la table ronde. Lancelot du lac. II. Le conte de la charrette', *Romania* 12 (1883) 459-534

Paris, Gaston, review of Wendelin Foerster, ed., *Erec und Enide*: *Romania* 11 (1881) 148-66

Parmisano, A. Stanley, 'A Study of the Relationship between the Attitudes toward Love and Marriage in Late 14th and Early 15th Century English Poetry and Contemporary Ecclesiastical Teaching on these Topics' (unpublished Ph.D. diss, Cambridge, 1968, no. 6488)

Pater, Walter, 'Two Early French Stories', in *The Renaissance* (1873; new edn, Oxford, 1986), pp. 1-19

Paterson, Linda O., 'L'épouse et la formation du lien conjugal selon la littérature occitane du XIe au XIIIe siècle; mutations d'une institution et condition féminine', *FS Pierre Bec*, pp. 425-42

Paues, Anna C., 'A newly discovered manuscript of the *Poema Morale*', *Anglia* 30 (1907) 217-37

Payen, J.C., 'La 'mise en roman' du mariage dans la littérature française des XIIe et XIIIe siècles: de l'evolution idéologique à la typologie des genres', in Van Hoecke and Welkenhuysen, pp. 219-235

Payen, J.C., 'La Pensée d'Abélard et les lettres romans du XIIe siècle', *Cluny Studies*, pp. 513-20

Pearsall, Derek, 'John Capgrave's *Life of St Katharine* and Popular Romance Style', *MeH* NS 6 (1975) 121-37

Pearsall, Derek, *Old English and Middle English Poetry*, The Routledge History of English Poetry vol. 1 (London, 1977)

Pedersen, Frederik, 'Did the Medieval Laity Know the Canon Law Rules on Marriage? Some Evidence from Fourteenth-Century York Cause Papers', *MS* 56 (1994) 111–52

Peterson, Douglas L., '*The Owl and the Nightingale* and Christian Dialectic', *JEGP* 55 (1956) 13–26

Petit de Julleville, L. *Histoire de la langue et de la littérature française des origines à 1900*, vol. 1: *Moyen Age* (Paris, 1896)

Pfander, Homer G., *The Popular Sermon of the Medieval Friar in England* (privately printed: New York, 1937)

Pfeffer, Wendy, 'When the Nightingale Stops Singing: The Evolution of an Image in the Medieval French Lyric', *Revue de l'Université d'Ottawa/University of Ottawa Quarterly* 51/2 (1981) 189–96

Pfeffer, Wendy, *The Change of Philomel: The Nightingale in Medieval Literature*, American University Studies, Series III, vol. 14 (New York, Berne and Frankfurt a. M., 1985)

Pierre Abélard; Pierre le Vénérable: Les courants philosophiques, littéraires et artistiques en occident au milieu du XIIe siècle: Abbaye de Cluny, 2 au 9 juillet, 1972, Colloques internationaux du C.R.N.S. (Paris, 1975)

Plummer, John F., 'The Woman's Song in Middle English and its European backgrounds', *VF*, pp. 135–54

Plummer, John F., *Vox Feminae: Studies in Medieval Women's Songs*, Studies in Medieval Culture 15 (Kalamazoo, Michigan, 1981)

Powicke, Maurice, *The Thirteenth Century 1216–1307* (Oxford, 1953; 2nd edn, 1962, rpt. 1991)

Pratt, Robert A., 'Jankyn's Book of Wikked Wyves: Medieval Antimatrimonial Propaganda in the Universities', *Annuale mediaevale* (1962) 5–27

Pratt, Robert A., 'The Development of the Wife of Bath', in *Studies in Medieval Literature: in honour of Albert Croll Baugh*, ed. MacEdward Leach (Philadelphia, 1961), pp. 45–79

Price, Jocelyn G., 'The *Liflade of Seinte Iuliene* and Hagiographic Convention', *MeH* NS 14 (1986) 37–58 [see also Wogan-Browne]

Raby, F.J.E., *A History of Secular Latin Poetry in the Middle Ages*, 2 vols (Oxford, 1934, rpt. 1957)

Reed, Thomas L., jr, *Middle English Debate Poetry and the Aesthetics of Irresolution* (Columbia and London, 1990)

Reichl, Karl, *Religiöse Dichtung im englischen Hochmittelalter: Untersuchung und edition der Handschrift B. 14. 39 des Trinity College in Cambridge*, Münchener Universitäts-Schriften, Philosophische Fakultät, Texte und Untersuchungen zur Englischen Philologie 1 (Munich, 1973)

Riddy, Felicity, ed., *Regionalism in Late Medieval Manuscripts and Texts: Essays celebrating the publication of 'A Linguistic Atlas of Late Mediaeval English'* (Cambridge, 1991)

Rigg, A.G., *A History of Anglo-Latin Literature: 1066–1422* (Cambridge, 1992)

Ritzer, Korbinian, 'Secular Law and the Western Church's Concept of Marriage', *Concilium* 5/6 (May, 1970) 67–75

Robbins, Rossell Hope, 'The Authors of the Middle English Religious Lyrics', *JEGP* 39 (1940) 230–8

Roberts, Jane, 'A Preliminary Note on British Library, Cotton MS Caligula

A. ix', in *The Text and Tradition of Layamon's 'Brut'*, ed. Françoise Le Saux, Arthurian Studies 33 (Woodbridge, 1994), pp. 1–14

Robertson, D.W. jr, 'The Concept of Courtly Love as an Impediment to the Understanding of Medieval Texts', *MCL*, pp. 1–18

Robertson, D.W., jr, *A Preface to Chaucer* (Princeton, 1962)

Robertson, D.W., jr, *Abelard and Heloise* (New York, 1972; London, 1974)

Robertson, D.W., jr, 'The Doctrine of Charity in Medieval Literary Gardens: a Topical Approach through Symbolism and Allegory', *Speculum* 26 (1951) 24–49

Robertson, D.W., jr, 'The Subject of the De Amore of Andreas Capellanus', *MP* 50 (1952–3) 145–61

Robertson, Elizabeth, *Early English Devotional Prose and the Female Audience* (Knoxville, 1990)

Rösler, Margaret, 'Alexiusprobleme', *ZFRP* 53 (1933) 508–11

Rösler, Margaret, *Die Fassungen der Alexius-legenden*, Wiener Beiträge zur Englische Philologie 21 (Vienna and Leipzig, 1905)

Rousseau, Constance M., 'The Spousal Relationship: Marital Society and Sexuality in the Letters of Pope Innocent III', *MS* 56 (1994) 89–109

Ruhe, Ernstpeter, and Rudolf Behrens, *Mittelalterbilder aus neuer Perspektive: Diskussionsanstöße zu amour courtois, Subjectivität in der Dichtung und Strategien des Erzählens: Kolloquium Würzburg 1984* (Munich, 1985)

Rumsey, Lucinder, 'The scorpion of lechery and *Ancrene Wisse*', *MÆ* 61 (1992) 48–58

Russell, J.C., 'The Patrons of *The Owl and the Nightingale*', *PQ* 48 (1969) 178–85

Rychner, J., '*La Vie de Saint Alexis* et le poème latin, *Pater Deus ingenite*', *Vox Romanica* 36 (1977) 67–83

Salter, Elizabeth, *English and International: Studies in the Literature, Art and Patronage of Medieval England*, ed. Derek Pearsall and Nicolette Zeeman (Cambridge, 1988)

Sampson, George, *The Concise Cambridge History of English Literature* (Cambridge, 1941, rpt. 1945)

Samson, Annie, 'The South English Legendary: Constructing a Context', in *Thirteenth Century England I: Proceedings of the Newcastle upon Tyne Conference 1985*, ed. P.R. Coss and S.D. Lloyd (Woodbridge, 1986), pp. 185–95

Sargent-Baur, Barbara Nelson, 'Erec's Enide: "sa fame ou s'amie"?', *RP* 33 (1980) 373–87

Scahill, John, 'Early Middle English Orthographies: Archaism and Particularism', *Medieval English Studies Newsletter* 31 (1994) 16–22

Scahill, John, 'The Friar, the Maid, the Writer and the Reader', *Poetica* 36 (1992) 1–14

Scheludko, Dimitri, 'Über die ersten zwei Strophen des Alexiusliedes', *ZFRP* 55 (1935) 194–7

Schlauch, Margaret, *English Literature and its Social Foundations* (Warsaw, 1956; rpt. 1967)

Schmitt, C.B., 'Theophrastus in the Middle Ages', *Viator* 2 (1971) 251–270

Schmolke-Hasselmann, Beate, 'Ring, Schwert und Gürtel im Albanipsalter', *ZFSL* 87 (1977) 304–13

Schnell, Rüdiger, *Andreas Capellanus: Zur Rezeption des römischen und kanonischen Rechts in 'De Amore'*, Münstersche Mittelalter-Schriften 46 (Munich, 1982)

Schotter, Anne Howland, 'Women's Song in Medieval Latin', *VF*, pp. 19–33

Sckommodau, Hans, 'Alexius in Liturgie, Malerei und Dichtung', *ZFRP* 72 (1956) 165–94

Scully, Terence, 'The *Sen* of Chrétien de Troyes' *Joie de la cort*', in Smith and Snow, pp. 71–94

Sheehan, Michael, 'Choice of marriage partners in the Middle Ages: development and mode of application of a theory of marriage', *SMRH* 1 (1978) 3–33

Sheehan, Michael, ' "Maritalis Affectio" Revisited', in Edwards and Spector, pp. 32–43

Sheehan, Michael, 'Marriage Theory and Practice', *MS* 40 (1978) 408–60

Sheehan, Michael, 'The Formation and Stability of Marriage in Fourteenth-Century England: Evidence of an Ely Register', *MS* 33 (1971) 228–63

Sheldon, E.S., 'Why does Chrétiens Erec Treat Enide so Harshly?', *RR* 5 (1914) 115–26

Shepherd, Geoffrey, 'All the wealth of Croesus . . .', *MLR* 51 (1956) 161–7

Shippey, Thomas Alan, 'Listening to the Nightingale', *Comparative Literature* 22 (1970) 46–60

Silvestre, Hubert, 'Die Liebesgeschichte zwischen Abaelard und Heloise: der Anteil des Romans', in *Fälschungen*, pp. 121–65

Silvestre, Hubert, 'Du Nouveau sur André le Chapelain', *RMAL* 36 (1980) 99–106

Sinclair, K.V., 'Anglo-Norman Studies: The Last Twenty Years', *Australian Journal of French Studies* 2/2 (1965) 113–55

Sisam, Celia, 'The Broken Leaf in MS Jesus College, Oxford, 29', *RES* NS 5 (1954) 337–43

Smith, Jeremy J., 'Tradition and Innovation in South-West-Midland Middle English', in Riddy, pp. 53–65

Smith, Nathaniel B., and Joseph T. Snow, 'Courtly Love and Courtly Literature', in Smith and Snow, pp. 3–14

Smith, Nathaniel B., and Joseph T. Snow, eds, *The Expansion and Transformations of Courtly Literature* (Athens, Georgia, 1980)

Spahn, Renata, *Narrative Strukturen im 'Guy of Warwick': Zur Frage der Überlieferung einer mittelenglischen Romanze*, ScriptOralia 36 (Tübingen, 1991)

Spanke, Hans, 'Zur Geschichte des altfranzösischen Jeu-parti', *ZFSL* 52 (1929) 39–63; rpt. *Studien zur lateinischen und romanischen Lyrik des Mittelalters* Collectanea 31 (Hildesheim, Zurich and New York, 1983), pp. 356–80

Sparnaay, H., *Hartmann von Aue: Studien zu einer Biographie*, 2 vols (Halle, 1933, 1938)

Spitzer, Leo, 'Erhellung des Polyeucte durch das Alexiuslied', *Archivum Romanicum* 16 (1932) 473–500

Stanley, Eric G., 'Parody in Early English Literature', *Poetica* 27 (1986) 1–69

Stanley, Eric G., 'The Date of Laȝamon's Brut', *N&Q* 213 (1968) 85–9

Stebbins, Charles E., 'Les grandes versions de la Légende de Saint Alexis', *Revue belge de philologie et d'histoire* 53/3 (1975) 679–95

Stebbins, Charles E., 'The "Humanity" of Saint Alexis in the separation scene of the 13th Century OF Poem (Paris Ms. 2162 BN)', *Revue belge de philologie et d'histoire* 49/3 (1971) 862–5

Stebbins, Charles E., ed., 'The Oxford Version of the Vie de Saint Alexis', *Romania* 92 (1971) 1–36

Stevens, John and Theodore Karp, 'Troubadours, Trouvères', *NGDMM*, XIX, 189–208

Stevens, John, 'The granz biens of Marie de France', in Lawlor, pp. 1–25

Stone, Lawrence, *Road to Divorce: England 1530–1987* (Oxford, 1990; rpt., 1992)

Storey, Christopher, 'La Vie de Sainte Euphrosine – a reminder of a neglected thirteenth-century poem', *French Studies* 31 (1977) 385–393

Stuard, Susan Mosher, ed., *Women in Medieval Society*, (University of Pennsylvania, 1976)

Sundby, Bertil, *The Dialect and Provenance of the Middle English Poem 'The Owl and the Nightingale': A Linguistic Study*, Lund Studies in English 18 (Lund and Copenhagen, 1950)

Swanton, Michael, *English Literature before Chaucer* (London and New York, 1987)

Thomas, Rudolf et. al., eds, *Petrus Abaelardus: Person, Werk, und Wirkung*, Trierer Theologischen Studien 38 (Trier, 1980)

Thomson, Rodney M., *Manuscripts from St Albans Abbey, 1066–1235*, 2 vols (Woodbridge, 1982)

Tintignac, C., *La thème du renoncement dans la 'Vie de Saint Alexis' et sa permanence dans les lettres françaises* (Paris, 1975)

Tolkien, J.R.R., '*Ancrene Wisse* and *Hali Meiðhad*', *E&S* 14 (1929) 104–26

Topsfield, L.T., 'Fin'Amors in Marcabrun, Bernart de Ventadorn, and the *Lancelot* of Chretien de Troyes', in Van Hoecke and Welkenhuysen, pp. 236–49

Uitti, Karl D., 'The Old French *Vie de Saint Alexis:* Paradigm, Legend, Meaning', *RP* 20/3 (1967) 263–295

Utley, Francis Lee, *The Crooked Rib: An Analytical Index to the Argument About Women in English and Scots Literature to the End of the year 1568* (Columbus, Ohio, 1944)

Utley, Francis Lee, 'Must We Abandon the Concept of Courtly Love?' *MeH* NS 3 (1972) 299–324

Utley, Francis Lee, 'Dialogues, Debates and Catechisms', *Manual*, III, 669–745

Utley, Francis Lee, 'Robertsonianism Redivivus', *RP* 19 (1965–6) 250–60

Vanderwerf, Hendrik, 'Jeu-parti', *NGDMM*, IX, 613

Van Hoecke, W., and A. Welkenhuysen, eds, *Love and Marriage in the Twelfth Century*, Mediaevalia Lovaniensia 8 (Leuven, 1981)

Verbeke, G., 'Peter Abelard and the Concept of Subjectivity', *Leuven Studies*, pp. 1–11

Vinaver, Eugène, *The Rise of Romance* (1971, rpt. Cambridge, 1984)

Vincent, P.R., 'The dramatic aspect of the Old French *Vie de Saint Alexis*', *SP* 60 (1963) 525–41

Vogel, Cyrille, 'Les rites de la célébration du mariage: leur signification dans la formation du lien durant le haut moyen âge', *Spoleto Studies*, pp. 397–465

Von Moos, P., 'Le silence d'Héloïse et les idéologies modernes', *Cluny Studies*, pp. 245–268

Von Moos, P., 'Cornelia und Heloise', *Latomus* 34 (1975) 1024–59

Waddell, Chrysogonus, 'The Reform of the Liturgy from a Renaissance Perspective', *RRTC*, pp. 88–109

Walther, H., *Das Streitgedicht in der lateinischen Literatur des Mittelalters*, Quellen und

Untersuchungen zur lateinischen Philologie des Mittelalters 5/2 (Munich, 1920); rpt. with supplementary material by Paul Gerhard Schmidt (Hildesheim, 1984)

Watson, Nicholas, 'The Methods and Objectives of Thirteenth-Century Anchoritic Devotion', in *The Medieval Mystical Tradition: Exeter Symposium IV*, ed. Marion Glasscoe (Cambridge, 1987), pp. 132–53

Weiss, Judith, 'The power and weakness of women in Anglo-Norman romance', in Meale, pp. 7–23

Wells, John Edwin, '*The Owl and the Nightingale* and MS Cotton', *MLN* 48 (1933) 516–9

Wenzel, Siegfried, *Preachers, Poets and the Early English Lyric* (Princeton, 1986)

Westphal-Wihl, Sarah, 'The Ladies' Tournament: Marriage, Sex, and Honor in Thirteenth-Century Germany', *Signs* 14/2 (1989) 371–98

Wiesen, David, *St Jerome as Satirist: A Study in Christian Latin Thought and Letters*, Cornell Studies in Classical Philology 34 (Ithaca and New York, 1964)

Wilcox, John, 'Defining Courtly Love', *Michigan Academy of Sciences, Arts and Letters* 12 (1930) 313–25

Wilson, R.M, *Early Middle English Literature* (3rd. edn, London, 1968)

Wilson, R.M., 'The Medieval Library of Titchfield Abbey', *Proceedings of the Leeds Philosophical and Literary Society* 5 (1940) 150–77, 252–76

Wilson, R.M., *The Lost Literature of Medieval England* (London, 1952, 2nd edn, 1970)

Winkler, E., 'Von der Kunst des Alexiusdichters', *ZFRP* 47 (1927) 588–97

Witt, Michael A., '*The Owl and the Nightingale* and English Law Court Procedure of the Twelfth and Thirteenth Centuries', *Chaucer Review* 16 (1982) 282–92

Wogan-Browne, Jocelyn, ' 'Clerc u lai, muïne u dame'': Women and Anglo-Norman hagiography in the twelfth and thirteenth centuries', in Meale, pp. 61–85 [see also Price]

Wood, Margaret, *The English Medieval House* (London, 1965, rpt. 1990)

Woodbridge, Benjamin M., 'Chrétien's Erec as a Cornelian Hero', *RR* 6 (1915) 434–42

Woolf, Rosemary, 'The Fall of Man in *Genesis* B and the *Mystère d'Adam*', *Studies in Old English Literature in Honor of Arthur G. Brodeur* (University of Oregon, 1963), pp. 187–99

Woolf, Rosemary, 'The Theme of Christ the Lover-Knight in Medieval English Literature', *RES* NS 13 (1962) 1–16

Woolf, Rosemary, *The English Religious Lyric in the Middle Ages* (Oxford, 1968)

Wrenn, C.L., 'Curiosities in a Medieval MS', *E&S* 25 (1940) 101–5

Wrenn, C.L., review of Huganir, *The Owl and the Nightingale . . .*: *MÆ* 1 (1931) 149–56

Wulff, A., *Die frauenfeindlichen Dichtungen in die romanischen Literaturen des Mittelalters bis zum Ende des XIII. Jahrhunderts*, Romantische Arbeiten IV (Halle a. S., 1914)

Yapp, Brunsdon, *Birds in medieval manuscripts* (New York, 1982)

Zaddy, Zara P., 'Pourquoi Erec se décide-t-il à partir en voyage avec Enide?' *CCM* 7 (1964) 179–185

Ziolkowski, Jan M., 'The Medieval Latin Beast Flyting', *MlJh* 20 (1985) 49–65

Ziolkowski, Jan M., *Talking Animals: Medieval Latin Beast Poetry, 750–1150* (Philadelphia, 1993)

Bibliographical Appendices

A. Metrical Lives of St Alexis in Middle English

I. VERNON
C.13; 612 lines; tail-rhyme
MSS: Oxford, Bodleian Library, MS Vernon 43; ibid., MS Laud 108; Naples, MS XIII, B. 29; Durham Cathedral, Cosin's Library, MS V.ii.14
Editions: Carl Hörstmann, 'Leben des h. Alexius nach MS Laud 108', *Archiv* 51 (1873) 101–110; Carl Hörstmann, 'Zwei Alexiuslieder', *Archiv* 56 (1876) 391–416, at pp. 394–401; J. Schipper, *Englische Alexiuslegenden aus dem XIV. und XV. Jahrhundert*, vol. 1, Quellen und Forschungen zur Sprach- und Culturgeschichte der germanischen Völker 20 (Strasbourg and London, 1877); F.J. Furnivall, *Adam Davy's 5 Dreams about Edward II*, EETS OS 69 (London, 1878), pp. 20–79

II. LAUD
Late C.14; 1152 lines; tail-rhyme
MS: Oxford, Bodley, MS Laud 622
Editions: C. Hörstmann, 'Alexiuslieder', *Archiv* 59 (1878) 71–106, at pp. 79–90; Furnivall, *Adam Davy's 5 Dreams*, pp. 19–79

III. NORTHERN HOMILY CYCLE [NHC]
Late C.14; 646 lines; couplets
MS: Oxford, Bodleian Library, MS Ashmole 42; ULC, MS Gg. V.31
Edition: Carl Hörstmann, *Altenglische Legenden* (Heilbronn, 1881), pp. 174–88

IV. TITUS
Early C.15; 422 lines; couplets
MS: BL MS Cotton Titus A. 26
Editions: Hörstmann, 'Alexiuslieder' (1878), pp. 90–101; Furnivall, *Adam Davy's 5 Dreams*, pp. 20–79

V. LAUD-TRINITY
Late C.14/C.15; 636 lines; tail-rhyme
MSS: Oxford, Bodleian Library, MS Laud 463; Oxford, Trinity College, MS 57
Editions: Hörstmann, 'Zwei Alexiuslieder', pp. 401–16; Furnivall, *Adam Davy's 5 Dreams*, pp. 20–79; J. Schipper, *Die zweite Version der mittelenglischen Alexiuslegenden* (Vienna, 1887)

VI. SCOTTISH LEGENDARY COLLECTION [SLC]
C.15; 560 lines; couplets
MS: ULC, MS Gg. II.6

Edition: W. Metcalfe, *Legends of the Saints*, Scottish Text Society, 3 vols (Edinburgh, 1896), pp. 441–57

B. French Versions of the Life of St Alexis

1. The "Alsis" Group

The following texts are united by the variation of "Alsis" for "Edessa" (see Elliott, *The Vie de Saint Alexis*, p. 13; Hemming, p. vii). The Latin metrical life, 'Pater deus ingenite. . .' also belongs to this group.

LAPV = The "eleventh-century" 'Chanson de Saint Alexis'

L   *St Albans Psalter*, Jesuit College, Hildesheim (mid. C.12)
A   Paris, BN, MS nouv. acq. fr. 4503 (C.12)
P1   Paris, BN, MS fr. 19525 (C.13)
P2   Manchester, John Rylands Library, MS fr. 6 (mid. C.13)
V   Vatican, Cod. Lat. 5334 (mid. C.12)

Related Thirteenth- and Fourteenth-Century Versions

S   Paris, BN fr. 12471 (C. 13); ed. Elliott, *The Vie de Saint Alexis*, pp. 93–137
M   (a) Paris, BN MS fr. 1553
     (b) Carlisle Chapter Library
     C.13; rhyme; ed. from Carlisle MS by Elliott, ibid., pp. 151–86
Q   [8 MSS] C.14: rhyming quatrains, 784 lines: ed. Gaston Paris and Leopold Pannier, *La vie de Saint Alexis: poème du XIe siècle et renouvellements des XIIe, XIIIe et XIVe siècles* (Paris, 1872), part IV

2. Non-"Alsis" Versions

C.12 PROSE VERSION
MS: BL MS Royal 20. D. 6, plus 8 others
Edition: Erich Lutsch, *Die altfranzösische Prosaversion der Alexiuslegende* (Berlin, 1913)

R [Octosyllabics]
Early C.13; 964 lines
MS: Paris, BN MS fr. 24508
Edition: Gaston Paris, 'La Vie de Saint Alexi en vers octosyllabiques', *Romania* 8 (1879) 163–80

ALEXANDRINES
O [C.13: 58 monorhymed laisses, 1043 alexandrine lines]
MS: Oxford, Bodleian Library, MS, Canonici Misc. 74
Edition: Charles E. Stebbins, *Romania* 92 (1971) 1–36

P [C.13: 60 monorhymed laisses, 1224 alexandrine laisses]
MS: Paris, BN, MS fr. 2162
Edition: Charles E. Stebbins, in *A critical edition of the 13th and 14th Centuries Old French poem versions of the 'Vie de saint Alexis'*, Beihefte zur Zeitschrift für romanische Philologie 145 (Tübingen, 1974), pp. 21–63

OCTOSYLLABICS
C.14: octosyllabic couplets, 1984 lines
MS: Bibliothèque de la ville d'Avranches, MS 224
Edition: Charles E. Stebbins, *A Critical Edition*, pp. 101–26

MIRACLE-PLAY
C.14: 2659 lines
Cangé MS
Edition: Gaston Paris and Ulysse Robert, *Miracles de Notre Dame par personnages*, 7 vols (Paris, 1883), VII, pp. 279–369

PROSE
MS: Paris, BN, MS fonds fr. 1534
Edition: G.C. Keidel, *An Old French Prose Version of 'La Vie de Saint Alexis'* (Baltimore, 1896)

C. A Select List of the Lives of St Alexis in Languages other than English or French

Syriac Version (C.5)
Fr. trans.: A. Amiaud, *La légende syriaque de Saint Alexis, l'homme de Dieu*, Bibliothèque de l'Ecole des Hautes Etudes 79 (Paris, 1889), based on BL MS Add. 17177

Earliest Greek Version
Biblioteca Nazionale Marciana, Venice Cod. VII. 33
Edition: Rösler, 'Alexiusprobleme', *ZFRP* 53 (1933) 508–11

Vita S. Alexii: ['Pan-Occidental' or 'Bollandist'] Latin Version (C.10)
Editions: *ASS*, July 17, pp. 251–3; Odenkirchen, pp. 34–51

Latin Version = 𝔄
Munich, Clm. 13070 (Regensburg); 17138 (Scheftlarn); 22248 (Windberg)
See H.F. Maßmann, *Sanct Alexius Leben in acht gereimten mittelhochdeutschen Behandlungen, nebst geschichtlicher Einleitung, so wie deutschen, griechischen und lateinischen Anhangen*, Bibliotek der gesammten deutschen National-Literatur 9 (Quedlinburg and Leipzig, 1843)

Latin Rhythmical Version: 'Pater Deus ingenite . . .' (C.11 MS)
MS: Vatican MS Pal. 828

Edition: E. Aßmann, 'Ein rhythmisches Gedicht auf den heiligen Alexius', *Festschrift Adolf Hofmeister*, pp. 31–8 (Halle, 1955); see also J. Rychner, 'La Vie de Saint Alexis et le poème latin, *Pater Deus ingenite*', *Vox Romanica* 36 (1977) 67–83

8 Middle German Versions: see Maßmann, *Sanct Alexius Leben*.
Of these, the 'D'-version, Konrad von Würzburg's *Sankt Alexis Leben* (C.13), has been edited more recently by P. Gereke (Altdeutsche Textbibliothek 20 (Halle, 1926))

D. Guy of Warwick: Complete Versions in English and French before 1500

GUI
Anglo-Norman, 1232–42; 12926 lines, couplets
13 MSS. inc. frags.: *Gui de Warewic*
Edition: A. Ewert, CFMA, 2 vols (Paris, 1932–3)

AUCHINLECK
English, Early C.14; 12416 lines, couplets/tail-rhyme
Auchinleck MS, Advocates' Library, Edinburgh, 19.2.1, ff. 108r–175v
Edition: J. Zupitza, *The Romance of Guy of Warwick edited from the Auchinleck Ms. in the Advocates' Library, Edinburgh and from Ms.107 in Caius College, Cambridge*, EETS ES 42, 49, 59, 3 vols (London, 1883, 1887, 1891)

CAIUS
English, Late C.15; 11095 lines, couplets
Caius College, Cambridge, MS 107 ff. 1–271
Edition: Zupitza, ibid.

ULC
English, Late C.15; couplets
ULC MS, Ff. 2.38, ff. 161r–239r
Edition: J. Zupitza, *The Romance of Guy of Warwick edited from Ms. Ff.2.38 in the University Library, Cambridge*, EETS ES 25–6 (London, 1875–6)

C.15 FRENCH PROSE
Early C.15
BN, Paris, MS Fr. 1476 (ancien 7552); BL MS Old Royal 15.E.6; also 2 C.16 printings
Edition: D.J. Conlon, *Le Rommant de Guy de Warwik et de Herolt d'Ardenne*, Univ. of North Carolina Studies in the Romance Languages and Literatures 102 (Chapel Hill NC, 1971)

JOHN LYDGATE
English, 592 lines, 8-line stanzas
6 MSS: printed from Oxford, Bodleian Library, MS Laud 683 by: J. Zupitza, 'Zur Literaturgeschichte des Guy von Warwick', *Sitzungsberichte der phil. hist.*

Classe. der Kais. Akademie 74 (Vienna, 1873) pp. 623–668, at pp. 649–65; *The Minor Poems of John Lydgate: Part II: Secular Poems*, ed. Henry Noble MacCracken, EETS OS 192 (London, 1934), pp. 516–38

C.16 FRENCH PROSE
A version printed by François Regnault (Paris, 1525); trans. Caroline Clive (1821), ed. William B. Todd, *Guy of Warwick: A Knight of Britain* (Austin, 1968)

E. 'The Wooing Group'

On ureisun of ure louerde [*UL*]	Lambeth 487
On wel swuthe god ureisun of God almihti [*UGA*]	Cotton Nero A.14
On lofsong of ure louerde [*LLo*]	Cotton Nero A.14
On lofsong of ure lefdi [*LLa*]	Cotton Nero A.14
The oreisun of seinte Marie [*OSM*]	Royal 17 A 27
The wohunge of ure lauerd [*WL*]	Cotton Titus D. 18

F. Reference Works

This list gives details of the short lyrics cited by titles in the course of this book. The lyrics are listed here in alphabetical order of their first lines.

Middle English

First Line	Title (Author)	Editions	IMEV
A mayde Cristes me bit yorne	The Luue-Ron (Thomas of Hales)	Morris, pp. 93–9; Dickins and Wilson, pp. 104–9	66
Herkneth alle gode men	A lutel soth sermon	Morris, pp. 186–9	1091
Hwan thu sixst on leode	The ten abuses The Abuses of the Age	Morris, pp. 184–5 (and see Wenzel, pp. 174–9)	4051
Hwenne ich thenche of domes-day	Doomsday *or* De die judicii	Morris, pp. 162–9; Brown, pp. 42–6; Reichl, pp. 408–14	3967
Hwenne so wil wit ofer-stieth	Will and Wit	Morris, p. 192; Brown, p. 65	4016

238

Ich am eldre than ich wes	Poema Morale	Morris, pp. 58–71	1272
[prologue:] Ihereth of one thinge	The Last Day or The(ne) Latemest Day or Death	Morris, pp. 168–85; Brown, pp. 46–54; Reichl, pp. 415–36	3517
In worschupe of that Mayden swete	Of Women cometh this Worldes Weal This World's Weal comes from Women	Furnivall, *Minor Poems*, pp. 704–8	1596
Man may longe lives wenen	Death's Wither-Clench or Long Life	Brown, pp. 15–8; Morris, pp. 156–9; Dobson and Harrison, pp. 122–30	2070
Off a trewe loue clene and derne	Of Clene Maydenhod Of Pure Maidenhood	Furnivall, *Minor Poems*, pp. 464–8	2605
On hire is al my lif ylong	An Orison to Our Lady or A Prayer of Penitence to Our Lady	Morris, pp. 158–63; Brown, pp. 56–60; Dobson and Harrison, pp. 130–6; Reichl, pp. 470–5	2687
[prologue:] Ihereth nu one lutele tale that ich eu wille telle [text:] Leuedi thu bere that beste childe that ever wes ibore	The Passion of Our Lord	Morris, pp. 37–57	1441

Old French

First Line (Author)	Editions	Linker	Raynaud
Bele mere, ke frai?	Jeffrey and Levy, pp. 242–4		
Chascuns qui de bien amer (Richard de Fournival, 1201–1259/60)	Lepage, no. III, pp. 41–9; Jeanroy, *Origines*, pp. 472–7.	223.4	759; 1281
Deduisant com fins amourous	Bec, *La Lyrique*, II, p. 15		
Je ne le seré de .VII, ans	Aebischer (see Bibl.)		
L'autrier tout seus chevauchoie mon chemin	Bec, *La Lyrique*, II. pp. 17–8	1038	1362
On doit bien aymer l'oysellet	Köhler (in Warnke, edn of Marie de France, *Lais*, pp. xc–xcvi)		

Occitan

First Line	Author	Editions	PC
Ab la dolchor del temps novel	Guilhem IX	Bond, pp. 36–9; Goldin, pp. 46–9; Riquer, pp. 118–20	183.1
Be me plairia, senh'En Reis	Giraut de Bornelh and Alfonso II, King of Aragon	Bossy, pp. 100–1	242.22/23.1a
Can l'erba fresch' e·lh folha par	Bernart de Ventadorn	Goldin, pp. 136–41; Press, pp. 78–82	70.39
Companho, farai un vers tot covinen	Guilhem IX	Bond, pp. 2–5; Goldin, pp. 20–3; Press, p. 12; Riquer, pp. 128–30	183.3
Estornel, cueill ta volada	Marcabrun	Goldin, pp. 60–5; Riquer, pp. 211–5	293.25
Farai chansoneta nueva	Guilhem IX	Bond, pp. 44–7; Goldin, pp. 40–3; Press, pp. 20–22; Riquer, pp. 124–7.	183.6
Farai un vers pos mi somelh	Guilhem IX	Goldin, pp. 26–32; Bond, pp. 18–24; Riquer, pp. 133–8	183.12
Ges l'estornels non s'oblida	Marcabrun	Goldin, pp. 66–70; Riquer, pp. 216–9	293.96
Gui d'Ussel, be·m pesa de vos	Maria de Ventadorn and Gui d'Ussel	Bogin, pp. 98–101	194.9/295.1
Mout jauzens me prenc en amar	Guilhem IX	Bond, pp. 32–5; Goldin, pp. 42–5	183.8
Na Carenza, al bel cors avinens		Schultz, p. 28; Bec, *FS Erich Köhler*, pp. 21–30; Bogin, pp. 144–5, 178–9; Dronke, *Women Writers*, pp. 101–3, 300–302; Rieger. pp. 155–6.	12.1
Pos vezem de novel florir	Guilhem IX	Bond, pp. 28–31; Goldin, pp. 36–41; Press, pp. 18–20; Riquer, pp. 121–3	183.11
Rossinhol el seu repaire	Peire d'Alvernhe	Riquer, pp. 316–20; Goldin, pp. 162–5	323.23

Latin

First Line	Title (Author)	Editions	Walther
Abrahae proles, Israelis nata	Planctus Dinae (Peter Abelard)	PL 178. 1817; Dronke, *Poetic Individuality*, p. 146	183
Aurea frequenter lingua *or* Pulcher valet ver in silva		Strecker, App. no. 1, pp. 111–3; Adcock, pp. 30–35.	1796
Aurea personet lira	(Fulbert of Chartres?)	Strecker, no. 10, pp. 29–32	1804
Clerus et presbyteri nuper consedere	Consultatio sacerdotum	Wright, *LPMap*, pp. 174–9	2929
In me, dei crudeles nimium		Dronke, 'Profane Elements', p. 571	8991
Iuvenilis lascivia		Dronke, *MRELL*, II, p. 361; Adcock, pp. 28–9	10029
Pater Deus ingenite		Aßmann, *FS Adolf Hofmeister*, pp. 31–8	13803
Phebus libram perlustrabat	Altercatio Yemis et Etatis	Walther, pp. 191–203,	14091
Prisciani regula penitus cassantur	De concubinis sacerdotum	Wright, *LPMap*, pp. 171–3	14734
Quam velim virginum si detur opcio	Arundel Lyric, no. 28	McDonough, p. 119; Adcock, p. 44	15175
Rumor novus Angliae partes pergiravit	De convocatione sacerdotum	Wright, *LPMap*, pp. 174–9	16929
Vix nodosum valeo	(Alan of Lille)	Häring: see Biblio., pt. 3	20763

Middle High German

First Line	Author	Editions
Der helden minne ir klage	Wolfram von Eschenbach	Neumann, pp. 88–9

Index